OXFORD THEOLOGY AND RELIGION MONOGRAPHS

Royal Priesthood in the English Reformation

MALCOLM B. YARNELL III

OXFORD
UNIVERSITY PRESS

OXFORD
UNIVERSITY PRESS

Great Clarendon Street, Oxford, OX2 6DP,
United Kingdom

Oxford University Press is a department of the University of Oxford.
It furthers the University's objective of excellence in research, scholarship,
and education by publishing worldwide. Oxford is a registered trade mark of
Oxford University Press in the UK and in certain other countries

© Malcolm B. Yarnell III 2013

The moral rights of the author have been asserted

First Edition published in 2013
Impression: 2

Published in the United States of America by Oxford University Press
198 Madison Avenue, New York, NY 10016, United States of America

British Library Cataloguing in Publication Data
Data available

Library of Congress Control Number: 2013938309

ISBN 978-0-19-968625-4

Links to third party websites are provided by Oxford in good faith and
for information only. Oxford disclaims any responsibility for the materials
contained in any third party website referenced in this work.

Printed and bound in Great Britain by Clays Ltd, St Ives plc

Preface

The seed for this book was produced within an intellectual conflict over the royal priesthood in a place and time far removed from that of sixteenth-century England. While Southern Baptist concerns drove a related master's thesis, it was a passion to discover, in common with the philosophy of Herbert Butterfield and Leopold von Ranke, the past 'as it really happened' that compelled this particular research. A methodical examination of the social and intellectual background and expression of the doctrine as it was diversely construed during the English Reformation has long been required. My mentors in history and theology at Southwestern Seminary and Duke University, respectively Distinguished Professor of Theology James Leo Garrett Jr. and Distinguished Professor of the History of Christianity David Steinmetz, encouraged research in this subject and instilled the priority of original context for speaking about a text. Upon turning to the doctrine of universal priesthood, it was quickly discovered that the *Sitz im Leben* had not necessarily driven the secondary presentations. So, in a sense, this is a revisionist thesis in a Rankean vein concerning an idea that has been presented in a multitude of conflicting ways, historically and historiographically.

While the seed and earliest growth of the book are found in Texas and North Carolina, it was within the Faculty of Theology at the University of Oxford that the idea was cultivated into a lengthy dissertation. Former Principal of Westminster College and my first supervisor, Kenneth Wilson, guided a wide-ranging theological and philosophical exploration, while Corpus Christi College Chaplain and Fellow Judith Maltby completed the supervision through mediating the English Reformation in all its magnificence. Professor of the History of the Church Diarmaid MacCulloch offered general guidance through the DPhil and its examination, and, along with Judith in her valuable and vigilant oversight, professionally shepherded the book's preparation for publication. If not for the personal encouragement of these two as well as that of Professor Paul Fiddes, my former Principal at Regent's Park College, this book would not have been completed. Two of my fellow students also deserve mention: Professor Alec Ryrie of Durham University has helped with numerous details through the years. Father William Wizeman, SJ, who recently passed away, provided invaluable assistance in the Counter-Reformation.

While such highly competent scholars aided this book's development, still others bestowed precious support. The research in England would never have begun without generous financial sustenance from Thomas and Dilys Wilson as well as the donors brought together by my pastor and mentor, Wayne

L. DuBose. With joy, I delivered the eulogies at the homegoings of both Tom and Dilys, yet sadly before they could see this book published. It is in honor of their lifelong enabling provision that this book is dedicated. Finally, if the beautiful and vivacious Karen Annette Searcy had not agreed to marry a shy Louisiana boy, he might never have become a student of history and theology, much less a gospel minister and father. Thank you, Karen, for being the most excellent wife and mother to our five children: Truett, Matthew, Graham, Kathryn, and the appropriately named Elizabeth.

Contents

Abbreviations

A&M	John Foxe, *The Acts and Monuments*, 4th edn, ed. by Josiah Pratt, 8 vols (London: Religious Tract Society, 1877)
ARG	*Archiv für Reformationsgeschichte*
Arnold	*Select English Works of John Wyclif*, ed. by Thomas Arnold, 3 vols (OUP, 1869–1871)
BIHR	*Bulletin of the Institute of Historical Research*
BL	British Library, London
Bodleian	Bodleian Library, Oxford
Burnet	Gilbert Burnet, *The History of the Reformation of the Church of England*, 3 vols (London, 1681, 1715)
C&S	*Thomas Cranmer: Churchman and Scholar*, ed. by Paul Ayris and David Selwyn (Woodbridge, Suffolk: Boydell Press, 1993)
CH	*Church History*
Concilia	*Concilia Magnae Britanniae et Hiberniae*, ed. by David Wilkins, 4 vols (London, 1737)
Cox, I	*Writings and Disputations of Thomas Cranmer, Archbishop of Canterbury, Martyr, 1556, Relative to the Sacrament of the Lord's Supper*, ed. by John Edmund Cox (PS, 1844)
Cox, II	*Miscellaneous Writings and Letters of Thomas Cranmer, Archbishop of Canterbury, Martyr, 1556*, ed. by John Edmund Cox (PS, 1846)
CQR	*Church Quarterly Review*
Cranmer	Diarmaid MacCulloch, *Thomas Cranmer: A Life* (YUP, 1996)
CSPS	*Calendar of State Papers, Spanish*, ed. by G.A. Bergenroth et al, 15 vols (1862–1964)
CUP	Cambridge: Cambridge University Press
CWE	*The Collected Works of Erasmus*, ed. by Richard J. Schoeck and Beatrice Corrigan (Toronto: University of Toronto Press, 1974–)
CWM	*The Complete Works of St. Thomas More* (YUP, 1963–)
Defence	*Archbishop Cranmer on the True and Catholic Doctrine and Use of the Sacrament of the Lord's Supper* [1550], ed. by Henry Wace (London: Thynne, 1907)
Documents	*Documents of the English Reformation*, ed. by Gerald Bray (Cambridge: James Clarke, 1994)
EETS	Early English Text Society, Original Series [Unless otherwise indicated]

ECAF	*Elizabeth I: Autograph Compositions and Foreign Language Originals*, ed. by Janel Mueller and Leah S. Marcus (London: University of Chicago Press, 2003)
ECW	*Elizabeth I: Collected Works*, ed. by Leah S. Marcus, Janel Mueller, and Mary Beth Rose (London: University of Chicago Press, 2000)
EHR	*English Historical Review*
Formularies	*Formularies of the Faith put forth by Authority during the Reign of Henry VIII*, ed. by Charles Lloyd (OUP, 1856)
FZ	*Fasciculi Zizaniorum Magistri Johannis Wyclif Cum Tritico*, ed. by Walter Waddington Shirley (London: Rolls Series, 1858)
HJ	*Historical Journal*
HTR	*Harvard Theological Review*
JBS	*Journal of British Studies*
JEH	*Journal of Ecclesiastical History*
JTS	*Journal of Theological Studies*, New Series
L&P	*Letters and Papers, Foreign and Domestic, of the Reign of Henry VIII*, ed. by J.S. Brewer et al (London, 1862–1932)
Lambeth	Lambeth Palace Library, London
LCC	*The Library of Christian Classics*, 26 vols (London: SCM Press, 1953–1969)
Liturgies	*The Two Liturgies, A.D. 1546, and A.D. 1552: With Other Documents Set Forth by Authority in the Reign of King Edward VI*, ed. by Joseph Ketley (PS, 1844)
LW	*Luther's Works*, ed. by Jaroslav Pelikan and Helmut T. Lehmann, 55 vols (Philadelphia: Fortress Press; St. Louis: Concordia, 1955–1986)
ODNB	Oxford Dictionary of National Biography
OUP	Oxford: Oxford University Press
P&P	*Past and Present*
PRO	Public Record Office, London
PS	Parker Society [Texts of the English Reformers] (CUP, 1841–1854)
PUP	Princeton, New Jersey: Princeton University Press
RH&RB	*The Writings of Robert Harrison and Robert Browne*, ed. by Albert Peel and Leland H. Carlson (London: Allen & Unwin, 1953)
RQ	*Renaissance Quarterly*
SCH	*Studies in Church History*
SCJ	*Sixteenth Century Journal*
SEWW	*Selections from English Wycliffite Writings*, ed. by Anne Hudson (CUP, 1978)
SP	State Papers

Statutes	*Statutes of the Realm*, ed. by A. Luders et al, 11 vols (London, 1810–1828) [Statutes are cited in the form: year of reigning monarch, chapter, section.]
Strype	John Strype, *Ecclesiastical Memorials; Relating Chiefly to Religion and its Reformation, Under the Reigns of King Henry VIII, King Edward VI, and Queen Mary the First*, 7 vols (London, 1816)
Trefnant	*Registrum Johannis Trefnant, Episcopi Herefordensis*, ed. by William W. Capes (London: Canterbury and York Society, 1916)
TRHS	*Transactions of the Royal Historical Society*
TRP	*Tudor Royal Proclamations*, ed. by Paul L. Hughes and James F. Larkin, 2 vols (YUP, 1964, 1969)
Unity	Reginald Pole, *Defense of the Unity of the Church*, transl. by Joseph G. Dwyer (Westminster, MD: Newman, 1965)
VAI	*Visitation Articles and Injunctions of the Period of the Reformation*, ed. by Walter Howard Frere and William McClure Kennedy, 3 vols (London: Longmans, Green and Company, 1910)
Walter, I	*Doctrinal Treatises and Introductions to Different Portions of the Holy Scriptures by William Tyndale, Martyr, 1536*, ed. by Henry Walter (PS, 1848)
Walter, II	*Expositions and Notes on Sundry Portions of the Holy Scriptures Together With the Practice of Prelates by William Tyndale, Martyr, 1536*, ed. by Henry Walter (PS, 1849)
Walter, III	*An Answer to Sir Thomas More's Dialogue, the Supper of the Lord After the True Meaning of John VI. and I Cor. XI. and Wm. Tracy's Testament Expounded by William Tyndale, Martyr, 1536*, ed. by Henry Walter (PS, 1850)
WLW	Wyclif's Latin Works, The Wyclif Society, 23 vols (London, 1883–1922)
YUP	London: Yale University Press

List of Plates

Plate 1. Reflecting a royal claim to authority, without a priestly intermediary and in the presence of biblical and royal saints, Richard II, the King of England, kneels to communicate directly with Jesus Christ, the King of Heaven, and receive the banner of resurrected kingship. The Wilton Diptych, late fourteenth century. Used by permission of the National Gallery.

Plate 2. Reflecting a clerical claim to authority, a priest distributes the consecrated host, the body of God with its attendant soteriological and apotropaic power, to the receptive laity. Illuminated manuscript, *Omne Bonum*, late fourteenth century. Used by permission of the British Library Board, Royal MS 6E, VI, fol. 337^v.

Plate 3. Reflecting a popular claim to authority, John Ball addresses the 1381 Peasants' Revolt. Ball queried in an egalitarian manner, 'Whan Adam dalf, and Eve span, Wo was thanne a gentilman?' Illuminated manuscript, Jean Froissart, *Chroniques de France et d'Angleterre*, Book II, late fifteenth century. Used by permission of the British Library Board, Royal MS 18E, I, fol. 165^v.

Plate 4. The King of Heaven invests spiritual authority in the church through the granting of the tiara to a pope attended by a cardinal and other clergy before a church (at left) and temporal authority in the state through the granting of the crown to a king attended by nobles and knights before a castle (at right). Illuminated manuscript, *Concordantia Discordantium Canonum*, twelfth century. Used by permission of the British Library Board/De Agostini.

Plate 5. The King of England, Henry VIII, authorized by heaven, distributes authority through the Word of God to Thomas Cranmer at the head of the clergy (at left) and to Thomas Cromwell at the head of the magistrates (at right). Title page of the second 'Great Bible', also known as 'Cranmer's Bible'. *The Byble in Englyshe, that is to saye the content of all the holy scrypture, both of ye olde and newe testament, truly translated after the veryte of the Hebrue and Greke textes* (London: Rychard Grafton and Edward Whitchurch, 1539). Used by permission of the British Library Board, C18, d.1.

Plate 6. This popular woodcut demonstrates some of the royal, clerical, and popular aspects of the English evangelical doctrine of royal priesthood. Drawing upon Josiah's lettered reformation of Israel's worship through Solomon's Temple, in the higher part of England's temple, Edward VI grants the submissively kneeling reformed clergy the Bible while the magistrates triumphantly stand (at bottom left). The new Josiah suppressed the 'Romish Church' through destroying her images and expelling her clergy (at top). The reformed vision of the church included people of both genders and all ages entering the house of common prayer, the clergy preaching God's Word and the laity reflecting upon it, and true worship through the two reformation sacraments, including a centered table for communion as opposed to an eastern altar for the sacrifice of the mass (at bottom right). John Foxe, *The second volume of the*

Introduction

'On the whole we may say doctrine conditions events and is not conditioned by them.'[1] In the midst of discussing Thomas Cranmer's rendition of the doctrine of the priesthood of all believers, Cyril Eastwood thus characterizes—and for the contextual historian, condemns—his own ambitious project to provide the authoritative historical summary of the doctrine.[2] Expanding his 1957 London University doctoral thesis, Eastwood surveys royal priesthood from the Old Testament to his own time.[3] The reader expecting analyses of what the doctrine *meant* will be disappointed for Eastwood is more concerned to tell you what it *means*. Eastwood's confusion between then and now, between his subjects' beliefs and his own, manifests itself variously. He depends almost exclusively on secondary sources and his rare reading of the primary sources can be quite simple and unreflective.[4] He thus dismisses the historical context in which his subjects operate. Those theologians whose work has not been treasured by a major Protestant tradition are, moreover, generally excluded.[5] As a result, his subjects' interpretations remain strikingly, and suspiciously, consistent with his own.

Similar misinterpretations of the historical understandings of the doctrine have been presented not only in theological treatises by both Catholic and Protestant theologians, but also in early modern English histories by both Whiggish and Revisionist historians. Eastwood stands within the historiographical tradition of Protestant liberalism shaped by Philip Schaff, Thomas Lindsay, Adolf Harnack, and Ernst Troeltsch. These four defined the authoritative Protestant historiography of the doctrine for the twentieth century.

---

[1] *The Priesthood of All Believers: An Examination of the Doctrine from the Reformation to the Present Day* (London: Epworth, 1960), 91–2.

[2] Theology does, and should, have an impact upon human action, but the historian must be careful not to read his or her own theology into the past.

[3] *The Royal Priesthood of the Faithful: An Investigation of the Doctrine from Biblical Times to the Reformation* (London: Epworth, 1963).

[4] E.g. *Priesthood of All Believers*, 155.

[5] Where are John Fisher, Thomas More, and the Council of Trent, or Caspar Schwenckfeld and Sebastian Franck?

Schaff lists the priesthood of all believers among the leading principles of the Reformation. Coupled with 'independent manhood' and democracy, this principle is the basis of all other freedoms; it entails personal access without any priestly mediation and culminates in congregationalism and vocations.[6] According to Lindsay, universal priesthood is the foundation upon which all Reformation doctrines are built. The definitive thought of Martin Luther endorses direct access to God without human mediators and outward helps.[7] Harnack stresses the rise of individualism during the Reformation. The 'rights of the individual', the shedding of outward constraints, and 'freedom of conscience' were all present in Luther's quest for freedom.[8] A similar understanding is adopted by Troeltsch, who traces the historical interplay of individualism and universalism in his influential analysis of Christian social theories. Relying on secondary sources, Troeltsch says John Wyclif did away with the 'objective priesthood' and depreciated 'the institutional aspect of the Church, in order to exalt the individual and personal immediacy of the soul's relationship with God'. The priesthood of all believers is the individualist principle in Reformation thought and little else.[9]

Such an atomistic, antimediatorial interpretation of the Reformation doctrine coincides well with Roman Catholic critiques. James Edward Rea reviewed a few manifestations of the doctrine and concluded that, as understood by late medieval heretics such as Wyclif and early modern reformers such as Luther, it is individualistic, internal, and anthropocentric. However, Rea, in a pre-Vatican II polemical mindset, is more concerned with refuting Protestant liberalism than with understanding his subjects.[10] As we shall see, this modern historiography of Wyclif as atomist, a type of historiography advanced by both Protestant and Catholic scholars, is rather perverse.

Among recent historians of the English Reformation, the doctrine is usually classified as the theological manifestation of anticlericalism. In the searing debate over anticlericalism and the expansion of Protestant beliefs in England, Christopher Haigh places the priesthood of all believers among the 'different branches of "anticlericalism"', along with Erastianism and the gut reactions of neglected parishioners.[11] In one of his few agreements with Haigh,

---

[6] Philip Schaff, *Modern Christianity: The German Reformation, A.D. 1517–1530*, 2 vols (Edinburgh: T&T Clark, 1888), I, 4, 16, 24–5.

[7] Thomas M. Lindsay, *A History of the Reformation*, 2 vols (Edinburgh: T&T Clark, 1906), I, 435–44; *The Church and Ministry in the Early Centuries*, 2d edn (London: Hodder and Stoughton, 1903), 35, 311–19.

[8] Adolf Harnack, *History of Dogma*, transl. by Neil Buchanan *et al*, 7 vols (London: Williams & Norgate, 1894–1899), VII, 184–6.

[9] Ernst Troeltsch, *The Social Teaching of the Christian Churches*, transl. by Olive Wyon (London: Allen & Unwin, 1931), 360–1, 470.

[10] *The Common Priesthood of the Members of the Mystical Body* (Westminster, Maryland: Newman, 1947).

[11] 'Anticlericalism and the English Reformation', *History*, 68 (1983), 392.

A.G. Dickens asserted anticlericalism was 'demanded by' and 'strengthened by' the doctrine.[12] In a local study of Bristol, one revisionist, Martha Skeeters, pictures a perfectly peaceful medieval community held together by an independent clergy. This community was tragically torn apart by the new doctrines of the Reformation, prominent among which is 'the priesthood of the believer', the theological manifestation of a destructive and individualistic laicism. Skeeters' conclusions are, however, suspect, for she relies on a purely modernized rendition of the doctrine, a rendition for which she provides a single reference to Paul Althaus.[13] Althaus, however, is adamant that Luther held a corporate version of the doctrine.[14] Paying little attention to medieval England, Rosemary O'Day laments the doctrine as an anticlerical continental innovation alien to England.[15] These are not the only contemporary historians who define the doctrine in terms of anticlericalism.[16] Unfortunately, most rely primarily on trial records—records laden with crass accusations and curt denials—and hostile treatises for their definition. Positive definitions offered by the period's theologians have gone relatively unappreciated. If theologians have typically ignored the context of the idea,[17] historians have largely bypassed the period's intellectual explorations of the idea.

In light of the facile treatment given to the doctrine by contemporary theologians and historians, the need for a reappraisal of the doctrine's historical meanings is evident. The greatest temptation for the historian of ideas is to create an ideological framework to which history must conform. Recognizing this danger and in response to those who create systematic descriptions divorced from 'historical-genetic reading', Bernard Lohse has modeled an historical theology that takes both history and theology seriously. In his study of Luther, Lohse surveys Luther's historical development before attempting a systematic review of Luther's theology.[18]

---

[12] 'The Shape of Anti-clericalism and the English Reformation', in *Politics and Society in Reformation Europe*, ed. by E.I. Kouri and Tom Scott (London: Macmillan, 1987), 392, 403. Dickens offers a mediating statement in 'The Early Expansion of Protestantism in England 1520–1558', *ARG*, 78 (1987), 187–222.

[13] *Community and Clergy* (OUP, 1993), 60, 234.

[14] *The Theology of Martin Luther*, transl. by Robert C. Schultz (Minneapolis: Fortress Press, 1966), 313–18.

[15] *The English Clergy* (Leicester: Leicester University Press, 1979), 190–245 (240).

[16] Susan Brigden, 'Youth and the English Reformation', in *The Impact of the English Reformation 1500–1640*, ed. by Peter Marshall (London: Arnold, 1997), 55–6; Anne Hudson, *The Premature Reformation* (OUP, 1988), 451.

[17] Harald Goertz's review of Luther's doctrine is shaped by the recent Lutheran debate over relating universal priesthood to ordained ministry. Goertz opts for a metaphorical understanding of Luther, doing little justice to the young Luther's desire to reify the doctrine *against* his opponents' metaphorical understanding. Goertz, *Allgemeines Priestertum und Ordiniertes Amt bei Luther* (Marburg: Elwert Verlag, 1997).

[18] *Martin Luther's Theology: Its Historical and Systematic Development*, transl. by Roy A. Harrisville (Minneapolis: Fortress Press, 1999), 3–10.

In agreement with Lohse's method, this study considers historical context in preparation for a later systematization. It confines itself to a period limited enough to attain a modicum of contextual insight, yet broad enough to discern a modicum of development. Our goal is to provide an historiography of an ideal, the idea of royal priesthood. This is accomplished by concentrating on a particular country spanning the transition from the Middle Ages to the early modern period. We shall survey the 'premature',[19] official,[20] and popular[21] phases of England's Reformation, concentrating on two theologians in particular.

John Wyclif, so-called 'Morning Star of the Reformation', initiates our discussion. As will be seen, the established interpretations of his theology of universal priesthood need correction. After reviewing late medieval developments and the immediate reception of Luther's doctrine in England, Thomas Cranmer receives the lion's share of our attention. Paying such homage to Cranmer is quite necessary. He is at the center of the English Reformation from its juridical beginning in Henry VIII's marital dilemma. He is also a prominent figure during subsequent discussions concerning the roles of king, clergy, and people in the mid-1530s, and during the establishment of evangelical doctrine under Edward VI. Although Cranmer was neither a prolific polemicist like Luther, nor a systematician like John Calvin, we hazard the assertion he was as important to England's Reformation as Luther and Calvin were in their respective regions.[22] The form of the liturgy was Cranmer's, and Cranmer led the evangelical negotiations with 'the powers that be' for the official definition of doctrine and for the availability of vernacular Scripture. We conclude with a survey of reactions to the doctrine under Mary I and Elizabeth I, the sacred queens of England.

RELATED THEMES

Three important hermeneutical concepts influence this discussion: individualism, anticlericalism, and sacred kingship. The first two have been inappropriately confused with the doctrine while the third has been absent from interpretations. These concepts are summarized here.

---

[19] Hudson, *Premature Reformation*.

[20] Maurice Powicke, *The Reformation in England* (OUP, 1941), 1.

[21] Among others, Christopher Haigh asserts that in England's 'Reformations', the people matter. His revisionist paradigm has helped create an industry struggling to determine whether and when the popular reformation occurred. *English Reformations* (OUP, 1993), 19.

[22] Peter Newman Brooks, 'Saint Martin and Saint Thomas: a comparison', *Faith and Worship*, 47 (1999), 3–8.

Individualism

First, consider individualism. 'Individualism' is a relatively recent word, coined in French philosophical circles and introduced into the English language during the nineteenth century by Francis de Tocqueville.[23] *Oxford English Dictionary* offers three definitions, the first being a psychological principle, the second a social, the third a metaphysical. Generally, we may define individualism as the exaltation of self above community. For some, individualism implies the individual is a self-determined whole. Moral philosophers, theologians, and social historians have, however, recently denied the plausibility of this definition. There is no human personhood apart from human community; conversely, true community enables personhood.[24]

Individualism, therefore, can never really be a total withdrawal of the individual from relationship to the other. Rather, there can be various attitudes concerning the relationship of individual to community. Ferdinand Tönnies offers a famous definition in his distinction between *Gemeinschaft* and *Gesellschaft*. *Gemeinschaft*, community, an organic concept often identified with the traditional village, occurs when the will of the community predetermines that of the individual. *Gesellschaft*, society, a mechanical concept often associated with modern bureaucracy, occurs when the will of the individual precedes that of the community.[25] In other words, individualism as a metaphysical reality can never exist but individualism as a disposition is possible. Our concern is with this latter definition, with individualism as disposition, and with whether royal priesthood was thus understood during our subject period. The prominence of this doctrine during the sixteenth century was subsequently correlated with the rise of individualism.

Identifying systemic individualism is an awkward task. Pierre Birnbaum and Jean Leca have delineated seven types of individualism: utilitarian, romantic, economic, political, ethical, sociological, and epistemological. These various types point accordingly to the problem of measuring individualistic thought.[26] Among various measures offered have been biography, artistic representation of personal features, and philosophy, as well as juridical independence and

---

[23] Alan Macfarlane, *The Origins of English Individualism* (Oxford: Blackwell, 1978), 167–8.

[24] Robert Spaemann, *Persons: The Difference between 'Someone' and 'Something'*, transl. by Oliver O'Donovan (OUP, 2006). Cf. Rowan Williams, *On Christian Theology* (Oxford: Blackwell, 2000), 69–72; Oliver O'Donovan, *The Desire of the Nations* (CUP, 1996), 122–3, 271–84; David Aers, *Community, Gender, and Individual Identity* (London: Routledge, 1988), 2–6; John D. Zizioulas, *Being as Communion* (Crestwood, New York: St. Vladimir's Seminary Press, 1985), 27–49; Alasdair MacIntyre, *After Virtue*, 2d edn (Notre Dame, Indiana: University of Notre Dame, 1984), 172.

[25] *Community and Society*, transl. by Charles P. Loomis (East Lansing: Michigan State University Press, 1957).

[26] 'Introduction', in *Individualism: Theories and Methods*, transl. by John Gaffrey (OUP, 1990), 1–14.

belief in unmediated, personal access to God. In light of such theoretical and methodological problems in defining and measuring individualism, the historiographical concept of 'the rise of individualism' appears dubious. According to Bertrand Badie, the concepts of community and individualism often have more to do with theoretical construction by the observer than with reality on the ground.[27] This is all too true for modern historiography of the late medieval–early modern period.

Again, is the increasing prominence of the doctrine of royal priesthood to be identified with the rise of individualism in England? Two other questions must be answered before we attempt to answer this question: when did individualism arise in England? And, when did royal priesthood come into prominence? Answers to the first question stretch from the twelfth to the nineteenth centuries. Relying primarily upon literature, Colin Morris placed 'the discovery of the individual' in the Renaissance of the twelfth century.[28] Walter Ullmann, surveying juridical concepts, and Alan Macfarlane, examining property rights, pinned it on the thirteenth century.[29] Jacob Burckhardt, reviewing art and literature, says that in the Italian Renaissance of the late thirteenth century through to the fifteenth century 'man became a spiritual *individual*, and recognized himself as such'. Beforehand, 'man was conscious of himself only as a member of a race, people, party, family, or corporation—only through some general category'.[30] According to historians of the Renaissance, individualism entered England through its appropriation of Italian humanism in the late fifteenth century and again in the late sixteenth century.[31]

The mysticism that became popular in England in the fourteenth and fifteenth centuries also contributed to a sense of inwardness. Sarah Beckwith sees two types of mysticism operating in this period. Positive mysticism stresses the mediation of symbols, while negative mysticism negates all mediation. Margery Kempe with her visible prophetic behavior represents positive mysticism, a mysticism which challenges the clerical monopoly on sacred power. Arranged against her are most of the other mystics who declined to oppose clerical monopoly, preferring instead to withdraw inwardly.[32] Jonathan Hughes' research into late medieval Yorkshire shows how the dominant mysticism was individualistic in nature and increasingly popular among the laity.[33]

---

[27] 'Community, Individualism and Culture', in *Individualism: Theories and Methods*, transl. by John Gaffrey (OUP, 1990), 103.

[28] *The Discovery of the Individual 1050–1200* (London: SPCK, 1972).

[29] Ullmann, *The Individual and Society in the Middle Ages* (London: Methuen, 1967); Macfarlane, *Origins of English Individualism*.

[30] *The Civilization of the Renaissance*, transl. by S.G.C. Middlemore (London: Allen & Unwin, 1944), 81.

[31] Cf. Alistair Fox, *The English Renaissance* (Oxford: Blackwell, 1997), 18–37, 59–92.

[32] *Christ's Body* (London: Routledge, 1993), 12–21.

[33] *Pastors and Visionaries* (Woodbridge, Suffolk: Boydell, 1988).

According to John Bossy, the loss of the traditional 'social axiom' can be blamed on the Reformation, specifically upon Luther's doctrine of forensic justification.[34] Bossy's oft-repeated emotive language of the loss of traditional community during the Reformation, most importantly in his article on 'The Mass as a Social Institution 1200–1700',[35] has been tempered in recent years,[36] but only after scathing critiques. Colin Richmond shows how fifteenth-century gentry took the supposedly communal worship of the traditional parish and privatized it by turning public relics into personal jewelry, by dividing the parish church with private pews, by removing the *Pax*—the kissing of which Bossy saw as a replacement for frequent communion, a 'communion' that is typically understood as expressing unity, but which he contradictorily interprets as divisive of community—into the household for private use, and by building their own altars in private chapels staffed by private priests who led private services.[37] Miri Rubin deconstructs Bossy's 'social miracle', showing how the religious fraternities were voluntary in nature and destructive of kinship relations. Rather than building community, Corpus Christi processions were often a forum for social conflict where interest groups jockeyed for proximity to the host, thereby stressing hierarchy and division rather than love and unity. She says the overuse of 'traditional community' in numerous studies means the concept 'has lost its cutting edge as a tool'.[38]

Max Weber's assignment of the rise of individualism to seventeenth-century English Calvinists became a platitude among many sociologists. Yet, Weber's thesis is built on a set of caricatures of English Calvinism and traditional priesthood. He alleged the doctrine of predestination brought the Calvinist to loneliness and despair over his own fate and hatred towards his neighbor. This 'disillusioned and pessimistically inclined individualism' was due to the belief that 'no one could help him', no priest, no sacraments, no church, no God. There were 'no means whatever' to reach God: God is absolutely transcendent, everything pertaining to the flesh is corrupt, and no mediation is offered between the two. On the other hand, the traditional priest was a 'magician who performed the miracle of transubstantiation, and who held the key to eternal life in his hand'. Weber's caricatures are misconceived at best, offensive at worst.[39] R.H. Tawney parroted Weber's thesis, seeing its ultimate

---

[34] *Christianity in the West 1400–1700* (OUP, 1985), 91–7.

[35] *P&P*, 100 (1983), 29–61.

[36] Bossy, 'Prayers', *TRHS*, 6th series, 1 (1991), 137–8.

[37] 'Religion and the Fifteenth-Century English Gentleman', in *The Church, Politics and Patronage in the Fifteenth Century*, ed. by Barrie Dobson (Gloucester: Alan Sutton, 1984), 197–9.

[38] 'Small Groups: Identity and Solidarity in the Late Middle Ages', in *Enterprise and Individuals in Fifteenth-Century England*, ed. by Jennifer Kermode (Stroud: Sutton, 1991), 134. Cf. Rubin, 'The Eucharist and the Construction of Medieval Identities', in *Culture and History 1350–1600*, ed. by David Aers (London: Harvester, 1992), 43–63.

[39] *The Protestant Ethic and the Spirit of Capitalism*, transl. by Talcott Parsons (London: Allen & Unwin, 1930), 104–5, 117.

outworking in the (Charles) Dickensian evils of the Industrial Revolution, when industrialists lost all social concern.[40] The Weber–Tawney thesis became so dominant that many social historians found it difficult to abandon or even modify.[41]

Like sociologists, philosophers have disagreed over the rise of individualism. Anthony Kenny points to the debates over divine personhood in the early church.[42] Others consider the rediscovery of Aristotle in the High Middle Ages important.[43] Indeed, from Augustine of Hippo (d.430) to Thomas Aquinas (d.1274), a notable move was made from the heavenly life as communal to the beatific vision as personal, but whether this can be ascribed to Aquinas' reading of Aristotle is unknown.[44] Others have suggested William of Ockham (d.1347) and nominalist philosophy.[45] Still others accuse the Enlightenment of the eighteenth century, encapsulated in Descartes' assertion, *cogito ergo sum*, I think therefore I am.[46] The case has also been made that America's western frontier created a hitherto unseen broad-based independence in philosophical, political, and religious thought.[47] In conclusion, as Charles Taylor masterfully demonstrates, the historical development of the philosophical movements of man-centered individualism and secular humanism are very complex.[48]

At this point, it should be clear that the entire effort to pinpoint the rise of individualism in the modern period is a tenuous affair. The means of measuring such a change shows that this is true not only for the modern period, but also for the entirety of Christian history. Many have measured the rise of individualism through biography, autobiography, and individualistic historiography. Thus, one might claim the seventeenth century, when spiritual journals became

[40] *Religion and the Rise of Capitalism* (London: Penguin, 1922), 179–96.

[41] C.J. Calhoun, 'Community: Toward a Variable Conceptualization for Comparative Research', *Social History*, 5 (1980), 105–29.

[42] *A Brief History of Western Philosophy* (Oxford: Blackwell, 1998), 103.

[43] Ullmann, *Individual and Society*, 122–4; Morris, *Discovery of the Individual*, 161.

[44] Augustine saw the end of all things as *tranquillitas ordinis*, a peaceful order, in which *pax hominum ordinata concordia*, the ordered concord of human peace, includes *pax caelestis civitatis*, the peace of the heavenly city. Aquinas emphasized the contemplative life in which intellectual creatures, 'for their own sake', finally experience the beatific vision of God. Augustine, *Civitas Dei*, bk. XIX, ch. 13; Aquinas, *Summa Contra Gentiles*, bk. III, ch. 112. These references are owed to Professor O. M. T. O'Donovan.

[45] Antony Black, 'The Individual and Society', in *The Cambridge History of Medieval Political Thought*, ed. by J.H. Burns (CUP, 1988), 601–2; Janet Coleman, 'The Individual and the Medieval State', in *The Individual in Political Theory and Practice*, ed. by Janet Coleman (OUP, 1996), 25–9.

[46] MacIntyre, *After Virtue*.

[47] Robert Bellah, *Habits of the Heart* (Los Angeles: University of California Press, 1987); Nathan O. Hatch, *The Democratization of American Christianity* (YUP, 1989).

[48] Charles Taylor, *Sources of the Self* (CUP, 1989), 303–90. Taylor finds three movements towards the self: inwardness, which began with Plato; the affirmation of ordinary life, which began with Luther; and, the voice of nature, which began in the late eighteenth century. On the critical decades in the rise of modern humanism, see Charles Taylor, *A Secular Age* (HUP, 2007), 221–34.

quite common, for the emergence of individualism. Before that, however, were the biographies and autobiographies of the Italian Renaissance. Even earlier was the personal *History of his Calamities* by Peter Abelard in the twelfth century, when arranging history around a singular figure was common.[49] But long before was written the most influential autobiography ever, Augustine's *Confessions*. Even the apostle Paul offered personal reflections in his epistles, and his method of evangelism included the relation of divine encounter in personal story.[50] Christianity, from its beginnings, has been both a person-affirming and a self-effacing religion.[51]

When did individualism arise? Rather than add another voice to the range of diverse answers offered by such prominent scholars, it is prudent to remain temporarily agnostic. Prudence also dictates provisional ignorance concerning the second question—when the doctrine of royal priesthood came into prominence—at least until more research is available.[52] In other words, claiming an historical concurrence between individualism and royal priesthood is fraught with difficulties. When coupled with the following research in the English Reformation, we discover the two concepts could be quite unrelated.

Anticlericalism

Second, consider anticlericalism. Besides being a purely negative term, 'anti-clericalism' is unfortunate because it is loaded with political meanings from the nineteenth-century context wherein it was first used. Its coinage and subsequent popularity has been ascribed to James Anthony Froude (d.1894), author of the 12-volume *History of England*. Froude helped establish the Whiggish interpretation, claiming the Reformation was a result of lay disgust with a corrupt and foreign-influenced clergy. But Froude was reacting to events in his own time, specifically to the clericalism of the Oxford movement and to the Irish nationalism he assumed was primarily instigated by Catholic priests.[53] In twentieth-century historiography, the influential A.G. Dickens

---

[49] Sverre Bagge, 'The Individual in Medieval Historiography', in *The Individual*, ed. by Coleman, 35–57.

[50] Acts 9, 22, 26; Galatians 2; II Corinthians 11.

[51] Morris, *Discovery of the Individual*, 10–12.

[52] A significant gap exists between the best English-language studies on universal priesthood in the early church and the Reformation. Cf. James Leo Garrett Jr., 'The Pre-Cyprianic Doctrine of the Priesthood of All Christians', in *Continuity and Discontinuity in Church History*, ed. by F.F. Church and T. George (Leiden: E.J. Brill, 1979), 45–61; James Leo Garrett Jr., 'The Priesthood of All Christians: From Cyprian to John Chrysostom', *Southwestern Journal of Theology*, 30 (1988), 22–33.

[53] Richard A. Cosgrove, 'English Anticlericalism: A Programmatic Assessment', in *Anticlericalism in Late Medieval and Early Modern Europe*, ed. by Peter A. Dykema and Heiko A. Oberman (Leiden: E.J. Brill, 1993), 576–80.

advanced the Whiggish interpretation. From the beginning of his career, Dickens believed anticlericalism reached a 'new intensity' in early sixteenth-century England, becoming a veritable 'tide' that swept all before it, 'devout and profane, Protestant and Catholic, rich and poor alike'.[54]

As noted before, Haigh's challenge to the anticlericalist understanding of the Reformation, even labeling it 'fiction', helped subvert the dominant historiography. After cursorily surveying polemical literature, parliamentary legislation, and ecclesiastical litigation in sixteenth-century England, Haigh concludes anticlericalism, 'in short, was not a cause of the Reformation; it was, however, a result'.[55] But Heiko Oberman, after reviewing forty-one articles from an international colloquium on anticlericalism, saw three periods of anticlericalism: (1) before the Reformation, there was a long tradition of medieval criticism; (2) during the Reformation, there was a programmatic goal to reform the clergy; (3) after the Reformation, when the clergy joined the state in molding the laity into subjects, a new type of anticlericalism arose.[56] The following study agrees more with Oberman's paradigm than Dickens' or Haigh's.

There are almost as many problems with the methodology and taxonomy of anticlericalism as there are with individualism. It is too prominent and useful a term to dismiss out of hand, and yet, as Dickens notes, 'Anti-clericalism has become an unduly capacious word.'[57] In response to this problem, a number of attempts have been made to develop a typology. J.J. Scarisbrick sees four types working during the Henrician years: (1) a crude, destructive variety based simply on selfish appetite; (2) a positive, secular type personified by Thomas Cromwell (d.1540), who wanted to use the church's wealth for altruistic purposes; (3) a positive, religious kind promoted by English humanism, which wanted a traditional reform of the clergy; and, (4) 'the anticlericalism of heresy', which began in Lollardy and received new life in English Lutheranism.[58] Although Scarisbrick's typology advances the discussion, it is too restrictive in accepting only traditionalist clergy as clergy. Lutheranism, moreover, did not desire the dissolution, but the reformation, of the clergy. Their anticlericalism was not universal.

Peter Marshall, Judith Maltby, and Patrick Hornbeck have furthered the discussion by recognizing that anticlericalism was, in the words of Maltby,

---

[54] *Lollards and Protestants in the Diocese of York 1509–1558* (OUP, 1959), 12. Cf. G.G. Coulton, *Ten Medieval Studies* (CUP, 1906), 137–52.

[55] 'Anticlericalism and the English Reformation', 391, 407.

[56] 'Anticlericalism as an Agent of Change', in *Anticlericalism in Europe*, x. On post-Reformation anticlericalism resulting from clerical incursions in politics, see Andrew Foster, 'The Clerical Estate Revitalized', in *The Early Stuart Church, 1603–1642*, ed. by Kenneth Fincham (London: Macmillan, 1993), 139–60. On anticlericalism in the early Enlightenment, see J.A.I. Champion, *The Pillars of Priestcraft Shaken* (CUP, 1992).

[57] 'Shape of Anti-clericalism', 379.

[58] *Henry VIII* (University of California Press, 1968; new edn, YUP, 1997), 243–4.

'a nuanced and intricate affair'.[59] They believe distinction must be made between anticlericalism as desire for the dissolution of the entire clerical estate and anticlericalism in its particular, temporal forms. Anticlericalism was most often pointed against individual clerics or against a section of the clergy, usually the prelacy and the regular clergy, rather than the entire institution. It was typically a simple protest against abuses of power perceived as existing among the clergy (e.g. tithes and abuses of mortuaries, self-serving litigation, and sexual failings) rather than an attempt to abolish the clergy. Many, like Thomas More (d.1535), were anticlerical in one context and proclerical in another.[60] Maltby concludes in her study of religious conformity that clergy and laity were more interested in a 'working relationship' than in clericalism and anticlericalism.[61] Hornbeck argued for the division of anticlericalism into two strands, advocates of 'antisacerdotalism' as opposed to the 'hyperclericalists'. However, this terminological proposal highlights the extremes and fails to allow for the inevitable gradations between the two.[62] Recognizing the need to make distinctions yet allow for gradation, we shall use the term 'radical anticlericalism' to describe the desire for the total dissolution of the clerical estate. 'Anticlericalism' is used to describe all other criticisms, which criticisms were often meant to reform rather than destroy. Simple anticlericalism could be pointed against individuals, against certain institutions within the clerical estate, or against clerical representatives of opposing traditions issuing from the Reformation.[63]

Besides distinguishing the different goals of various anticlericalisms, we must also identify the different proponents of anticlericalism. As we shall see, complaint against clerical abuses could be best pronounced by the clergy themselves. This enigma allowed one historian to coin the oxymoronic, yet useful, term of 'clerical anticlericalism'.[64] The appropriation of complaint against the clergy by the clergy was intimately connected with their prominent position in the hierarchical scheme of salvation and with the proclamatory means of salvation. This means has been described as 'complaint', 'satire', and 'criticism'. Although the clergy criticized all three medieval estates, their vitriolic idealism was most

---

[59] Judith Maltby, *Prayer Book and People in Elizabethan and Early Stuart England* (CUP, 1998), 228–9.

[60] Peter Marshall, *The Catholic Priesthood and the English Reformation* (OUP, 1994), 214–15.

[61] *Prayer Book and People*, 34, 230.

[62] J. Patrick Hornbeck II, *What is a Lollard? Dissent and Belief in Late Medieval England* (OUP, 2010), 144. Hornbeck's analysis of the terminology of 'lollardy' is helpful, and his proposal regarding Ludwig Wittgenstein's 'family resemblance' model of language is interesting. Hornbeck ch. 1. Unfortunately, his treatment of universal priesthood reduces it to a mere antisacerdotalism. Hornbeck, 166.

[63] For instance, Richard Overton excoriated Roman, Episcopal, and Presbyterian clergy while reserving tepid praise for Independent, Anabaptist, and Brownist clergy. *An arrow against all tyrants* (1646), in *The English Levellers*, ed. by Andrew Sharp (CUP, 1998), 65.

[64] Peter Iver Kaufman, 'John Colet's *Opus de Sacramentis* and Clerical Anticlericalism', *JBS*, 22 (1983), 1–22.

often pointed at those who held the means of salvation: themselves. These distinctions will be teased out in more detail throughout this book.

Sacred Kingship

Third, consider sacred kingship. The concept of national king as priest may seem to modern ears an odd digression in a discussion of the Christian doctrine of all believers being priests and kings; however, it was not so strange to people in late medieval and early modern England. Sacred kingship was a crucial support for European monarchies. Early modern historians usually brush aside this entire subject. Franklin le van Baumer, in an influential monograph, which provides no evidential basis and strives against the natural reading of primary sources, asserted that Henry VIII 'consistently' denied personal spiritual power.[65] Most modern scholars have followed le van Baumer, citing a distinction between *potestas ordinis* and *potestas iurisdictionis*, power of orders and power of jurisdiction.[66]

As we shall see, first coined in the Middle Ages to separate papal juridical power from priestly sacramental power, the *potestates* distinction came to England through canon law. Although the distinction was raised to clarify the relationship of king and clergy in the 1537 *Bishops' Book*, it was removed from Henry's 1543 revision. At other times, Henry flatly rejected efforts to distinguish spiritual and temporal powers. It was only during Elizabeth's reign that the distinction received new attention, but even then it did not solve all the problems. The *potestates* distinction left a very crucial question unanswered: who shall define doctrine? England's archbishops were forced to respond and their answers caused trouble.

For all his revisionism, this is one area where Haigh has held the line with the older historiography. Anglican theologians have tended to ignore or gloss over the problematic relationship between king and clergy,[67] and Haigh has left this reading unchallenged. Henry, according to Haigh's historiography of reluctant Reformation, was a theological conservative.[68] As we shall see, however, Henry was no conservative in the sacrament of orders. Indeed, he was quite revolutionary and his revolt from Rome had consequences for English attitudes toward clerical status and function.

[65] *The Early Tudor Theory of Kingship* (YUP, 1940), 82–3.
[66] E.g. G.R. Elton, *The Tudor Constitution* (CUP, 1965), 333n; Scarisbrick, *Henry VIII*, 279; Dickens, *Thomas Cromwell and the English Reformation* (London: Hodder and Stoughton, 1959), 87.
[67] E.T. Davies, *Episcopacy and Royal Supremacy* (Oxford: Blackwell, 1950), 7–11; Paul F. Bradshaw, *The Anglican Ordinal* (London: SPCK, 1971), 10; Edward P. Echlin, *The Story of Anglican Ministry* (Slough: St. Paul Publications, 1974); *Documents*, 113.
[68] *English Reformations*, 155.

ALL BELIEVERS AS PRIESTS AND KINGS

In a critical study of the biblical concept of royal priesthood, John Hall Elliott concludes many of the doctrines that have been associated with the doctrine in subsequent historical writings—baptism, Christ's unique priesthood, ministerial office, eucharistic sacrifice—do not rely upon a strictly scriptural basis for such associations. The primary text upon which other biblical references[69] depend is Exodus 19.5, the 'Exodus formula', where Israel received the divine promise in covenant. However, I Peter 2.4–10 is the preferred proof-text in Christian discourse. Luther used the latter text in a radical anticlerical sense but Elliott asserts it is more about an elect and holy community than personal freedom from clerical tyranny.[70]

Sacrifice is connected with priesthood in most religions, and Christianity is no exception. In sacrifice, a living creature or token of a creature is dedicated for a holy task on behalf of another. After consecration, the vicarious victim is killed and offered to the deity by the 'priest', a religious official, family senior, or other individual. The purpose of this rite is to facilitate communication with a deity or deities in order to access or remove power.[71] In the New Testament, the elect and holy community presents very real spiritual sacrifices, such as the offering of self; deeds of charity; pecuniary gifts; praises, confession, and prayer; and, converts gained through mission. These sacrifices are offered by the church to God on behalf of the world.[72] A crucial question in Christian history is when, where, and by whom these spiritual sacrifices are to be made.[73] Most medieval Christians assumed lay sacrifices were included within the more powerful offering of the eucharistic sacrifice made only by the priest in the ceremony of the mass. Heretics and reformers disagreed.

In the mediatorial scheme, on the reverse side of sacrifice (a human movement towards deity) is the representation of deity before humans. In Christianity, this human mediation of divine power usually involves proclaiming the Word and administering the sacraments to the community. Again, the crucial question is when, where, and by whom these divine representations are to be made. Most medieval Christians assumed the proclamation of the Word and the administration of the sacraments, for the most part, were the preserve of

---

[69] Isaiah 61.6, 66.21; I Peter 2.5, 9; Revelation 1.6, 5.10, 20.6.

[70] *The Elect and the Holy* (Leiden: E.J. Brill, 1966). Cf. T.F. Torrance, *Royal Priesthood*, 2d edn (Edinburgh: T&T Clark, 1993).

[71] J.H.M. Beattie, 'On Understanding Sacrifice', in *Sacrifice*, ed. by M.F.C. Bourdillon and Meyer Fortes (London: Academic Press, 1980), 29–44.

[72] Romans 12.1, 15.16; I Corinthians 16.14; Philippians 4.18; Colossians 1.28; Hebrews 13.15–16; Revelation 8.3–4, 14.4–5.

[73] R.P.C. Hanson, *Eucharistic Offering in the Early Church* (Bramcote, Nottinghamshire: Grove Books, 1979); Rowan Williams, *Eucharistic Sacrifice: The Roots of a Metaphor* (Bramcote: Grove Books, 1982).

those within holy orders. According to ecclesiastical law, this meant Rome approved the bishops who supervised the priests allowed to perform these activities of soteriological power. However, emergencies might preclude clerical preserve, most commonly in the case of baptism, and occasionally in the case of confession.[74] Moreover, a distinction was eventually made between preaching as public activity and teaching as private activity, the latter being conditionally open to laity. These definitions became problematic when would-be reformers of church and clergy were stifled in their efforts.

Finally, taxonomical issues require attention. We allow the term 'royal priesthood' a dual function: generally, it summarizes the doctrine that all Christian believers are, or will be, priests and kings. The term has also been used synonymously with sacred kingship, most prominently in the writing of Martin Bucer when referring to Edward VI. 'Universal priesthood', 'common priesthood', and 'priesthood of all believers' synonymously describe the concept that all Christians are, in some sense, priests. 'Common priesthood' and 'all Christians are priests' were favored in the period but 'universal priesthood' and 'priesthood of all believers' have gained currency more recently. Some terms were not used in the period, but the concepts were prevalent and we take the liberty in this study to summarize those concepts in shorthand. 'Universal kingship' and 'kingship of all believers' describe the belief that all Christians are, in some sense, kings. 'Common' is used before some tasks previously reserved for priests but subsequently claimed for laity; for example, 'common proclamation', 'common baptism', 'common confession'. 'Lay presidency' designates the celebration of eucharistic communion by laypeople. 'Royal' before a term specifies roles or tasks previously reserved for priests but afterwards claimed by the king; for example, 'royal ordination' and 'royal proclamation'.

Although the primary goal of this study is historical, one should not be tempted to think this entire discussion is irrelevant to modern concerns. Consider three events within the last few decades. *Lumen Gentium*, the dogmatic constitution on the church issued by Vatican II, affirms 'the common priesthood of the faithful' before affirming clerical hierarchy. This rather liberal document raised the expectations of many Roman Catholics, especially lay theologians and progressive priests. Subsequent backpedaling at the 1985 Extraordinary Synod and the 1987 Synod on the Laity, encouraged by the hierarchicalism of John Paul II, proved disappointing. One priest asked how the church expects laity to become involved when all decisions are finally made by clergy.[75] In an entirely different context, a resolution on 'the priesthood of

---

[74] Amédée Teetaert, *La Confession aux Laïques dans L'Eglise Latine depuis le VIIIe jusq'au XIVe Siècle* (Paris: Gabalda, 1926).

[75] *Lumen Gentium*, ch. 2; Jerry Joyce, *The Laity: Help or Hindrance?* (Dublin: Mercier Press, 1994), 111.

the believer' by the 1988 Southern Baptist Convention in San Antonio, Texas, generated strong emotions. Believing the resolution allowed ministerial authority to stifle lay initiative, Southern Baptist 'moderates' marched en masse to the Alamo, sang 'We Shall Overcome', and burned their messenger credentials to symbolize their last stand against the pastoral tyranny of Southern Baptist 'conservatives'.[76] Finally, Bishop Colin Buchanan summarizes as hysterical the reactions to a recent decision in the diocese of Sydney, Australia to consider lay presidency. 'Apparently an Anglican diocese which legitimates lay presidency will cause whole provincial constitutions to unravel, will undermine the historic threefold ministry, and will commit all sorts of good people to attending communion services where they cannot be sure that it is a true sacrament which is being celebrated.'[77] These three cases demonstrate that the 'correct' interpretation of Scripture's 'royal priesthood' remains a lively issue.

[76] A.E. Farnsley, *Southern Baptist Politics* (University Park: Pennsylvania State University Press, 1994), 75–84.

[77] 'Editorial', *News of Liturgy*, 299 (1999), 1. Cf. *Lay Presidency at the Eucharist?*, ed. by Trevor Lloyd (Bramcote: Grove Books, 1977).

1

John Wyclif's Universalist Approach to Universal Priesthood

This chapter addresses John Wyclif's doctrine of universal priesthood and the modern misunderstandings of it, especially the assignment of modern individualism and a thorough antiecclesiasticism to this medieval reformer. Wyclif (d.1384) has become a cipher for those advocating a post-Reformation, post-Enlightenment individualistic interpretation of the royal priesthood. Dyson Hague's words stand as a common interpretation of Wyclif:

> by this theory, which established a direct relation between man and God, Wycliffe swept away the whole basis of a mediating priesthood, the very foundations on which the mediaeval Church was built. More than this. In this great work on The Divine Dominion it seems to me that Wycliffe went deeper, far deeper than the mere feudal, political, ecclesiastical. For in it he uprooted from the foundation the very basic idea of mediaeval theology, the enslaving power of a mediatorial priesthood.[1]

Hague is not one of Wyclif's more reputable biographers, but even such established Wyclif scholars as Herbert Workman and Rudolf Buddenseig attributed modern views to a medieval theologian. Buddenseig claimed that Wyclif's translation of the Bible resulted in certain principles: 'the liberation of the individual from the hands of the priest, the Right of Private Judgment, the Sufficiency of Holy Scripture with regard to salvation, and the transfer of the ultimate authority in religious matters from the Papal Church to the single believer.'[2] This may have been an historical result, but it is doubtful that this was Wyclif's intent. Workman goes further, assigning the Enlightenment doctrine of private judgment to Wyclif himself.[3] 'We note the individualism of Wyclif's

---

[1] *The Life and Work of John Wycliffe*, 2d edn (London: Church Book Room, 1935), 17–18.

[2] *John Wiclif, Patriot and Reformer* (London: Allen & Unwin, 1884), 76.

[3] Workman, *John Wyclif: A Study of the English Medieval Church*, 2 vols (OUP, 1926), II, 153. Helpfully corrected in J.I. Catto, 'Wyclif and Wycliffism at Oxford 1356–1430', in *The History of the University of Oxford*, vol 2, *Late Medieval Oxford*, ed. by J.I. Catto and Ralph Evans (OUP, 1992), 175–262.

system. The organic whole finds little or no place; every man stands face to face with the Will of God; individualism permeates every act of his life.'[4]

Leaving Wyclif's biographers, we find many historical theologians who argue similarly in their reviews. James Edward Rea believed Wyclif's teaching that 'every man must be a theologian' fathered the Lollard common priesthood and is 'fundamentally individualistic, purely internal and anthropocentric'.[5] Cyril Eastwood, employing a naive antihistorical method, drafted Wyclif into the line-up for his modern understanding of the doctrine.[6] Ernst Troeltsch differs little in his assessment.[7]

However, more recent scholars, beginning with Paul de Vooght,[8] have indicated that the modern concept of individualism was not exactly on Wyclif's mind. Reginald Poole tried to reconcile two competing ideologies with the peculiar statement, 'Individualism is therefore only another aspect of Wycliffe's communism.'[9] Others seek to reconcile Wyclif's supposed individualism with his communal focus by showing conflict or change in the theologian's own mind or by positing a major contradiction between his thought and his practice. However, Anthony Kenny and Maurice Keen maintain the profound realism in Wyclif's philosophy helped him adopt the positions that defied the church militant of his day.[10] This chapter builds on

---

[4] Workman, *Wyclif*, II, 19.

[5] John Wyclif, *De Civili Dominio*, ed. by Reginald L. Poole and Johann Loserth, 3 vols (WLW, 1900), I, 402; Rea, *Common Priesthood*, 235.

[6] *Royal Priesthood of the Faithful*, 171–8.

[7] *Social Teaching of the Christian Churches*, 360–1.

[8] *Les Sources de la Doctrine Chrétienne d'après les Théologiens du XIV Siècle et du Début du XVe* (Paris: Desclèe de Brouwer, 1954), 168–200 (196–9).

[9] Although Poole begins the transition to a better understanding of Wyclif's own position, he is still bound to a modernist interpretation. He solves his dilemma by dismissing Wyclif's philosophy and interpreting the Reformation as essentially individualistic, a view he then casts back upon Wyclif.

> In using the word *individual* we are indeed departing from the strict meaning of Wycliffe's words, and introducing an apparent contradiction to that doctrine of community which lies at the root of his exposition. Such is however the purport of his language, as we should now understand it: to Wycliffe himself the individual Christian was nothing save by virtue of his membership of the Christian body; but since he divorced the idea of the church from any necessary connexion with its official establishment and left it purely spiritual, to say that a man's relation to God is determined by his union with the church, is the same as to say that he stands on his own private spiritual footing. Individualism is therefore only another aspect of Wycliffe's communism; and thus, however visionary and unpractical the scheme may be in which he framed it, however bizarre in many of its details, the fundamental principle of his Doctrine of Dominion justifies its author's title to be considered in no partial sense as the father of modern Christianity.

Illustrations of the History of Medieval Thought and Learning (London: SPCK, 1920), 266.

[10] Kenny, *Wyclif* (OUP, 1985); Kenny, 'The Realism of *De Universalibus*', in *Wyclif in His Times*, ed. by Kenny (OUP, 1986), 17–29. 'Wyclif's philosophical views—his realist or Platonist metaphysics—are in consequence the key to much of his theological work. In particular they are the key to his views on a number of subjects which have—or rather had—very practical applications: lordship, the Church, the papacy, the office of kingship, and above all the authority

their work to show that John Wyclif's doctrine of universal priesthood was primarily communal in nature, not individualistic. Furthermore, it is demonstrated that he never intended to rid the church of the order of priesthood and indeed held this position into his latter days. We begin by rediscovering the philosophical, political, and theological foundations upon which Wyclif's doctrine of universal priesthood was built.

WYCLIF'S PHILOSOPHICAL FOUNDATION

In contrast to Wyclif's supposed individualism, what strikes most of Wyclif's modern philosophical commentators is his enthusiasm for realism. The two major systems of the medieval period were realism and nominalism. Realism may be traced from Plato through Augustine and Aquinas, while nominalism is found in certain Aristotelian texts and William of Ockham. In simple terms, realists taught that the universals in which individuals participate have an actual existence. Nominalists disagreed; universals are merely conceptual tools manufactured by the mind to explain commonalities between individuals.[11] With realism, the metaphysical is affirmed wholeheartedly; with nominalism, it is denied or becomes an agnostic or fideistic exercise. Nominalism carried the day for many, perhaps contributing to the individualism often identified with Modernity.[12]

The structure of medieval university education required the student to master philosophy before proceeding to theology. Conceptually, then, philosophy was the basis for theology, and insofar as one proceeded to civil or ecclesiastical service, practice followed from theology. Furthermore, the first topic of theology that one encountered in the standard textbook was the doctrine of God, followed by the doctrines of creation and humanity.[13] There is a natural thought progression from the universal to the particular, from the theoretical to the practical, from deity to humanity. Wyclif took this method to heart and embraced the realism that originally formed it. His realism was reinforced by his reading of Augustine, the Neo-Platonist

of the Bible.' Keen, 'Wyclif, the Bible, and Transubstantiation', in *Wyclif in His Times*, 1–16. Cf. J.A. Robson, *Wyclif and the Oxford Schools* (CUP, 1961), 141–95.

[11] 'Universals have no existence in reality. They are convenient mental fictions, signs standing for many particulars at once.' Meyrick H. Carre, *Realists and Nominalists* (OUP, 1946), 107.

[12] The *via moderna* was the philosophical school influential upon Luther. Although Luther rejected the Pelagianism of the *via moderna*, he incorporated its nominalism into his personal soteriology. Alister McGrath, *The Intellectual Origins of the European Reformation* (Oxford: Blackwell, 1987), 108–21.

[13] G.R. Evans, *Philosophy and Theology in the Middle Ages* (London: Routledge, 1993), 51–118.

theologian whose thought dominated the early medieval West, and of Augustinians such as Thomas Bradwardine (d.1349), whose determinism also informed Wyclif's predestinarianism.[14]

Wyclif's philosophical works, composed between 1365 and 1372, were collected into *Summa De Ente*, consisting of some thirteen treatises arranged in two books.[15] The first book considers being and humanity; the second, God and the divine attributes. The first book includes seven treatises, of which *Tractatus de Universalibus* is considered the most important.[16] Since Wyclif considered his conversion to realism in religious terms and held the system to the end of his life, it may be considered the key to his later thought.[17] His purpose in Chapter 1 of this treatise is to eliminate errors about universals. There are three general classifications of universals: universal by causality, universal by community, and universal by representation. The second in this ordered trilogy, universals by community, or metaphysical universals, are the genus (e.g. animal) and species (e.g. man), which provide the similarities and distinctions of creation. The final classification, universals by representation, consists of the signs by which human minds grasp and communicate the truths of reality. Nominalists embraced the third but denied the second classification. Realists embraced both, attributing knowledge of universals to the agent intellect that is a gift of the uncreated intellect, God. However, Wyclif is chiefly interested in the first classification.

Universals by causality are attributes created in the mind of God. In God is 'the intellectual or ideal being of every creature'.[18] It is important to grasp here that everything in Wyclif's unique doctrines returns to this axiom. The ideal in the immutable mind of God is the basis of every truth: the membership of the church has been predestined and fixed in the mind of God;[19] the Bible is the literary extension of the living Word of God and is, therefore, infallible;[20]

---

[14] Workman, *Wyclif*, I, 119–25. For the intellectual influences on Wyclif, see Robson, *Wyclif and the Oxford Schools*; Gotthard Lechler, *John Wiclif and His English Precursors*, transl. by Peter Lorimer, 2 vols (London: Kegan Paul, 1878), I, 27–120.

[15] Among those works bearing Wyclif's name, the current consensus is that only the published Latin writings may safely be attributed to his direct authorship. The English works are ascribed to his Lollard disciples. Margaret Aston, 'Wyclif and the Vernacular', *SCH*, Subsidia 5 (1987), 281–330; Anne Hudson, 'Wyclif and the English Language', in *Wyclif in His Times*, 85–103.

[16] Kenny, *Wyclif*, 9.

[17] Beryl Smalley, 'The Bible and Eternity: John Wyclif's Dilemma', *Journal of the Warburg and Courtauld Institutes*, 27 (1964), 78–81. The author of *Fasciculi Zizaniorum* was among the first, other than John Kenningham, to recognize the importance of Wyclif's realism to his later doctrines. The first in his list of Wyclif's thirteen heresies is 'that if anything was or will be, it is'. *FZ*, 2–3; Joseph H. Dahmus, *The Prosecution of John Wyclif* (YUP, 1952), 20.

[18] Wyclif, *On Universals (Tractatus de Universalibus)*, transl. by Anthony Kenny (OUP, 1985), 1.

[19] Gordon Leff, 'John Wyclif: The Path to Dissent', *Proceedings of the British Academy*, 52 (1966), 157–60.

[20] Smalley, *Bible and Eternity*, 81–4.

the substance of the eucharist cannot be annihilated since it has been created in the mind of God;[21] and all time is grasped by God instantaneously since he exists above or beyond time.

Developing this last point illuminates Wyclif's thought. He says, 'Every creature which was at any time to be is said to be in its particular causes at the beginning of the world.' In what way is a creature said to be at the beginning? 'Their first and most exalted being is the eternal mental being which they have in God. Every such being is an item of divine life, and is in reality God himself, according to the text of John 1, "What was made, in Him was life".'[22] Since God first creates the creature as an ideal in His mind, and God always is and lives beyond time, then the ideal always exists. 'And thus it seems reasonable to say that God is always creating his creatures, because he is always making them in the way that a light makes light.' Again, 'the existence of the creature, even though it is temporal, causes in God an eternal mental relationship, which is always in the process of being caused and yet is always already completely caused.' In other words, all that has existed, that exists now, or that will exist in time is currently present to, and maintained by, God.[23] 'All these and similar things are obvious from the infallible principle that with God all things which have ever been or will ever be are present, and thus, if something has been or will be, it is at the appropriate time.' As a corollary, it can never be annihilated, since annihilation would entail not only an impoverishment of creation but also the loss of divine integrity. In his later arguments over transubstantiation, he would conclude that annihilation, a prominent interpretation of transubstantiation, is, therefore, blasphemy.[24]

Since God created universals and individuals, they will continue to exist. The theory of universals is so important that lack of love for universals is the root of all sin. However, while concerned for universals, Wyclif does not ignore *supposits*, individuals. They, too, have substances which are related to the universal substance, but which are distinct because 'they receive contraries as changes take place within them'. Supposits originate from and share or participate in the universals. They truly exist but are of a lower priority.[25]

In Chapter 3 of this treatise, his philosophy of universals impacts his theology and ethics. In agreement with Augustine, Wyclif 'teaches how we are to love common things'. The more universal goods are better because they

---

[21] Heather Phillips, 'John Wyclif and the Optics of the Eucharist', *SCH*, Subsidia 5 (1987), 45–58.

[22] *On Universals*, 48–9, 130, 134.

[23] Although these statements may lead us to consider pantheism, Wyclif never gave such a full definition and was careful to distinguish between creator and creation. *On Universals*, 147, 162.

[24] *On Universals*, 163–4, 140–50. Cf. Kenny, 'Realism and Determinism in the Early Wyclif', *SCH*, Subsidia 5 (1987), 165–77.

[25] *On Universals*, 10–15, 155–78. God 'has utterly distinct knowledge of everything there is.' *On Universals*, 24–5.

are prior by nature and are of greater concern to God. 'From all this it is clear—I think—that all envy or actual sin is caused by the lack of an ordered love of universals.' Wyclif offers two ethical examples of how this love of universals above individuals should display itself.

> [First,] what everyone must principally love in his neighbour is that he is a human being, and not that he is his own son, or someone useful; for according to Augustine it is being a man which is what is common and is in an especial manner the work of God, since it precedes every particular human being, while being your son, or your mistress, is something you have brought about yourself.

> [Second,] if proprietors who are devoted to particulars were more concerned that a well-ordered commonwealth should thrive, than that their kinsfolk should prosper, or their relations or the people linked to them by locality or by some other individuating condition, then beyond doubt they would not press, in the disordered way they do, for their own people to be raised to wealth, office, prelacy and other dignities. They would aim a little higher, and want such preeminence indifferently for anyone of their species, provided that was the more appropriate thing for the general public.

He concludes, therefore, that 'beyond doubt, intellectual and emotional error about universals is the cause of all the sin that reigns in the world'. Salvation from this sin is not an inward turn to mystical contemplation but an outward turn to communal action. Betterment of the human community is more important than personal soteriology or the advancement of one's closest contacts. (Later, he will affirm that salvation is in the hands of God and cannot be known for sure but may be indicated by right living within the community.) Therefore, 'if the will, in place of its private good, preferred, in due order, the common or better good, it would not sin.'[26]

When asked why other scholars do not hold this same truth, Wyclif responds with four reasons: the darkening of the reason, the ears of the sophists, the arrogance of many people, and a lack of instruction. Indeed, his philosophy comes to him, he says, out of direct religious experience. God has revealed this truth to him, converting him from a sinful outlook. From this philosophical foundation, Wyclif developed his theology in general[27] and his doctrine of universal priesthood in particular. Before proceeding, it should be noted that Wyclif's primary aim in life was to reform the institutions of church and society that he loved so dearly. He was not setting out a soteriology of individuals, but a reformation of institutions.[28] Significantly in terms of this

---

[26] *On Universals*, 21–2.

[27] Samuel Harrison Thomson suggested in 1931 that Wyclif's philosophy was the basis for his theology, a point recently demonstrated at length by Stephen E. Lahey. Thomson, 'The Philosophical Basis of Wyclif's Theology', *Journal of Religion*, 11 (1931), 86–116; Lahey, *Philosophy and Politics in the Thought of John Wyclif* (CUP, 2003); Lahey, *John Wyclif*, John Wyclif (OUP, 2009), 199.

[28] William Farr, *John Wyclif as Legal Reformer*, (Leiden: E.J. Brill, 1974).

present study, his reform efforts, although pointed towards a community of equality in Christ, were to be responsibly instituted through the laws of England and its monarch.[29]

DOMINION AND GRACE

One major aspect of 'royal priesthood' is royalty. How did Wyclif understand kingship? First of all, Christ is the highest King, the King who became a commoner. In *De Benedicta Incarnacione*, Wyclif contends that Christ took upon himself the common humanity of all men, 'the manhood as it is in the *forma exemplaris* of the Divine Idea'. The humanity of Christ being the 'universal man' becomes the basis of the humanity of all his brethren, and individual human beings are thereby bonded together. With this basic definition, any essential distinctions between humans dissipate,[30] but social distinctions necessarily remain.

In *De Officio Regis*, he outlines how the three estates of the medieval period began. Priests, kings, and people were not always separate but became so through an historical process: At the beginning of the world, all were *reges et sacerdotes*, kings and priests, but temporal dominion was handed over to individual kings after the Fall. With the giving of the law, the church, which includes Israel, was given *distinccionem inter clerum et laycos*, the distinction between clergy and people. Then beginning with *legis gracie*, the law of grace, the church was endowed with a *maiorem distinccionem* between clergy and people through the conferring of the indelible character on the clergy. The clergy at this time were 'pure and propertyless like rational souls who aspire to heaven.' This divine order, however, was upset when the clergy began to acquire property, for the king alone should rule over the temporal realm while priests should rule spiritually. Kings do not normally celebrate the sacraments, and priests should never aspire to exercise royal power, which includes dominion over property.[31]

There is a subtle distinction in Wyclif's thought, for although priests must never function as kings, kings may function as priests. As a general rule, kings do not celebrate the sacraments, but they must discipline the priests and may periodically ordain priests according to various Old Testament precedents.[32]

---

[29] Michael Wilks, 'Predestination, Property, and Power: Wyclif's Theory of Dominion and Grace', *SCH*, 2 (1965), 220–36.

[30] Workman, *Wyclif*, I, 138–9.

[31] *[P]ure exproprietarie tanquam animal racionale ad celestia aspirante. De Officio Regis*, ed. by Alfred W. Pollard and Charles Sayle (WLW, 1887), 137–49; other references in Wilks, 'Royal Patronage and Anti-Papalism from Ockham to Wyclif', *SCH*, Subsidia 5 (1987), 151n.

[32] *De Officio Regis*, 144.

Sacramental power is normally reserved to priests but the king has total jurisdictional power. The laws of the king apply to the clergy within his realm, for ecclesiastical legislation *pertinat ad regem, qui debet esse sacerdos et pontifex regni sui*, pertains to the king, who ought to be priest and high priest for his realm.[33] According to Augustine, 'The king is adored on earth as the vicar of God'. The king is, therefore, the vicar of Christ's deity, which places him above the priest who is the vicar of His humanity.[34] As a result, the king must be a priest but a priest must not be a king.[35] When priests assume secular power, they become laity in reality and priests in name, thereby confusing mother church.[36]

Wyclif elaborated on both civil dominion and divine dominion in his major treatises, *De Civili Dominio* and *De Divino Dominio*. Drawing upon a famous polemic against the friars, *De Pauperie Salvatoris*, by Richard FitzRalph (d.1360),[37] Wyclif concluded that all dominion is actually God's. Human beings lost the original gift of dominion, natural lordship, at the Fall and now only hold it as a stewardship when in the state of grace. Whatever a sinful man does is sin and since God holds all dominion, he will not entrust the sinful man with dominion as he disapproves of sin. However, through God's permissive will, the sinful man may hold things for a time even if he does not hold real dominion.[38]

As opposed to Aristotle and Aquinas, who find the origin of civil law in human nature, Wyclif places its origination in sin. Though divinely instituted, civil dominion is in itself a sinful enterprise. When kings exercise dominion, they sin but not mortally. There are two types of human dominion after the Fall, civil and evangelical. Evangelical dominion is that of the clergy, indeed of all true Christians. Since the church should not be involved in sin, it can have

---

[33] *De Officio Regis*, 152. 'And from this premise Wyclif had little difficulty in defining the regalian rights of the king over his clergy: his position as the source of ecclesiastical property; his rights of patronage—to reserve benefices, to appoint bishops, to tax the clergy, and to extract oaths of allegiance from them; his duty to make laws for the regulation of the priesthood; his capacity to punish delinquent clerics; his power to revoke his original grants by withholding ecclesiastical revenues or by outright confiscation of church property in time of need—all the very familiar features of an ecclesiastical polity over which the prince stands supreme as king and priest.' Wilks, 'Predestination, Property and Power', 234–5. Cf. Wilks, 'Royal Patronage and Anti-Papalism', 163.

[34] *Rex adoratur in terris quasi vicarius dei.* Augustine, *De Questionibus Veteris et Nove Legis*, ch. 20. Wyclif, *De Officio Regis*, 12–14.

[35] *Unde non plus confunderetur, minoraretur vel extingueretur sacerdotis auctoritas quam presumendo assumere in eodem sacerdote istam duplicem potestatem.* 'Priestly authority is no more confused, threatened or extinguished than where in their priesthood they assume this twofold power.' *De Officio Regis*, 141.

[36] *Patet etiam quomodo multi hodie sunt nudo nomine clerici cum vita et proprietate possessionis sunt laici, et ista duplicitas creditur confudere matrem nostram. De Officio Regis*, 149.

[37] Workman, *Wyclif*, I, 126–32.

[38] L.J. Daly, *The Political Theory of John Wyclif* (Chicago: Loyola University Press, 1962), 68–70.

no involvement in civil dominion. Practically, this entails the 'medicinal' disendowment of the hierarchy and the monastic orders. Since perhaps one-third of all lands were in the hands of ecclesiastics, this was social dynamite.

The church consists of the lords, who exercise civil dominion with the temporal sword; the priests, who exercise evangelical dominion with the spiritual sword; and the commons. Both types of dominion, civil and evangelical, proceed from the same source, Jesus Christ. Furthermore, since Old Testament kings ruled their priests, temporal lords must monitor clerical ethics. However, temporal lords must also respect the clergy's spiritual ministrations. Wyclif envisioned concord, not discord, between the two powers. The secular lord gives physical alms for sustenance; the cleric gives his more valuable spiritual alms in return.[39] Both were to honor each other in different ways: the clergy were to honor the king's palpable dignity; secular rulers were to honor the clergy's superior life and greater virtue.[40]

This formula might have worked in the scholastic laboratory but two other Wycliffite conclusions—that 'no one in mortal sin is lord of anything' and that the good Christian has dominion of all goods whatever his social status—caused problems in the field, when heard by others.[41] Although Wyclif rigorously applied his strictures against sinful dominion to the church, he refused to apply them to the state. Others failed, or refused, to grasp this distinction. There is a division of scholarly opinion concerning the impact of Wyclif's teachings on the peasants involved in the revolt of 1381, but he obviously did not help the situation.[42] We know that Wyclif based his appeal for the disendowment of the church on the needs of the impoverished people and taught that 'the poor are the basis of the pillar of state'.[43] His purpose in calling on the crown to effect the needed reform was for the benefit of all people and not the crown itself.

Considering the vehemence of Wyclif's preaching and the fairly rigid social structure of the day, Wyclif might have inadvertently added fuel to the smoldering fire of social resentment. There were class tensions within English society due to the undermining of traditional feudal rights that accompanied

---

[39] *The Political Theory of John Wyclif*, 71–88.

[40] *De Officio Regis*, 14–15.

[41] One basis for Wyclif's egalitarianism was his contention that before sin there was no need for civil law. The best form of government is aristocracy rather than monarchy because the former reflects the original state, but sin has necessitated monarchy. Dahmus, *Prosecution*, 24; Lahey, *Philosophy and Politics in the Thought of John Wyclif*, 161–2.

[42] 'There is little reason to think that his teaching was responsible for the rising, still less that the rebels had his active encouragement or support.' K.B. McFarlane, *John Wycliffe and the Beginnings of English Nonconformity* (London: English Universities Press, 1952), 99. Steven Justice, relying on a treatise and a sermon of Wyclif's which were meant for wide distribution in the mid-1370s, believes his violent language was 'misapplied' by the rebels. *Writing and Rebellion: England in 1381* (London: University of California Press, 1994), 67–101.

[43] *Writing and Rebellion*, 85n.

the rising demand for labor and a concurrent rise in wages. A new poll tax exacerbated the matter.[44] The misapplied theology of Wyclif and the preaching of John Ball—who is supposed to have said, 'Whan Adam dalf, and Eve span, Wo was thanne a gentilman?'—may have fanned the flames [see Plate 3], but it is doubtful this was Wyclif's intention.[45] There are some uncanny resemblances between his egalitarian communism and the preaching of the rebels, but Wyclif generally looked to the lords to solve the problems for the people.[46] The people's problems would all be solved by royal disendowment of the church. Utopia for him was not democracy but a virtuous aristocracy.[47] Of the three types of governments he envisioned (aristocratic, monarchical, and priestly) he considered monarchy inevitable and priestly government reprehensible.[48] Democracy was not an option.

Wyclif limits universal kingship in numerous ways. In a sermon on Revelation 1, the only sense in which Christians may be kings is *in patria* or *ad patrium*, that is, in relationship with the father. Moreover, evangelical kingship is fulfilled only when the church militant is eschatologically transformed into the church triumphant.[49] Although evangelical, or natural, lordship belongs to the *predestinati*, it is not to be claimed now but shared. True Christian lordship communicates itself now and realizes itself fully only in future. Moreover, evangelical lordship is not for personal use; it is a 'community of lordship'.[50] By emphasizing its Godward direction, by suspending its exercise into the eschaton, and by noting its communal dimension, Wyclif kept his version of the kingship of all believers, 'evangelical lordship', free of radical application.

THE COMMUNITY OF THE PREDESTINED

There is a naive consensus among some scholars that anyone who preaches against the clergy is obviously antisacerdotal, anticlerical, or antiecclesiastical.[51]

---

[44] As the nation was fighting against France at the time and the papacy was at Avignon, some felt payments to the papacy supported the enemy. Wyclif taught that during emergencies the church must return donations and relieve taxation on the poor. Keen, *English Society in the Later Middle Ages 1348–1500* (London: Penguin, 1990), 1–76, 217–39.

[45] R.B. Dobson, *The Peasants' Revolt of 1381*, 2d edn (London: Macmillan, 1983), 374.

[46] Justice, *Writing and Rebellion*, ch. 2.

[47] Howard Kaminsky, 'Wyclifism as Ideology of Revolution', *CH*, 32 (1963), 66.

[48] *De Civili Dominio*, bk. 1, ch. 27; *From Irenaeus to Grotius*, ed. by Oliver O'Donovan and Joan Lockwood O'Donovan (Cambridge: Eerdmans, 1999), 506–7.

[49] *Per istam autem locionem sumus complete facti regnum quod est ecclesia triumphans. Sermones*, ed. by Johann Loserth, 4 vols (WLW, 1887–1890), IV, 182–3.

[50] *De Civili Dominio*, bk. 1, ch. 7; bk. 3, ch. 5; *From Irenaeus to Grotius*, 488–91.

[51] Gordon Leff, *Heresy in the Later Middle Ages* (Manchester: Manchester University Press, 1967), II, 494ff; Malcolm Lambert, *Medieval Heresy*, 2d edn (Oxford: Blackwell, 1992), 219, 224.

Considering the sheer volume of Wyclif's clerical denouncements, it is easy to attribute all of his activity to these negative conceptions. However, Gerald Owst and Penn Szittya have shown that orthodox churchmen could be just as vehement in their denunciations.[52] One wonders why these orthodox churchmen are not generally considered 'anticlerical' as well. Furthermore, Wyclif was not 'against the church' or 'against the priests' as the terms suggest; rather, he wanted to correct the abuses of the church and return the ministry to true spiritual leadership, and his theology lent itself to this task.

The metaphysical grounding of Wyclif's theology in realism is also evident in his ecclesiology. Since the division of humanity between *predestinati*, the predestined to salvation, and *praesciti*, the foreknown to damnation, is within the immutable mind of God, there can be no change from one status to another by any human effort. Neither can there be any real effort to separate the two groups now, other than separating oneself from plainly wicked clergy.[53] There were three mysteries hidden from human persons: whether they are predestined to glory or not; the time of their death; and, the time of the day of judgment. Furthermore, the clergy cannot be sure they or anyone else are part of the elect. Therefore, heirarchical excommunication is a useless exercise unless God has already pronounced judgment. Ordination secures nothing without righteousness, and one could conceivably become a priest without being ordained by a wicked bishop.[54] The marks of true priesthood are the lack of sin, the practice of evangelical poverty, and the preaching of the Word. Wyclif thereby minimized holy orders, as well as the other sacraments, but he did not dispense with them.[55]

One of Wyclif's favorite means of denouncing his opponents is to label them *privatas sectas*. The 'private sects' he addresses are, in general, the Caesarean clergy, monks, friars, and canons. Another taxonomy of 'private sects' was confined to the four major mendicant orders.[56] In *De Apostasia*, the four mendicant orders (Carmelites, Augustinians, Franciscans, and Dominicans) are denounced as 'private religions'. The true religion, founded on the

---

[52] Owst, *Preaching in Medieval England* (CUP, 1926), 21–38; Szittya, *The Antifraternal Tradition in Medieval Literature* (PUP, 1986).

[53] Wilks, 'Predestination, Property and Power', 224–8.

[54] *De Simonia*, ed. by Michael Henry Dziewicki and Dr Herzberg-Frankel (WLW, 1899), 112–13; *On Simony*, transl. by Terrence A. McVeigh (New York: Fordham University Press, 1992), 162–3.

[55] Cf. Leff, *Heresy*, 516–45.

[56] Paradoxically, the 'private sects' reinforced Wyclif's concern for the common good. Prior to his antimendicant phase, in the 1371 Parliament, two Austin friars, arguing for disendowment of the church because of the need to finance the war with France, said that by natural and divine law all goods are common. Private property has the sanction only of custom and human legislation. When the need arises, 'private property must yield to the general good'. It is believed that Wyclif attended this Parliament, adopted their terminology and subsequently applied the argument to the church hierarchy. Aubrey Gwynn, *The English Austin Friars in the Time of Wyclif* (OUP, 1940), 214–15.

observance of Christ's law, has been replaced by these private and idolatrous
religions. Wyclif calls on his 'good comrades' to come out of the false private
religions and follow the one true order of Christ alone. Faithful religious must
follow Scripture, rather than 'apocryphal inventions', and 'shun as poison the
practices which set more store on these later rites than on God's law, and
which is more zealous for the state of their own private sect than for the
common good'.[57] As he later proclaimed, there should not be multiple sects
dividing the church; all should be members *in unicam sectam domini Iesu
Cristi*, in the singular sect of the Lord Jesus Christ.[58]

Because of Wyclif's attacks on papacy, prelacy, and religious orders, Workman concludes his ecclesiology is 'without hierarchy, and without divisions.
Distinctions of a sort there must be, but such distinctions should not be of
spiritual status.... Essentially all are one, just as presbyter and bishop originally were one.'[59] Workman reads Wyclif correctly, to a point, but he fails to see
that Wyclif did hold to a consistent distinction between clergy and laity.
Moreover, Wyclif's purpose was not to exalt individuals but the community.
The problem with the private sects was that they did not have the communal
good in mind but their own.

Developing a Trinitarian model of community, Wyclif demonstrates how
the private sects destroyed the bonds of communal love. 'There are three
bonds of love by which the living faithful are gathered to one another,
undoubtedly the bond of blood, the bond of affinity, and the bond of charity.'
The first bond, that between parent and child, corresponds to the Father, who
begets to himself a natural Son. The second bond, that of marriage, corresponds to the Son, who assumed humanity to marry the church. The third
bond occurs when the Holy Spirit, who is charity or love, links together two
formerly independent persons, *substancialiter*, substantially.[60] What galls
Wyclif is that a diabolical twofold bond has been constructed to attack and
replace the divine threefold bond. The twofold bond is comprised of the four
mendicant sects with their legal traditions. In this way the four divisive sects
sought to replace the one true and universal *sectam domini Iesu Cristi*.[61]

Wyclif's attack would have radically altered the institutional church in
England, if the state had taken it to heart. However, Pope Gregory XI was

---

[57] *Et hii cavent tamquam venenum quod plus ponderent ritus adiectos quam legem dei et plus
zelent pro statu private secte quam pro bono publico. De Apostasia*, ed. by Michael Henry
Dziewicki (WLW, 1889), 44; Gwynn, 267.

[58] *De Fundatione Sectarum*, in *Polemical Works*, ed. by Rudolf Buddenseig, 2 vols (WLW,
1883), I, 21–5; Szittya, *Antifraternal Tradition*, 181–2.

[59] Workman, *Wyclif*, II, 93.

[60] *Tria sunt vincula amoris, quibus fideles viantes ad invicem colligantur, scilicet vinculum
consanwineitatis, vinculum affinitatis et vinculum caritatis. De Triplici Vinculo Amoris*, in
Polemical Works, I, 161–2.

[61] *Polemical Works*, 143.

quick to condemn Wyclif, informing the court of Edward III that Wyclif's principles were 'conducive to the weakening of the entire ecclesiastical order'. Gregory then employed a powerful and long-lived argument, a domino theory of church and state, asserting that not only is the church in danger but Wyclif's principles also 'threaten the destruction of the entire state'. The secular lords must act quickly 'as well as for their own merit before God and their honor in this life'.[62] The temporal lords probably took no action against Wyclif because of his strong Erastianism, but his followers would prove another matter.

THE EUCHARIST

Intimately bound up with any discussion of universal priesthood is the role of the eucharist, the defining cultural symbol of the Middle Ages, an era in which symbolism influenced everything.[63] The eucharist was understood according to the doctrine of transubstantiation made authoritative at Lateran IV in 1215, but there were various interpretations of the doctrine of transubstantiation. According to Aquinas, the substance changed and the accidents were upheld by quantity. Alternatively, John Duns Scotus believed the substance of the elements were annihilated, leaving the accidents to be miraculously upheld by God.[64] Scotus' view prevailed in Oxford. In 1378, Wyclif condemned the Scotist understanding, branding it a modern innovation. He reasoned that the substance and the accidents remain unchanged after consecration. Annihilation conflicts with realism and with the integrity of God, for God does not deceive our senses; the theory of cognition and the integrity of God must be preserved. Therefore, transubstantiation, which Wyclif took to mean Scotist annihilation, must be rejected. Gary Macy has classified the late medieval views of transubstantiation as 'coexistence', 'substitution', and 'transmutation'. 'Coexistence', similar to Luther's consubstantiation, was effectively shut out by the condemnation of Wyclif at Constance.[65]

---

[62] Bull of 22 May 1377; Dahmus, *Prosecution*, 45. Although Gregory died soon after and the Schism delayed any prosecution of Wyclif by the papacy, the same arguments were used against Wyclif after 1381, against the Lollards after the Oldcastle rising of 1414, and against the reformers in the sixteenth century. This continued coupling of church and state against egalitarian reforms can be seen in James VI and I's axiom of 'no Bishop, no King'. *A History of Conferences and Other Proceedings Connected with the Book of Common Prayer, From the Year 1558 to the Year 1690*, 3d edn, ed. by Edward Cardwell (OUP, 1849), 183–4, 202–3.

[63] Rowan Williams, 'Religious Experience in the Era of Reform', in *Companion Encyclopedia of Theology*, ed. by Peter Byrne and Leslie Houlden (London: Routledge, 1995), 576.

[64] Keen, 'Wyclif, the Bible, and Transubstantiation', 7–8.

[65] 'The Dogma of Transubstantiation in the Middle Ages', *JEH*, 45 (1994), 11–22.

Wyclif believed transubstantiation turns the eucharist into an idolatrous blasphemy since it teaches people to adore the absurd.[66] Some assume Wyclif thus denies the Real Presence, but he did not. Rather, he tried to put the presence of God in the eucharist on a higher plane of understanding than the merely carnal.[67] Christ is not physically present, but spiritually or sacramentally or figuratively, and is received by faith.[68] *Figura* does not mean unreal, or less real, as might be expected. For Wyclif, a thorough-going realist, the figurative or the spiritual may be hidden from us, but it remains the higher plane of reality.[69]

Wyclif's opponents feared any change in eucharistic theology, for if the priest cannot make the body of Christ, then his authority over the salvation-seeking laity is diminished. Building on the works of Dionysius, the pseudo-Areopagite, the entire medieval sacerdotal and social structure was believed to rely on this priestly power to make the body of God.[70] Wyclif, however, denies his condemnation of transubstantiation will destroy priestly authority. Rather, 'priestly authority would be kept and comprehended within its proper limits'. The basis of clerical authority is not the power to make the bread into Christ's body, but the 'spreading abroad' of Christ's holiness and blessedness through his body, the church.[71] In rejecting annihilation, Wyclif was not ridding the church of eucharistic presidency; rather, he was objecting to certain philosophical definitions of the eucharist, and to their popular abuses.

SCRIPTURE AND PROCLAMATION

Wyclif worked out the biblical implications of his metaphysics in debate with the Carmelite friar and theologian, John Kenningham (d.1399).[72] In that debate, Wyclif displayed a very high view of Scripture, for Scripture has its origin with God. This has led to a divergence of opinion on how 'fundamentalist' Wyclif was. For instance, Robson argues,

> the Word of Scripture was God Himself, an emanation of the Supreme Being 'transposed into writing'. [Indeed,] the word of God was divinely inspired; more, it was the material form of the eternal Word, itself a divine exemplar existing prior to the composition of the Scriptures in historic times. Each syllable of

---

[66] See Chapter 1 of this book.

[67] Catto, 'John Wyclif and the Cult of the Eucharist', *SCH*, Subsidia 4 (1985), 269–86.

[68] *De Eucharistia*, ed. by Johann Loserth (WLW, 1892), 14–17. Cf. Leff, *Heresy*, 549–7.

[69] *De Apostasia*, 223.

[70] Exemplified in a reply to the 1395 Lollard attack on the eucharist. Roger Dymmok, *Liber Contra XII Errores et Hereses Lollardorum*, ed. by H.S. Cronin (WLW, 1922), 91–2, 108–10.

[71] *De Eucharistia*, 15; *On the Eucharist*, in *LCC*, XIV, 64–5.

[72] Workman, *Wyclif*, II, 120–2.

Scripture is true because it is a divine emanation: Wyclif had come to accept literal fundamentalism.[73]

However, Robson appears to overstate the case for Wyclif's 'fundamentalism'. Smalley specified a more relevant model for Wyclif's doctrine of Scripture. She identified an important metaphor according to which Wyclif argued that the words of Scripture are a 'mirror' whereby the truth shines. The imagery of the Bible as reflective preserves a connection between God and the written text while simultaneously specifying a difference.[74]

Wyclif was shocked by what he perceived to be the lack of respect for Scripture in his day. He considered the clergy ignorant or dismissive towards it because they wanted to keep the laity unaware of priestly sin.[75] He said the Bible should be available in the vernacular to clergy and laity alike in order to dispel this ignorance of the 'logic of Scripture'. Although optimistic about the ability of the agent intellect in all people to receive the gift of knowledge from the uncreated intellect, he recognized that many would err in translation and interpretation. The clerical suppression of Scripture is an error rooted in pride.[76] The vernacular language must be used since the truth of God can be clothed in many languages.

Interpretation itself is not simply an exercise of the individual receiving divine illumination, although this is indeed necessary. Rather, the truth of Christ's law is found in following a threefold process: 'faith in Scripture', 'lively reasoning', and 'the effective witness of the saints'. In practice, Wyclif relied on all three, as evidenced by his continued use of logic and the teaching of the Fathers when interpreting Scripture. 'The effective witness of the saints' in his hands sounds much like the *sensus fidelium* of Vatican II and is much more dynamic than mere 'fundamentalism' or 'private judgment'. He emphasized the literal sense but readily used the figurative, the tropological, the allegorical.[77] (Wyclif's conception of *sola scriptura* is related to our concerns but differs in its focus on Scripture rather than orders.) There has been a lively debate concerning Wyclif's supposed embrace of *sola scriptura*. Paul de Vooght has the better of the debate because of his historical sensitivity. Wyclif's detractors have usually judged him according to later conceptions and for polemical purposes.[78]

---

[73] Robson, *Wyclif and the Oxford Schools*, 146, 163–8.

[74] *Ipse enim sunt speculum in quo veritates eterna relucent.* Smalley, *Bible and Eternity*, 81.

[75] *De Officio Pastorali*, ed. by Gotthard Victor Lechler (Leipzig, 1863), 36; *On the Pastoral Office*, in *LCC*, XIV, 51.

[76] *Et ita defectus fidei scripturae est causa superbiae. Trialogus Cum Supplemento Trialogi*, ed. by Gotthard Lechler (OUP, 1869), 163; *Tracts and Treatises of John de Wycliffe, D.D.*, transl. by Robert Vaughan (London: Wycliffe Society, 1845), 130.

[77] *LCC*, XIV, 82.

[78] De Vooght, *Les Sources*, 196–9; Michael Hurley, '*Scriptura Sola*: Wyclif and His Critics', *Traditio*, 16 (1960), 275–352; Eric Doyle, 'William Woodford on Scripture and Tradition', in *Studia Historico-Ecclesiastica*, ed. by Isaac Vazquez (Rome: Pontificum Athenaeum Antonianum, 1977), 481–504. De Vooght replied to Hurley in 'Wyclif et la *Scriptura Sola*', *Ephemerides Theologicae Lovanienses*, 39 (1963), 50–86. In the latest statement on the issue, Jeremy Catto,

Wyclif's novelty was not his placing of the interpretation of Scripture in the hands of the individual. Wyclif has been accused of this, but he never went to such an extreme. Rather, he placed Scripture in the hands of the community as opposed to the 'private sects'. Every Christian must indeed be a theologian, but he must receive as much training in theology and metaphysics as possible.[79] The Bible is to be his object of understanding and the sense of the Catholic church his support. Wyclif's novelty was not the surrender of the community in favor of the individual but his opposition of Scripture as understood by the Fathers to recent church tradition.[80] He believed that the church hierarchy and councils could err because of their individual nature and it was the task of the laity as the militant part of the universal church to reclaim the ancient truths.[81] Wyclif wanted to rescue the church from hierarchical individualism and return it to true community by including the laity in the recovery of the ancient tradition. Even in his final, beleaguered years he continued to stress the priority of the public good of the community over the private good of the individual.[82]

This emphasis on Scripture led to his emphasis on preaching. According to Wyclif, true priests, especially those directly responsible for the cure of souls, must look into the mirror of Scripture and vigilantly foresee and forewarn their flock about the dangers facing them.[83] Wyclif's emphasis on clerical preaching was, however, nothing new. The friars were founded as 'orders of preachers' and the hierarchy had long promoted the virtues of proclamation and instruction.[84]

WYCLIF'S DOCTRINE OF UNIVERSAL PRIESTHOOD

In the context of his overall philosophical theology, the statements of Wyclif concerning universal priesthood may now be properly situated. In a number of places, he implies universal priesthood and even states *quod omnis*

---

who wrote his Oxford dissertation on Wyclif's opponent, William Woodford, asserted that *De Veritate Sacrae Scripturae*, 'unlike *De civili dominio*, was not a call to reform on the part of the church, but a declaration of independence for himself and his followers on the scriptural basis of self-evident, if not self-explanatory truth.' 'Wyclif and Wycliffism at Oxford', 209. For Wyclif's hermeneutical model, see G.R. Evans, 'Wyclif on Literal and Metaphorical', *SCH*, Subsidia 5 (1987), 259–66.

[79] *De Veritate Sacrae Scripturae*, ed. by Rudolf Buddenseig, 3 vols (WLW, 1906), I, 378; II, 141, 145, 166; de Vooght, *Les Sources*, 168–200.

[80] Leff, 'Path to Dissent', 157.

[81] Leff, *Heresy*, 520–4.

[82] The individual finds his welfare served in self-sacrifice for the sake of the community. *Trialogus*, 102–3; *Tracts and Treatises*, 114.

[83] Szittya, *Antifraternal Tradition*, 174–5.

[84] Owst, *Preaching in Medieval England*, 39–46.

predestinatus laycus est sacerdos, that every predestined layman is a priest.[85] This is based on the testimony of 'Augustine, Chrysostom, and other saints'. It is imperative to our understanding of Wyclif's doctrine of universal priesthood that in this passage from the 1380 *De Eucharistia* he was arguing for a certain understanding of the eucharist; universal priesthood is but a subsidiary argument. Since the laity 'could'—Wyclif is clear that he is employing the logician's method of potentiality and is not promoting an actuality—administer the eucharist, this indicates transubstantiation in the hands of the ordained priest is a fallacy. The focus, therefore, should not be on the power of the priest but the faith of the recipient. Moreover, the church has reasonably required that only 'priests according to religious status and the dignity of custom' should consecrate the sacrament. Universal priesthood may lead to a purified ordained ministry, but it does not destroy order.

> None (it might be said) of the faithful doubts indeed that God may give to the layman the power of consecrating, just as the layman, since he could be a priest (as the logicians say), could consecrate. Indeed, it seems according to the testimony of Augustine, Chrysostom, and other saints that every predestined layman is a priest; and much more, that a devout layman, when consecrating, since he could be giving holy ministry to the church, could have the reckoning of a priest. But even so, as the church has reasonably varied in the words of consecration from all four evangelists, while preserving the meaning, it opens out of the faith of the Scripture what ought to be done; thus it [the church] has reasonably ordained that only priests, according to the religious state and dignity of custom, could consecrate this sacrament.[86]

Contrary to the context of the phrase, 'every predestined layman is a priest', Gordon Leff concludes this 'was tantamount to a denial of the priesthood as an order. As such it must be accounted the single most destructive and heretical feature of Wyclif's teaching.'[87] Wyclif's doctrine of the universal priesthood as understood by Leff might indeed make Wyclif the 'greatest heresiarch of the

---

[85] *De Eucharistia*, 98. Margaret Aston summarizes similar passages from Wyclif's *De Potestate Pape* and reasons that the universal priesthood is a 'hypothetical contingency'. 'Lollard Women Priests?' in Aston, *Lollards and Reformers* (London: Hambledon Press, 1984), 67–9. Cf. Williell R. Thomson, *The Latin Writings of John Wyclyf: An Annotated Catalog* (Toronto: Pontifical Institute of Mediaeval Studies, 1983), 296.

[86] *Nullus (inquam) fidelis dubitat quin Deus posset dare layco potenciam conficiendi, sicut laycus cum possit esse sacerdos (ut dicunt loyci) possit conficere. Ymmo videtur iuxta testimonium Augustini, Crisostomi et aliorum sanctorum quod omnis predestinatus laycus est sacerdos, et multo magis devotus laycus conficiens, cum daret ecclesie sacrum ministerium, haberet racionem sacerdotis. Verumptamen sicut ecclesia racionabiliter variavit in verbis confeccionis ab omnibus hiis quatuor evangelistis servando sentenciam, quod patet ex fide scripture debere fieri, sic racionabiliter ordinavit quod soli sacerdotes propter religiositatem et dignitatem in moribus hoc sacramentum conficerent. De Eucharistia*, 98–9. Cf. *LCC*, XIV, 84.

[87] Leff, *Heresy*, 520. Cf. Leff, 'Path to Dissent', 161.

later middle ages'.[88] However, in spite of Leff's strident assertions, Wyclif never denied the priesthood as an order, nor did he replace it with an orderless universal priesthood. His references to universal priesthood were always couched in the scholastic form of potentiality; subjunctives and verbs of possibility abound. If anything, the only concrete service for a universal priesthood might be a transition to a new ordained ministry.

Leff's error is apparently repeated by Richard Southern in his otherwise excellent biography of Wyclif's forerunner, Robert Grosseteste. Southern alleges that Wyclif 'illegitimately' misrepresented Grosseteste with his doctrine of universal priesthood. 'Grosseteste did not support Wyclif's views of the right of the laity to take over and administer ecclesiastical revenues; or on the lack of necessity for confession to a priest; or on the priesthood of all believers; or on the Eucharist.'[89] But a comparison between Grosseteste's sermon to the clergy and Wyclif's reference to that sermon does not reveal a chasm in understanding, although there may be a development. In his third *Dictum*, Grosseteste—a reforming bishop who confronted the papacy and called on his priests to live truly like priests—affirmed that the priesthood belongs to all Christians 'generally' and 'spiritually', but it belongs 'particularly' and 'literally' to those who are priests or who ought to be priests.[90]

In a disputation soon after Wyclif's 1377 condemnation by Gregory, Wyclif defended Grosseteste's distinction between *predestinati* and *praesciti*. As part of that argument, Wyclif employed Grosseteste's universal priesthood to empower a priestly order separate from wicked bishops. Wyclif says one could practice priesthood without episcopal ordination but this should not be done rashly and pretentiously. 'And to many it seems that, dismissing presumptuous rashness, the sons of God could in the present circumstances use the office of priests, even if they were not consecrated by a Caesarean bishop.'[91] As in *De Eucharistia*, Wyclif's discussion of universal priesthood is again couched in the scholastic terms of logical possibility. Again, the doctrine

---

[88] 'Path to Dissent', 143. 'John Wyclif is the outstanding example in the later middle ages of an heresiarch.' Leff, *Heresy*, 494.

[89] *Robert Grosseteste*, 2d edn (OUP, 1992), 306. Beryl Smalley concluded that Wyclif did not employ Grosseteste only for polemical purposes but rather that he received 'genuine mental satisfaction' from reading Grosseteste. 'The Biblical Scholar', in *Robert Grosseteste, Scholar and Bishop*, ed. by D.A. Callus (OUP, 1955), 95–6.

[90] *Licet autem verfus ifte fic generaliter & spiritualiter omnibus membris Chrifti competat; fpecialiter tamen nobis habentibus curam animarum, qui non folum fpiritualiter, fed & ad literam, facerdotes fumus vel effe debemus.* 'One may moreover note that thus generally and spiritually it [priesthood] belongs to all members of Christ; nevertheless, it belongs particularly to us who have cure of souls, who not only spiritually, but also literally, are priests or ought to be.' *Fasciculus Rerum Expetendarum & Fugiendarum*, ed. by Edward Brown, 2 vols (London, 1690), II, 301.

[91] *Et multis videtur quod dimissa presumpcione temeraria filii Dei possent inpresenciarum uti officio sacerdotis, licet ab episcopo cesareo non fuerint consecrati. Responsiones ad Argumenta Radulfi Strode*, in *Opera Minora*, ed. by Johann Loserth (WLW, 1913), 176–8.

is not a primary but a subsidiary argument. And again, his real hope is for a righteous priesthood, not an orderless church. Universal priesthood may only be used as a transition to a righteous particular priesthood when wicked bishops dominate the church. Moreover, the responsibility for reforming the church in the case of wicked bishops belongs to the monarchy, which should appoint competent bishops.[92]

Rather than a formless ministry, Wyclif wanted to return the ministry to its ancient foundation. The priest's evangelical power is in his closeness to living out the Word of God and in the faithful preaching of the Word, as opposed to the mechanical understanding of the soteriological power of eucharistic consecration and the unrighteous exercise of civil power by the Caesarean clergy. Wyclif argued that episcopal consecration was normal but not absolutely necessary. He never denied sacramental orders, but he did deny the false reservation of ordination to wicked prelates.[93] This led him to search the Scriptures and Christian history for the basis of legitimate orders, and he concluded that the only legitimate orders are those of bishop, or presbyter, and deacon. On what basis then can one become a priest if the wicked prelate hinders ordination? The answer: by the direct consecration of the High Priest Jesus. In *De Quattuor Sectis Novellis*, Wyclif says all the predestined are priests to the Father, but this does not allow one to disdain the rites and services of ordained priests, nor does it allow the faithful to discount episcopal consecration, apart from a particular revelation by God. On the other hand, unless God imperceptibly ordains a priest, episcopal consecration is insufficient to make one a true priest. As an alternative to episcopal consecration, Wyclif broaches ordination by priests who may assist divine ordination.[94] He is not clear on the outward form of this ordination, nor is he clear on whether the *sacerdotes* who may ordain are presbyters or *predestinati*; nevertheless, he retains an ordained priesthood.

---

[92] Lahey, *Philosophy and Politics in the Thought of John Wyclif*, 179; Lahey, *John Wyclif*, 220.

[93] *De Simonia*, 112–13; *On Simony*, 162–3.

[94] *Sed hic instant mundani, quod iuxta hoc laicus est sacerdos et facta episcoporum sensibilia superfluunt.—Hic dicitur, quod quilibet predestinatus est sacerdos in patria nec debet propterea omnes ritus et opera sacerdotibus limitata exercere, nec debet fidelis sine revelacione consecracionem episcopi sui contempnere. Sed hoc debet credere, quoomodocunque episcopus suus operatus fuerit, nisi deus insensibiliter ordinet. Consecracio sensibilis parum valet, et sic assistente ordinacione divina quilibet sacerdos potest eque conferre sacramenta ecclesiastica sicut papa, sicut ceteri apostolii eque bene ordinaverunt episcopos sicut Petrus.* 'But in this present world, although the layman is also a priest, and episcopal deeds are perceived as unnecessary, this is said: every predestined person is a priest to the Father, but priests should not be kept from exercising all ceremonies and works on that account, nor should the faithful disdain episcopal consecration without revelation. But this should be believed, that perceptible consecration is not effective enough, however a bishop may have worked, unless God imperceptibly ordains. Thus, any priest could assist divine ordination by conferring the sacraments of the church equally with the pope, just like the other apostles ordained bishops just as well as Peter.' *Polemical Works*, I, 259.

Modern commentators have difficulty with Wyclif because in his specula-tion he never spells out, for instance, how this new style of ordination might work in a visible manner other than that a true priest is recognizable in holy living and the preaching of the Word. This dangling thread has lulled later interpreters who, with one eye on the extremes of Lollardy, which claimed Wyclif as a precursor,[95] and another eye on their own modern predispositions for or against Protestant liberalism, have forced Wyclif into a mold not of Wyclif's making. Wyclif has, therefore, been claimed as the 'Morning Star of the Reformation'[96] and as the father of individualism.

This is not to say that Wyclif embraced the ecclesiastical hierarchy, but rejecting a hierarchy is one thing, while embracing liberal individualism is quite another. If anything, Wyclif moved towards a third option between an overarching hierarchy and a fractious individualism; that is, he toyed with an incipient congregationalism responsibly related to its social system. On the one hand, there is in his thought a movement towards congregational election in such statements as 'there would be free election by the parishioners and the choice of the curate would be limited by merit alone. I care little for the appointment by the pope or his bishop.' On the other hand, Wyclif carefully defers to the social order, conceding to temporal lords the power to intervene if parishioners quarrel or depart from truth.[97] As Wyclif's most recent biographer concluded, 'his social ideals were far from incendiary.'[98]

Wyclif's major concern was to reinstate the pastoral role as the central focus of the priesthood so that the people as a whole would benefit. The office of the priest is to preach the gospel, pray for his subjects, and purge and protect them.[99] He was disgusted with the forms and methods of the medieval hier-archy, which he believed encouraged a grasping for wealth and a lack of concern for the welfare of souls. He attacked that hierarchy at its root by denying the miracle of transubstantiation, the necessity of private confession to a cleric, the existence of private sects, and the use of excommunication by the hierarchy. In the end, the only hope he saw for an improved ministry was through forced disendowment and the return to evangelical poverty. He did not denigrate the particular priesthood but elevated it above the entrapments of this world.[100]

---

[95] Even such careful historians as Anne Hudson and Margaret Aston have periodically spoken of a 'coherence' between the radical theological character of Lollardy and the 'intention' of Wyclif. Hudson, *Premature Reformation*, 1–2, 62, 279, 508; Aston, *Lollards and Reformers*, 69.

[96] This tradition stretches back to sixteenth-century reformers and traditionalists who rarely read Wyclif, but used him as a symbol for what was right or wrong with the Reformation. Aston, *Lollards and Reformers*, 243–72; Kenny, 'The Accursed Memory: the Counter-Reformation Reputation of John Wyclif', in *Wyclif in His Times*, 147–68.

[97] *De Officio Pastorali*, 43–5; *LCC*, XIV, 56–7.

[98] Lahey, *John Wyclif*, 189.

[99] *De Officio Pastorali*, 27, 34; *LCC*, XIV, 44, 48.

[100] Wilks, 'Royal Patronage and Anti-Papalism', 159; Wilks, 'Wyclif and the Great Persecu-tion', *SCH*, Subsidia 10 (1994), 56–7.

From a late work, which influenced the Lollard *Twelve Conclusions* and triggered the university's subsequent condemnation of Wyclif,[101] we see that even during his most polemical stage Wyclif never relinquished the particular priesthood. *Trialogus* was written during his Lutterworth period, specifically in late 1382 or early 1383.[102] The three personalities in conversation are *Alithia*, Truth; *Pseustis*, Falsehood; and *Phronesis*, Wisdom. *Alithia* seeks answers commensurate with his name; *Pseustis*, a disciple of Antichrist, prefers deception; and *Phronesis*, representing Wyclif himself, formulates long answers for the refutation of *Pseustis* and the edification of *Alithia*. In Book 4, Chapter 15, the sacrament of orders is introduced by a probing question from *Alithia*. *Phronesis* says there are three senses of *ordo*. First, in apparent agreement with Dionysius' general outline,[103] he says that since there are orders among the angels, there must also be orders among all creatures. Second, there are the orders of the novel religions of Antichrist, by which he presumably means the private religions. Third are the orders of the church.[104]

The contemporary understandings of church order are categorized according to a threefold formula: those necessary distinctions that are founded in the primitive church; those unnecessary Caesarean innovations that have become sinful; and, those common opinions that are not considered in Scripture, but are not necessarily to be rejected. Only the two orders of priest and deacon were necessary in the early church and are thus necessary for the church now. The subsequent distinctions of pope, cardinals, patriarchs, archbishops, bishops, archdeacons, and all other offices are unnecessary and should be reformed by the king since they promote the realm of Antichrist. The ceremony of ordination and the bestowal of the indelible character belong to the third

---

[101] Under the heading of the sacrament of orders, only two of the 267 articles condemned at Constance deal specifically with the universal priesthood. Both are careful to address the universal priesthood in terms of scholastic potentiality. *Non occurrit ex scriptura, quare sanctus laicus vel sacerdos non posset talia benedicere & consecrare.* 'It does not occur in Scripture, why the holy layman or priest could not as such bless and consecrate.' *Deficientibus praeletis, ut cifris, Christus ordinat quamcunque, quemcunque, quandocunque voluerit. Sequens igitur Christum in moribus secure potest de ipso confidere, quod deficiente praelato Caesareo, sit a Christo legitime ordinatus.* 'With deficient prelates, as now, Christ ordains however, whomever, whenever he wishes. It follows therefore that of himself one may rely safely on Christ in a manner; because of the deficient Caesarean prelate, he could be ordained legitimately by Christ.' *Fasciculus Rerum Expetendarum*, I, 269. Among the early conciliar and papal condemnations of Wyclif—the eighteen articles condemned by Gregory in 1377; the 24 articles condemned at the Blackfriars synod in 1382; the eighteen articles condemned at the London synod in 1397; the forty-five articles condemned at the Prague synod in 1403, at the Council of Rome in 1413 and at Session 8 of the Council of Constance in 1415; and the 267 articles condemned at the Oxford synod in 1411 and Session 15 of Constance—these are the only instances that the doctrine is mentioned. Wyclif's medieval opponents did not understand Wyclif's doctrine in the modern sense and deemed it of little importance.

[102] Thomson, *Latin Writings*, 79.

[103] David Luscombe, 'Wyclif and Hierarchy', *SCH*, Subsidia 5 (1987), 233–44.

[104] *Trialogus*, 295–6; *Tracts and Treatises*, 163–4.

category and apparently may be retained.[105] The distinction that Wyclif emphasizes between clergy and laity is not that of the indelible character, however, but that of manner of life and grade in society. 'Since, then, all believers, are, undeniably, to follow Christ in their character, the clergy must of necessity follow him in their own order, especially in his humble poverty.'[106]

Wyclif's conception of the other sacraments also influences his discussion of a universal priesthood. *Pseustis* concludes from *Phronesis*' idea that since in the eucharist God is only sacramentally present, then a layman might be able to consecrate the sacrament as well as a priest. 'It seems to me that you depart alike from the church and from Scripture, since, according to your statements, a layman might officiate in this sacrament like a priest, and the church would then be in doubt which host to worship.'[107] *Phronesis* casts the logic of *Pseustis* back at him: indeed, the laity might as well be confecting whenever priests who are ignorant confect. While playing his habitual 'game of cat and mouse' to tease his readers,[108] Wyclif alleges the early Christians who were breaking bread from house to house may not have all been priests. Laypersons may have even been consecrating the eucharist. 'But leaving this as uncertain it appears to me that this office suits holy priests.'[109] He thus dismisses the universal priesthood from practicing lay presidency as 'uncertain' and reaffirms the divine institution of the priestly office since Christ at the Last Supper gave that task to the particular priesthood. Lay presidency is not part of the faith even if perhaps a possibility.[110]

Thus, even in his most polemical stage Wyclif retained a particular priesthood along with universal priesthood. The powers of this universal priesthood are held in uncertainty and potentiality, and these powers are limited by divine institution and reasonable custom.

---

[105] *Trialogus*, 296–7; *Tracts and Treatises*, 164–5.

[106] *Cum ergo non valet negare, quin oportet omnes fideles sequi Christum in moribus, patet quod in gradu summo oportet clericos specialiter in paupertate humili sequi ipsum. Trialogus*, 302; *Tracts and Treatises*, 168.

[107] *Videtur mihi quod delira ab opinione ecclesiae et fide scripturae, cum juxta tuum dicere aeque posset laicus conficere ut sacerdos; et sic ecclesia foret utrobique ambigua, quam hostiam adoraret. Trialogus*, 280; *Tracts and Treatises*, 155.

[108] Wilks, 'Predestination, Property, and Power', 225. 'Like Ockham, Wyclif took particular pleasure in indulging in lengthy speculation about divine possibilities (thereby creating great alarm and confusion) but knowing full well that this speculation was to have no immediate results for human life.' 'Predestination, Property, and Power'. 228.

[109] *Sed dimittendo istud incertum apparet mihi quod sacerdotes sanctos decet istud officium. Trialogus*, 280; *Tracts and Treatises*, 155.

[110] *Verumtamen quia istud non est fides, non oportet quod credatur ab ecclesia, sed quod probabiliter supponatur. Trialogus*, 281. 'Nevertheless, because this is not an article of faith, there is no necessity for its being believed by the church: but it may be left as a probable supposition.' *Tracts and Treatises*, 155.

CONCLUSIONS

In a positive light, Wyclif drew towards a spiritual interpretation of these important doctrines by focusing on God instead of the church. In a negative light, Wyclif failed to propose a viable alternative to the visible hierarchical structures of the church. His only recourse was to call for the secular lords to take matters into their own hands and correct abuses by the disendowment of clerical possessions and the monitoring of clerical morals.[111] This was to be done for the sake of the poor and not for private advancement.

Finally, we compare our conclusions with the work of an historiography that too often casts its own philosophy back on that of a former age. For example, Edward A. Block contends that Wyclif was a radical dissenter in the sense of a hyperindividualistic, spiritualistic destroyer of the institutional church. Unfortunately, he depends on a few late Latin works and the dubiously assigned English manuscripts, which are more likely the work of later Lollards. Moreover, like Gordon Leff, whom we previously considered,[112] Block relies overmuch on cognates and synonyms of the qualifying verbs 'imply' and 'indicate'. The 'invisible church', 'the right to interpret Holy Scripture according to the dictates of his conscience', and 'connection with the Church [as] not essential to salvation'[113] may be popular theological conclusions today, but against Block we must contend that Wyclif never actually said such things. Wyclif's redefinition of the sacraments and their effectiveness may be connected logically to the abolition of a mediating hierarchical priesthood, but it is a logic that is not Wyclif's.

This represents a problematic type of modern scholarship, which tends to connect points, darken lines, and embellish portraits never pictured in the medieval sage's mind. Block even equates Wyclif with such radical dissenters

---

[111] This is why he begins his treatise on the pastoral office with a call for the Christian to purge the church militant of false shoots and structure it for the better blessing of the church. *De Officio Pastorali*, 1; *LCC*, XIV, 32.

[112] (Italics in the following quotations are mine.) Wyclif's universal priesthood is '*tantamount*' to a denial of the priestly order. *Heresy*, 520. 'This was a blow struck at the entire sacramental life of the Church; although Wyclif conceded that priestly mediation was necessary as the result of the fall, and never openly disavowed the sacraments, the whole *tendency* of his thought was to depreciate them.' 'Path to Dissent', 166. 'This *inevitably* opened the way to taking God's law into one's own hands.' 'Path to Dissent', 161. 'Though Wyclif denied that it derogated from priestly power, its total *effect* was as a further attack upon the church.' 'Path to Dissent', 179. Even in his last article on the subject, when he was forced to take account of Wyclif's philosophy, Leff still failed to distinguish later movements from Wyclif's intention. 'The centre of his own heresy [is that] he *effectively* deprived the Church of a visible identity as an institution, or even a temporal origin.' 'The Place of Metaphysics in Wyclif's Theology', *SCH*, Subsidia 5 (1987), 225. 'He *effectively* made the Bible [...] the mediator between the individual believer and God.' 'The Place of Metaphysics in Wyclif's Theology', 227. Individualism is '*the ultimate effect*' of all of Wyclif's doctrines. 'The Place of Metaphysics in Wyclif's Theology', 232.

[113] Edward A. Block, *John Wyclif: Radical Dissenter* (San Diego, California: San Diego State College Press, 1962), 32, 41, 27.

as John Bunyan and John Milton; however, the antiecclesiasticism that Block defines is not found in the thought of Wyclif nor among congregational post-Restoration dissenters. Block concludes, 'Like Milton, Wyclif leaves each man face to face with his Maker, directly responsible and accountable to Him alone; like Milton, Wyclif in this way strips a mediating Church of any valid reason for continuing to exist.'[114]

The conclusions of Leff and Block may pass as polemical theology but they fail to meet the rigorous demands of historical theology. Unfortunately, such conclusions have even periodically appeared in the work of careful historical theologians, though the effect there is tempered by a more typical reliance upon the primary sources properly read in context.[115] Rather than a proponent of crass egocentrism and harsh anticlericalism in his doctrine of universal priesthood, as the dominant post-Reformation historiography claimed, it is more likely that John Wyclif was a reformer searching for a way to make the Christian church a living reality for the English nation in which he lived and for the parish congregation in which the ageing priest died as he celebrated the eucharist.[116]

---

[114] *John Wyclif: Radical Dissenter*, 43.

[115] G.R. Evans concludes from *De Quattuor Sectis Novellis* that '"everyone predestined" for heaven is a priest in this life and does not need the sacraments celebrated by the priests of the Church.' *John Wyclif: Myth and Reality* (Oxford: Lion Hudson, 2005), 225, 288 n66. However, the citation Evans provides in this instance says nothing about the sacraments. Rather, drawing upon Matthew 12:25, Wyclif indicates that the lower orders, *vulgares*, are the basis of the kingdom and, *debet secundum legem dei a partibus superioribus stabiliri, a sacerdotibus spiritualiter et a dominis corporaliter*, 'according to the law of God, they ought to be established by the superior parts, spiritually by the priests and corporally by the lords.' *Polemical Works*, I, 242. And, in a rare instance, even Lahey imports a modern acidic understanding of universal priesthood into his otherwise excellent discussions. *Philosophy and Politics in the Thought of John Wyclif*, 187.

[116] Lahey, *John Wyclif*, 29.

2

Royal Priesthood in Late Medieval England

St Mary's Church, Fairford, Gloucestershire is the only English parish church retaining a complete set of late medieval stained glass. The faces of Henry VII, his family, and clergy have been discovered among the biblical saints. Fairford's 'books of the people', as Gregory I defined such images, illustrate medieval faith and society. As the creed progresses, it becomes evident that two events dominate the narrative: Calvary above the altar and the Last Judgment in the great west window. The windows above the nave illuminate the march to judgment. To the left of Christ stand the twelve persecutors of the faith; to his right, the twelve confessors. Fairford's windows in their architectural context offer us a picture of medieval society, for priests and kings dominate the nave, the people's place.[1] Likewise, priests and kings dominated medieval society. Late medieval English society considered itself in corporate, even organic, terms. Wyclif and the Lollards, indeed most people, divided the visible church, coterminous with society, into soldiers, clerks, and workers. These three estates, or degrees, exercised three separate offices: knighthood, priesthood, and labor.[2] Orthodox churchmen roughly agreed with Wyclif's threefold division, often quibbling over details,[3] while commanding individuals to respect the bounds of their offices.

John Russell, Bishop of Lincoln, in preparing three drafts of a parliamentary sermon for Edward V and Richard III, outlined this social theory in order to calm the turbulence created by the Lancastrian–Yorkist strife. Because man is a social being, evidenced by his use of language, he needs a 'policie' to coordinate his public body. The English body is composed of three parts: prince, nobles, and people; alternatively, lords spiritual, lords temporal, and commons. The people, naturally tremulous, likened to water, must be calmed by aristocratic rule, likened to islands. The nobles depend for their authority

---

[1] Edward Keble, *St Mary's Church*, 3rd edn (Shropshire: R.J.L. Smith, 1997).
[2] Wyclif, *De Officio Regis*, 58–9; *The Lanterne of Ligt*, ed. by L.M. Swinburn, EETS 151 (OUP, 1917), 40, 74; Keen, *English Society in the Later Middle Ages*.
[3] Thomas Netter, *Doctrinale Fidei Catholicae*, 3 vols (Venice, 1757; reprint, Farnborough: Gregg Press, 1967), II, 12; Aquinas, *Summa Theologica*, II-II, qns 183–4.

on proximity to the prince. An Old Testament metaphor exemplifies this divine theory of authority. At the top of England's Mount Sinai is the king, who, *quasi deus noster in terris*, as our God on earth, may only be approached by nobility. The nobles, in the roles of Moses and Aaron, mediate royal law to the people, who must avoid the mountain since they cannot withstand divine speech. Developing a New Testament communal metaphor, Russell says the English body is both mystical and political, and its one head is the king, who cures the body's ills. If the estates function as they should, supporting the others through their specific roles, then the body finds harmony. Justice is available to the people through their representatives, the same nobles ordained to keep the people busy fulfilling their respective offices. If the people do not understand a particular decision of the head, as mediated by the nobility, they must obey anyway. Anyone stepping beyond his office is a 'roten membre'.[4]

While outlining late medieval social theory, Russell's drafts raise more questions than they answer. What if the body is sick and the head and his mediators conflict? How does that other divine vicar, the high priest of Rome, relate to England's king? Who judges the inevitable disputes between priests and knights? What are the exact offices that individuals should inhabit and never leave? If all Christians are kings and priests, how are social divisions to be maintained? As this chapter surveys the late medieval English doctrines of royal priesthood, it answers some of these questions while showing others were inevitably unanswerable. While the theory of the three estates was widely affirmed, its boundaries were tested and sometimes violated by representative commentators from the estates. Our survey begins with priestly kings, proceeds to kingly priests, and concludes with the royal priestly people.

PRIESTLY KINGS (AND LAWYERS)

Kings

The identification of kingship with priesthood finds precedence not only in Christian Scripture but also in pagan Anglo-Saxon society. The conversion of Europe to Christianity occurred in stages, with kings and warriors leading the way; England was no exception.[5] The key to this conversion, and periodic apostasy, wherein the people apparently followed the choices of their king, was due in part to the king's position as priest to his people. The Germanic king's descent from the pagan god, Woden, and his ability to make sacrifices for the

---

[4] S.B. Chrimes, *English Constitutional Ideas in the Fifteenth Century* (CUP, 1936), 167–91.

[5] Richard Fletcher, *The Conversion of Europe from Paganism to Christianity 371–1386 AD* (London: HarperCollins, 1997), 160–92.

luck, or welfare, of the tribe, paralleled the indelible character and peace-making function of the Christian priesthood. The pagan priest–king retained many of his former functions in law, finance, worship, and war when he converted. After conversion, a distinction between priesthood and kingship was made, but this never resulted in a total separation, for the king was still the sacred protector possessing a mixed character. Indicative of this continuation and the difficulty with which the distinction between English priesthood and kingship was made, is the fact that two separate court systems, one ecclesiastical and one royal, were not established until well after the Norman conquest.[6]

Even after the conquest, the distinction between *regnum* and *sacerdotium* was never finalized. It has been rightly asserted that the relationship between kingship and priesthood is 'the dominant problem of medieval political thought'.[7] Due to the hierarchical tendencies of the late medieval church,[8] this ultimately amounted to a conflict between the claims of popes and those of emperors and kings. In the fifth century, Pope Gelasius spoke of two coordinate powers by which this world is ruled. Christ was both priest and king, but he never entrusted both powers in one hand. These dual powers, each divine in origin, were mutually submissive; in spiritual matters kings were to submit to the priesthood; in temporal matters priests must submit to kings. Gelasian dualism became something of a truism.[9] The two cooperative powers wielded distinct swords; the king wielded the material while the priesthood wielded the spiritual. With the Gregorian reforms of the eleventh century, however, this dualist consensus cracked. Priests denied the rectitude of lay investiture, prompting extensive literary battles and political brinkmanship. Scholars on both sides believed reconciliation lay in a division of jurisdictions [see Plate 4]. Canon law and civil law, with their competing claims, subsequently became major industries with their own educational faculties and large roles in government.[10] Nonetheless, the 'boundaries between canon law and civil law remained highly permeable throughout the Middle Ages.'[11]

In England, the *York Tractates*, written by an anonymous Norman scholar around 1100 to defend Henry I's investiture of Anselm of Canterbury, made bold claims on behalf of kings. 'Consecrated at the holy altar with sacred

---

[6] William A. Chaney, *The Cult of Kingship in Anglo-Saxon England* (Manchester: Manchester University Press, 1970).

[7] Ewart Lewis, *Medieval Political Ideas*, 2 vols (New York: Cooper Square, 1974), II, 506.

[8] Aquinas concluded 'the government of one is best'. *On the Government of Rulers, De Regimine Principum*, transl. by James M. Blythe (Philadelphia: University of Pennsylvania Press, 1997), I, 7.

[9] John A. Watt, *The Theory of Papal Monarchy in the Thirteenth Century* (New York: Fordham University Press, 1965), 12–22.

[10] J.A. Watt, 'Spiritual and Temporal Powers', in *Cambridge History of Medieval Political Thought*, 370–1; Dorothy M. Owen, *The Medieval Canon Law* (CUP, 1990), 1–14.

[11] James A. Brundage, *Medieval Canon Law* (London: Longman, 1995), 176.

unction and benediction', kings are ordained by divine authority to rule, judge, and administer the church. Bishops, on the other hand, are ordained to teach. Baptism confers both regal and sacerdotal dignity on every Christian, thus both regal and sacerdotal authorities are necessary in the church. Because both kings and priests have a 'common unction', they are both Christs. The anonymous Norman, however, distinguishes between the anointing of these two Christs. This distinction is based upon Christ's two natures and two offices. The priesthood of Christ correlates to Christ's human nature; his divine nature correlates to his kingship. Due to the divine nature's higher status, 'likewise among men the royal power is greater and higher than the priestly.' Both priests and kings are vicars of Christ, but kings are vicars of Christ's divinity while priests are vicars only of his humanity.[12]

Such bold claims for England's king abound. The common law theorist, Henry of Bracton (d.1268), recognized dual powers but accorded final arbitration to the king. The king is the vicar of God and his judges are vicars of Christ. In legal disputes, even disputes concerning priests, the king arbitrates. (However, although the king is above the realm, which realm includes the priesthood, the law is above the king and he must use the judges of his realm in settling disputes of jurisdiction.) In recognizing a dualist system of powers and courts, Bracton yet accorded final jurisdiction to the royal court.[13] In royal conflicts with the papacy, the highest representative of the priesthood—particularly in those conflicts between Henry II and Archbishop Thomas Becket over the prosecution of clergy, and between John and Innocent III over the election of bishops—the kings made tactical retreats but retained ultimate control. The English solution to the relationship between *regnum* and *sacerdotium* has been described as 'effectively dualism at the king's command'.[14]

In the fourteenth century, John's recognition of papal oversight was restricted by Parliament. Parliament's statute of Provisors, which restrained papal provisions in violation of royal provisions to prelatical office, and the statute of Praemunire, which forestalled appeals against royal decisions to the papacy, were first passed in, respectively, 1351 and 1353. The statute of Provisors was subsequently reaffirmed in 1390 and 1401, the statute of Praemunire in 1364 and 1393. The statutes claim much for the realm against the papacy but should not be interpreted as attempts to rupture relations. Rather, the conflict reveals a 'deadlock between two unlimited prerogatives' and a 'conflict of two rival systems of patronage'.[15] Edward III, Richard II, and Henry IV pressured papal privileges but settled for the mutual benefit of both

---

[12] *De Consecratione Pontificum et Regum*, transl. by Lewis, *Medieval Political Ideas*, II, 562–6; Ernst H. Kantorowicz, *The King's Two Bodies* (PUP, 1957), 42–61.

[13] *The King's Two Bodies*, 143–64.

[14] Watt, 'Spiritual and Temporal Powers', 391–4.

[15] W.A. Pantin, *The English Church in the Fourteenth Century* (CUP, 1955), 91, 94.

king and pope. The king retained ultimate juridical power in England, even if he had to account for a querulous papacy.

The priestly, even divine, claims, made for medieval English kings began with their coronation service. Royal coronations were liturgical events with major intimations conferring priestly status upon the king. The form in which he was anointed, the *ordo*, has striking similarities to the consecration of a bishop.[16] He was considered a descendant of saintly King Edward the Confessor.[17] He could heal scrofula with the royal touch and epilepsy through blessing cramp rings; the former practice lasting into the Stuart era, the latter ending after Mary I.[18] The oil used in his unction, an anointing explicitly compared to the christening of biblical prophets, priests, and kings,[19] took on increasingly divine attributes. Anointing the king's head proved controversial. As a sign of papal vassalage, John was not anointed on the head, but the practice was subsequently restored.[20] Even the coronation robes were similar to priestly and episcopal vestments. When Edward I's tomb was opened, he was wearing a priest's stole.[21]

Richard II (d.1400), attempting to bolster his position against the encroaching nobility, stressed the divine origin of kingship, thus exemplifying an 'escalation in the mystique of monarchy'.[22] Portraiture, language, cult, and ceremony contributed to his efforts. His portraits resembled icons and stressed the divine origin of his authority. In the Wilton Diptych, Christ grants him the banner of resurrected kingship [see Plate 1]. In the 'Coronation' portrait, he is shown holding orb and sceptre with a Christ-like face.[23] Richard introduced a new vocabulary of address, primarily 'majesty' and 'prince', in an attempt to stress his God-like position.[24] Believing rebellion against the king is rebellion against God, he compared his own sufferings to Christ's, *imitatio Christi*.[25] He ordered that during feasts as he sat upon his throne in royal array, 'yf he loked

---

[16] *The Coronation Order of King James I*, ed. by J. Wickham Legg (London: F.E. Robinson, 1902), xvii–xxix.

[17] Percy Ernst Schramm, *A History of the English Coronation*, transl. by Leopold G. Wickham Legg (OUP, 1937), 116, 123–5.

[18] John N. King, *Tudor Royal Iconography* (PUP, 1989), 185–7.

[19] Eleanor Shipley Duckett, *Saint Dunstan of Canterbury* (London: Collins, 1955), 103; *Coronation Order of James*, 22–3.

[20] Schramm, *English Coronation*, 128–33, 136.

[21] *Coronation Order of James*, xxxvi–xxxviii.

[22] Roy Strong, *Coronation: A History of Kingship and the British Monarchy* (London: HarperCollins, 2005), 112.

[23] Nigel Saul, 'The Kingship of Richard II', in *Richard II: The Art of Kingship*, ed. by Anthony Goodman and James Gillespie (OUP, 1999), 49–50; John Drury, *Painting the Word* (YUP, 1999), 9–21.

[24] Saul, 'Richard II and the Vocabulary of Kingship', *EHR*, 110 (1995), 862–4, 876.

[25] Simon Walker, 'Richard II's Views on Kingship', in *Rulers and Ruled in Late Medieval England*, ed. by Rowena E. Archer and Simon Walker (London: Hambledon Press, 1995), 59–60.

on eny mann, what astat or degree that evir he were of, he moste knele'.[26] Like other kings, Richard supported the cults of English saint-kings, such as that of Edward II.[27] In spite of such extravagance, Richard was considered orthodox, even if he turned a blind eye to Lollard knights in his court and opposed Archbishop Arundel, the hammer of the Lollards. He did not interfere with doctrine, rather he desired supreme temporal power in the land.[28] An anonymous Latin chronicler concluded that in exceeding his ancestors and reaching for Solomon's glory, he was, in an allusion to the Babylonian king Belshazar, weighed and found wanting at the height of his glory.[29] Upon his death, he was buried in Dominican attire.

The indelible character implanted during coronation strengthened Richard's claim for divine authority. It is said he wanted Arundel to recoronate him with the holy oil supposedly given to Thomas Becket by the Virgin Mary, recently discovered among his possessions. Arundel refused, citing divine anger with repeating a sacrament conferring character.[30] In refuting the Donatist Petilianus, Augustine had defined unction as a sacrament conferring a holy status on a king, thus David honored the wicked king Saul.[31] Robert Grosseteste conceded coronation was a sacrament, for it gave the king a sevenfold gift from the Holy Spirit. Although in the thirteenth century the sacraments were limited to seven and coronation was defined as a sacramental, this did not eradicate the common belief that in coronation a king was given an indelible character. He was no longer a mere layman.[32]

Neither was the king fully a priest. Grosseteste warned Henry II that his consecration, though similar to a bishop's, did not grant him the power to perform any priestly offices. Grosseteste's explicit denial signals the existence of contrary beliefs. Since Grosseteste, in the same letter, elevated priests above kings, his claims must be seen as part of the continuing polemical battle between *regnum* and *sacerdotium*. Theologians did not always reflect popular belief.[33] European kings, though not full-fledged priests, functioned as deacons or subdeacons during the mass, and this strengthened popular conceptions of sacred kingship.[34] During the English coronation service, the king made at least two offerings at the altar, a mark of gold and St Edward's chalice

[26] *An English Chronicle*, ed. by John Silvester Davies (London: Camden Society, 1856), 12.

[27] R.N. Swanson, *Church & Society in Late Medieval England* (Oxford: Blackwell, 1989), 99–100.

[28] Richard G. Davies, 'Richard II and the Church', in *Richard II: Kingship*, 83–106.

[29] *English Chronicle*, 133.

[30] Marc Bloch, *The Royal Touch*, transl. by J.E. Anderson (London: Routledge, 1973), 137–40.

[31] *Answer to Petilian*, II, xlvii, 110–12.

[32] Walter Ullmann, *Principles of Government and Politics in the Middle Ages* (London: Methuen, 1961), 140; Bloch, *Royal Touch*, 113–14; Strong, *Coronation*, 119.

[33] *English Coronation Records*, ed. by Leopold G. Wickham Legg (London: Constable, 1901), 66–8.

[34] Bloch, *Royal Touch*, 117; *Coronation Order of James*, xxxviii–xl.

with a paten.[35] Similarly, in the *Sarum Missal*, the deacon presented the paten and chalice to the priest for the sacrifice.[36] Medieval coronation orders justified this by reference to Melchisedek, priest–king of Salem.[37]

Kings not only received the consecrated host from the Archbishop of Canterbury, they also drank from St Edward's chalice at the hands of the Abbot of Westminster. It has been questioned whether medieval English kings ever received both elements during the mass at their coronation. The Leggs based their conclusion of indefinition on the fact the king could receive *corpus et sanguinem Domini* under one kind, *sub utraque specie* being a seventeenth-century interpolation. However, it would have taken unusual and undocumented steps to move the unconsecrated wine from St Edward's chalice to a chalice for consecration and then place unconsecrated wine and water back in St Edward's chalice. The reference in *Liber Regalis*, the Latin coronation rite, to the king's partaking of a chalice *post percepcionem sacramenti* does not exclude the possibility the wine was also part of the same sacrament.[38] After all, the prelates were careful to lift a large silk towel to catch any spillage.[39] In light of the Leggs' untenable argument from silence, English kings likely received both kinds as did their French cousins.[40]

When the magnates deposed Richard, a deposition affirmed by the people,[41] he ultimately appealed to the sacred character conferred by his royal unction. He told Lord Chief Justice William Thirning, the realm's messenger, that although renouncing all the honors and dignity of a king, he could not renounce 'those special dignities of a spiritual nature which had been bestowed upon him, nor indeed his anointment'. He could neither renounce his character nor cease to retain it. Startled by this last-ditch effort for an enduring claim to the throne, Thirning reminded Richard of his written renunciation. Richard 'simply smiled' and changed the conversation.[42] Richard's inalienable claim to the throne contributed to the continued uprisings occurring in his name during the early fifteenth century.[43]

---

[35] *English Coronation Records*, 236; *Coronation Order of James*, 12, 40.

[36] *The Sarum Missal in English*, transl. by Frederick E. Warren (London: Alexander Moring, 1911), 30–1.

[37] *Three Coronation Orders*, ed. by J.W. Legg (London: Henry Bradshaw Society, 1900), 48–9; *English Coronation Records*, 103, 125; Genesis 14.17–20.

[38] *Coronation Order of James*, xli; *Three Coronation Orders*, 48–9; *English Coronation Records*, lxii, 105, 126, 236.

[39] *English Coronation Records*, 237.

[40] *English Coronation Records*, lxii.

[41] Medieval England never practiced democratic deposition; the people could only 'assent' to what the magnates determined. B. Wilkinson, 'The Deposition of Richard II and the Accession of Henry IV', *EHR*, 54 (1939), 215–39.

[42] Thomas Walsingham, 'Record and Process', in *Chronicles of the Revolution 1397–1400*, ed. by Chris Given-Wilson (Manchester: Manchester University Press, 1993), 188–9.

[43] *English Chronicle*, 23–6.

Sir Arnold Savage, Speaker of the House of Commons in 1401, employed theological language to advance civil government. He compared the three estates of the realm to the Holy Trinity, forming a trinity in unity and a unity in trinity. Savage also compared Henry IV's rule through law to a priest's administration of the sacrifice of the mass. As the priest at the end of the mass said, *Ite, missa est,* and the people respond, *Deo gratias,* so should the people respond to Henry's promise to rule justly.[44] Claiming divine authorization for his rule, Henry IV had himself anointed with Becket's holy oil,[45] setting a standard practice for succeeding Lancastrian and Yorkist kings. Royal coronation might put *rex* above *sacerdotium,* but not above *legem*: even his especial anointing would not allow Henry IV to arbitrarily murder Richard Scrope, Archbishop of York. A cult for Scrope quickly spread as a protest to centralized power.[46] Henry's leprous death was seen as divine judgment,[47] but this centralization of power continued under his son.

In his examination of Henry V's government, Jeremy Catto concludes Henry brought the church directly under the purview of the state. Henry purified popular religion of its Lollard heresy, founded monasteries to promote personal devotions, employed bishops who brought a strong political administration to their dioceses, standardized the liturgy according to Sarum usage, and advanced public policy through religious ritual. Catto concludes, 'In all but name, more than a century before the title could be used, Henry V had begun to act as the supreme governor of the Church of England.'[48] The humanist Nicolas de Clamanges concurred, informing Henry, 'The Lord laid down that royalty should be priestly, for through the holy unction of chrism Christian kings must be considered holy, after the likeness of priests.'[49]

Henry VI inherited broad powers upon his accession in 1422. When Reginald Pecock, Bishop of Chichester, was brought to trial for heresy, it began with a lay appeal to Henry. John, Viscount Beaumont, wrote the king informing him that he must emulate his father's prosecution of heresy, assuring him he would thereby prosper on earth and 'be exaltid to regne eternally with our Lord Ihesu Criste'. The king should prosecute even against his prelates' wishes.[50] Henry instituted proceedings against Pecock, barred the Archbishop of Canterbury

---

[44] Chrimes, *English Constitutional Ideas,* 68–9; Kantorowicz, *King's Two Bodies,* 227. Sir John Fortescue similarly compared the realm to a chantry. J.R. Lander, *The Limitations of English Monarchy in the Later Middle Ages* (London: University of Toronto Press, 1989), 12–14.

[45] Walsingham, *Annales Ricardi Secundi,* in *Chronicles of the Revolution,* 201–2.

[46] Hughes, *Pastors and Visionaries,* 305–7.

[47] *English Chronicle,* 31–8.

[48] Catto, 'Religious Change under Henry V', in *Henry V: The Practice of Kingship,* ed. by G.L. Harriss (OUP, 1985), 97–115.

[49] Bloch, *Royal Touch,* 122.

[50] Beaumont to Henry VI, 24 June 1457; Wendy Scase, 'Reginald Pecock', in *English Writers of the Late Middle Ages,* ed. by M.C. Seymour (Aldershot, Hampshire: Variorum, 1996), 103–5, 120–2.

from restoring him, gave the pope 'Instructions' to reject his restoration, and ordered Oxford University to repress his followers. Pecock's clerical opponents said he was a threat to 'not oonly the pouair and iurisdiction of regalie and preesthode, [but also] thauctorite of al holy scripture'. Theological authority and political power, spiritual and temporal, were inextricably intertwined; a threat to one threatened all. This domino theory of authority both compelled and empowered kings to pursue the deposition of priests. Henry VI could repress Pecock's teachings because 'in oure Iunction and coronacion we be sworne principaly aboue al other things texalte and glorifie the name of almighty God and to defende his chirche and the catholique doctrine'.[51]

Ullmann notes an increased emphasis on the divine aspect of coronation during the fifteenth century.[52] The changes in the ceremony all supported a theocratic elevation of the king, not against the church but against the people, most likely in response to his loss of real power in the localities. The movement towards divine approbation involved *laudes regiae*, liturgical songs which have been described as 'nothing less than the ritual veneration of the quasi-sanctified person' of the king.[53] The Lancastrian coronations impressed contemporaries, especially when kings donned prelatical vestments.[54]

During the Yorkist–Lancastrian wars, royal unction and female priesthood also became propaganda weapons.[55] Sir John Fortescue (d.1476), Chief Justice and occasional common law theorist, defended Henry VI's claim to the throne with the propriety of royal unction. Edward IV's rival claim depended on two female ancestors. Fortescue said Henry VI is 'the Lord's Christ or the Lord's anointed' for he was anointed with Becket's holy oil as proved in his healing powers. Royal ordination, like priestly ordination, requires three things: 'a due minister, that is, the bishop with intention; a due form of ordination and unction; and due matter, that is, a person fit to receive such order and unction'. Since a woman cannot be a priest, and Edward's claim necessarily goes through two women, then Edward is not 'due matter' for consecration.[56] Such patriarchal presuppositions contributed to Henry VIII's anxiety over his successor.

---

[51] Catto, 'The King's Government and the Fall of Pecock, 1457–58', in *Rulers and Ruled*, 216, 219–20.

[52] *Liber Regie Capelle*, ed. by Ullmann (London: Bradshaw Society, 1961), 22–43.

[53] *Verus Vox, Rex Edwardus*

> *Rectus Rex, Rex Edwardus*
> *Justus, juridicus et legitimus Rex, Rex Edwardus*
> *Cui omnes hos subjici volumus*
> *Suaeque humillima iuguns admittere subernationis.*

Lander, *Limitations of English Monarchy*, 44, 53–5.

[54] Schramm, *English Coronation*, 135–6; *English Coronation Records*, xl; Giles Gossip, *Coronation Anecdotes* (London, 1823), 28–9.

[55] Paul E. Gill, 'Politics and Propaganda in Fifteenth-Century England', *Speculum*, 46 (1971), 333–47.

[56] *De Titulo Edwardi Comitis Marchiae*, in *The Works of Sir John Fortescue, Knight, Chief Justice of England and Lord Chancellor to Henry the Sixth*, ed. by Thomas Fortescue, 2 vols (London, 1869), 85–6.

Henry VII, founder of the Tudor line, also had a high view of royal unction. He was reluctant to punish the pretender, Lambert Simnel, because Simnel had been anointed in Dublin. A Milanese envoy reported, 'They say that His Majesty, out of respect for the sacred unction, wants to make a priest of him.' Thus, an anointed king without a kingdom might become a priest. Henry VII got on well with the church, perhaps because the chapters always elected and the popes always confirmed his prelatical nominees. His prominent privy councilor, Edmund Dudley (d.1514), said that the king 'doth appoint and make the Bishops'; moreover, 'he assisteth his maker and redeemer, of whom he hath all his power and authority'. Kenneth Pickthorn concludes Henry VII and the church cultivated 'amicable co-operation'.[57] Taking heart from Henry II's success in canonizing Edward the Confessor and emulating Richard's efforts on behalf of Edward II, the first Tudor king boosted his own divine claims by promoting a royal cult for Henry VI. Henry VIII and Thomas Cranmer pursued a similar trend toward royal dominance.[58]

Lawyers

The amicable relationship between king and clergy apparently depended on the king's decision to cooperate with the church rather than vice versa. Real juridical power resided with the king as became apparent in the courts. From the eleventh to the fourteenth centuries, there was vigorous competition between two English legal systems, canon law and common law. From the mid-fourteenth century, there was a slow attrition of ecclesiastical jurisdiction, culminating in its final defeat under Henry VIII.[59] Church courts were generally concerned with sexual, probate, and heresy matters. These provided opportunities for competition, but the most vexing issues were 'benefit of clergy', the right of clergy even in minor orders to escape royal justice by demanding ecclesiastical privilege, and 'sanctuary', which allowed criminals, including traitors, immunity from prosecution if they could reach designated areas before capture.[60] The royal courts fought back with the previously mentioned statutes of Provisors and Praemunire and with 'writs of prohibition', royal instruments to transfer ecclesiastical cases to common law jurisdiction.[61]

---

[57] Pickthorn, *Early Tudor Government: Henry VII* (CUP), 8–9, 175–82.

[58] Schramm, *English Coronation*, 123–4, Swanson, *Church & Society*, 288–9; King, *Tudor Royal Iconography*, 26–7.

[59] Swanson, *Church & Society*, 141–2. The Royal Injunctions of 1535 terminated Canon Law studies in the universities. 37 Henry VIII, ch. 19 allowed civil lawyers to run ecclesiastical courts. Owen, *Medieval Canon Law*, 1, 70.

[60] Chrimes, *English Constitutional Ideas*, 285–8; Swanson, *Church & Society*, 149–58, 166–74.

[61] *Church & Society*, 182–7.

Behind these battles lay competing claims to divine authorization and priesthood made by both clergy and common lawyers. That the former is true is commonplace; the latter claim is less well known. Common lawyers, the judges and advocates operating in the royal courts, considered their tasks in theological terms and their persons in priestly terms. Late medieval common lawyers were a special brand of priesthood charged with dispensing divine law. In one illustrated manuscript, coif wearing serjeants-at-law are interspersed among the prelates displaying the sacrament to a newly enthroned Edward II.[62] Their appearance in such a holy setting, even if on the fringes, suggests their impinging importance.

In the fifteenth century, ecclesiastics abandoned the field of political theology. While preserving church doctrine and prelatical hierarchy against Lollardy, they left political thought to an increasingly literate laity, including John Fortescue.[63] Fortescue delineated his political theology in a number of Latin and English works. Regarding kingship, his most informative work is *De Laudibus Legum Anglie*.[64] Following medieval theory, he equates civil law, specifically English common law, with divine law. The king receives law from the priests, 'that is from men catholic and literate'.[65] 'For a priest is by etymology said to be one who gives or teaches, and because human laws are said to be sacred, hence the ministers and teachers of the laws are called priests.'[66] These ministers of justice help humanity attain the *summum bonum* by the virtue of justice, the entire legal process being a divine grace.[67] Although the prince should know the laws, he must leave the details to the serjeants-at-law and their apprentices, just as he leaves 'the mysteries of theology to ecclesiastical prelates'.[68]

After praising the antiquity and superiority of English common law to Roman civil law, Fortescue offers an extended comparison of the legal profession with the priesthood. Like clergy in university, lawyers study law, but at Inns of Court and Chancery. They are superior to clergy, who learn only Latin, for they must master English, French, and Latin. Lawyers study both legal science and Scripture, and live in voluntary societies offering strict discipline. Their doctors receive the degree of 'serjeant-at-law' in a ceremony comparable to coronation or ordination. Their vestments, 'like the priests', include a coif that may not be removed, even in the presence of the king, for they obey a

---

[62] Corpus Christi College, Cambridge MS 20. *English Coronation Records*, inside cover. Cf. *Three Coronation Orders*, xxxi–xxxvii.

[63] Jean-Philippe Genet, 'Ecclesiastics and Political Theory in Late Medieval England', in *Church, Politics and Patronage*, 23–43.

[64] Of two modern translations, Chrimes's is preferred. *On the Laws and Governance of England*, ed. by Shelley Lockwood (CUP, 1997), 1–80; *De Laudibus Legum Anglie*, ed. by S.B. Chrimes (CUP, 1942).

[65] The king, *a sacerdotibus levitice tribus assumere iubetur exemplar legis, id est a biris catholicis et literatis*, 'is commanded to receive a copy of the law from the priests of the Levitical tribe, that is, from men catholic and learned'. *De Laudibus*, ch. 1.

[66] *De Laudibus*, ch. 3.   [67] *De Laudibus*, ch. 4.   [68] *De Laudibus*, ch. 8.

higher law than the king. The coif indicates possession of an indelible character, created during their consecration to their new degree or estate, this degree or estate being explicitly distinguished from an office. As with religious orders, these justices spend the remainder of their lives as contemplatives of Scripture and law, thereby conveying grace to the kingdom.[69] The conferral of the coif of which Fortescue speaks has been compared to 'a laying on of hands, the outward symbol of an apostolic succession'.[70] Fortescue ends *De Laudibus* as if the entire discourse were a liturgical event, 'giving thanks and praise to Him who began, continued, and finished it, whom we call Alpha and Omega, and whom every spirit should praise. Amen.'

This sacred legal order, with its origins in the crusading orders and from which the Chief Justices were chosen by the king, included among its apprentices a number of Lollards. Henry Bothe of Lancashire, John Prince of Windley, William Glasier of Barton, Thomas Praty of Solihull, and John Friday of Wigston, all apprentices-at-law, were accused of publicly preaching heresy. Thomas Compworth, esquire of Oxfordshire, practiced common discipline by refusing to pay tithes to the abbot of Oseney. Although prosecuted for heresy, he survived to practice law and became quite wealthy. Maureen Jurkowski believes lawyers were attracted to Lollardy because of the influence of both the Inns in London and heretics in their localities. Comparable literary skills and clerical disendowment schemes made Lollardy appealing.[71] Lollard sermons compared the legal 'charters' of Scripture and church, deeming the latter to be self-serving clerical innovations.[72] For some lawyers then, their own title to a sacred ordering gainsaid clerical mediation.

Serjeants-at-law have never been connected with heresy, perhaps because, as has been noted, gentry were rarely prosecuted for heresy due to their status.[73] Prominent families in English religious and social history were represented in the order. In the fifteenth century, these include Nicholas Gower, William Gascoigne, William Cheyne, William Paston, and several de la Poles. In the sixteenth century, we note John More, Richard Elyot, Thomas Audley, and Nicholas Bacon.[74] Surviving transcripts of 'exhortations' or 'calls', ordination speeches, by the Chief Justices show a continuing sense of priesthood. In 1521, Sir Robert Brudenell defined lawyers as 'ministers of the law'

---

[69] *De Laudibus*, chs. 48–51; J.H. Baker, *The Order of Serjeants at Law: A Chronicle of Creations with Related Texts and a Historical Introduction* (London: Selden Society, 1984), 19–23, 49–51, 67, 87–104.

[70] *Order of Serjeants at Law*, 89.

[71] Jurkowski, 'Lawyers and Lollardy in the Early Fifteenth Century', in *Lollardy and the Gentry in the Later Middle Ages*, ed. by Margaret Aston and Colin Richmond (Stroud: Sutton Publishing, 1997), 155–82.

[72] Emily Steiner, 'Lollardy and the Legal Document', in *Lollards and Their Influence in Late Medieval England*, ed. by Fiona Somerset et al (Woodbridge: Boydell, 2003), 155–74.

[73] Margaret Aston and Colin Richmond, 'Introduction', in *Lollardy and Gentry*, 20.

[74] Baker, *Order of Serjeants at Law*, passim.

necessary for the welfare of the nation. Another Henrician justice agreed, detailing the sacred significance of their vestments. In 1540, Sir Edward Montague compared the Chief Justice to Moses and serjeants-at-law to Christ, John the Baptist, and Paul. Following his 'highe vocation', the justice interprets both law and Scripture for the commonwealth.[75]

Justices saw themselves both as mediators of divine law and representatives of the king. Edward IV and Henry VII concurred, for common lawyers were employed in increasing numbers during their administrations.[76] A serious rupture between the lawyers' allegiance to law and their allegiance to king did not occur until the seventeenth century. Meanwhile, Fortescue was able to hold together ultimately competing concepts of authority.[77] Society was divinely ordered; thus, the confluence of God, king, and law was part and parcel of his thought. As for competing claims between king and clergy, Fortescue was able to draw upon both, as occasion required. To extricate himself from the embarrassing claims he made against Edward IV, who had recently captured Fortescue, he wrote a public apology. Fortescue says Edward could claim the throne through a woman after all, for the woman in question was under the authority of the pope. Since the pope was both *rex et sacerdos* and wields both the spiritual and temporal swords, then he could provide for the feminine deficiency in Edward's claim to unction.[78] Fortescue provides examples of how patriarchy can be self-defeating and how political necessity is often the mother of theological invention. His theological principles camouflaged temporal matters with eternal disguise.[79]

Common law support for papal primacy was highly occasional, for common lawyers saw themselves as the final court of appeal. They cited as precedent the king's mixed personhood, which encompasses both kingship and priesthood. During the tenth year of Henry VII's reign, Chief Justice Brian overruled a bishop for falsely imprisoning a defendant and misusing *De Haeretico Comburendo*, the 1401 law for burning heretics. Brian ruled that since the king is a mixed person, united with the priesthood of holy church, his court has jurisdiction in this case.[80] Fortescue employed a similar argument in allowing

---

[75] *Order of Serjeants at Law*, 280–8, 289–93, 294–302.

[76] E.W. Ives, 'The Common Lawyers in Pre-Reformation England', *TRHS*, 5th series, 18 (1968), 145, 155.

[77] Norman Doe, *Fundamental Authority in Late Medieval English Law* (CUP, 1990), 10; R.W.K. Hinton, 'English Constitutional Doctrines from the Fifteenth Century to the Seventeenth', *EHR*, 75 (1960), 410–25.

[78] *The Declaracion Made by Sir John Fortescu Knyght*, in *Works of Fortescue*, I, 535; Gill, 'Politics and Propaganda', 346.

[79] Anthony Gross, *The Dissolution of the Lancastrian Kingship* (Stamford, Lincolnshire: Paul Watkins, 1996), 70–90.

[80] 'Car il dit, *quod Rex est persona mixta*, car est *persona unita cum sacerdotibus* saint Eglise; en quel cas le Roy poit maintener son jurisdiction per prescription.' 10 Henry VII, pl. 17; quoted by Chrimes, *English Constitutional Ideas*, 387.

the king to fill vacant bishoprics and canonries. The king may fulfill the role of a bishop in such cases because he is a *persona mixta*.[81]

William Lyndwood, the fifteenth-century canon law theorist whose *Provinciale* (1430) was adopted by both provinces, slightly disagreed. Lyndwood served both church and crown and spent much time reconciling their competing jurisdictions. He periodically allowed the king to limit ecclesiastical jurisdiction, yet the king was also responsible for helping the bishops enforce their jurisdiction.[82] However, when considering whether kings may control clerical temporalities, he asserts they could not; rather, the church tolerates the king's temporary power over these temporalities. Yes, the king possesses a priesthood by reason of his unction. Nevertheless, his *persona mixta* 'does not give him power concerning *spiritualia*, that is, concerning those things which pertain to the rule of the church and the ministry of sacraments and sacramentals; neither does it give him power concerning the exercise of ecclesiastical jurisdiction'. Refuting common law precedence, Lyndwood says the king's priesthood is strictly limited in the ecclesiastical arena. His mixed personage does not allow the transference of spiritual jurisdiction.[83] Thomas Netter, Provincial Prior of the Carmelites and opponent of the Lollards, agreed with Lyndwood.[84]

KINGLY PRIESTS

Power

Like their royal counterparts, late medieval popes exalted themselves both spiritually and temporally. Previously, the bishops of Rome were satisfied with the title, 'Vicar of St Peter', but from the middle of the twelfth century he was *vicarius Christi* and kings were disabused of such pretension.[85] Although titles may not impress the modern reader, titular claims to divine authorization might clinch an argument for the medieval listener. Throughout the Middle Ages, popes jockeyed with emperors and kings for the claim to be both *rex et sacerdos*.[86] For instance, during his convoluted attempts to mediate between

---

[81] *Defensio Juris Domus Lancastriae*, in *Works of Fortescue*, I, 514.

[82] John A.F. Thomson, *The Transformation of Medieval England 1370–1529* (London: Longman, 1983), 323–34.

[83] Cf. Lyndwood, *Provinciale* (Oxford, 1679), 126; *Lyndwood's Provinciale*, ed. by J.V. Bullard and H. Chalmer Bell (London: Faith Press, 1929), 50.

[84] *Doctrinale*, II, 79.

[85] R.W. Southern, *Western Society and the Church in the Middle Ages* (London: Penguin, 1970), 104–5.

[86] Perhaps the best study on this centuries-long conflict is provided in Joseph Canning, *A History of Medieval Political Thought 300–1450* (London: Routledge, 1996).

rival aspirants to the Holy Roman Empire, Innocent III (d.1216) claimed authority to arbitrate since he was the only person to be both regal and sacerdotal.[87]

Innocent III was not making any new claims with his appropriation of the language of *vicarius Christi* and *regale sacerdotium*. He did, however, make them exclusive possessions of the papacy. Moreover, he considered all power, whether practiced by kings or priests, as flowing through his office.[88] This *plenitudo potestatis*, plenitude of power, was defined in a number of ways. It found biblical precedent in Christ's conferral of the power of the keys, for binding and loosing sin, upon Peter. Thus, the power of forgiveness is mediated through Peter and his successors in Rome. Biblical precedent was also found in Christ's request for swords and his statement that two were enough. Canonists identified these two swords as *gladius spiritualis et gladius materialis*, spiritual sword and temporal sword. Although the pope could not bear the material sword himself, the prince could only use it *ad nutum sacerdotis*, at the command of the priesthood. The king is thus a mere minister of the pope, a vicar of the papacy. For Innocent III, this effectively meant dualism under the pope.[89]

Innocent IV (d.1254) went further, grasping authority to wield both swords. Dualism, coordinated rule by separate kings and priests, took a theoretical back seat to the principle of *regimen unius persone*, rule by one person. The church is one body; therefore, it can only have one head, and the pope inherits that headship from Christ. Papal apologists believed the functions of both priest and king centered in one person could be traced through Noah, Melchisedek, Abraham, Moses, Samuel, David, and, eventually, Jesus Christ. Christ communicated this succession of royal priesthood through Peter to the popes. The office of this all-powerful pope is *vicarius Christi*, which includes both Christ's kingship and priesthood; therefore, his jurisdiction extends universally.[90] All spiritual matters ended in his judgment as did any temporal matter coming to his attention, *ratione peccati*, by reason of sin. *Ratio peccati* became an increasingly capacious concept.[91] This papal confidence resulted in the greatest claim by a medieval pope, when in his 1302 bull, *Unam Sanctam*, besides asserting the superiority of spiritual over temporal, Boniface VIII

---

[87] Jane Sayers, *Innocent III: Leader of Europe 1198–1216* (London: Longman, 1994), 54–5.

[88] *Innocent III: Leader of Europe 1198–1216* , 88, 197; Friedrich Kempf, 'Innocent III's Claim to Power', in *Innocent III: Vicar of Christ or Lord of the World?*, 2d edn, ed. by James M. Powell (Washington, DC: Catholic University of America Press, 1994), 173–7.

[89] Brian Tierney, *Church Law and Constitutional Thought in the Middle Ages* (London: Variorum, 1979), I, 596–612; Watt, 'Spiritual and Temporal Powers', 370–4.

[90] Watt, *Papal Monarchy*, 58–73; Michele Maccarrone, 'Innocent III Did Not Claim Temporal Power', in *Innocent III: Vicar or Lord?*, 73–8.

[91] Lewis, *Medieval Political Ideas*, II, 524–5.

concluded 'it is entirely necessary to salvation for every human creature to be subject to the Roman Pontiff'.[92]

James of Viterbo agreed with this hierocratic papalist position. He was greatly concerned with defining how and through whom all power was communicated and retained. The pope is central to his theory of the divine communication of political power: 'the whole of the power of government which has been communicated to the Church by Christ—priestly and royal, spiritual and temporal—is in the Supreme Pontiff, the Vicar of Christ'.[93] These powers are divided into two categories, *potestas iurisdictionis* and *potestas ordinis*. In claiming temporal powers for the clergy, canonists created a nomenclature for priestly and royal powers.[94] *Potestas ordinis*, the power of orders or priesthood, accords its holder the ability to preach the Word and dispense the sacraments, especially the right to make sacrifice. *Potestas iurisdictionis*, the power of jurisdiction, is regal power. *Potestas iurisdictionis* is further divided into royal power over temporal things and royal power over spiritual things.

Potestas ordinis was transmitted by Christ to the apostles and, through the laying on of the bishop's hands, according to Acts 20, to the clergy. *Potestas iurisdictionis* over temporals is transmitted by God to kings either through communal election or by direct divine action. *Potestas iurisdictionis* over spirituals, the keys of binding and loosing from sin, were given by Christ to Peter and his successors. 'For the power to bind and release is a judicial power which certainly belongs to kings. In a singular and pre-eminent way, however, this royal power was given to the blessed Peter, and, in him, to each of his successors.' Bishops have a limited *potestas iurisdictionis* but the pope has a simple and unlimited kingship.[95] With these definitions, Viterbo excluded kings from the priesthood while allowing priests to exercise regal powers. Later, we shall see how these definitions were both useful and problematic for the English reformers.

In medieval England, some clergy stood close to the reins of power. It was not unusual for educated clergy to perform multiple roles in church and state, and receive episcopal appointment, canonries, or multiple benefices.[96] English archbishops, scions of nobility, came into their own in the late fourteenth and early fifteenth centuries. William Courtenay, Archbishop of Canterbury, was able to begin the suppression of Wyclif and the Lollards, against the wishes of John of Gaunt, because of his aristocratic birth. Thomas Arundel, Archbishop

---

[92] *James of Viterbo on Christian Government: De Regimine Christiano*, ed. by R.W. Dyson (Woodbridge: Boydell Press, 1995), xiv.

[93] *De Regimine Christiano*, II, 9; Dyson edn, 131.

[94] Ullmann, *Principles of Government*, 41–2.

[95] *De Regimine Christiano*, II, 3; Dyson edn, 65–70.

[96] Peter Heath, *The English Parish Clergy on the Eve of the Reformation* (London: Routledge, 1969), 50–3; A. Hamilton Thompson, *The English Clergy and their Organization in the Later Middle Ages* (OUP, 1947), 15.

of York and Canterbury in succession, was highly instrumental in Richard II's downfall and was intimately involved in the government of Henry IV.[97] Kings used their clergy in the highest offices of the land. Under Henry VII and early in Henry VIII's reign, prelates played a dominant role. Henry VII used Richard Fox, Richard Nix, and John Morton to shore up his base of power and rob the magnates of theirs, especially on the northern and Welsh marches. Peter Iver Kaufman notes a complex 'interpenetration of religious and political life' when Fox was Bishop of Durham.[98]

One of Wyclif's major complaints concerned the combination of temporal and spiritual powers among the upper clergy. His arguments against *clerus caesareus* centered on their disorderly concern with possessions and the consequent neglect of the cure of souls.[99] The Lollards agreed. A priest that 'encumbren and entriken himself in worldli bisynesse and office' works 'agen the pure staat of presthod'.[100] The sixth of the *Twelve Conclusions*, the Lollard agenda presented to Parliament in 1395, pictured a strict separation of powers, 'for temperelte and spirituelte ben to partys of holi chirche, and therfore he that hath takin him to the ton schulde nout medlin him with the tothir'. Thus, Parliament was advised 'that alle maner of curatis bothe heye and lowe ben fulli excusid of temperel office, and occupie hem with here cure and nout ellis'.[101]

Roger Dymmok, a Dominican prior under Richard II, disagreed with this strict dualism. Dymmok believed that since Christ was both *rex et sacerdos*, then his priests in the church, *regale sacerdotium*, may also succeed to a throne or to any lesser office. Since Christ did not tell Peter to throw his sword away, but merely sheath it for a time, then priests may wield both the temporal and spiritual swords.[102] Repeatedly, Dymmok conflates priesthood and kingship. Among the pastors of the church responsible for diligently watching after the lower degrees of society are holy doctors and kings. Both clergy and knights act with moral authority in their secular activities. An indelible character, which signifies royal dignity and power, is given to both kings and bishops when they are installed. Dymmok was apparently looking for self-advancement in writing his refutation of *Twelve Conclusions* but without success.[103]

Richard Fitzjames, Bishop of London under Henry VII and Henry VIII, best known for his support of his chancellor's violent defense of clerical jurisdiction

---

[97] Margaret Aston, *Thomas Arundel* (OUP, 1967), 336–75; *English Chronicle*, 13–20.

[98] *The 'Polytyque Churche'* (Macon, Georgia: Mercer University Press, 1986), 119–39.

[99] *De Quattor Sectis Novellis*, in *Polemical Works*, 243–4; *De Officio Regis*, 28.

[100] Egerton MS 2820, fol. 49; quoted by Anne Hudson, *'Hermofodrita* or *Ambidexter'*, in *Lollardy and Gentry*, 45.

[101] *SEWW*, 26.

[102] Dymmok, *Liber Contra XII Errores et Hereses Lollardorum*, ed. by H.S. Cronin (WLW, 1921), 146–9.

[103] *Liber Contra*, 314–15, 128; Fiona Somerset, 'Answering the *Twelve Conclusions*', in *Lollardy and Gentry*, 52–76.

in the Richard Hun case,[104] agreed with Dymmok. In a sermon published by Wynkyn de Worde, Fitzjames advocated priestly rule. There are four 'Jhūs' in Scripture, three of whom prefigure the fourth, Jesus Christ. First, Joshua, son of Nun, 'myghty prynce', saved the people through might. Second, Joshua, son of Josedech, 'the grete preest of the lawe', saved them through obedience. Third, Jesus, son of Sirach, one of the great 'philosofers', saved them through wisdom. And Jesus Christ saved them through all three. It is Fitzjames' definition of the second Jhūs' role that dominates his survey. The aspiring bishop believes 'thenne were bysshops rulers of the people & pryncis helpers & coadiutors'. Bishops 'beere deuowte obedience unto almyghty god, & teche other the same'.[105] How? By having rule committed to them by God. In a subtle shift, he makes the king a helper in enforcing obedience on the people.[106] Of course, 'Some men here present, ye & not a fewe, woll peraventure muse, why & to what entent I brynge in thys longe story of Jhus Josech, the grete preest of ye olde lawe'. Why, of course, so they can learn obedience from the bishops, whom they should obey.[107]

Thomas Netter stood somewhere between the royalist Wyclif and such advocates of kingly priesthood as Fitzjames. Although his entire work refutes one Wycliffite doctrine after another, he will not conflate royal and priestly powers. He agrees with Wyclif that priests are not lords. Yet, he agrees with clerical advocates that secular lords must obey priests. Moreover, priests are preferred above kings. (It was a commonplace among pre-Reformation clergy that their dignity is greater than 'kynges or emperours: it is egall with the dignity of angels', even above angels.[108] Some Lollard priests also claimed this dignity.[109]) Against Wycliffism, Netter says one cannot separate the honor due priests from that due kings. One cannot simultaneously exalt kings and oppress priests. Like dominoes, the dual powers stand and fall together; their dignities are distinct yet codependent.[110]

Office

There were eight stages of advancement from lay to full priestly status. The first tonsure, a shaving of the hair to resemble a crown, confirmed one as a

---

[104] Edward Hall, *Henry VIII*, 2 vols, ed. by Charles Whibley (London: Jack, 1904), I, 129–42.

[105] *Sermo Die Lune in Ebdomada Pasche* (Westminster: de Worde, 1495), sigs aiiii^v–av^r.

[106] *Sermo Die Lune*, sig. avi^v.

[107] *Sermo Die Lune*, sig. bi^v.

[108] John Colet, 'The Sermon of Doctor Colete made to the Convocacion at Paulis', in J.H. Lupton, *Life of John Colet* (London: George Bell, 1887), 297; Swanson, 'Problems of the Priesthood in Pre-Reformation England', *EHR*, 417 (1990), 864n.

[109] 'The Sermon of William Taylor 1406', in *Two Wycliffite Texts*, ed. by Anne Hudson, EETS 301 (OUP, 1993), 11.

[110] Netter, *Doctrinale*, II, 74.

member of clerical orders. Afterwards, one progressed through the minor orders: doorkeeper, lector, exorcist, and acolyte. Major orders included subdeacons, deacons, and priests.[111] Of greater dignity within the priesthood were cathedral canons, diocesan officials, bishops, archbishops, cardinals, and the pope.[112] There was some equivocation over whether bishops belonged to a different order than priests,[113] but the orthodox universally agreed that only bishops (or their vicars-general) held the power of ordaining priests.[114] Through this monopoly and their juridical powers, the episcopate was integral to the functioning of medieval church and society. Of course, the appointment of a bishop required papal approval. Thus, the church formed a juridical unity from papal curia to parish.

Within the priesthood proper, there were, generally speaking, two classes. Lower class priests often came from yeoman or peasant stock and were without a parish living. Such an unbeneficed chaplain might serve as a parish clerk, parish priest, assistant parish priest, chantry priest, household priest, or gild priest. Higher class priests, often the second-born offspring of nobility, gentry, and merchants, were generally better educated and obtained benefices through preferment, but were subject to charges of absenteeism, pluralism, and simony due to the structure of the patronage system.[115] Here we have primarily considered secular priests but those living under a monastic rule often became priests, too. These 'regular priests' were given special dispensations by the papacy to operate within the parish but outside the jurisdiction of diocese and parish. This could engender ill feelings between regular and secular priests.[116]

The major ministrations of the medieval priesthood were three: confession, sacrifice, and teaching.[117] These were not the only tasks belonging to a cure of souls but they were the most important ones. There was some disagreement over the priority of the ministrations and the powers of the priesthood within them. A staunchly orthodox Oxford don, Thomas Gascoigne, listed priestly duties as preaching, offering hospitality, praying, and communal peacemaking.[118] The widely recognized central duty and power of the orthodox priesthood was the

---

[111] Heath, *English Parish Clergy*, 13–15.   [112] Thompson, *English Clergy*, 1–100.

[113] Paul F. Bradshaw, 'Medieval Ordinations', in *The Study of Liturgy*, revised edn, ed. by Cheslyn Jones et al (OUP, 1992), 378.

[114] Lyndwood, *Provinciale*, II, 4.

[115] John R.H. Moorman, 'The Medieval Parsonage and its Occupants', *Bulletin of the John Rylands Library*, 28 (1944), 7–8; Heath, *English Parish Clergy*, 27–49; Tim Cooper, *The Last Generation of English Catholic Clergy* (Woodbridge: Boydell Press, 1999), 37–93.

[116] Heath, *English Parish Clergy*, 175–82.

[117] Marshall, *Catholic Priesthood*, 5–107.

[118] Swanson, 'Problems', 846–7; Winifred A. Pronger, 'Thomas Gascoigne: I', *EHR*, 53 (1938), 606–26; idem, 'Thomas Gascoigne: II', *EHR*, 54 (1939), 20–37.

making of the body of God in the mass.[119] Lollards defined the priest's responsibilities as 'prechyng and preying with hert, and gyvyng of sacramentis, and lernyng of Gods lawe, and gyvyng gode ensaumple by clennesse of lif'.[120] The orthodox might begin their discussions with the seven sacraments. Our discussion is organized around the three major ministrations of the priesthood: confession, the mass, and preaching.

Annual confession was made mandatory for all Christians in 1215 by the bull *Omnis Utriusque Sexus*, promulgated by Innocent III to support the Fourth Lateran Council. It has been asserted that such a requirement for pastorally-supervised personal introspection was indicative, if not causative, of a 'rise of individualism' in the Middle Ages.[121] Catholic historians have pointed instead to the social functions of confession, especially the restoration of communal peace.[122] In a major study, Thomas Tentler concluded social control was definitely the goal of confession, but it was accomplished through personal self-examination. Confessors had at their disposal huge manuals for categorizing sin and resolving 'cases of conscience'.[123] The confessional simultaneously promoted individual reflection and social harmony. In England, the focus of confession shifted from communal peace to personal peace with God. This atomism occurred, ironically, as part of Arundel's effort to suppress Lollardy and enforce orthodoxy. Along with their use of the church courts to combat heresy, the circle of clergy around Arundel appropriated mysticism within their program of national religion. Laity were encouraged to focus inwardly, leaving outward religion for priests.[124]

Confession, of course, was prerequisite for communion, and in this process the priest not only served as mediator but was divinized.[125] In his ordination, the priest was specifically given the power to sacrifice. It is this power—to make and offer the body of Christ to God on behalf of people, both living and dead—that gave priesthood its central place in the medieval cultus. In the sacrifice of the mass, supernatural power for both spiritual and physical needs

---

[119] In a popular morality play, the main character did not find peace facing death until he made penance and received the sacrament of the mass from the priest. 'Five Wits' said God gave the priesthood a power higher than that of angels: 'With five words he may consecrate God's body in flesh and blood to make, and handleth his Maker between his hands.' 'Everyman', in *The Pageant of Medieval England: Historical and Literary Sources to 1485*, ed. by Francis Godwin James (Gretna, Louisiana: Pelican, 1975), 178.

[120] Arnold, III, 145.

[121] Morris, *Discovery of the Individual*, 70–9. Oscar D. Watkins, *A History of Penance*, 2 vols (London: Longmans Green, 1920), I, 477, II, 536–8, 735.

[122] John Bossy, *Christianity in the West*, 35–56; Peter Biller, 'Confession in the Middle Ages', in *Handling Sin*, ed. by Biller and A.J. Minnis (York: York Medieval Press, 1998), 29–30.

[123] Tentler, 'The *Summa* for Confessors as an Instrument of Social Control', in *The Pursuit of Holiness in Late Medieval and Renaissance Religion*, ed. by Charles Trinkaus and Heiko A. Oberman (Leiden: E.J. Brill, 1974), 103–26.

[124] Hughes, *Pastors and Visionaries*, 151–3, 196–7.

[125] Swanson, 'Problems', 857–9.

was made available in the physical form of the wafer. Spiritually, through the physical or spiritual reception of the host, the repentant believer was incorporated into Christ [see Plate 2].[126] Physically, the very sight of the host could be used as a magical—the elusive 'apotropaic' is Eamon Duffy's preferred adjective—talisman for a variety of purposes, from ensuring safety in childbirth and travel to healing the sick and fighting fires.[127] Edward Hall says the consecrated host was elevated to quell a riot in Calais in the mid-1520s, but being Welshmen, the rioters 'wer so rude that thei nothyng them regarded'.[128] This is a vivid reminder that priests wielded power that not only saved souls and healed physical ailments but also preserved society. Of course, most laypeople communicated orally only once every year, and then only the host. The priest received both kinds at each mass.

Different frequencies and modes of reception were not the only barriers placed between priest and people.[129] Architecturally, the roodscreen inhibited participation between people's nave and priest's chancel, visually isolating the people—Duffy's recharacterization of the roodscreen as backdrop rather than barrier is physically untenable.[130] The foreign nature of liturgical language, Latin, compelled the worship of the people to become separate from that of the priest. This was explicitly recognized in one popular primer: 'Clerks hear on a manner, But lewd men behove another to learn.'[131] Almsgiving, the offerings of the people, became less frequent.[132] Private masses were exactly that, dedicated to private purposes; although including the universal church in their prayers, these masses were primarily intended for individuals and families to escape purgatory.[133]

Such separation enhanced the priest's mediatorial role. In some sense, he became Christ. The priest, as Christ, offers the sacrifice to God on behalf of the church. Moreover, he, as Christ, offers the sacrament to the people on behalf of God.[134] The priest's monopoly on the sacramental power of making the body of God was part and parcel of his mediatorial role. The people could offer their spiritual sacrifices, alms, and prayers to God at the eucharist but only

---

[126] Miri Rubin, *Corpus Christi: The Eucharist in Late Medieval Culture* (CUP, 1991), 12–14, 77.

[127] Duffy, *The Stripping of the Altars* (YUP, 1992), 100–2, *passim*; Thomas, *Religion and the Decline of Magic* (London: Penguin, 1973), 36–40; Swanson, 'Problems', 856–7.

[128] *Henry VIII*, I, 297.

[129] P.J. Fitzpatrick, 'On Eucharistic Sacrifice in the Middle Ages', in *Sacrifice and Redemption*, 135.

[130] *Stripping*, 109–12. Christine Peters refers to 'the undoubtedly important function of the screen, as a barrier between nave and chancel, in enhancing the mystery of the mass.' *Patterns of Piety: Women, Gender and Religion in Late Medieval and Reformation England* (CUP, 2003), 105.

[131] *The Lay Folks Mass Book*, ed. by Thomas Frederick Simmons, EETS 71 (London: Trübner, 1879), 17.

[132] Joseph A. Gribbin, 'Lay Participation in the Eucharistic Liturgy of the Later Middle Ages', in *Ministerial and Common Priesthood in the Eucharistic Celebration* (London: Saint Austin Press, 1999), 51–2.

[133] K.L. Wood-Legh, *Perpetual Chantries in Britain* (CUP, 1965), 305, 312–13.

[134] Marshall, *Catholic Priesthood*, 43, 69.

through the priest as corporate representative. They received, in turn, the *Pax* and the blessing, but only by virtue of the priesthood.[135]

Among theologians there was much speculation concerning the doctrine of transubstantiation, the change of the elements of bread and wine into the body and blood of Christ.[136] Allegorical explanations of the gestures made and vestments worn by the priest were also popular.[137] Surprisingly, there was little definition of the concomitant action of any priesthood, namely sacrifice. Medieval theologians, such as Aquinas, spoke of the sacrifice of the mass as representing, commemorating, and even having the nature of the sacrifice of Christ on the cross. Since Christ's sacrifice was unique, he was not crucified again in the mass, but his sacrifice was therein made available to the people. The efficacy of the sacrifice was available to those who did not commune, even to those not present.[138]

By emphasizing an indefinite sacrifice and an invisible transubstantiation, an aura of mystery surrounded the eucharist, especially the consecrated host. To further accentuate the physical presence of the body of Christ, the elevation of the host was introduced in the thirteenth century. The feast of Corpus Christi became a major part of the church calendar and, after being introduced in 1318, its celebration in England became widespread in the fifteenth century. In this way, the host became a holy commodity at the disposal of the priesthood, and complaints of idolatry surfaced.[139]

During his examination before Arundel, the Lollard priest William Thorpe decried such devotion. Once, when Thorpe was preaching, the sacring bell was rung and many ran from him to catch a glimpse of the elevated host. Thorpe hotly reminded them the virtue of the eucharist lay in their belief about it rather than in gazing at it. In other words, internal faith generated by preaching excels ignorant excitement for ceremony. Thorpe considered preaching essential for priests: 'it is euery preestis office and cheef dette for to preche bisili, frely and treuli the word of God'. Priests who do not preach share in the damnation of the lost; therefore, priests may safely ignore episcopal licensing.[140]

The Lollards were not alone in their emphasis on preaching. Many orthodox theologians considered preaching to be the priesthood's premier task. Gascoigne believed heresy would develop as a result of the lack of preaching; therefore, priests must preach. He wanted the episcopal licenses commanded by Arundel's constitutions condemned. Gascoigne joined an important group of London priests in continuing Henry V's religious program of *doctrina*, teaching the people, and joined in condemning Reginald Pecock for his

---

[135] Bossy, 'Mass as a Social Institution', 35–6.
[136] See 'The Eucharist', pp. 29–30 of this book.
[137] Fitzpatrick, 'Eucharistic Sacrifice', 137–8; *Lay Folks Mass Book, passim.*
[138] Fitzpatrick, 'Eucharistic Sacrifice', 138–41.
[139] 'Eucharistic Sacrifice', 143–5; Gribbin, 'Lay Participation', 60–2; Rubin, *Corpus Christi*, 199–204.
[140] 'The Testimony of William Thorpe 1407', in *Two Wycliffite Texts*, 40–52.

defense of non-preaching prelates.[141] Denouncing the London preachers as *clamatores in pulpitis*, pulpit-bawlers, Pecock became the only English bishop prosecuted for heresy before the Reformation.[142]

Anticlericalism

One major strand of medieval preaching employed the method of complaint to enable conversion. Gerald Owst said, 'Of all the important types of composition in English literature, there is perhaps none which still presents a history so neglected, so disjointed and so little understood at its earliest stages as that of Satire and Complaint.'[143] Among Reformation historians, Owst's pioneering studies in this arena are unacknowledged. Whiggish historiography sees anticlericalism as ballooning at the beginning of the Reformation; Revisionist historiography sees anticlericalism as a result of Reformation; Owst shows that complaint directed against the clergy was a vibrant contributor to Christian history long before the Reformation. Boniface VIII began *Clericos Laicos*, his famous bull of 1296, with the words, 'Antiquity teaches that the laity have been exceedingly hostile to the clergy'.[144] Against Boniface's version of events, however, we find the greatest proponents of anticlericalism in England were the clergy themselves. The propagators of vernacular complaint were priests, at first mostly regular, later secular. They directed their vitriol against every estate, including priests. 'It was the Catholic clergy of every species in the Church who for centuries had been accustomed, from their own pulpits, to scold their fellow-clergy—indeed the hierarchy as a whole—in terms no less flagrant and sometimes no less indecent than the most scurrilous Reformer.' This was not the work of isolated heretics but a church-wide clerical phenomenon.[145]

This clerically induced anticlericalism was manifold in its manifestations. Secular priests and prelates railed against regulars for papally granted privileges that undermined the secular position, especially when friars heard parishioners' confessions. In his antiregular tirades, Wyclif stood in the tradition of William of St Amour, secular opponent of the Dominican Aquinas, and of Richard FitzRalph, Bishop of Armagh.[146] William Langland, a clerk in minor orders and author of *Piers Plowman*, was as vehemently set against the friars as

---

[141] Pronger, 'Gascoigne: II', 30–1; Catto, 'Fall of Pecock', 205, 213–14.

[142] Scase, 'Pecock', 95–102; V.H.H. Green, *Bishop Reginald Pecock* (CUP, 1945), 49–69.

[143] Owst, *Literature and Pulpit in Medieval England*, revised edn (Oxford: Blackwell, 1961), 210.

[144] *De Regimine Christiano*, Dyson edn, vii.

[145] Owst, *Literature and Pulpit*, 214–37, 285.

[146] Wyclif gives credit for his antifraternalism to St Amour, Ockham, Grosseteste, and FitzRalph. *De Ordinatione Fratrum*, in *Polemical Works*, I, 91–3; Szittya, *Antifraternal Tradition*;

Wyclif.[147] The monks and friars attacked each other while countering the blows of secular priests. Lollards defended secular priests while railing against both the prelacy and the religious orders. The prelates took particular delight in suppressing their Wycliffite critics.[148] Gascoigne was a 'notorious' critic of the church, identifying the chief evils in parish life as the impropriation of tithes, pluralism, and non-residence.[149]

John Colet, humanist Dean of St Paul's, envisioned the reformation of the church, and denounced the clerical evils of pride, lust, covetousness, and secular occupation. What makes Colet's denunciation so profound is that he was speaking, *ad clerum*, to a 1512 Convocation convened to discuss new measures for combating heresy among the laity. He had the temerity to identify the real crisis as primarily clerical rather than lay. Lay heresy is the consequence of a wicked priesthood.[150] However, Colet was not sponsoring a lay-led, but an episcopal, reformation. If bishops would reform themselves, the clergy would follow, and the people would not be far behind. Existing canons should be enforced rather than new ones issued. If the clergy would only live up to their ideal, they would receive from the laity obedience, honor, and tithes, and the peace and liberty which accompany unction. Colet's agenda has been oxymoronically but aptly dubbed 'clerical anticlericalism'.[151]

Why such an emphasis on criticism by pre-Reformation preachers? Were priests in the Middle Ages naturally contentious? William Langland offers insight into the motives of these critical pre-moderns. For all of his anticlericalism, Langland believed in the divine sanctioning of priesthood. Preachers and popes are spiritual guides and examples who show the way of salvation: 'these should be God's salt to preserve men's souls'. The problem for Langland, however, is indicated by his use of the hortatory subjunctive. Langland had a high ideal for the priesthood, but reality was not measuring up to it. Friars, scholars, canon lawyers, and prelates were sadly deficient in their character and activity. Even Mohammed was a Christian cleric gone bad.[152]

Langland believed that if the priesthood was corrupt, then the people were doomed. The church is like a tree: the priests are roots; the people are branches dependent on the clergy for nourishment. Wicked priesthood results in a wicked society. Conversely, a healthy priesthood engenders a healthy

---

Edith Wilks Dolnikowski, 'FitzRalph and Wyclif on the Mendicants', *Michigan Academician*, 19 (1987), 87–100.

[147] Scase, *Piers Plowman and the New Anticlericalism* (CUP, 1989).

[148] Scase, 1–14.

[149] Pronger, 'Gascoigne: I', 615–16.

[150] 'Sermon of Doctor Colete', 295–9.

[151] 'Sermon of Doctor Colete', 299–304; Kaufman, 'Colet's *Opus de Sacramentis* and Clerical Anticlericalism.'

[152] Langland, *Piers Plowman: A New Translation of the B-Text*, transl. by A.V.C. Schmidt (OUP, 1992), 174–5, 180–2.

society.[153] Langland was semi-Pelagian in his soteriology, and while he believed in predestination he also believed in the priestly mediation of grace and the active lay reception of grace.[154] Like many in this period, both orthodox and heterodox, he came close to the Donatist position, the belief that priestly mediation was hindered by the wickedness of the priesthood.[155] Since priesthood is necessary for lay salvation and the priesthood missed the ideal, it needs correction.

Restoring an ideal priesthood can only be accomplished through criticism. In Passus X, 'Wit' searched for 'Do-well', 'Do-better', and 'Do-best', three guides to personal salvation. 'Clergy' told Wit that Do-best is he who may 'rebuke wrongdoers' because his life is perfect and blameless. Langland's works-oriented soteriology equates criticism with evangelism. In Passus XI, we learn criticism generates shame, which fosters penance. For a person to act, he must know his deficiencies and see an example of holy living. If Do-best, the exemplary priest, criticizes, then salvation is possible. In Passus XII, we learn that Do-best can only be a cleric. Thus, for salvation to reach the people, the clergy must first criticize themselves and reach perfection. Afterwards, wicked people may be saved.[156]

Langland despaired of priests ever reaching perfection. Therefore, God gave the latest dispensation of grace to Piers Plowman. Perhaps the world will be saved through this layperson. In the last Passus, 'Conscience', while assuming the harmonious working of laity and clergy, realizes some clergy are good and others are bad.[157] He wonders whether Piers may be a better confessor than the clergy. Conscience calls out to the clergy for help but leaves the embattled and nearly-defeated Christian community to look for Piers, who by now has become a Christ-figure.[158]

The same type of idealism which Colet and Langland displayed was integral to Wyclif's protest. Wyclif was disappointed with himself and other clergy because they could not meet the high standards for preaching and works of mercy that a wide circle of northern clergy considered necessary for the fulfillment of their office. Even Philip Repingdon, onetime Lollard then Bishop of Lincoln and Cardinal, willingly took Margery Kempe's criticism and begged

---

[153] *Piers Plowman*, 169–70.

[154] Robert Adams, 'Langland's Theology', in *A Companion to Piers Plowman*, ed. by John A. Alford (London: University of California Press, 1988), 90–5.

[155] Popular theology lurched between mechanistic and Donatistic understandings when the sacramental mediation of priesthood was emphasized. Marshall, *Catholic Priesthood*, 44–57.

[156] *Piers Plowman*, 101–4, 124–5, 128–30; Adams, 'Langland's Theology', 96–7.

[157] The Fairford windows oppose evil priests and kings against good priests and kings; judiciously, the evil figures were drawn from antiquity while the good were more recent. Even the York mystery plays showed evil priests in action, convincing Pilate that the fool-king Jesus was both traitor and heretic. *York Mystery Plays*, ed. by Richard Beadle and Pamela M. King (OUP, 1984), 139–53, 204–7.

[158] *Piers Plowman*, 253–4.

for her prayers. Late medieval English clergy were suffering from an epidemic of self-criticism.[159]

John Colet

We end our review of the second estate by examining Colet's ideal priesthood. Colet, mentioned already, held himself and all clergy to a high standard, later lauded by Erasmus Desiderius (d.1536): 'Against these temptations he fought so successfully with the help of philosophy and sacred study and watching, fasting, and prayer, that he passed his whole life unspotted by the defilements of this world.'[160] According to Erasmus, Colet's program was built on philosophy, Scripture, and exemplary living. He began with pseudo-Dionysius, a sixth-century Syrian monk whose supposed canonical status conferred great authority on his mystical, hierarchical theology. Dionysius coined the term 'hierarchy', literally, the rule of priests. He believed the clergy guided the individual in the approach to God, but eventually individuals must go on their own.[161] Colet appropriated the Dionysian system, giving it a conjugal twist. According to Colet, the two sacraments through which all others are understood are ordination and marriage. Ordination is the foundational sacrament; matrimony is the teleological sacrament; the other sacraments can be instituted only by orders and realized only in marriage.[162]

Colet says God is 'Order'. He is the priest of priests and the source of all priesthood. The making of priests is the *raison d'être* of the priesthood. 'Hence it is that priesthood is actually, if I may so express it [*sacerdotificans*] priest-making: for all priesthood is from God, the priest of priests.' To make other priests, the priest must imitate God in purity, light, and goodness. Priesthood is the same thing as matrimony. In divine fecundation, the priesthood 'impregnates' the laity 'in a kind of holy coitus'. The clergy, 'husbands in Jesus', make the female priesthood, the laity, holy through 'spiritual marriage'. The active, male, clerical priesthood cleanses, illumines, and perfects the passive, female, lay priesthood through the sacraments. Their offspring is justice, a spiritual sacrifice.[163] Cleansing is administered by the lower orders, the lowest

---

[159] Hughes, *Pastors and Visionaries*, 161–71; *The Book of Margery Kempe*, transl. by B.A. Windeatt (London: Penguin, 1985), I, 15.

[160] Erasmus to Justus Jonas, 13 June 1521; *CWE*, VIII, 237.

[161] 'Dionise Hid Divinite', in *The Cloud of Unknowing and Other Works*, ed. by Clifton Wolters (London: Penguin, 1961), 201–18; Leland Miles, *John Colet and the Platonic Tradition* (London: Allen & Unwin, 1962), 158–206; Sears Jayne, *John Colet and Marsilio Ficino* (OUP, 1963), 116–17.

[162] 'Catechyzon', in Lupton, *Colet*, 287; *De Sacramentis*, chs. 1–2, 4, in John B. Gleason, *John Colet* (London: University of California Press, 1989), 274–7, 302–5.

[163] Colet, *De Sacramentis*, 270–9, 304–5.

of the three hierarchies; illumination is the work of deacons, the middle hierarchy; perfection is the duty of priests, the highest hierarchy.[164] All believers are priests but clergy are an active and sanctifying *vir*, husband, while laity are a passive and obedient *uxor*, wife. Together, in the cooperation of *vir* and *uxor*, the church sacrifices or propagates the sacrifices of justice and holiness. Thus, they show themselves spiritually married to Jesus.[165] Jesus himself is both masculine and feminine; masculine in his Godhead; feminine in his humanity. He is also 'the sacrament of sacraments, the sacramental principle himself'.[166]

Colet's ecclesiology was corporocentric and fragile. He believed fallen man is naturally atomistic. Sin separates individuals from one another, 'each one, in reliance on himself, following the bent of his own inclination'. Sinful, atomistic individuals are why society is turbulent, constantly shifting. In the new covenant, individuals are brought to social harmony in Christ. The Holy Spirit is the only one who can provide *virtus conglutinans*, the cementing power that provides 'order' and 'beauty of regularity' for redeemed society. The Spirit is present to all at once and fully present to each one. Whatever happens to one is immediately felt by all. Christians must use their individual spiritual gifts for the good of the whole body.[167] While the social body is vital, its proper functioning depends on each individual. Ultimately, society may fracture merely through one sin. 'And by all comune reason, yf thou kepe this conuenient order to God and his creatures, they shall kepe theyr order to the; but yf thou breke thyne order to them, of lykelyhood they shall breke their order to the.'[168]

Colet's society repeatedly fractured. In 1511 and 1512, he was an expert witness for the prosecution of John Brown and Edward Walker, both condemned as heretics. Brown and Walker were relinquished to the secular arm for burning, for believing among other things that priests are given no more power than laypeople to minister the sacraments, including the eucharist.[169] In spite of this, Colet's sermons were appreciated by Lollards. During the famous trial and funeral of Richard Hun in 1511, apparently murdered by the bishop's commissary, Colet remained silent. Then came his denunciation of clerical evils in the 1512 Convocation sermon. Soon after, lordly Bishop Fitzjames accused Colet of sedition, who escaped condemnation only through Archbishop William Warham's protection. His clerical opponents subsequently decried his

---

[164] *De Sacramentis*, ch. 3; Gleason edn, 278–85.

[165] *De Sacramentis*, ch. 4; Gleason edn, 306–9.

[166] *De Sacramentis*, ch. 4; Gleason edn, 302–3, 328–9.

[167] *De Corpore Christi Mystico*, in *Opuscula Quaedam Theologica*, ed. by Lupton (London: George Bell, 1876), 29–48, 183–96; *Enarratio in Epistolam S. Pauli ad Romanos*, ed. by Lupton (London: George Bell, 1873), 58–91.

[168] 'A ryght fruitfull monicion', in Lupton, *Colet*, 306; *Enarratio ad Romanos*, 83–4.

[169] *Kent Heresy Proceedings 1511–12*, ed. by Norman Tanner (Maidstone: Kent Archaeological Society, 1997), 43–58.

sermons for criticizing war before Henry VIII. He did not forsake the hierarchy, however, for he preached during the installation of Thomas Wolsey as Cardinal in 1515, offering him high praise.[170] Colet, like most political theologians in late medieval England, desired a harmonious relationship between God and man, king and priest, and priest and people. Unfortunately, the ideal was elusive and disappointment led to conflict and criticism. We now turn to the third estate, the people.

A ROYAL AND PRIESTLY PEOPLE?

In light of the dominant social theory, in what sense could members of the third estate participate in both royalty and priesthood? As we shall see, encroachments by the third estate into the higher estates were severely delimited, even as the concept of a universal kingship and priesthood was retained. Heretics were also careful to circumscribe their statements, especially with regard to kingship, though they often challenged the priesthood. Even then, Lollards rarely tested the boundaries of eucharistic consecration. Richard Rex properly restricts his conclusions: 'There seems, moreover, to have been an inchoate doctrine of the priesthood of all believers among the Lollards, which might have rendered any formal ministry redundant.'[171] This doctrine was indeed inchoate, for it was not implemented in late medieval England, but it was certainly considered.

Universal Kingship

John Stafford, Bishop of Bath and Wells, informed Parliament in 1436 of three coronations: 'The first of these is in the baptising of a Christian, in sign of which they are anointed and receive the chrism.' The others are the priestly reception of the tonsure and the king's reception of a jeweled crown.[172] The equation of baptismal anointing with making all Christians into prophets, priests, and kings stretches back at least to Hippolytus' *Apostolic Tradition*. This tradition was affirmed in both the Eastern and Western baptismal rites, giving all Christians a share in Christ's threefold office.[173] Viterbo, following a gloss on Revelation 1.5, agrees with this threefold lordship. Secular princes

---

[170] Kaufman, 'Clerical Anticlericalism', 18–22; Lupton, *Colet*, 178–98.

[171] Richard Rex, *The Lollards* (Basingstoke: Palgrave, 2002), 82.

[172] *Rotuli Parliamentum*, IV, 495; transl. in Bertie Wilkinson, *Constitutional History in the Fifteenth Century* (London: Longmans, 1964), 213.

[173] *Apostolic Tradition*, ch. 5; quoted in Leonel L. Mitchell, *Baptismal Anointing* (London: SPCK, 1966), 6, 65, 106, 135, 140, 153.

rule their subjects by divine disposition; pastors rule the faithful people entrusted to them; and, individual believers 'are kings simply because, with God's help, they rule over themselves'.[174] John of Paris (d.1306), dualist opponent of papalist Viterbo, applies royal priesthood 'to all faithful and just men who, in constituting a unity with Christ their head, are kings and priests in him.... Or again: they are called a kingdom, because Christ their king rules in them'.[175]

Orthodox discussions of the kingship of the faithful exhibit some similarities. First, they occur within the context of discussions concerning hierocratic political theology. Second, they treat the issue summarily. Third, they define universal kingship as participation in the kingship of Christ, which participation begins with baptism. Fourth, they each immediately and virtually dismiss a reified popular kingship, usually by spiritualizing, internalizing, or atomizing it. *Opus Arduum*, penned *c.*1389 by an unknown Wycliffite in prison and printed by Luther, offers another means for dismissing a reified universal kingship, eschatological fulfillment.[176] The author allows for a minor current fulfillment through Lollard resistance to episcopal preaching licenses. Revelation 1.5 gives 'power to resist our enemies, who attack preaching'. But later references in the Apocalypse show universal kingship is delayed and internalized. In 5.10, 'God has made us a kingdom' means 'he will reign in us and we in him'. 'And we will reign over the earth, . . . nevertheless in the end, . . . not by earthly power, . . . but by heavenly power.' On 20.6, he allows for either a premillennial or postmillennial reign of the saints, but again, such a reign is in the future.[177]

But was Lollardy so subservient? In its early days they had a strong presence in the royal court. Kenneth McFarlane traced the successful careers of several Lollard knights in the governments of Edward III, Richard II, and Henry IV.[178] Michael Wilks believes Wyclif's theology of clerical disendowment was but one expression of the 'official policy' of the royal court. What happened to change this pro-court Lollardy? 'Lollard' was a term of derision, first appearing on the continent. The English prelatical party adopted it as a means of misrepresenting their opponents as illiterate, populist, and subversive.[179] The domino theory of clerical and temporal lordship propounded by Gregory XI became an orthodox commonplace in the fifteenth century. With

---

[174] Over each of these kings is Christ, the King from whom all power flows, and the pope is his vicar. *De Regimine Christiano*, II, 3; Dyson edn, 68.

[175] *On Royal and Papal Power*, transl. by J.A. Watt (Toronto: Pontifical Institute of Mediaeval Studies, 1971), ch. 18, 189.

[176] Curtis V. Bostick, *The Antichrist and the Lollards* (Leiden: E.J. Brill, 1998), 51.

[177] *Commentarivs in Apocalypsin*, ed. by Martin Luther (Wittenberg, 1528), fols 4ʳ, 48ᵛ–49ʳ, 195ᵛ.

[178] McFarlane, *Lancastrian Kings and Lollard Knights* (OUP, 1972), 137–226.

[179] Wilks, 'Royal Priesthood: The Origins of Lollardy', in *The Church in a Changing Society* (Uppsala: Swedish Society of Church History, 1978), 63–80. On the terms 'Lollard' and 'Wycliffite', see Leff, *Heresy*, 346; Hudson, *Premature Reformation*, 2–4.

the inane rebellion of Sir John Oldcastle against Henry V, credence was lent to orthodox propaganda; Wycliffism became Lollardy.[180]

Earlier Wycliffite sources show they were generally far removed from illiteracy and revolution. One sermon, *Synne is for to Drede*, affirms the traditional orders of priests, knights, and laborers. Each order is necessary for the maintenance of the church. Temporal lords 'ben vikers of godhed of Crist' and must keep priests and laborers true to their vocations. Priests must encourage knights to rule temporally and must themselves never govern. The commons are prohibited from resisting even tyrannical rulers. 'I have not redde in Gods lawe that sogettis schhulden feght with hor worldly soveraynes.'[181] *Twenty-Five Articles* agreed that priests must preach and administer sacraments and knights must govern the church.[182] Wycliffites did not dispense with a particular priesthood, but supported disendowment by temporal rulers to return the clergy to their pristine state of poverty and spiritual service. Langland concurred with the goal of clerical disendowment.[183] Wycliffites affirmed the ideal of community through communal representation. As the community's representatives, knights rule society. Any social changes must necessarily begin, proceed, and end with their leadership. Like the orthodox preachers of complaint, Wycliffite preachers might criticize members of all three estates, but their criticism affirmed the old estates theory. They primarily wanted the estates to function as intended.[184] Against modern misperceptions, Simon Ford has demonstrated Wycliffites were neither egalitarian nor democratic. Rather, they were 'far more traditional than radical'.[185]

Wycliffites explicitly rejected individual judgment in favor of communal judgment. This is most evident in their calls for the withholding of tithes from wicked clergy. Only when the community acts in tandem may it discipline their clergy. 'And certis me thenkes that parischenes may in certeyne case withholde dymes fro hym that is calde the persone [parson].... But not iche parischen schulde, whan ever he wolde, holde fro hys person be hys owne juggement.' It is the community, led by gentry, which judges and disciplines clergy.[186] These works simultaneously exalt temporal sovereignty and communal accord. 'We owen obedience to oure souereyns'; moreover, 'Holi chirche is a forme of al rigtwisenes, that is to seie a comune acorde of alle

---

[180] W.T. Waugh, 'Sir John Oldcastle', *EHR*, 20 (1905), 434–56, 637–58.

[181] Arnold, III, 142–7.

[182] *Twenty-Five Articles*, arts 11, 14; Arnold, III, 472, 479. Dated c.1389 by Hudson, *Premature Reformation*, 210–11.

[183] Hudson, *Premature Reformation*, 334–42; Adams, 'Langland's Theology', 109–11.

[184] *Of Servants and Lords*, in *The English Works of Wyclif hitherto Unprinted*, ed. by F.D. Matthew, EETS 74 (London: Trübner, 1880), 226–43.

[185] Simon N. Ford, 'Social Outlook and Preaching in a Wycliffite *Sermones Dominicales* Collection', in *Church and Chronicle in the Middle Ages*, ed. by Ian Wood and G.A. Loud (London: Hambledon Press, 1991), 185–6.

[186] *Seven Werkys of Mercy Bodyly*, in Arnold, III, 167, 177. Hudson's example of individual judgment in the withholding of tithes is not Wycliffite. Hudson, *Premature Reformation*, 343.

good thingis; and this chirche preieth in comune and worschith hir werkis in comune'.[187]

The Fairford church windows reminded people of the temporal irrelevance of their kingship. Below the Last Judgment, another judgment window shows the beheading of the Amalekite who slew Saul. King David had ordered the Amalekite's death, in spite of Saul's status as David's enemy and in spite of the Amalekite's gift of the royal crown, because the Amalekite touched the Lord's anointed.[188] The anointing of baptism gave people no bodily power over those possessing royal unction. In his attempt to escape prelatical persecution, Oldcastle, like so many others in this period, forgot this truth, and Lollardy went into its dark days. Perhaps a clue to Oldcastle's behavior may be found in the thought of John Fortescue.

Fortescue garnered his concept of royal priesthood from Thomas Aquinas.[189] In *The Deference Bi Twene Dominium Regale and Dominium Politicum et Regale*, Fortescue's theory of *dominium*, lordship, begins with royal priesthood. 'The childeryn of Israell, as saith Seynt Thomas, aftir that God hade chosen thaim *in populum peculiarem et regnum sacerdotale*, were ruled bi hym vndir Juges *regaliter et politice*, in to the tyme that thai desired to haue a kynge, as tho hade al the gentiles, wich we cal peynymes, that hade no kynge but a man that reigned vppon thaim *regaliter tantum*.' Fortescue envisioned three types of government: politically alone, or rule by popular judges; royally alone, or rule by kings alone; and royally and politically, or rule by kings with judges acting on behalf of the people.[190] The best type of government is *regaliter et politice*, royal and political; that is, rule by king and judges, the latter acting as the people's representatives.

Fortescue refers often to the Israelite judges and to Christ's heavenly rule as precedents for England. The period of the judges was established in Exodus 19, when God as king elected Israel to rule with him as a royal priesthood. When Israel chose to be ruled by a human king alone in I Samuel 8, they began to suffer because they rejected God's rule *regaliter et politice*.[191] Fortescue's ideal political system of government *regaliter et politice* has been likened to constitutional monarchy. He believed royal power originated when the people, through their judges, purposefully gathered as a mystical body. The king was

---

[187] *The Lanterne of Ligt*, 40, 74.   [188] Keble, *St Mary's Church*, 12; II Samuel 1.

[189] Fortescue refers to *De Regimine Principum*. Aquinas wrote the first book and part of the second; the remainder being completed by Ptolemy of Lucca (d.1327). Aquinas said, 'Therefore, a regal priesthood derives from him, and, what is more, all the faithful of Christ, insofar as they are his members, are called kings and priests'. *De Regimine Principum*, I, 15.9; Blythe edn, 3–5, 100.

[190] *Deference*, ch. 1. Plummer's edition is preferred. *On Laws and Governance*, Lockwood edn, 84; *The Governance of England*, ed. by Charles Plummer (OUP, 1885), 109. Cf. *De Regimine Principum*, IV, 1.

[191] *De Naturae Legis Nature*, in *Works of Fortescue*, I, 203–6; *Deference*, chs. 1–3.

elected by the people to seek the common good; thus, he cannot enact laws or govern without their judges. Although universal kingship was given a role in Fortescue's ideal government, they must always act communally through judges.[192]

Across the spectrum—by clerics, heretics, and common lawyers—the people were affirmed as being kings due to their baptismal participation in Christ's kingship. Their kingship, however, was always severely restricted. Universal kingship was primarily individual, internal, spiritual, or eschatological. Only through their representatives among kings, nobility, and gentry were they able to claim any temporal relevance for their kingship. Lollard universal kingship might issue forth in rebellion through Oldcastle, but only because Oldcastle was, apart from his religious outlook, a typically troublesome magnate in politically turbulent fifteenth-century England.[193] We now consider universal priesthood.

Universal Priesthood

Paul Dabin summarizes the doctrine of universal priesthood among patristic and medieval theologians. Universal priesthood concerned participation in Christ's priesthood and was inaugurated in baptism and perfected in confirmation. It allowed the Christian to participate in the sacraments, and brought moral and religious obligations. Universal priesthood does not, however, prejudice the incommunicable powers of order and jurisdiction conferred on the hierarchy. The doctrine becomes erroneous whenever laity assume the power to offer the divine mysteries, or when they usurp or suppress clerical functions.[194]

Bede, the English church father par excellence, refers to the doctrine often in his glosses. Baptism, being 'stamped with the oil of gladness' or 'mystical chrism', makes one a greater priest than Old Testament priests. Spiritual gifts have not been reserved for individual prophets and priests only; they are given 'for all indistinctly, from both sexes, in all conditions, for all persons'. Universal priesthood allows all Christians, clergy and laity, to participate in the eucharist. Since all are priests, all may offer themselves as spiritual sacrifices to God during the mass. They may also help build the altar for the worship of God. Although universal priesthood exceeds Aaronic priesthood, it does not eliminate clergy.

---

[192] J.H. Burns, 'Fortescue and the Political Theory of *Dominium*', *HJ*, 28 (1985), 777–97; Gill, 'Politics and Propaganda', 333; Hinton, 'Constitutional Doctrines', 410–17; Chrimes, *Constitutional Ideas*, 314–22; *Works of Fortescue*, 359–60.

[193] One chronicler reports a Yorkist rebellion failed because, 'Though they were by no means against the Lord, they were nevertheless against his Christ, namely the most serene lord king'. Wilkinson, *Constitutional History*, 131.

[194] *Le Sacerdoce Royal des Fidèles dans la Tradition Ancienne et Moderne* (Paris: Desclèe de Brouwer, 1950), 51–2.

Stressing unity, Bede says Peter called the people a royal priesthood 'because they are one in the body of the one who is the supreme king, the true priest'. The clergy, however, are a distinct priesthood *in lege nomen et officium*, by legal name and office.[195] A number of Bede's passages on universal priesthood found their way into the *Commonplace Books* of Thomas Cranmer.[196]

Even during their acrimonious rebuttals against the exaggerations of lay critics, orthodox theologians carefully maintained all Christians were, in some sense, priests. Since I Peter 2 'has been said of all the faithful, then every faithful person is a priest'. Yet, 'while every good person is in general a priest, he may not confect the body of Christ and offer it, but must work in himself with God to offer the sacrifice of the mind to God, according to Romans 12'.[197] Like many others, this orthodox writer spiritualizes and internalizes universal priesthood.[198] Since preaching, mass, and confession were the major ministrations of the clergy, they will form the basis of our discussion. A number of debates between orthodox divines and Lollard theologians, specifically Walter Brut and John Purvey, show the problems and solutions raised by a literal concern with Wyclif's teaching that every predestined layperson is a priest.

Purvey, once believed to have been a virtual second Wyclif,[199] has since proved less prominent. He recanted his opinions in 1400, accepted a living from Arundel at West Hythe, Kent in 1401, but disappeared again in 1403. He died on 16 May 1415 in Newgate Prison for his part in the Oldcastle rebellion, leaving behind a library of banned works.[200] Purvey advocated a radical version of universal priesthood that focussed on the ability of all Christians to preach. However, since the only evidence we have of Purvey's theology comes from his opponents, any conclusions must be tempered. Another difficulty is presented by John Foxe's inadequate translation of Purvey's trial records. Foxe excluded the most damning sections of Purvey's heresy of orders, and Foxe's Victorian editors added notes claiming Purvey spoke of private not public ministry.[201]

---

[195] *Le Sacerdoce Royal des Fidèles*, 150–7.

[196] BL Royal MS 7B, XI, fols 189ʳ–190ʳ. Cf. *Patrologia Latina*, ed. by J.P. Migne (Paris, 1844–55), XCIII, 49, 134–5, 192.

[197] *Ad oppositum sic . . . genus electum regale sacerdocium gens sancta primo Pe 2do ergo dictum est omnibus fidelibus ergo omnis fidelis est sacerdos. Confirmatur . . . diceram omnis sacris sacerdos est Ergo omnis bonus generatim dum sacerdos non opus potest conficere corpus Christi et illud offerre sed opus potest seipsum deo offerre hostia mentum deo ad Ro 12o. Utrum quilibet laicus iustus sit sacerdos nove legis*, BL Harley MS 31, fol. 217ʳ.

[198] Viterbo, *De Regimine Christiano*, II, 3; Dyson edn, 63. Paris, *On Royal and Papal Power*, ch. 18; Watt edn, 189.

[199] Margaret Deanesly, *The Lollard Bible and Other Medieval Biblical Versions* (CUP, 1920), 266–97.

[200] Hudson, *Lollards and Their Books* (London: Hambledon Press, 1985), 85–110; Maureen Jurkowski, 'New Light on John Purvey', *EHR*, 110 (1995), 1180–90.

[201] On the difficulties in using Foxe, see Thomas Freeman, 'Texts, Lies, and Microfilm: Reading and Misreading Foxe's "Book of Martyrs"', *SCJ*, 30 (1999), 23–46. John Foxe, *The Ecclesiastical history contayning the Actes and Monumentes* (London, 1563), V, 192–3; *A&M*, III, 286, 286n, 288n, 289.

Richard Lavenham compiled Purvey's heresies after reviewing his *libelli*.
Whether these were books written by Purvey, or perhaps only annotated, are
unknown. Lavenham says Purvey believed 'all good Christians, being predestined, have truly been ordained priests or made by God to offer Christ to
themselves and themselves to Christ, and to teach the gospel to their neighbors, by word and by example'.[202] Up to this point, the accusation against
Purvey is by no means heretical. It carries Wyclif's definition of true Christians but this was not necessarily heresy. It, moreover, reflects the orthodox
internalization of sacrifice. Lay teaching of the gospel to a neighbor by word
and example is also not unusual. The propriety of lay teaching depended on its
relationship to preaching. Teaching was a private activity, conditionally open
to laymen, while preaching was a public activity, restricted to clergy.[203]

Purvey's heresy began with his denial of Roman priesthood. His disdain for
traditional priesthood with its episcopally imposed indelible character led him
to consider other means of ordination. Churches need presbyters and 'God
knows how to and may, when it pleases him, make priests without human
operation'. He developed Wyclif's speculation concerning direct ordination by
Christ. While the presbyter's ordination may be invisible, the people have visible
evidence of the true presbyter when they see him imitate Christ and the
apostles.[204] Purvey stepped over the line into heresy by confusing priest with
presbyter, trapping himself into egalitarian government and universal administration of the sacraments: 'And whoever is a holy man, who is a member of
Christ and will be saved, is a true presbyter ordained by God; no worldly bishop
need ever lay hands on him.' In confusing *sacerdos* with *presbyteros*, he asserts
the presbyterate of all Christians. English etymology had always confused priest
with presbyter, but Latin etymology kept them distinct. Adding insult to injury,
Purvey said, 'laymen may legitimately minister all the sacraments necessary to
salvation'.[205] At his trial, Purvey abjured both the conflation of priesthood with
presbyterate and the universality of sacramental powers.[206]

Years later, Thomas Netter reviewed some works he claimed were by
Purvey. Netter's review came during his long treatment of church offices. In
his first chapter on preachers, Netter says Purvey, Wycliffite *Doctor eximius*,
conceded 'to anyone, without any discrimination of grade, sex or condition,
and without the Prelate's permission, the preaching office'. In his commonplace collection of Scripture, doctors, and canon law, Purvey said, 'all priests
ought to preach', and then ascribed the preaching office 'similarly to levites,
readers and to every singular clerk, kings, dukes, every singular prince, heads

---

[202] *Haeresis et Errores*, III, 1; FZ, 387.
[203] Owst, *Preaching in Medieval England* (CUP, 1926), 4; *SEWW*, 19, 22.
[204] *Haeresis et Errores*, III, 2; FZ, 387–8.
[205] *Haeresis et Errores*, IV, 4; FZ, 390.   [206] *Confessio et Revocatio*, III, 1; FZ, 402.

of household and laity of whatever kind'. He even extended this office to women, whom Netter believes the apostles plainly excluded.[207] Purvey cited a number of authorities for female proclamation, including the apocryphal book of Judith, where we find Judith teaching the priests. The Judith reference irked Netter into exclaiming, *JUDITH IN EXTREMO PERICULO SACERDOTIUM docuit; tamen non officio, sed subventionis affectu,* Judith instructed the priesthood in extreme danger; nevertheless, not by office, but to relieve her passion.[208] Netter cited two reasons why women are generally not permitted the preaching office: it is a deformity of natural order, and women naturally lead men away from the truth. Women may teach, but only in private and only to women, sons, and brothers. His general principle for instruction is 'one is to teach by office and authority, another by necessity and friendliness: one at church, another at home'. Preaching is 'evidently not allowed to women due to sex, magisterium, and office; laymen are not allowed due to office'.[209]

Netter's approval of female proclamation to relieve passions was manifested in a contemporary, Margery Kempe of Lynn. Margery was orthodox in doctrine if enthusiastic in practice. Speaking as God's 'secretary' caused her to be examined five times for heresy between 1413 and 1417. Netter once banned a friar from teaching Margery any more Scripture.[210] She took it upon herself to rebuke publicly the ungodly, including episcopal households. She informed Arundel she was allowed to speak of God by Scripture, pope, and church. However, speaking for God publicly did not make her a preacher, she said, for she never went into a pulpit.[211] Standing in a long tradition of orthodox female prophets, the opposition she faced only proved she was really God's chosen instrument.[212] In one of her visions, Christ told her he would give her the grace to answer every cleric with love. This promise proved valuable. After publicly rebuking Arundel's officials, she was threatened with burning, but she convinced Arundel of her orthodoxy and even privately rebuked him.[213] Proclamation was also practiced by women Lollards, though not as widely as once thought.[214] Kempe shows orthodox women could publicly proclaim truth. Orthodox women, however, had to claim divine authorization and,

---

[207] *Doctrinale,* II, 70.1.
[208] Netter refers to *sacerdotium* while the Vulgate says *presbyteron. Doctrinale,* II, 73.2–4; Judith 8.10.
[209] *Doctrinale,* II, 73.4.
[210] *Book of Margery Kempe,* I, 69.
[211] Diane Watt, *Secretaries of God* (Cambridge: Brewer, 1997), 37–42.
[212] *Secretaries of God,* 23–6, 30–2, 49–50.
[213] *Book of Margery Kempe,* I, 5, 16.
[214] Cross, '"Great Reasoners in Scripture": The Activities of Women Lollards 1380–1530', *SCH,* Subsidia 1, (1978), 359–80; Shannon McSheffrey, *Gender & Heresy* (Philadelphia: University of Pennsylvania Press), 109–24.

although their messages were accepted, they were seen as empty vessels who could add nothing to their message, as the male clergy might.[215]

Preaching was not the only priestly preserve under assault. The priestly monopoly over the sacraments had never been complete. Canon law allowed for lay baptism of infants in the likelihood of death. It was stressed, however, *quod extra casum necessitatis*, that other than in case of necessity, priests ought to minister baptism.[216] Using emergency baptism as the thin end of a broad wedge, Walter Brut allowed the lay administration of all sacraments. This Welshman was arrested by John Trefnant, Bishop of Hereford, in 1391 and brought to submission in 1393. Educated in Oxford, Brut defended his positions ably in Latin.[217] As in his treatment of Purvey, Foxe selectively translated Brut's beliefs. He carefully omitted the most controversial part, Brut's defense of women priests.[218] Brut's positions were taken seriously, for at least seven refutations were compiled by orthodox churchmen, four specifically naming Brut.[219]

Brut's trial began with six charges formulated by his opponents. The first said 'every Christian, even a woman, existing without sin, may confect the body of Christ as well as a priest'.[220] After Brut's preliminary Latin defense, Trefnant requested clarification. Brut's lengthy second defense begins by affirming Trefnant's authority but reminds him God can reveal truth to laymen. The pivotal truth this layman discovered is that since the Aaronic priesthood ceased with Christ, all ceremony had ceased, including tithes,

---

[215] Carolyn Muessig, 'Prophecy and Song', in *Women Preachers and Prophets through Two Millennia of Christianity*, ed. by Beverly Mayne Kienzle and Pamela J. Walker (London: University of California Press, 1998), 146–58.

[216] *Provinciale*, I, 7.3; 1679 edn, 41–2.

[217] *Pace* McFarlane, Brut was a clear and complex thinker in spite of his penchant for apocalypse. *Wycliffe and English Nonconformity*, 135–8. Cf. Hudson, '*Laicus Litteratus*: The Paradox of Lollardy', in *Heresy and Literacy 1000–1530*, ed. by Peter Biller and Hudson (CUP, 1994), 222–36.

[218] Brut's trial and works are recorded in *Trefnant*, 278–394. Large portions are translated in Foxe's Book of Martyrs in the editions after 1563. Foxe declares the omission of *Trefnant*, 345–7, is 'for breuitie'. John Foxe, *The Ecclesiastical history contayning the Actes and Monumentes* (London, 1570), V, 614. Cf. idem, (1576), V, 504; (1583), V, 521; *A&M*, III, 131–88.

[219] The replies of John Neuton and William Colvyll, current and former chancellors of Cambridge University, are recorded without specific attribution in Trefnant's Register. The first reply is primarily concerned with lay administration of confession. The second ranges through all thirty-seven articles drawn up of Brut's heresy. *Trefnant*, 368–94. Four discussions, the second mentioning Brut by name, are recorded in BL Harley MS 31: *Utrum liceat mulieribus docere viros publice congregatos*, 'Whether women may teach public congregations of men', fols 194ᵛ–6; *Utrum mulieres sint ministri ydonei ad conficiendum*, 'Whether women may be suitable ministers to consecrate the eucharist', fols 196ᵛ–205; *Utrum quilibet laicus iustus sit sacerdos noue legis*, 'Whether any just layman whatsoever may be a priest of the new law', fols 216–18; *Utrum mulieres conficiunt vel conficere possunt*, 'Whether women have confected or may confect', fols 218–23. The seventh, a fragment of a response to Brut, has been attributed to William Woodford. Paris BN Latin 3381, fols 115–24ᵛ. Hudson, '*Laicus Litteratus*', 222–5; Aston, *Lollards and Reformers*, 52–8.

[220] *Trefnant*, 279; *A&M*, III, 132.

circumcision, and priestly command of the sword. Kingship and law, priesthood and sacrifice were completed in Christ.[221] Following this are redefinitions of confession, eucharist, and orders.[222]

During his discussion of the eucharist, he affirms traditional estates theory. The eucharist is a similitude, figure, sacrament, and memorial of Christ but transubstantiation is doubtful. Transubstantiation has deceived people into believing priests have a marvelous power. This power of consecration encourages priests to exalt themselves beyond their estate. The real problem in eucharistic belief is the priesthood reaching beyond its estate, both spiritually and temporally.[223] In his discussion of orders, Brut again radically separates the Aaronic and Christian priesthoods. The orthodox often hearkened to older priesthoods as precedents for Christian priesthood. Dymmok referred his readers to both Old Testament and pagan sects in defense of a sacrificial priesthood over against universal priesthood. Similarly, the second defense by one Brut opponent defers to other sects' hierarchical priesthoods.[224] In response, Wycliffites like Brut distinguished the old and new covenants so radically that any priesthood separate from the people was deemed unacceptable.

According to Brut, the sacrifice of Christ was not only unique but unrepeatable. The orthodox agreed Christ's sacrifice was unrepeatable, but Brut accused them of repeating Christ's sacrifice with each mass. Such repetition denies the uniqueness of Christ's offering for human sins.[225] A Cambridge chancellor realized the uniqueness of Christ's sacrifice was the central issue upon which Brut's heresy of universal priesthood depends. Asserting that laypeople, male and female, have ministerial power over Word and sacraments necessarily excludes the sacrifice of the mass. If Christ is not *nunc realiter sacrificatur cotidie in altari a sacerdotibus*, now really sacrificed daily on the altar by priests, then the entire sacerdotal system of the medieval church is denuded of power.[226] Transubstantiation, the elevation of the host, the terror of confession prior to communion—all depended upon the ability of the priest to transcend time and space and bring the redeeming body and blood of Christ from the cross to place him before God and people. Without this power, sacerdotal hierarchy was severely compromised. According to Dymmok, mass and priesthood stand and fall together. Sacerdotal hierarchy requires the priestly monopoly of making a wafer of bread into the body of God.[227]

Brut's speculation concerning lay presidency terrified the orthodox. By removing the mysterious barrier of the indelible character, Brut endangered the priestly estate, downgrading it to a mere function. However, Brut was always careful to express his views in speculative terms. He hedged with the

---

[221] *A&M*, III, 139, 141, 149–52, 160–4.   [222] *A&M*, III, 166–73, 173–6, 176–86.
[223] *A&M*, III, 175–6.
[224] *Liber Contra*, 109–10; *Utrum quilibet*, BL Harley MS 31, fol. 216ʳ.
[225] *A&M*, III, 178.   [226] *Trefnant*, 382–3.   [227] *Liber Contra*, 108–9.

doctrine of emergency. In his discussion of female presidency, he explained, 'However, it is not proper for them to proceed to act, provided that others are constituted to this by the church.... But it is a good agreement that it is not proper for them, neither for laymen, to do this where there are those who are constituted by the church to minister the sacraments.'[228] The famous fourth of *Twelve Conclusions* similarly speculated after denying transubstantiation: 'For we suppose that on this wise euery trewe man and womman in Godis lawe make the sacrament of the bred withoutin one sich miracle.'[229]

Lollards realized they were meddling with an awesome cultural symbol in the mass, aptly described by Miri Rubin as 'a special type of sacrament, an arch-sacrament.'[230] They speculated about lay presidency, but vehemently denied practicing such. The Lollard priest William White was accused of persuading his lay disciple, John Scutte, to consecrate the eucharist for White and a few others. Though it was the twelfth accusation, he 'totally denied this article from the beginning'.[231] William Ramsbury—a layman illicitly tonsured in 1385 by another layman, Thomas Fishbourn—repeatedly celebrated mass but always excluded the words of consecration.[232] Henry Knighton tells of a woman in London whose daughter celebrated mass but she, too, excluded the words of consecration.[233] Friar Daw accused Lollards of allowing women to say mass. Jack Upland hotly retorted that Daw could never prove it.[234] Speculation concerning lay presidency continued even after the Lollards lost their educated leadership.[235] Hawisa Mone, like other disciples of White, abjured in 1430 her opinion that 'every man and every woman beyng in good lyfe oute of synne is as good prest and hath [as] much poar of God in al thynges as ony prest ordred'.[236] In 1441, another Lollard denied the necessity of the priesthood, but coupled his denial with a complaint against three other sacraments.[237] In the Kent heresy proceedings of 1511 and 1512, all five of the burnt heretics were

---

[228] *Trefnant*, 346–7.   [229] *SEWW*, 25.

[230] Rubin, *Corpus Christi*, 36.   [231] *FZ*, 423–4.

[232] Nothing explicitly connects Ramsbury with Lollardy. Hudson, 'A Lollard Mass', in *Lollards and Their Books*, 111–23.

[233] *Knighton's Chronicle*, 540–1.

[234] Aston, *Lollards and Reformers*, 64–5.

[235] The loss of their intellectual leadership began with the prosecution of Nicholas Hereford, Philip Repingdon, and John Aston by Archbishop Courtenay in the 1380s but the *coup de grace* was administered by Arundel's Oxford Constitutions.

[236] *Heresy Trials in the Diocese of Norwich, 1428–31*, ed. by Tanner (London: Royal Historical Society, 1977), 142. Ten of the 60 followers of William White abjured the heresy of universal priesthood. *Heresy Trials in the Diocese of Norwich*, 42, 52, 57, 67, 86, 147, 153, 166, 177, 179, 205. Cf. Aston, *Lollards and Reformers*, 49–70.

[237] John Jurdan said, 'the sacrament of ordre ordeyned for ministers to be in the church is vayne, voyde, superflewe and not necessarie'. Highlighting Jurdan, Hornbeck argues that the Lollard universal priesthood was 'a form of antisacerdotalism'. However, Jurdan never mentioned the universal priesthood and emphasized baptism rather than ordination. *The Register of John Stafford, Bishop of Bath and Wells, 1425–1443*, 2 vols, ed. by Thomas Scott Holmes (London: Somerset Record Society, 1915–1916), II, 266–7. Hornbeck, *What is a Lollard?*, 142,

accused of affirming, 'there is no more power given by God to a priest than to a layman, in ministering the church's sacraments, celebrating masses or performing other sacred functions'.[238] All five initially denied this charge, but Robert Hilles accused William Carder of saying 'the auctorities and power of preests upon sacraments and other things by them mynistred was no more worth than if they had be doon by a layman, and that they had no more power than another'. Carder, their most prominent leader, was among those burnt. Nine Kent heretics either abjured or died for holding this opinion.[239] Lollard speculation aimed at the priestly monopoly over presidency may never have been practiced, but this did not forestall persecution.

Lay Empowerment

Although the hierarchy sought to limit lay initiative, especially by prosecuting Lollardy, it was slowly losing its hegemony. This is especially evident in the areas of education, devotion, and voluntary religion. Ironically, it was the church that had done so much to bring about lay advances in these areas. By educating the laity, the clergy gave them an increasing ability to articulate theology on their own. By teaching them how to contemplate divine mysteries, the clergy gave the laity their own means of access to God. Lay literacy and lay mysticism put pressure on the clerical monopoly of preaching and confession. With lay control over religious institutions, the stage was set for eventual bottom-up changes in governance. Increasingly, the only arena in which the clergy could claim a clear monopoly was in the mass. In the sixteenth century, this, too, proved vulnerable.

The university system, originally a clerical preserve, contributed to the loss of clerical distinctiveness in education. The intellectual elite battled on many fronts: against those below, the unlearned (*rustici, vulgi, plebs*), they claimed a natural superiority; against the elites above, secular and priestly, they advanced through challenge and assimilation. Part of their assimilation of priesthood involved redefining *clerus*. Originally, *clerus* meant 'one chosen by lot', and came to designate priests. However, in European universities during the twelfth century, *clerus* also meant 'scholar'. By the fourteenth century, less than half of the clergy in some universities were even tonsured. The lines between clergy and laity were being dissolved in the universities.[240]

166–71,173. Intriguingly, Jurdan, a 'clerk', earlier presented a priest to Bishop Stafford for institution. *Register of Stafford*, II, 224.

[238] *Kent Heresy Proceedings*, 2, 9, 17, 44, 51.

[239] *Kent Heresy Proceedings*, 11, 27, 28, 30, 34, 37, 41, 52–3, 117.

[240] Alexander Murray, *Reason and Society in the Middle Ages* (OUP, 1978), 163–5.

The dissolution occurred below university level, too. Lateran IV ordered priests to teach the faith. In response, Archbishop Pecham's Lambeth constitution of 1281, *Ignorantia Sacerdotum*, blaming priests for lay ignorance, ordered an ambitious educational program. Vernacular texts were composed for this program.[241] Duffy's magisterial work on primers shows how religious faith and literacy were subsequently intimately connected.[242] During the fifteenth century, laypeople increasingly took the reins of the educational system. Government, funding, leadership, curriculum, and pupils came within their domain.[243] While many schools were established to provide for mass priests, the laity benefited immensely from their establishment.[244] By the sixteenth and seventeenth centuries, great strides in literacy were being made in England, especially in London.[245]

Advances in education brought personal confidence to the laity. The root of Pecock's heresy was his elevation of reason above Scripture, creed, and the Fathers.[246] He encouraged Lollards not to oppose Scripture to priesthood, but his speculations concerning priesthood and Scripture appeared to threaten both.[247] The mode of his argumentation encouraged lay independence in thought. The laity must develop their reasoning skills and 'obeie to doom of resoun'.[248] Moreover, they should offer sacrifices to God by themselves, or with the aid of 'a preest or a lay man'. The eucharistic offering was now optional rather than necessary for offering spiritual sacrifices.[249] Through vernacular engagement with Lollard ideas current in London, the Bishop of Chichester adopted their vernacular book habits and thereby 'risked compromising his authority.'[250]

As in education, the laity were also being empowered in their devotion, especially through personal mysticism. Mystical thought, long part of the Christian tradition,[251] entered the English vernacular through Richard Rolle, a hermit who gained a wide following among clergy and, through confessional

---

[241] G.H. Russell, 'Vernacular Instruction of the Laity in the Later Middle Ages in England', *Journal of Religious History*, 2 (1962), 98–119.

[242] *Stripping*, 207–98; Duffy, *Marking the Hours: English People & Their Prayers 1240–1570* (YUP, 2006).

[243] Nicholas Orme, *Education and Society in Medieval and Renaissance England* (London: Hambledon Press, 1989), 23–31; Keen, *English Society*, 217–39.

[244] J.A.H. Moran, *The Growth of English Schooling 1340–1548* (PUP, 1985), 223.

[245] David Cressy, *Literacy and the Social Order* (CUP, 1980).

[246] He abjured the 'presumyng of myne natural wytte, and preferryng my iugement and naturalle reason'. *English Chronicle*, 75–7. Cf. Pecock, *The Reule of Crysten Religioun*, EETS 171 (OUP, 1927), 460–6.

[247] J. Fines, 'Bishop Reginald Pecock and the Lollards', in *Studies in Sussex Church History*, ed. by M.J. Kitch (Sussex: Leopard's Head Press, 1981), 57–75.

[248] Pecock, *Book of Faith*, ed. by J.L. Morison (Glasgow, 1909), 174–5; quoted by Fines, 'Pecock', 68–9.

[249] *Reule*, 329, 261–2.

[250] Mishtooni Bose, 'Reginald Pecock's Vernacular Voice', in *Lollards and Their Influence*, 217–36.

[251] Rowan Williams, *The Wound of Knowledge* (London: Darton, Longman & Todd, 1979), 128.

and cults, among laity.[252] The mystic's goal was 'an equally immediate and experimental union with God by love'.[253] The English mystical method, though not antithetical to sacerdotal mediation, preferred the Dionysian means known as *via negativa*, which involved escape from society and denial of the physical. Moreover, though the eucharist could be an aid to escape, it was one amongst many.[254] This explains why one of the most popular English texts, the translation of Thomas à Kempis' *Imitatio Christi*, largely circulated without its fourth book during the fifteenth century.[255] Only in the fourth book is there an orthodox discussion of the sacraments affirming the necessity of offering spiritual sacrifices through the priest's offering of Christ in the mass.[256] It was up to Lady Margaret Beaufort to translate the fourth book, from the French, and make it available to the reading public in 1503.[257]

Walter Hilton, a canon lawyer in Arundel's circle, recognized the dangers of asacramental mysticism, and tried to compensate, but his solution was only a stopgap. A direct experience of God is available to the laity on the basis of *imago dei*, the image of God in every soul.[258] The means of contemplation, aided 'by goodwill and by a deep desire', are reading, meditation, and prayer.[259] Hilton attempts to balance his asacramentalism with warnings to leave judgment to the clergy and to conform to the church, but makes exceptions for emergency and conscience.[260] The novice must use the set prayers of the church, but the expert contemplative, 'the pure man or woman', is a priest who lights her own fire of love on the altar of her soul.[261] The qualification of unmediated access by reminders to use the church and its priesthood are a consistent feature: in the heavenly pecking order,[262] in confession,[263] and in soteriological knowledge.[264] Although Hilton simultaneously promoted public conformity and private devotion,[265] the very definition of public as hindrance to personal experience of God paradoxically encouraged lay independence.

---

[252] Hughes, *Pastors and Visionaries*, 174–366.

[253] David Knowles, *The English Mystical Tradition* (London: Burns & Oates, 1961), 2.

[254] Rolle, *The Fire of Love*, transl. by Clifton Wolters (London: Penguin, 1972), 46–7, 82–5; *Cloud*, 18–27. Marion Glasscoe, *English Medieval Mystics* (London: Longman, 1993), 75–6, 84, 88.

[255] Roger Lovatt, 'The Imitation of Christ in Late Medieval England', *TRHS*, 5th series, 18 (1968), 97–121.

[256] *The Imitation of Christ*, transl. by Leo Sherley-Price (London: Penguin, 1952), bk. 4, chs. 5, 8, 9.

[257] *The Imitation of Christ*, 25. Surprisingly, Lady Margaret's translation work is not considered in a volume dedicated to such Tudor initiatives by women. *Silent But for the Word*, ed. by Margaret Patterson Hannay (Kent, Ohio: Kent State University Press, 1985).

[258] *The Ladder of Perfection*, transl. by Leo Sherley-Price (London: Penguin, 1957), I, 5, 9.

[259] *The Ladder of Perfection*, I, 12, 15; II, 1, 24.

[260] *The Ladder of Perfection*, I, 17, 22.

[261] *The Ladder of Perfection*, I, 27–32.

[262] *The Ladder of Perfection*, I, 61–2.

[263] *The Ladder of Perfection*, I, 66; II, 7.

[264] *The Ladder of Perfection*, II, 27, 30.

[265] J.P.H. Clark, 'Late Fourteenth-Century Cambridge Theology and the English Contemplative Tradition', in *The Medieval Mystical Tradition in England*, ed. by Marion Glasscoe (London: Brewer, 1993), 1–16.

Through continuing research into wills and churchwarden acccounts, scholars have recently detected shifts in popular orthodox piety during the late Middle Ages. Popular devotion was increasingly dedicated to Jesus Christ himself, and as an adult accessible upon the cross rather than as an infant accessed through the mediation of the Virgin Mary.[266] Although the saints were retained, they began to function more as exemplars and less as intercessors.[267] This shift toward Christocentrism was especially noticeable in orthodox communities, such as Tenterden, where Lollardy was also present. While orthodox Christians retained the mass, they favored the Jesus Mass and began to turn away from forms of intercession associated with the cult of saints.[268]

Lollards complained of the destructive nature of 'priuat religion',[269] yet, after their defeat by the church hierarchy, Lollards themselves turned inwards. One of their most frequent heresies was the denial of the necessity of auricular confession. Brut's first attack on sacerdotal monopoly conferred the keys of auricular confession on all Christians in baptism. He allowed confession to priests or laypeople, but direct confession to God was best.[270] In the Norwich heresy trials, confession was the sacrament questioned most. In the Kent heresy trials, it came second only to the eucharist.[271] Foxe's relations of Lollard trials are filled with denials of auricular confession. John Swetstock, an orthodox preacher, listed it as Lollardy's second most important heresy.[272] Thus, amongst orthodox and heretics, there is a definite inward devotional turn.

As with education and devotion, likewise religious governance took on more of a lay character. Colet's refoundation of the school attached to St Paul's is famous for its submission to lay government, because, according to Erasmus, he found less corruption in married people.[273] In spite of its theoretical hierarchy, religion in late medieval England was increasingly voluntaristic. Household chapels for the more wealthy laity, perhaps important to the later emphasis on the father as responsible for household religion, were becoming increasingly popular.[274] Numerous studies have shown how religious gilds provided for the voluntary association and discipline of the laity in lay-founded and lay-governed institutions. The proliferation of chantries in this period often led to lay control of the priesthood.[275] Some clergy treated

---

[266] Peters, *Patterns of Piety*, 74.   [267] *Patterns of Piety*, 98, 110.

[268] Robert Lutton, *Lollardy and Orthodox Religion in Pre-Reformation England* (Woodbridge: Boydell, 2006), 198–9.

[269] *SEWW*, 24.

[270] *A&M*, III, 168–70.

[271] *Norwich Heresy Trials*, 11; *Kent Heresy Proceedings*, xxv.

[272] Roy M. Haines, '"Wilde Wittes and Wilfulnes"', *SCH*, 8 (1972), 150.

[273] *Statuta Paulinae Scholae*, in Lupton, *Colet*, 272, 280; *CWE*, VIII, 236–7.

[274] R.G.K.A. Mertes, 'The Household as a Religious Community', in *People, Politics and Community in the Later Middle Ages*, ed. by Joel Rosenthal and Colin Richmond (Gloucester: Alan Sutton, 1987), 123–39.

[275] Wood-Legh, *Perpetual Chantries*, 304, 314; Bossy, *Christianity in the West*, 57–63.

these multiple semi-sectarian structures within the church with suspicion. They competed with existing parish churches and often became the basis of new parishes. They might even elect and dismiss their priests.[276]

In light of this lay empowerment, Arundel's Oxford Constitutions of 1409 look more like a last stand than a decisive victory. Best known for their restriction of vernacular Bible translations, these constitutions brought into one instrument a number of previous attempts to limit religious independence. The first, second, and third constitutions subject all preaching to episcopal licensing. Other constitutions forbade unlicensed celebration of the sacrament, deviance from orthodox sacramental theology, and disputation of papal decrees. Wyclif's works were banned and Oxford University's privileges limited.[277] Arundel and his successors used their ecclesiastical courts and *De Haeretico Comburendo*, the heresy law passed by Parliament in 1401, to good effect.[278] Yet, as we shall see, these rearguard actions were ultimately defeated in the English Reformation.

---

[276] Gervase Rosser, 'Parochial Conformity and Voluntary Religion in Late-Medieval England', *TRHS*, 6th series, 1 (1991), 173–89; *Book of Margery Kempe*, I, 25.

[277] *A&M*, III, 242–8.

[278] 2 Henry IV, ch. 15; Aston, *Arundel*, 332–5, 376–7; E.F. Jacob, *Archbishop Henry Chichele* (London: Thomas Nelson, 1967), 69–71.

3

Common Priesthood in the Early English Reformation

Discussions of royal priesthood in the early years of the English Reformation revolved around the potentially radical social consequences of an egalitarian application of the doctrine. Erasmus of Rotterdam, humanist critic of medieval religion, prepared for more radical doctrines through his call for all Christians to have access to a vernacular Bible, function as theologians, and personally appropriate the cognitive dimensions of the Christian faith. Within a few years, Martin Luther surpassed Erasmus, advocating a doctrine of royal priesthood that struck at the roots of the entire religious structure. Luther's consideration of John Hus, who had developed John Wyclif's thought for the Bohemian context, appeared to establish a heretical succession to the polemical delight of conservative controversialists. Furthermore, Luther's ecclesiastical rebellion seemed to undermine civil politics, substantiating the papacy's old argument that any reified universal priesthood would also destroy traditional kingship. Henry VIII made a name for himself on the continent and in England by excoriating Luther for such reckless doctrines, and English conservatives amplified Henry's arguments, claiming evangelicalism was too radical to be tolerated. English conservatives like John Fisher, Thomas More, and Edward Powell did not go so far as to deny the doctrine of royal priesthood, but carefully circumscribed its meaning and exercise, including the restriction of vernacular translations of Scripture. In response, English evangelicals like Thomas Garrett, John Lambert, and William Tyndale defended the new teaching against conservative opprobrium, but pursued the radical implications of the doctrine nonetheless, undermining the traditional priesthood, eliminating any role for mediation, and atomizing the community. However, the most radical results came with the thoroughgoing anticlericalism of the secularist lawyer, Simon Fish, even as conservative laity also demonstrated lay judgment against the clergy.

ERASMUS

Traditional historiography places Renaissance before Reformation. Indeed, the humanists' doctrine of royal priesthood laid the groundwork for the reformers' doctrine. Italian humanists first made forays into England during the fifteenth century, bringing a love for letters and a critical spirit. The English reacted favorably by patronizing humanist scholars, founding libraries and schools, and making pilgrimage to Italian universities.[1] John Colet was one such pilgrim, but his doctrine of universal priesthood, excluding the conjugal motif, was fairly traditional, as previously noted. It was Colet's Dutch friend, Desiderius Erasmus, who popularized certain doctrines that anticipated Luther's vision of priesthood. Erasmus visited England at least twice, teaching in both Oxford and Cambridge and endearing himself to nobles and prelates. His influence on subsequent thinkers, whether conservative or radical, should not be underestimated.[2]

Erasmus' theological reflection challenges irreverent ritualism. He composed *Enchiridion Militis Christiani* (1501) for an impious German noble, recommending personal faith and morality. *Enchiridion* was an instant classic, appearing in numerous Latin editions and vernacular translations,[3] including an English one by William Tyndale.[4] Drawing on mysticism, Erasmus reorients religion from the external to the internal. True religion requires an internal appropriation of *philosophia Christi*. Mere external formality does not qualify. *Philosophia Christi* is attained in battle against vices through personal conformity with Christ's exemplary life. Reflecting the humanist concern for *ad fontes*, Erasmus says Christ's life is available in the original source, Scripture. Scripture functions as a simple mirror wherein one examines oneself for conformity. The Erasmian ideal is personalistic and dismissive of clerical dependence: the goal is personal access to God; the means, reading and self-examination.[5]

An influential and subtly subversive program developed from these basic Erasmian ideals. His ideal of self-knowledge, the internal appropriation of Christian truth by every Christian, required vernacular Bibles. In *Paraclesis*, the preface to his 1516 edition of *Novum Testamentum*, Erasmus demanded the universal availability of Scripture in the vernacular. The 'first step' towards

---

[1] Quentin Skinner, *The Foundations of Modern Political Thought*, 2 vols (CUP, 1978), I, 193–201.

[2] James Kelsey McConica, *English Humanists and Reformation Politics* (OUP, 1965); Maria Dowling, *Humanism in the Age of Henry VIII* (London: Croom Helm, 1986); Margo Todd, *Christian Humanism and the Puritan Social Order* (CUP, 1987).

[3] McConica, *Erasmus* (OUP, 1991), 49.

[4] David Daniell, *William Tyndale: A Biography* (YUP, 1994), 43.

[5] *CWE*, LXVI, 24–55; Johan Huizinga, *Erasmus and the Age of Reformation* (PUP, 1984), 49–54; McConica, *Erasmus*, 49–61.

pure religion is personal understanding, which in turn requires popular access to Christ's teaching. 'Since baptism is common in an equal degree to all Christians', doctrine is not reserved for scholastic theologians. 'Only a very few can be learned, but all can be Christian, all can be devout, and—I shall boldly add—all can be theologians.' 'The farmer', 'weaver', and 'traveler' must personally handle the 'mysteries' of Christ.[6] In *Praise of Folly*, Erasmus reserves his bitterest sarcasm for trained theologians who pretend that they have a monopoly on truth. These scholastic 'sophists' ignore Scripture and dwell upon extrabiblical ideas such as indelible characters.[7]

Although Erasmus criticizes traditional priests for their exaggerated pretensions to power, he affirms their role in propagating the faith. Priests, princes, and people form concentric circles of mutual responsibility.[8] Against traditionalists, he believes the priest's primary role is more teacher, example, and pastor than consecrator of sacraments. Indeed, he finds the dominant eucharistic devotion alarming.[9] Transubstantiation is among the 'tortuous obscurities' of scholastic theologians.[10] There is a Real Presence in the eucharist, but whether the mass is a sacrifice is simply speculation. It is a *repraesentatio* of Christ's sacrifice, which leads to our *commemoratio*, then to *contemplatio* in personal faith and *imitatio* in acts of love.[11] Erasmian devotion focuses, not on the host, but the Word: 'Let us all, therefore, with our whole heart covet this literature, let us embrace it, let us continually occupy ourselves with it, let us fondly kiss it, at length let us die in its embrace, let us be transformed in it.'[12]

Rather than defining the mass as a sacrifice, Erasmus emphasizes the people's sacrificial responses to the memory of Christ's sacrifice. Spiritual sacrifices are internal and individual. God is won 'by pure affections', not by meaningless rituals. 'Rational sacrifices' are mental not physical, and entail 'subduing your evil desires' and 'brutish and worldly passions' through 'confession of sins'. Other acts of 'rational worship' include 'pure prayers', 'newness of understanding', 'righteousness', and 'thanksgiving'. Spiritual sacrifices soar to the Father 'from the altar of a sincere heart' and are accepted through the Son's mediation.[13] Although Erasmus does not explicitly connect spiritual sacrifices with universal priesthood, he affirms both doctrines.[14] All Christians

---

[6] *Paraclesis*, in *Christian Humanism and the Reformation*, 3rd edn, ed. by John C. Olin (New York: Fordham University Press, 1987), 101–4.

[7] *Praise of Folly*, transl. by Betty Radice (London: Penguin, 1971), 86–95.

[8] McConica, *Erasmus*, 61–2.

[9] John B. Payne, *Erasmus: His Theology of the Sacraments* (Richmond, Virginia: John Knox Press, 1970), 106–7.

[10] *Praise of Folly*, 88.

[11] Payne, *Erasmus: Theology of Sacraments*, 25, 134.

[12] *Paraclesis*, 108.

[13] *CWE*, XLII, 69; XLIV, 89; LVI, 321–22; LXIII, 192–3.

[14] *Contra* Germain Marc'hadour, 'Erasmus as Priest', in *Erasmus' Vision of the Church*, ed. by Hilmar M. Pabel (Kirksville, Missouri: Sixteenth Century Journal Publishers, 1995), 140.

are made priests through the anointing of baptism.[15] Christian priesthood gives individuals direct access to the throne of God. Laymen may baptize and intercede for the priest during the eucharist. Laypeople may also teach one another; however, teaching is the especial duty of clergy.[16] Yet Christ is 'the one and only teacher', so 'let us be disciples of Him alone'.[17]

These last three notions—the distinct teaching roles of clergy, people, and Christ—are individually affirmed yet never integrated. This loose assemblage of roles echoes Erasmus' repudiation of a rigid ecclesiology. He downplays hierarchy, often treating popes and prelates harshly.[18] The final arbiter of Christian doctrine is not the papacy but the consensus of the faithful.[19] The church itself is the congregation of all faithful people, and both lay and clerical vocations are equally holy.[20] Erasmus' *congregatio* is more like Tönnies' *Gesellschaft* than *Gemeinschaft*,[21] especially when he envisions individuals disjointedly plucked from their original communities. The church is a 'union of interdependent individuals who have been elected from the various sects and nations into the fellowship of Christ'. He affirms traditional organic ecclesiology but highlights the difference of functions and gifts employed in edification.[22]

With such egalitarian tendencies, should Erasmian humanism be considered anticlerical? Erasmus was definitely critical of clerical abuses in general. Scholastic theologians and religious orders were hapless victims of his wit, but he supported other clergy.[23] He preferred a few, highly qualified priests to a mass of ignorant ones. An illegitimate son of a priest, Erasmus was himself ordained in 1492, though he rarely celebrated the mass. Erasmus elevated orthodox reformers as exemplary models. John Colet, opponent of dead ritualism and clerical abuses, was his model priest. John Fisher, Bishop of Rochester, was Erasmus' paradigmatic bishop; a proponent of episcopally led reformation, Fisher regularly guided his flock through preaching. Thomas More, critic of abuses, both lay and clerical, and, later, vigorous prosecutor of heretics as Chancellor of the Realm, was Erasmus' model layman.[24]

In spite of his subsequent rough treatment by the Council of Trent, Erasmus was a 'Catholic reformer'. He eventually opposed Luther, due to the latter's dogmatic spirit and schismatic actions.[25] Clerical abuses and lifeless ritualism should be corrected but such vices are more tolerable than discord in the church.[26] In a late letter, Erasmus resurrected the monopoly of theologians, as

---

[15] *CWE*, LXIII, 88.   [16] Payne, *Erasmus: Theology of Sacraments*, 104–7.
[17] *Paraclesis*, 107.   [18] *Praise of Folly*, 107–11.
[19] Payne, *Erasmus: Sacraments*, 31–2; Marc'hadour, 'Erasmus as Priest', 122–3.
[20] McConica, *Erasmus*, 98.
[21] See Introduction to this book.
[22] *CWE*, XLII, 70–1.
[23] *Praise of Folly*, 86–104.
[24] Marc'hadour, 'Erasmus as Priest', 115–49.
[25] Basil Hall, *Humanists & Protestants* (Edinburgh: T&T Clark, 1990), 52–85.
[26] Hilmar M. Pabel, 'The Peaceful People of Christ', in *Erasmus' Vision*, 82–3.

opposed to the handling of 'mysteries' by 'cobblers', but his retraction went unheeded.[27] His anticlericalism was of a reforming, nondestructive type.

THE HERETICAL SUCCESSION

The primary proponent of universal priesthood in the early Reformation, Martin Luther, Augustinian monk of Wittenberg, could have learned his doctrine from a number of sources. Educated with humanists at Erfurt, Luther received Erasmus' *Novum Testamentum*, with its accompanying *Paraclesis*, and followed it in his theological development.[28] He was also attracted to German mysticism, which promoted a spiritualized universal priesthood.[29] However, Luther's own radical version was formulated after reviewing the conciliar process against John Hus at Constance.

Polemicists of the period assumed a heretical succession beginning with Wyclif and ending in Luther, with Hus as intermediary.[30] There is some dependence of thought between the three, but less than contemporaries assumed,[31] especially in their doctrines of universal priesthood. Gordon Leff, while repeating his misunderstanding of Wyclif's doctrine, shows that, although Hus borrowed from Wyclif's works, he was more concerned with fighting church abuses than following Wyclif in doing theology on the basis of realist philosophy.[32] Even in his 'most daring and sharpest work', *De Simonia*,[33] which includes extracts from Wyclif's work of the same name, Hus left the basic medieval sacerdotal structure untouched.[34] In *De Ecclesia*, Hus again judiciously appropriates Wyclif, excluding the English heretic's discussion of universal priesthood. He calls for princely reform of the church and affirms private judgment, but again leaves the sacerdotal structure intact.[35]

---

[27] McConica, *Erasmus*, 71.

[28] Heiko A. Oberman, *Luther: Man between God and the Devil* (London: Doubleday, 1992), 123–4, 171, 214.

[29] *The Theologica Germanica of Martin Luther*, ed. by Bengt Hoffman (New York: Paulist Press, 1980).

[30] David V.N. Bagchi, *Luther's Earliest Opponents* (Minneapolis: Fortress Press, 1991), 179; *A&M*, III–IV.

[31] Although Luther defended Wyclif, he probably never read any of his works. On Luther's relation to Hus, see Scott H. Hendrix, '"We are all Hussites"? Hus and Luther Revisited', *ARG*, 65 (1974), 134–61.

[32] 'Wyclif and Hus: A Doctrinal Comparison', in *Wyclif in His Times*, 105–26. Cf. William R. Cook, 'John Wyclif and Hussite Theology', *CH*, 42 (1973), 335–49.

[33] Per Vaclav Novotny, as quoted by Matthew Spinka, *John Hus: A Biography* (PUP, 1968), 169.

[34] *LCC*, XIV, 196–208.

[35] *Tractatus de Ecclesia*, ed. by S. Harrison Thomson (Cambridge: Heffer, 1956); *The Church*, transl. by David S. Schaff (London: Allen & Unwin, 1915).

In a disputation over whether Moses was a priest, Hus gives his clearest statement on priesthood. He says some are priests, *institucione vel consecucione*, by institution or appointment. They placate God by offering sacrifice *pro populo*, on behalf of the people, whom they also teach. Others are priests, not by institution, *sed sui devota oblacione et humili devocione*, but by their pious oblation and humble devotion. Aaron, Christ, and Christian clergy are priests by institution; Moses and all good Christians are priests by devotion. That the good Christian is priest and king, *simpliciter*, simply, and *ex illo genere*, by membership in Christ, is maintained by the Decretals and numerous fathers. Hus' most controversial statement concerns a third type of priest, one who is priest by institution but not piety. The fathers said every good Christian is a priest but not every priest is a good Christian. Therefore, like Judas Iscariot, *non sunt veri sacerdotes, sicut nec veri christiani*, they are not true priests if they are not true Christians.[36] The pope must discipline such evil priests, and if he fails, nobles must intervene.[37]

Thus, Hus was generally orthodox on priesthood. However, his refusal to obey his bishop and stop preaching was considered scandalous, and papal excommunications were ineffective. In 1412, Michael de Causis, a native of Prague, presented articles against Hus to the papal curia. Hus responded to most of them with the cry, *mentitur*, fabrication![38] After Hus appeared at the Council of Constance, de Causis presented another set of inflammatory articles to facilitate Hus' arrest. Though clearly contrived, and thus ignored by Hus, they achieved their purpose. While these articles were superseded by accusations drawn from his writings, they were attached as an addendum to the official condemnation.[39] The first supposed error concerns transubstantiation, which Hus never denied. The second concerns lay administration:

> Moreover he saith, that other men beside priests may minister the sacrament. This article is evident, forasmuch as his disciples do the same at Prague, who of themselves do violently take the sacrament out of the treasury, and communicate among themselves, when the holy communion is denied unto them. By this and other things also it is sufficiently evident, that he hath taught that every man, being without mortal sin, hath the power of orders or priesthood, forasmuch as such only as have taken orders ought to minister unto themselves. And because he proceedeth from small matters unto great and weightier, it doth consequently appear and follow, that those who be in the state of grace can bind and loose.[40]

---

[36] *Utrum Moyses Legislator Fuit Sacerdos*, in *M. Jan Hus*, ed. by Jan Sedlak (Prague: Stybla, 1915), II, 107–15.

[37] *LCC*, XIV, 272–5.

[38] *Documenta Mag. Joannis Hus*, ed. by Franciscus Palacky (Prague: Tempsky, 1869), 169–74.

[39] Leff, *Heresy*, II, 652–4, 680–4.

[40] *Primi Articuli*, in *Documenta Hus*, 194–5; *A&M*, III, 436.

There was indeed a case in Prague of a woman who snatched the host from a priest and administered it to herself and others, and accusations that cobblers were hearing confessions, but Hus was not directly involved.[41] The remaining articles concern the definition of church, Donatism, and lay election and discipline of priests. Tragically, Hus' denials concerning these and the official articles mattered not, for he was judicially murdered on 6 July 1415. In the accompanying sermon, the Bishop of Lodi lambasted Hus' transference of ecclesiastical jurisdiction to the laity.[42]

A century later, a young Luther was orthodox concerning priesthood, though critical of its failings. He believed a layman may pretend to priesthood, 'but because he has not been consecrated and ordained and sanctified, he performs nothing at all, but is only playing church and deceiving himself and his followers'.[43] In his 1517 protest against indulgences, traditionally considered the beginning of the Reformation, Luther hinted at spiritual egalitarianism, but retained the priest's representative role.[44] By the time his excommunication was being prepared, he was toying with the idea that all Christians may absolve in confession, but common confession was the recognized extent of his doctrine of universal priesthood.[45]

During the crucial summer of 1519, Luther and his compatriot, Andreas Karlstadt, entered a disputation with John Eck at the University of Leipzig. After hearing Luther oppose Scripture to papal definitions of faith, Eck accused the Wittenberger of mimicking Wyclif and Hus. Luther had never studied Hus, but during lunch, he reviewed Leipzig's copy of the documents from Constance. Resuming debate, Luther now affirmed the articles preached by Hus were *plane Christianissimi et evangelici*, clearly very Christian and evangelical. The presiding prince, George of Saxony, whose lands the Hussites once invaded, cried out with disgust, 'Plague take it!', and Luther moved one step closer to condemnation.[46]

Luther told an anonymous Bohemian at Leipzig he wished further exposure to Hus' writings. By 3 October, Luther received a set of knives and a copy of Hus' *De Ecclesia* from two Bohemian priests, Jan Poduska and Vaclav Rozd'alovsky. He devoured the work, had it reprinted, and presented a copy to his friend George Spalatin.[47] Spalatin was important for Luther's survival: a close

---

[41] Spinka, *Hus: Biography*, 251–4.   [42] *A&M*, III, 486–8.

[43] *Lectures on Romans* (1515–1516), in *LW*, XXV, 235.

[44] *Ninety-Five Theses*, theses 7, 37; Gert Haendler, *Luther on Ministerial Office and Congregational Function*, transl. by Ruth C. Gritsch (Philadelphia: Fortress Press, 1981), 27–8.

[45] *Exsurge Domine* (1520), article 13, in *LW*, XXXII, 50.

[46] *Der Authentische Text der Leipziger Disputation*, ed. by Reinhold Otto Seitz (Berlin: Schwetschke, 1903), 82–3; Scott H. Hendrix, *Luther and the Papacy* (Philadelphia: Fortress Press, 1981), 87; Robert Herndon Fife, *The Revolt of Martin Luther* (New York: Columbia University Press, 1957), 327–94.

[47] Thomson, 'Luther and Bohemia', *ARG*, 44 (1953), 160–81.

friend of Luther, he was the trusted chaplain of Luther's prince, elector Frederick 'the Wise' of Saxony. Luther often prepared Spalatin and the court privately before publicizing his next theological innovation. In a letter to Spalatin dated 18 December 1519, sandwiched between letters concerning Bohemian theology, Luther floated the rudiments of his new doctrine of royal priesthood, simultaneously reducing the seven sacraments to two and granting all Christians the ability to preach the Word and administer sacraments.[48] A letter to John Lang the next day concerned an argument Luther was having with Jerome Emser, George of Saxony's chaplain.[49] Emser would later prove the whetting stone upon which Luther sharpened his new doctrine.[50] It was during his period of enamor with Hus that Luther developed his radical views. Ironically, it may have been the half-truths of de Causis contained in the conciliar documents that inspired him.

During the slow progress of his excommunications, beginning with the lesser one of August 1518 and the final one, *Exsurge Domine*, issued in June 1520 but not received until December, Luther prepared his defenses.[51] Remembering the reward for heresy, Luther knew his only chance lay in convincing the temporal powers of their responsibility to stop papal injustice. The most influential treatise of the German Reformation was written with these needs in mind. In *Appeal to the Christian Nobility of the German Nation* (June 1520), Luther undermined the juridical foundation of the church. He assails three walls protecting the papacy, the first being any essential distinction between laity and clergy:

> It is pure invention that pope, bishop, priests, and monks are called the spiritual estate while princes, lords, artisans and farmers are called the temporal estate. This is indeed a piece of deceit and hypocrisy. Yet no one need be intimidated by it, and for this reason: all Christians are truly of the spiritual estate, and there is no difference among them except that of office.

Luther consistently denies this ancient distinction and its supporting doctrines. The Romanist *characteres indelibiles*—that ineradicable mark impressed upon the ordinand, which identifies him as separate from people—is merely an invention. All Christians are consecrated priests in baptism and are thus of equal standing. Nobody may practice their priesthood publicly without common consent.[52] This doctrine, however, was tangential. It supported his chief aim of encouraging the nobility to act 'without hindrance' against papacy, episcopate, and priesthood. 'Whoever is guilty, let him suffer.'[53] After denying the papal lock on biblical hermeneutics and the calling

---

[48] D. *Martin Luthers Werke. Briefwechsel* (Weimar, 1930–), I, 594–6.

[49] D. *Martin Luthers Werke. Briefwechsel*, 596–8.

[50] See 'The Reformation Development of the Priesthood of All Believers' (my unpublished master's thesis, Duke University, 1996), 15–19.

[51] Oberman, *Luther*, 185–7.   [52] *LW*, XLIV, 127–9.   [53] *LW*, 131.

of councils, he identifies ecclesiastical abuses in detail[54] and the remedies the nobility can provide.[55] His solutions are similar to those offered by Hus and Wyclif—princely correction of the church and disendowment of the clergy. He even offers a strident defense of Hus.[56]

Appeal to the Christian Nobility was written in German for the princes; his next treatise, *Babylonian Captivity of the Church* (October 1520), was written in Latin for theologians. *Appeal to the Christian Nobility* tore down the juridical walls erected by the papacy against temporal interference; *Babylonian Captivity* attacked the sacramental system through which clerical jurisdiction received social legitimacy. Addressing each sacrament, he reduced them from seven to two, retaining only baptism and the mass as necessary, while equivocating over penance.

Concerning the mass, *Babylonian Captivity* encourages utraquism, denies transubstantiation, and considers its equation with a good work and sacrifice 'by far the most wicked abuse of all'. The mass is, rather, a testament containing a promise by Christ, which everyone must personally accept. *Pace* Hus, he says it is definitely not a good work done *pro populi* by the priest. The mass is not a sacrifice, in the sense of the host being offered to God; rather, our sacrifices of alms and prayers are distinct from the mass itself. Christ's sacrifice ought not be identified with the mass. The priest retains a central place in eucharistic worship as the one who offers our sacrifices to God, but Luther believes, concerning the sacramental grace that comes through the sacrament, 'we are all equals, whether we are priests or laymen'.[57]

In a few pages, Luther bombards the sacrament of orders with every weapon at his disposal. The Dionysian hierarchies undergirding orthodox speculation are dismissed as Platonist not Christian. 'Such allegorical studies are for idle men'; let theologians study Scripture instead.[58] As in *Appeal to the Christian Nobility*, those fictitious indelible characters lack scriptural foundation. A layman may become a priest, then a layman again.[59] Christ wants priests to preach and baptize more than consecrate; indeed, the primary ministry of priest and bishop is proclamation.[60] The so-called 'sacrament' of orders is 'a seed bed of implacable discord' separating clergy from laity. It has promoted a 'detestable tyranny' that destroys Christian brotherhood.[61] 'We are all equally priests, that is to say, we have the same power in respect to Word and sacraments. However, no one may make use of this power except by the consent of the community or by the call of a superior.' Every Christian is

---

[54] *LW*, 139–56.   [55] *LW*, 156–217.   [56] *LW*, 194–200.

[57] *LW*, XXXVI, 35–57. Luther developed more fully his doctrine of the mass, as a sacrament only tangentially connected with sacrifice and whose efficacy lies in personal faith not priestly mediation, in *A Treatise on the New Testament* (July 1520), but *Babylonian Captivity* was more prominent. *LW*, XXXV, 75–111.

[58] *LW*, XXXVI, 109–10.   [59] *LW*, 111, 117.

[60] *LW*, 113–15.   [61] *LW*, 111–12.

'anointed and sanctified' with the Holy Spirit and may personally handle the sacrament. Although we call those who legitimately exercise their power, 'priests', they are really only 'ministers chosen from among us'.[62]

In his third great treatise of 1520, *Freedom of a Christian* (November), Luther developed this last point. The terms 'priest', 'cleric', 'spiritual', and 'ecclesiastic' are unjust; let them be called 'ministers', 'servants', and 'stewards' instead.[63] He next elaborates on common kingship. Every Christian is a king, 'lord of all things without exception', but with two qualifications. First, kingship is by participation in the high kingship of Christ, a participation brought about only by faith. Second, since Christ's kingdom is spiritual only, Christian kingship is invisible only; current magisterial arrangements may not be challenged. True Christian kingship is measured only in noble surrender— 'power is made perfect in weakness'—and its greatest expression is martyrdom. Of far greater excellence than Christian kingship is Christian priesthood. The priesthood of believers means 'we are worthy to appear before God' and perform two priestly functions: 'to pray for others and to teach one another divine things'. This common priesthood involves unmediated access to Christ, who in turn mediates with God. Christ directly teaches Christians; Christians may, therefore, teach others. Christ is in the Father's presence; Christians may, therefore, approach with petitions and intercessions.[64] Unfortunately, the Roman priesthood unduly separated priests from people, establishing a tyranny 'as if laymen were not also Christians'.[65]

In other works of the early 1520s, Luther furthered his doctrine of royal priesthood, characteristically emphasizing common priesthood, while ignoring or dismissing common kingship. In *Sermons on First Peter* (1522), he allows an external difference between priest and people, but before God there is no distinction. He counters fears that promoting common priesthood means women might preach by asking them to remain silent in church. As consolation, he insists that, before God, social distinctions of sex, vocation, and age are nonexistent. There are three functions in priesthood: offering oneself as a sacrifice, praying for others, and preaching the gospel. Preaching is 'the chief function' of the public priest, while 'the true priestly office' of all Christians is selflessly practiced 'when we sacrifice that villainous rogue, the lazy old ass, to God'.[66]

In a treatise written for Bohemia, *Concerning the Ministry* (1523), Luther tenders his most radical definition of common priesthood. Evans says, 'The emphasis here was upon the equality of individuals, not upon the collective character'.[67] According to Luther, there are seven functions which every Christian may perform: teaching, preaching, and proclaiming the Word;

---

[62] *LW*, 113, 116.   [63] *LW*, XXXI, 356.   [64] *LW*, 354–5.
[65] *LW*, 356.   [66] *LW*, XXX, 53–6, 62–6.
[67] *Problems of Authority in the Reformation Debates* (CUP, 1992), 218–19.

baptizing; consecrating and administering the eucharist; binding and loosing sins, formerly a juridical exercise, but now reconceived as preaching; offering spiritual sacrifices; interceding through prayer; and, judging doctrine, by which he means personally determining the fidelity of a priest's teaching, followed by discipline of the current priest and election of a new one.[68]

Such doctrines of universal priesthood were the leading subjects during the earliest years of the Reformation, being supplanted by the doctrine of justification by faith only after the German Peasants' Wars (1524–1525). Luther's doctrine of common priesthood became a truism for many Germans in the 1520s. Laypeople of all vocations took up the call to preach,[69] writing numerous theological pamphlets.[70] With his defense of the communal dismissal and election of priests, Luther unwittingly touched an old nerve among the lower classes.[71] There was an existing but embattled tradition of village control of chapels and of communal constitutional thought in pre-Reformation Germany. The peasants equated their tradition with Luther's teaching and appealed to his authority.[72] They subsequently organized and presented demands to the nobility. The most famous set of demands, *Twelve Articles*, written by a lay preacher, Sebastian Lotzer, on behalf of the Memmingen peasantry, begins with a call for communal election and dismissal of priests. This was repeated by many of the peasant groups, and they backed their demands with arms.[73]

Accompanying the Peasants' Wars were the alternatively individualist and communal teachings of Spiritualist and Anabaptist theologians. Like the peasants, they took Luther's common priesthood further than he envisioned, allowing for communal election and dismissal of clergy, relatively unrestricted preaching, and experimentation with the sacraments.[74] In 1525, Luther and his young ally, Philip Melanchthon, condemned the peasants' demand for common election.[75] Luther issued such scurrilous tracts as *Against the Robbing and Murdering Horde of Peasants*: 'Therefore let everyone who can, smite, slay, and stab, secretly or openly, remembering that nothing can be

---

[68] *LW*, XL, 21–36.

[69] Siegfried Hoyer, 'Lay Preaching and Radicalism in the Early Reformation', in *Radical Tendencies in the Reformation*, ed. by Hans J. Hillerbrand (Kirksville: Sixteenth Century Journal Publishers, 1986), 84–97.

[70] Steven Ozment, *Protestants: The Birth of a Revolution* (London: Doubleday, 1993), 45–66.

[71] *LW*, XXXIX, 301–14; Haendler, *Luther on Ministerial Office*, 55–66.

[72] Peter Blickle, 'Reformation and Communal Spirit', in *The German Reformation*, ed. by C. Scott Dixon (Oxford: Blackwell, 1999), 133–68.

[73] Blickle, *The Revolution of 1525: The German Peasants' War from a New Perspective*, transl. by Thomas A. Brady, Jr. and H.C. Erik Midelfort (London: Johns Hopkins University Press, 1981), 195–201.

[74] Yarnell, 'Reformation Development', chs. 4–5.

[75] *LW*, XLVI, 37–8. A copy of Melanchthon's tract found its way into Oxford's Bodleian Library. Melanchthon, *Widder die Artikel der Bawrschaft* (1525), sig. C1; Ozment, *Protestants*, 138, 243.

more poisonous, hurtful, or devilish than a rebel. It is just as when one must kill a mad dog.'[76] With these words, Luther set himself behind magisterial reformation and against popular reformation. In spiritual matters, freedom must precede order; in political matters, the reverse holds.[77] Hereafter, Luther downplayed common priesthood, returning most of the above-mentioned functions to a supervised priesthood under the control of those 'emergency bishops', the princes.[78]

FIDEI DEFENSOR

Even modern Protestant scholars agree reformation made little headway in England during the 1520s.[79] Periodic Lollard-burnings smothered theological innovation. Traditional religion was under pressure for internal reform but external threats were dismissed. Thomas More later accused England's leading churchman—Thomas Wolsey, Papal Legate, Cardinal, Archbishop of York, and Chancellor of the Realm—of treating heretics leniently.[80] Through merchants and humanists, Luther's writings entered England in 1518 and 1519. Erasmus was cautiously discussing Luther's writings with More, Wolsey, and others. However, curiosity became alarm in 1520, following Luther's excommunication and his radical treatises, especially *Babylonian Captivity*.[81] In March of the following year, William Warham, Archbishop of Canterbury, complained the universities were toying with Lutheranism. Changing roles, Cambridge, previously undefiled by Oxford's Wycliffism, 'is now thought to be the original occasion and cause of the fall of Oxford'.[82] Driven by diplomatic and internal reasons, England's establishment soon arranged a spectacular burning of Luther's books at Paul's Cross, attended by some 30,000 people. John Fisher preached a rousing sermon and Wolsey, standing under his golden canopy, waved a manuscript the king was composing against Luther.[83]

Although Henry VIII was kept from attending the bonfire by illness, he soon surprised Europe with *Assertio Septem Sacramentorum*, *Assertion of the*

---

[76] *LW*, XLVI, 50.   [77] Blickle, *Revolution*, ch. 13; Ozment, *Protestants*, 146.

[78] H.H.W. Kramm, 'Church Order and Ministry under Luther, and in the early Lutheran Church' (unpublished doctoral thesis, Oxford University, 1941), 323–46; Yarnell, 'Reformation Development', ch. 1.

[79] Carl R. Trueman, *Luther's Legacy: Salvation and English Reformers* (OUP, 1994); Dickens, *English Reformation*, 325–34.

[80] Richard Marius, *Thomas More* (London: Collins, 1986), 366–7.

[81] Bagchi, '*Eyn Mercklich Underscheyd*: Catholic Reactions to Luther's Doctrine of the Priesthood of All Believers, 1520–25', *SCH*, 26 (1989), 155–65.

[82] Warham to Wolsey; *L&P*, III, i, 193.

[83] Carl S. Meyer, 'Henry VIII Burns Luther's Books, 12 May 1521', *JEH*, 9 (1958), 173–87.

Seven Sacraments.[84] The debate over whether Henry actually wrote the treatise is as old as Luther's accusation to that effect. The current consensus is that he probably wrote it with the help of More,[85] Fisher, and others.[86] The earliest reference to Henry's *scribendo contra Lutherum* came in a letter from Richard Pace to Wolsey of 7 April 1521.[87] The final presentation copy was sent to Leo X with an apology that, in spite of being a layman, it was his princely duty 'to defend the church, not only with his arms, but with the resources of his mind'.[88] The contradiction of a layman taking an active role in theology was conveniently overlooked. Traditionalists normally reserved vitriol for 'striped laity', educated laymen pretending to theology, but made exception for Henry.[89] They welcomed his *Assertion* because it placed England firmly with the orthodox.[90] Leo rewarded Henry and his successors with the title of *Fidei Defensor*, Defender of the Faith, as still found on British coinage.

Assertion responds to Luther's *Babylonian Captivity*, but continental conservatives first broached the themes dominating Henry's defense of orthodoxy. They had argued for the 'fundamental unity of authority' between the spiritual and temporal regiments. In other words, God established a codependency between the clerical and royal *ordinatio*. Their historiography, too, convinced them any attack on spiritual order inevitably leads to an assault on temporal order: the Donatists led a revolt against the Roman empire; Wyclif encouraged the Peasants' Revolt of 1381; Hus ushered in the bloody Bohemian wars.[91]

Assertion echoes this domino theory. Luther is a 'Bohemian' and must be treated accordingly.[92] Henry's chief motive in responding to Luther is, as William Clebsch phrases it, 'preserving religious uniformity as instrumental to social and political unity'.[93] Since the foundation of unity is order, Henry is at his 'bitterest' in his defense of the sacrament of orders against common priesthood.[94] The continental controversialists' searching question struck a

---

[84] *Assertio Septem Sacramentorum* (Rome, 1521; reprint, Ridgewood, New Jersey: Gregg Press, 1966). A 1688 translation by T.W. Gent is available in *Miscellaneous Writings of Henry the Eighth, King of England, France & Ireland*, ed. by Francis Macnamara (Berkshire: Golden Cockerel Press, 1924), 22–154.

[85] More later reminded Henry he only edited *Assertion*, warning the king to leave the pope's 'authority more slenderly touched'. *A Man of Singular Virtue Being A Life of Sir Thomas More by His Son-in-Law William Roper*, ed. by A.L. Rowse (London: Folio Society, 1980), 74–5.

[86] MacCulloch downplays Henry's role, but notes, 'Later, throughout the years of the Reformation, the king was an assiduous corrector of others' theological drafts, and an improver in the margins of others' ideas.' 'Henry VIII and the Reform of the Church', in *The Reign of Henry VIII: Politics, Policy and Piety*, ed. by MacCulloch, (London: Macmillan, 1995), 159–80.

[87] *L&P*, III, i, 1220.

[88] Henry to Leo, 21 May 1521; *L&P*, III, i, 1297.

[89] Bagchi, *Luther's Earliest Opponents*, 89–90.

[90] Bagchi deems it 'sheer opportunism'. *'Eyn Mercklich Underscheyd'*, 164.

[91] Bagchi, *Luther's Earliest Opponents*, 93–114.

[92] *Assertio*, sigs biii^v, di^v–dii; *Miscellaneous*, 28, 52, 56.

[93] *England's Earliest Protestants 1520–1535* (YUP, 1964), 20.

[94] Neelak Serawlook Tjernegal, *Henry VIII and the Lutherans* (St Louis: Concordia, 1965), 14.

worrisome chord: Does the priesthood of all believers also mean 'the kingship of all subjects'?[95] After the turbulent fifteenth century, the English considered hierarchy absolutely necessary.[96] Therefore, as seen in official propaganda and royal proclamations, the watchwords of the Tudor monarchs were 'order' and 'obedience', to guarantee 'quietness' among the people. Richard Rex detects, with the second Tudor, an 'increased emphasis on obedience in the theology and preaching of the Church of England'.[97] Being interdependent, the ecclesiastical and civil orders must be simultaneously protected. Thus, Henry considered Luther's royal priesthood a wicked doctrine.

In two preliminary chapters, on indulgences and on papal authority, Henry searchingly questioned the various contentions of Luther and the papacy, then opted for the weight of history.[98] Individuals such as Luther should obey the pope, the high priest and judge placed over them by God.[99] The bulk of the treatise is a defense of the seven sacraments, of which he is preeminently concerned with the sacraments of the altar and orders. These two sacraments are as inextricably linked as are the temporal and spiritual orders. Therefore, he must defend the definition of the mass as a 'good work' and a 'sacrifice', or 'oblation',[100] effected by priestly transubstantiation,[101] in order to preserve society. He believes the real reason for Luther's new teaching is self-defense. 'Under the pretence of favoring the laity, he endeavors to stir them up to a hatred against the clergy.'[102]

In attacking the clergy, the German friar attacks the nobility. Coming in a seemingly odd place, during his discussion of the mass, one senses that in this passionate, poetic outburst Henry highlights his primary concern: Luther's 'accustomed force rages, he strives to breed discord and move seditions to excite the commonality against the nobility. And that he may the more easily stir them up to a revolt, he, by his foolish and weak policy, falsely pretends that he has Christ for Captain of the whole army in the camp, and that the trumpet of the Gospel sounds only for him.'[103] Henry defended the existing socio-religious order against Luther's anarchic individualism. This is even more evident in his discussion of orders: 'In the Sacrament of Orders, Luther keeps no manner of order, but gathering together from here and there all the

[95] Bagchi, *Luther's Earliest Opponents*, 100.

[96] Keen, *English Society in the Later Middle Ages*, 1–5, 195–8.

[97] *Henry VIII and the English Reformation* (London: Macmillan, 1993), 25–6.

[98] Henry's defense of the papacy is framed in the form of questions, as are most of his defenses of the papal hierarchy in this work. Perhaps even at this early stage Henry was questioning the papacy itself.

[99] *Assertio*, sig. ci; *Miscellaneous*, 48.

[100] *Assertio*, sigs gii^v^–iii^r^; *Miscellaneous*, 73–82.

[101] *Assertio*, sigs dii^v^–fii; *Miscellaneous*, 59–66.

[102] *Assertio*, sig. ciii^r^; *Miscellaneous*, 52–3.

[103] *Assertio*, sig. fiii; *Miscellaneous*, 67–8.

treasuries of his malice, he pours them out against it.' Luther's doctrine of common priesthood is *impiam doctrinam*, a wicked doctrine, that

> tends directly to the destruction of the Faith of Christ by infidelity. For what designs he else, who disputes that there is no difference of priesthood between the laity and the priest? And that all men are priests alike, that all men have the same power in what Sacrament soever, that the ministry of the Sacraments is not given to the priests but by the consent of the laity, that Sacrament of Orders is nothing else but the custom of electing a preacher in the Church.[104]

Henry does not renounce lay priesthood, but objects to the confusion of lay and clerical priesthoods. The key to understanding Henry here is the word 'power', for power in the sense of 'power over' or 'dominion'[105] may be legitimately exercised only by those in civil and ecclesiastical orders. To deny orders is to confuse people on who may legitimately wield power. Luther 'extols the laity to the priesthood for this only reason, that he may reduce priests to the rank of the laity'. However, only priests may use the power of priesthood, even if all are priests by some other definition. Henry's definition of 'power' quibbles with Luther's sense of 'office'. 'Office' derives from equal status according to Luther, while for Henry, there is a necessarily real distinction in status as well as function. Luther's denial of the indelible character as conceived within the Dionysian hierarchy made Henry fear for the entire sacramental and civil structure.[106]

Fidei Defensor also attacks Luther's hermeneutical method. 'Who would not laugh at this doltish divine?' Does I Peter 2.5–9 connote we are all really priests? Does 'ye are gods' make us equal to God? Does royal priesthood make us all kings? Luther believes, 'In a word, all Christians are kings in the same manner that they are priests; for it is not only said "Ye are a royal priesthood", but also "a priestly kingdom".' To make all people priests and kings equally is a doctrine designed by 'the serpent', a direct threat to the king's beloved order, especially the temporal order, at the top of which he placed himself.[107] The idea of the election of priests and bishops is just as problematic. Are then kings to be elected?[108] Henry's concern for order also dominates his discussions of the remaining sacraments. *Assertion* ends by reminding Luther he should be more concerned with the 'public good of all others' than 'his own private glory'. Sadly, Luther's real intent is 'to dissolve by his tumults, brawls and

---

[104] *Assertio*, sigs qiiii–ri^r; *Miscellaneous*, 125.

[105] Evans, *Problems of Authority*, ix.

[106] 'But his denying Orders to be a Sacrament is as it were the fountain to all the rest, which being once stopped up, the other small springs must of necessity become dry of themselves.' *Assertio*, sigs ri^r, riiii^v–siii; *Miscellaneous*, 126. Bagchi, '*Eyn Mercklich Underscheyd*', *passim*.

[107] *Assertio*, sig. siiii^v; *Miscellaneous*, 136.

[108] *Assertio*, sigs ti^v–tii^r; *Miscellaneous*, 137–8.

contentions the whole Church of Christ', church and society being coterminous entities.[109]

Assertion was a powerful tool for the Catholic party, in England and on the continent. Henry warned Europe's rulers that Luther's royal priesthood was as antimagisterial as it was antisacerdotal. He repeated this warning in a 1523 letter to the Saxon princes, declaring that, in the spirit of Wyclif and the Bohemians, Luther's attack on the clergy was an attack on all orders. 'The poison is producing dissension in the Church, weakening the power of the laws and the magistrates, exciting the laity against the clergy, and both against the Pope, and has no other end than to instigate the people to make war on the nobles, while the enemies of Christ look on with laughter.'[110]

Henry's *Assertion* was twice translated into German—once by Thomas Murner, once by Emser—and went through numerous Latin editions.[111] Under pressure from the Saxon princes, Luther made a few half-hearted efforts to reconcile with Henry, but the same issues separated king and reformer throughout the 1520s. Henry saw the central issue as authority versus anarchy; for Luther, it was obedience to gospel versus obedience to human law. Luther's first effort in 1522 was an unmitigated disaster. Henry was a 'new God', 'fool-king', and 'lying buffoon' whose 'ignorance' and 'insolence' reveal overweening pride.[112] It amused Luther to find Henry, 'lay-king', doing exactly what he had promoted: the English king was leading the reformation of the church in his realm.[113] He renews his attack against only those two sacraments, the mass and orders, which Henry defended most. Henry may argue for order and tradition, but Luther maintains 'freedom of conscience' and the Word above all.[114] Since Henry is troubled by common judgment and common election, Luther reasserts them. 'To know and judge concerning doctrine belongs to all men, even to individual Christians.' Yet, even if orders is not a sacrament, 'institution to ministry and preaching is still necessary'. It does not matter whether institution is by a single apostle, the bishop, or the people, but 'it would appear to be done more rightly by the election and consent of the people'.[115]

In late 1525, after the Peasants' Wars and under pressure from his prince, Luther again attempted rapprochement; however, his second letter was more 'an offer of apology rather than a definite apology'.[116] Henry replied in 1527

---

[109] *Assertio*, sigs xi^v–xiii^r; *Miscellaneous*, 150–1.   [110] *L&P*, IV, i, 40.

[111] Rex, 'The English Campaign against Luther in the 1520s', *TRHS*, 5th series, 39 (1989), 99.

[112] *Luther's Reply to King Henry VIII*, transl. by E.S. Buchanan (New York: [n.pub.], 1928), 5–6, 12, 14, 30.

[113] *Luther's Reply to King Henry VIII*, 1–3.

[114] *Luther's Reply to King Henry VIII*, 47.

[115] *Luther's Reply to King Henry VIII*, 50–1, 55–6.

[116] Edwin Doernberg, *Henry VIII and Luther* (London: Barrie and Rockliff, 1961), 53.

and an English translation of this correspondence appeared the following year. Henry reiterated his divine vocation to maintain his subjects' welfare, both materially and spiritually. Although the church hierarchy most ordinately cares for souls, temporal princes must be involved, for where royal favor is lacking, 'there raigned heresies sensualyte voluptie, inobedyence, rebellyon, no recognition of superiour, confusyon and totall ruyne in the end'.[117] He criticized Luther for leaving his vows as a monk and marrying a nun; such disregard for sacred vows by Luther incited the peasants in Germany. Luther believes he is only teaching 'charyte towarde our neyghbour' and 'obedyence unto the heedes and rulers of countrees', but Henry was unconvinced.[118] As late as 1529, Henry was still publicly in the Roman camp, but that would soon change.[119]

THREE ENGLISH CONSERVATIVES

'The largest single controversy of the Catholic literary campaign' was waged over Luther's *Babylonian Captivity* and Henry's *Assertion*. Traditionalists, many of them continental scholars under Henry's patronage, contributed some thirty-one tracts to the debate.[120] Among the English, vindications of the king's doctrine came from the official pens of Fisher and More, who were joined by Edward Powell, Oxford's leading intellectual. Fisher's works were the most theological; More's were more rhetorical (often agonizingly so); and, Powell's treatise was philosophical. Each author deserves individual treatment, but we offer here a collage of their opinions on royal priesthood.

The relevant works by the Bishop of Rochester[121] include *The Sermon of Iohan*, preached at the bonfire for Luther's books;[122] *Confutation of Luther's Assertions*,[123] a 200,000-word review of the forty-one articles against Luther in *Exsurge Domine*;[124] *Defence of the Priesthood* (1525),[125] a response to Luther's

---

[117] *Answere Unto A Certaine Letter of Martyn Lther* (London, 1527), fols 1–7.
[118] *Answere Unto A Certaine Letter of Martyn Lther*, fol. 22; Doernberg, *Henry and Luther*, 56.
[119] *TRP*, no. 122.
[120] Bagchi, *Luther's Earliest Opponents*, 122; Rex, 'English Campaign', 99–105.
[121] *The Life of Fisher*, ed. by Ronald Bayne, EETS extra series, 117 (OUP, 1921); Edward Surtz, *The Works and Days of John Fisher* (Cambridge, Mass.: Harvard University Press, 1967); Richard Rex, *The Theology of John Fisher* (CUP, 1991).
[122] *The English Works of John Fisher*, ed. by John E.B. Mayor, EETS extra series, 27 (London: Trübner, 1876), 310–49.
[123] *Assertionis Lutheranae Confutatio* (Antwerp: Hillen, 1523). Privileged by both Charles V and Henry VIII.
[124] Strype, I, 59–61.
[125] *Sacri Sacerdotii Defensio Contra Lutherum*, in *Corpus Catholicorum*, IX (Münster, 1925), 1–83; *The Defence of the Priesthood*, transl. by P.E. Hallett (London: Burns, Oates & Washbourne, 1935).

attack on the sacrifice of the mass and visible priesthood in *The Misuse of the Mass* (1521);[126] and *A Sermon had at Paulis* (1526).[127] The relevant works of More[128] include *Responsio ad Lutherum* (1523);[129] *Letter to Bugenhagen* (1525);[130] *A Dialogue Concerning Heresies* (1530);[131] and *The Confutation of Tyndale's Answer* (1532–1533).[132] Henry and Wolsey commissioned Powell, 'the most prominent Oxford theologian of the time', along with five other Oxford scholars, to refute Luther's 'new Wycliffism'. Powell's two volumes prevailed and were published in 1523. Though overshadowed by Fisher and More and ignored by Luther, Powell was an important opponent of evangelicals such as Hugh Latimer, whom he tagged 'Lollard' during an explosive controversy in Bristol. His recalcitrant opposition to Henry's divorce prompted his execution in 1540.[133] His *magnum opus* is *Propugnaculum Summi Sacerdotii*.[134]

Although Luther constantly denied any visibility to common kingship,[135] his English opponents accused him of either hermeneutical inconsistency, at best, or outright dishonesty, at worst. Garnering political capital, they claimed Luther's common kingship encouraged rebellion.[136] All three placed Luther in the heretical and rebellious succession in which Wyclif and the Bohemians figure most prominently.[137] In 'the greatest heap of nasty language ever put together',[138] More developed this theme. Luther, repeating the Bohemian heresy, does not respect kings.[139] His 'liberty' is really 'license' and leads to social chaos. More believes that, to resist anarchy on the one hand and tyranny on the other, society must obey the law embodied in the one true church, receiving grace through her sacraments.[140] Luther has replaced ecclesiastical authority with radical individualism. Luther's doctrine that every man must 'rely entirely on himself alone' opposes 'the whole church, spread throughout

---

[126] *LW*, XXXVI, 127–230.

[127] *A Sermon had at Paulis by commandment of the most reverend father in god my lorde legate* (1526).

[128] Roper, *Man of Virtue*; Marius, *Thomas More*; Peter Ackroyd, *The Life of Thomas More* (London: Chatto & Windus, 1998).

[129] *CWM*, V, i.

[130] *CWM*, VII, 17–101.

[131] *CWM*, VI, i.

[132] *CWM*, VIII, i–ii.

[133] Guy Fitch Lytle, 'John Wyclif, Martin Luther and Edward Powell', *SCH*, Subsidia 5 (1987), 465–79; Skeeters, *Community and Clergy*, 38–46.

[134] *Propugnaculum Summi Sacerdotii Evangelici, ac Septanarii Sacramentorum* (London, 1523).

[135] 'For all Christian people admit that all of these passages cannot possibly have reference to visible kings.' *LW*, XXXVI, 140.

[136] Rex, *Theology of Fisher*, 135.

[137] Fisher, *Sermon of Iohan*, 312, 344; Powell, *Propugnaculum*, fols 157^v–163^r.

[138] Francis Atterbury, referring to More's *Responsio ad Lutherum*. Quoted by Ackroyd, *More*, 223.

[139] *CWM*, V, 2–3, 40–1.

[140] Dermot Fenlon, 'Thomas More and Tyranny', *JEH*, 32 (1981), 453–76.

the whole world'.[141] He prophesies catastrophe in Germany: first, the princes will covet and inordinately appropriate church property; next, the people will turn on the princes; finally, the people will turn on themselves in bloodshed and confusion.[142] Within a year, the first two parts of More's dark prophecy were fulfilled. He dismissed the Lutherans' subsequent attempts to shift the focus from universal priesthood to justification by faith and vocations.[143]

Fisher informed Luther that if one interprets common kingship metaphorically, common priesthood must be similarly construed. It is impossible to reify one and allegorize the other.[144] Powell has a field day with this argument. 'Why have you not gathered from [these scriptures] that all Christians together are equally kings, and have equal royal authority, just as also priests, when scripture equally affirms both?'[145] The obvious answer is that Luther fears for his head by offending kings with such irreverence. Powell reminds him that Augustine's hermeneutical method requires Scripture to hold something as true in one place as it does in another.[146] Luther never adequately answered this question.

Conservatives were anxious to retain a distinct priesthood. This distinction must not only be functional, something with which Luther agreed, but also ontological. They maintained the essential distinction between priest and people through a number of interdependent teachings: Dionysian hierarchies, episcopal ordination, indelible characters, and the descent of a particular priesthood. Although Luther dismisses Dionysius, Powell is sure the Neo-Platonist was a contemporary of the apostles and must be accorded concomitant status.[147] Like Colet[148] and Fisher,[149] Powell believed the Dionysian hierarchies, both heavenly and ecclesiastical, are the only means through which grace descends upon mankind.

> The clergy is established as the middle order between prelates and people, so that it first receives purgation, illumination, and perfection from the prelacy, and afterwards diffuses it to the people. The people are the lowest in this ecclesiastical hierarchy, so that while they receive the hierarchical actions of prelates and clergy, they cannot themselves act upon one another or upon any below them, nor return it to those above.[150]

---

[141] *CWM*, V, 610–23.   [142] *CWM*, V, 688–93.   [143] *CWM*, VII, 17–101.

[144] *Defensio*, 49, 61; *Defence*, 75, 100.

[145] *Quare ergo es eo non collegit cunctos Christianos es equo esse reges, et regali authoritate pares: sicut et sacerdotes: cum scriptura utrumque aequaliter affirmet? Propugnaculum*, fol. 131^v.

[146] *Propugnaculum*, fols 131^v–132^r.

[147] *Propugnaculum*, fols 120^r, 126^v.

[148] See 'John Colet', pp. 66–68 of this book.

[149] *Defensio*, 17; *Defence*, 16.

[150] *Clerus autem inter praelatos et populum, ideo medius statuitur: ut a praelatis purgationem, illuminationem, et perfectionem primum recipiant: quas postea in populum ipse diffundat. Populus vero cum in illa subcelesti Hierarchia insimus sit: sic a prelatis et clero operationes illas hierarchicas suscipit: ut nec eas vel inferiori prebeat: nec vicissim superiori retribuat. Propugnaculum*, fol. 155^v. Translation by Bagchi, *'Eyn Mercklich Underscheyd'*, 161–2.

Prelacy is supremely important since bishops distribute the power of grace to the clergy. Fisher defines the church as simultaneously congregational and hierarchical: 'For what else was the Church, but a congregation composed entirely of prelates and subjects?'[151] Bishops are heirs to the apostles while the pope is heir to Peter. Episcopacy is necessary since through episcopal ordination, not communal election, the grace empowering priests is transferred.[152] The ninth axiom of *Defence* summarizes the orthodox view of the episcopal imposition of hands: 'The Holy Spirit willed that grace should be attached to an outward visible sign so that when the sign is duly performed we know by faith that grace is at the same moment bestowed.'[153] Fisher's Trinitarian understanding of revelation is similarly elitist: the Father instructed Israel through the prophets; the Son taught the church through the apostles, fathers, doctors, and councils; the Spirit now teaches through holy bishops and doctors. For Luther to introduce private judgment is to add a fourth person to the Trinity.[154]

If episcopal laying-on of hands is the visible sign, the indelible character is the invisible grace. Interestingly, the humanist Fisher does not affirm indelible characters in *Defence*, since, in rebutting Luther, he relies upon scriptural language. Rather than indelible character, he speaks of grace, powers, gifts, and special privileges endowed upon the apostles and their successors.[155] These unique endowments enable the clergy to watch over, rule, and teach the flock for which they received a charge.[156] The humanist More, too, prefers to speak about *collatio gratiae*, 'the bestowing of grace' in ordination, omitting *characteres indelibiles*.[157] Powell alone provided an explicit defense of the indelible character.[158]

These conservatives affirm the existence of a particular Christian priesthood. The schemes were various but the result was similar: God has established a Christian priesthood distinct from the priesthood of all Christians. In his 1521 sermon against Luther, Fisher envisions two stages of mediation between God and man. He believes the Old Testament shadows of priesthood were reified in the church: Christ and Peter make concrete the typological priesthoods of Moses and Aaron. Moses was the mean between God and Aaron, while Aaron was the mean between Moses and the people; therefore, Christ is the mean between God and Peter, while Peter is the mean between Christ and the people. Christ, 'in his absence', commits the cure of all Christians to Peter and his successors.[159] Fisher elsewhere reminds Luther that, in Exodus, a royal priesthood is affirmed simultaneously with a

---

[151] *Defensio*, 20; *Defence*, 21.   [152] *Confutatio*, fol. 88ʳ.

[153] *Defensio*, 39; *Defence*, 58.   [154] *Sermon of Iohan*, 3rd instruction.

[155] *Defensio*, 26–30; *Defence*, 33–40.   [156] *Defensio*, 24–6; *Defence*, 29–32.

[157] *CWM*, V, 652–3.   [158] *Propugnaculum*, fols 149ʳ–53ᵛ.

[159] *Sermon of Iohan*, 316–19.

particular priesthood. The first epistle of Peter separates shepherds from their flocks at the same time it affirms universal priesthood.[160] The fathers, Greek and Latin, kept a visibly separate priesthood.[161] Powell attacks the issue of high priesthood from three angles: natural law, Mosaic law, and evangelical law. The natural and Mosaic laws and priesthoods were completed in Christ, who in the evangelical law created *pontificum maximum*, the highest priest-hood, which we call the papacy.[162] Varying from Powell, Fisher concedes to Luther that natural law allows for communal election of priests but Christian law demands the descent of priesthood through hierarchy.[163]

Of course, reformers cared little for such *schemata*. The Roman church's laws, priesthood, and sacrifices were the very antithesis of Christian law, priesthood, and sacrifice.[164] One of the few English Lutherans, William Tyndale, easily dismissed Fisher's equation of Aaron with pope by reminding him the book of Hebrews specifically taught Aaron was a shadow of Christ. Furthermore, Christ gave his priesthood to all Christians.[165] As so often happens in such conflicts, the combatants simply talked past one another and in the process of refutation and counter-refutation, original meanings were lost. When Luther asserted there was no such thing as an outward, visible priesthood, he was responding to the two distinct priesthoods offered by Jerome Emser. Emser saw only two priesthoods, a spiritual one common to all Christians and a visible one of those tonsured and anointed according to Roman rites. Luther simply appropriated Emser's twofold paradigm, denying Emser's visible priesthood.[166] When Fisher read Luther's response to Emser, he assumed Luther was dispens-ing with all distinctions between clergy and people. *Defence of the Priesthood* is, therefore, primarily an apology for the existence of a clerical order in the church.[167] Luther, however, never denied the need for clerical office; he was merely denying Emser's version of it. Luther retained a functional distinction between priest and people, even if they are essentially equal.[168] Conservatives could not believe the rude ex-monk was capable of any such subtlety. Worse, Luther's rigid separation of function and essence, office and authority sabotaged traditional ontology.

By 'traditional ontology', we refer to the Dionysian hierarchies that were tethered by medieval theologians to eucharistic worship. Grace comes through the priesthood and the most important function of that priesthood occurs during the consecration of the mass. Conservatives believed in the 'essential unity and identity of Christ's sacrifice on the cross with the sacrifice of the mass'. The host offered daily is the same sacrificial victim offered upon the cross; moreover, while celebrating, '*qua* mediator the priest's action was not

---

[160] *Confutatio*, fol. 100ᵛ.   [161] *Defensio*, 10–20; *Defence*, 4–21.
[162] *Propugnaculum*, fols 7ᵛ–24, 144ᵛ–148ʳ.   [163] *Confutatio*, fol. 88ʳ.
[164] *LW*, XXXVI, 218–19.   [165] Walter, I, 209.   [166] *LW*, XXXVI, 138–41.
[167] *Defensio*, 8–9, *passim*; *Defence*, 1–3, *passim*.   [168] *LW*, XXXVI, 159.

distinct from that of Christ's'.[169] Since Luther divorced sacrifice from the mass, appealing rather to the congregation's separate spiritual sacrifices, they believed he was attacking the very source of post-baptismal grace for all Christians, living and dead.[170] This issue is so important the polemicists devote the lion's share of attention to the mass and orders.[171]

Respectful of Scripture, conservatives rarely denied a royal priesthood common to all Christians.[172] Their problem was how to affirm royal priesthood without destroying traditional priesthood. Their solution was to make some ad hoc affirmations, mostly tentative, and many denials, mostly vehement. Their affirmations of royal priesthood were variously egocentric, pugilistic, metaphoric, spiritualistic, and vaguely generic. Fisher offers an egocentric definition: 'All Christians, then, are kings and priests, but to themselves, not to others'. Again, 'every Christian is a priest to himself'. Fisher's individualist interpretation was designed to deflect any lay involvement in the mediatorial visible priesthood. Priests are mediators while the people have no mediatorial responsibilities. As we shall see, Fisher's opponent, Tyndale, took this individualism one step further, defining self-offering in a fideistic, antimediatorial sense.[173]

Fisher deflects lay encroachment in the sacerdotal sphere by affirming pugilism on behalf of clerically-defined faith: 'All Christians are anointed; anointed, however, to fight, not to preach the gospel.'[174] Both Powell and Fisher affirmed another pugilism—battle against one's own sinful nature—as the only legitimate role for common kingship.[175] In a more peaceful mode, they encouraged people to offer spiritual sacrifices, but these must not detract from the sacrifice of the mass.[176] In general, conservatives stress the metaphorical nature of royal priesthood. There is no visible or public expression for the doctrine.[177] Powell cannot find enough nouns to describe its purely figurative status: *tropus, metonymias, similitudo, figura, typus*.[178] Fisher also considers a vaguely generic interpretation—the believers' union in Christ gives

---

[169] Rex, *Theology of Fisher*, 91, 129–32.

[170] Fisher placed the transmission of grace during penance, but as penance was preparation for communion, the distinction mattered little. Bagchi, *Luther's Earliest Opponents*, 132–41; Evans, *Problems of Authority*, 167–96.

[171] Henry VIII, *Assertio*, sigs ci^v–iiii^r, qiiii–tiii^r; *Miscellaneous*, 51–85, 125–39. Powell, *Propugnaculum*, fols 25–71^r, 119^v–163^r. Cf. *CWM*, V, 608–11. Fisher, *Defensio*, 50; *Defence*, 76.

[172] Only one traditionalist denied it. Bagchi, *Luther's Earliest Opponents*, 138.

[173] Fisher, *Defensio*, 50; *Defence*, 75–6.

[174] *Defensio*, 39; *Defence*, 57.

[175] Powell, *Propugnaculum*, fol. 132^v. Fisher, *Defensio*, 61; *Defence*, 100.

[176] Powell, *Propugnaculum*. Fisher, *Confutatio*, fols 100^v–101^r; *Defensio*, 43–8, 67–70; *Defence*, 65–73, 110–15. Cf. Fisher's pre-Reformation discussion of the sacrifice of a contrite heart. *Exposition of the Seven Penitential Psalms*, transl. by Anne Barbeau Gardiner (San Francisco: Ignatius, 1998), 131–9.

[177] Fisher, *Confutatio*, fol. 101^r; *Defensio*, 49; *Defence*, 75.

[178] *Propugnaculum*, fol. 132^r.

them a general right to the name of royal priesthood. Ultimately, however, Fisher leaves the matter of a positive definition unresolved.[179]

Thomas More affirmed the 'common corps of Christendom', a doctrine with similarities to the Vincentian Canon of the early medieval church and the *consensus fidelium* of modern Catholicism. Vincent of Lérins defined the test of true doctrine as *quod ubique, quod semper, quod ab omnibus creditum est,* what has been believed everywhere, always, by all.[180] After encountering problems caused by misunderstandings over the common priesthood defined by *Lumen Gentium* of Vatican II, modern Catholic theologians prefer to speak of *consensus fidelium* as the witness which the people bear with (not opposed to) the bishops in support of true doctrine.[181] More made a similar move towards a difficult-to-reify common priesthood when he spoke of the test of doctrine as that which is 'the general counsell of the whole body of Christendome'.[182] This counsel is manifest not only in general church councils but also in that which has been established from antiquity. Papal primacy was one such establishment and it must be accepted as authoritative on that basis.[183] The ecclesiastical succession of doctrine and leadership must not be challenged by individual heretics. The people witness when supporting the tradition maintained by the hierarchy.[184] In this way, More could hoist Luther on his own petard: 'Those who you say have the right of judging doctrines all judge unanimously that that doctrine of yours by which you teach that no one has the right of founding law is an impious and foolish doctrine'.[185] More and Fisher agree the church's doctrine remains faithful through the Spirit's guidance.[186]

Although their positive definitions were tentative, even elusive, conservatives were neither tentative nor elusive with their negative assertions concerning royal priesthood. The layperson may never consecrate the mass.[187] Confession must only be made to ordained priests, because they possess the keys. Personal confession to God or to laypersons is insufficient.[188] Universal priesthood does not give the laity the right to elect and depose priests.[189] The

---

[179] *Christo (quo rex & sacerdos est) uniti sint, & eius unionis genera regale sacerdotium eos appellavit. Confutatio,* fol. 100ᵛ.

[180] *Commonitorium*, II, 3.

[181] John J. Burkhard, '*Sensus Fidei*: Theological Reflection since Vatican II', *Heythrop Journal,* 34 (1993), 41–59, 123–36.

[182] *The Correspondence of Sir Thomas More*, ed. by E.F. Rogers (PUP, 1947), 524–5.

[183] *The Correspondence of Sir Thomas More*, 48–9.

[184] Brian Gogan, *The Common Corps of Christendom: Ecclesiological Themes in the Writings of Sir Thomas More* (Leiden: E.J. Brill, 1982).

[185] *CWM*, V, 610–11. Cf. Fisher, *Confutatio*, fols 89–90ᵛ.

[186] *CWM*, VIII, 261; Fisher, *Sermon of Iohan*, 3rd instruction.

[187] *CWM*, VI, 294, 353–4.

[188] Fisher, *Confutatio*, fols 75–6.   [189] *CWM*, VI, 289–90; Fisher, *Confutatio*, fol. 88ʳ.

laity should refrain from engaging 'in the medlynge, dysputynge, and expownynge of holy scrypture', leaving such sacred activity to priests.[190]

These denials were not viewed as the imposition of clerical tyranny; rather, conservatives believed the clergy must necessarily monopolize certain functions for the common good. Fisher unwound Luther's opposition of personal faith to priestly mediation. Luther believes 'forgiveness depends entirely upon faith and not on the office or power of the priest'.[191] Rejecting this dichotomy, Fisher says personal faith is improved by the mediation of the priest. Priests necessarily loose and remit sin.[192] Moreover, in spite of his hierocratic tendency, Fisher was not wholly set against lay proclamation. He defended female prophets like Hildegard of Bingen and Bridget of Sweden since their words were verified by signs and miracles. Ironically, the downfall of this apologist for masculine sacerdotalism began with his all too gullible support of the Holy Maid of Kent.[193]

Similarly, More was not wholly set against the laity having Scripture translations even though they so often led to common proclamation and dissension. Vernacular Bibles in themselves are not objectionable; however, 'myscheuous' translations are.[194] The translations and glosses he assigns to Wyclif are objectionable because 'he purposely corrupted that holy texte, malycyously plantyng therin suche wordys as myght in the reders erys serue to the profe of such heresyes as he went about to sow'.[195] Tyndale's New Testament is similarly objectionable, specifically in its consistent mistranslation of three important words. First, Tyndale replaces 'prestys' with 'senyors', the latter being a French word mockingly signifying any old man. Behind this signification substitution, More perceives the radical Lutheran doctrine of universal priesthood with its denial of 'all holy order' and its affirmation of common election, common discipline, lay presidency, and common confession. Tyndale was really saying 'euery man woman and chylde may do as well as any preste'.[196] Tyndale, translator of the worst heresies of Luther,[197] also wants to replace the definite 'chyrche' with an indefinite 'congregacyon', and the works-oriented 'charyte' with the broader concept of 'loue'.[198] More concedes vernacular translations might be helpful for laypeople to prepare for the hearing of sermons,[199] but those translations must receive episcopal approval. Translating is a difficult task and can easily lead to heresy, so there is wisdom in leaving such things to episcopal oversight, as the Oxford Constitutions demand. More prepared his readers for Henry's promise to give them an official translation, if they forsook erroneous opinions.[200]

---

[190] *CWM*, VI, 334. Cf. Fisher, *Defensio*, 70–83; *Defence*, 116–37.
[191] *LW*, XXXII, 50.   [192] Fisher, *Confutatio*, fols 86ᵛ–87ʳ.
[193] Surtz, *Works and Days of Fisher*, 34–5.   [194] *CWM*, VI, 286.
[195] *CWM*, 314.   [196] *CWM*, 285–6, 289–90.
[197] *CWM*, 303.   [198] *CWM*, 286–8.
[199] *CWM*, 339.   [200] *CWM*, 330–44. Cf. *TRP*, no. 129.

On the other hand, Powell considered any vernacular Bible a danger, for it would make Luther's 'absurd' doctrine of common priesthood a reality. Powell assumes the doctrine that all believers should be theologians was Lutheran or Wycliffite, ignoring its Erasmian basis.

> For since all people, even the dregs of the vulgar, have been equally constituted priests by Luther, which is indeed indicative of his entire work, so that he has affirmed all are equally teachers; then, unless the New and Old Testaments are translated into the barbaric languages, which the filthy common people will be able to understand, he will never be able to effectively make this happen.[201]

Angered by any threat to scholarly elitism, Powell opposed the vernacular Bible. He believed it would only support the radical Lutheran doctrine of common priesthood.[202]

English conservatives reserved some vitriolic rhetoric for women priests. Fisher criticizes Luther for 'conjuring up his female priests from nowhere'. Everyone knows 'this ministry does not belong to women'. Peter appointed only men because 'women were unable to be appointed to this ministry'. Luther only 'wishes to curry favour with the ladies'.[203] In his 1529 *Dialogue Concerning Heresies*, More accentuates the Lutheran teaching that 'euery crysten woman ys a preste'. This is ridiculous for everyone knows a woman who hears confession cannot keep counsel but will scatter gossip all over town.[204] In 1530, Tyndale defended women who baptized, preached, and administered the eucharist in emergency situations but admitted 'women be no meet vessels to rule or to preach'. Accusing More, he laments, 'O poor women, how despise ye them!'[205] Tyndale's answer flustered his opponent and in *Confutation of Tyndale's Answer*, More returned to this theme repeatedly. Women should not normally baptize 'syth god sent out onely men to baptyse'. Although a woman may baptize in an emergency, 'in consecratynge neuer woman dyd yt, nor good man byleued that any woman myghte do yt'.[206] 'For his heresye rekeneth euery woman a preest, and as able to say masse as euer was saynt Peter.... And all be that neyther woman may be preest, nor any man is preest or hath power to say masse,... Tyndale hath begonne his heresyes, and sent his erronyous bokes about, callyng euery chrysten woman a preest.' Tyndale's doctrine is so pernicious that 'nowe in some places of Englande the symplest woman in the parysshe' is singing the mass.[207]

---

[201] *Nam cum omnes plebeos et feces vulgi, constituit Lutherus equaliter esse sacerdotes: opere quippe precium sibi omnino erat: ut eos cunctos eque affirmaret esse doctores: quod nisi novum et vetus testamentum, in barbaras traducantur linguas: quas intelligere sordes vulgi queant, id effici nunquam potuisse, satis ipse advertebat. Propugnaculum,* fol. 158ʳ.
[202] Lytle, 'Wyclif, Luther and Powell', 475.   [203] *Defensio,* 80; *Defence,* 131–2.
[204] *CWM,* VI, 351, 353.   [205] Walter, III, 18.
[206] *CWM,* VIII, 259–61.   [207] *CWM,* VIII, 594.

ENGLISH EVANGELICALS

Was the Lutheran doctrine of universal priesthood, the worst aspects of which More assumes Tyndale imported, implemented in England? There are two answers to this question. First, certain aspects of that doctrine were affirmed and implemented, but More's accusation that laypeople were actually saying mass is unsubstantiated.[208] Second, Luther's doctrine of universal priesthood may have informed English evangelicals, but it was evident in the years preceding Luther's revolt, and afterwards, that some interpretations of the doctrine were decidedly non-Lutheran. Maria Dowling, John Davis, and Diarmaid MacCulloch tell us 'evangelical' is a better description of the early English reformers than 'Lutheran' or 'Protestant' since there were various influences at work during this time.[209] The Wycliffite and Lutheran heresies were subject to commixture during the 1520s.[210] However, evangelical thinkers often bypassed the doctrine, though it was available from both traditions. They refused to proclaim universal priesthood either because they disliked it or feared suffering. Perhaps they could see that, as John Fines and Susan Brigden suggest, the doctrine could be inappropriately wielded by the impetuous.[211] Such factors mean there are few systematic explanations by evangelicals.

Among the laity, the doctrine was more often Wycliffite than Lutheran in origin. In 1509, Richard Hillman was accused in Coventry of saying a priest was only a priest when saying mass and afterwards was no more than a layman, having no more power than a layman.[212] One of the articles offered against Richard Hun in 1514, after his death, was that he believed 'poor men and idiots', who should have vernacular Bibles, are more apt to understand it than prelates, monks, and theologians.[213] In 1511 William Smith, Bishop of Lincoln, accused Thomas Man, a successful peripatetic Lollard evangelist, of teaching 'that all holy men of his sect only were priests'. Man was tried before the court of Bishop Fitzjames of London and burned at Smithfield in March

---

[208] After More's fall, John Gale, rector of Thwaite, Suffolk, proposed a radical version of the doctrine. On 4 March 1537, he said 'that any man can consecrate the body of Christ and that holy water and holy bread have no strength'. However, he does not seem to have led anyone to actually do so. His outburst seems more a protest against consecrating the mass himself than encouraging laypeople to do it. William Drury to Cromwell, 3 April 1537; *L&P*, XII, i, 818.

[209] Dowling, *Humanism in the Age of Henry VIII*, i; Davis, 'The Trials of Thomas Bylney and the English Reformation', *HJ*, 24 (1981), 787–90; *Cranmer*, 2. Foxe prefers the contemporary titles 'known-men' or 'just-fast-men'. *A&M*, IV, 217–18. Cf. Susan Brigden, 'Thomas Cromwell and the "Brethren"', in *Law and Government under the Tudors*, ed. by Claire Cross, David Loades and J.J. Scarisbrick (CUP, 1988), 31–49.

[210] Dickens, *Lollards and Protestants*, 37–52.

[211] Davis, 'Lollardy and the Reformation in England', and Brigden, 'Youth and the English Reformation', in *Impact of the English Reformation*, 37–54, 55–84.

[212] *Impact of the English Reformation*, 135.

[213] *Impact of the English Reformation*, 186.

1518.[214] Thomas Geffrey, an admirer of Colet, and Richard Vulford were accused, during the trials prosecuted by John Longland in Lincoln from 1518 to 1521, of long believing 'God neither made priests, for in Christ's time there were no priests'.[215]

During the persecutions of 1528, Cuthbert Tunstall, Bishop of London, examined one John Tyball on April 28. Tyball possessed both Wycliffite tracts and English Scripture translations well before Tyndale began his work, and from them he gathered the opinions that 'a prieste had no power to consecrate the body of Christe'; 'that yt was as good to confesse himself alone to God, or els to any other layman, as to a prieste'; and 'that pristhode was not necessary: for he thowght that every layman myght mynister the sacramentes of the churche, as well as any priste'. He tried converting several parish priests and monks to his views, succeeding somewhat with John Smyth and Richard Fox, both of Bumpstead.[216] In 1530, one James Algar, or Ayger, told a theologian 'that euery true Christen man, lyuing after the lawes of God, and obseruyng his Commaundementes, is a Priest as well as he'. Algar proceeded to deny the soteriological efficacy of masses for the dead, swearing 'he would do it with his own handes while he was aliue'. Such Pelagian assertions would have been anathema to the fideistic Luther. Like many other lay proponents of the doctrine, Algar was more Lollard than Lutheran. He abjured his opinions before the commissary of the Bishop of London.[217]

When Tunstall translated to Durham in 1530, he took his persecution north with him. Roger Dichaunte, a Newcastle merchant, abjured before Tunstall the belief that 'euery christen man is a preste and haithe power to consecrate the Bodye of owr lorde, and to doo all other thinges whiche prestes alone now use too doo'.[218] Lambert Hooke, or Sparrow, a Dutchman, abjured in late 1533 in Archbishop Edward Lee's court the belief 'there ys no preste but God onelye'.[219] A year later, another Dutchman, Gyles Vanbellaer, admitted to believing that God is the only priest and that priests have no power to consecrate the body of Christ on earth for he dwells only in the faithful Christian. Therefore, Vanbellaer concluded, every faithful Christian man may baptize and hear confession.[220] Dickens relates other cases in the northern courts where lay presidency and common confession continued to be affirmed well into the 1540s.[221] These lay opinions differ little from those of two priests from the diocese of Salisbury in 1499. They believed 'prestes and

---

[214] Thomson, *Later Lollards*, 93, 170–1; A&M, IV, 209.   [215] *Later Lollards*, 230.

[216] Strype, V, 364–7.

[217] Foxe, *Ecclesiastical History* (1570), VIII, 1159.

[218] *The Registers of Cuthbert Tunstall, Bishop of Durham 1530–59, and James Pilkington, Bishop of Durham, 1561–76*, ed. by Gladys Hinde, Surtees Society 161 (London: Andrews, 1952), 35.

[219] Dickens, *Lollards and Protestants*, 19.

[220] *Lollards and Protestants*, 20.   [221] *Lollards and Protestants*, 24, 44–5, 48.

bysshoppes have no more auctorite thenne a nother laymann' who follows Christian truth; therefore, auricular confession is unnecessary and can be made directly to God.[222] A glance through the first part of John Fines' *Biographical Register* reveals widespread belief in universal priesthood as empowering common confession, common proclamation, and lay presidency from the 1520s through to the 1550s.[223]

At the Inns of Court, those semi-clerical lay fraternities, we find a mixed bag of orthodox and evangelical lawyers. Representing one extreme is Thomas More; at the other is James Bainham. Bainham, supporter of Tyndale and other evangelical priests, was brought before the new Bishop of London, John Stokesley, in December 1531. He admitted to believing in common confession. After abjuring and being recaptured in April 1532, he denied the mass was a propitiatory sacrifice and championed providing vernacular Bibles for every man and woman. Bainham was burnt at the stake on 30 April, reportedly begging God to forgive More for persecuting him.[224] Robert Plumpton believed Tyndale's New Testament was the key to salvation and affirmed common proclamation.[225] As we saw in Chapter 2, the Inns had a tradition for developing religious self-dependence among its members. That Thomas Elyot, Christopher St German, Richard Taverner, and Edward Hall became major supporters of Henry's royal supremacy should be of little surprise. Neither should it be surprising the leading lay reformers under Elizabeth, Nicholas Bacon and William Cecil, came from the Inns. Lawyers had long been weaned from dependence on sacerdotal mediation. They were a 'narrow' interest group[226] in number but not influence. They successfully challenged the tithe structure in London,[227] and, as we shall see, were instrumental in curtailing clerical independence under Henry and defining the Elizabethan settlement.

Few of the early evangelical clergy did more than flirt with the doctrine and, unlike the laity, their renditions were more Lutheran than Lollard in character. Thomas Bilney, one of the most influential early evangelical priests from Cambridge,[228] and Thomas Arthur, his colleague, were asked during their

---

[222] *Lollards and Protestants*, 9.

[223] *A Biographical Register of Early English Protestants and Others Opposed to the Roman Catholic Church 1525-1558* (Abingdon: Sutton Courtenay Press, 1981).

[224] *A&M*, IV, 697-705. For historiographical problems in Foxe's account, see Thomas S. Freeman, 'The Importance of Dying Earnestly: The Metamorphosis of the Account of James Bainham in "Foxe's Book of Martyrs"', *SCH*, 33 (1997), 267-88.

[225] R.M. Fisher, 'Reform, Repression and Unrest at the Inns of Court, 1518-1558', *HJ*, 20 (1977), 792.

[226] Haigh, 'Anticlericalism', 398-9.

[227] Susan Brigden, 'Tithe Controversy in Reformation London', *JEH*, 32 (1981), 286.

[228] Davis, 'Bylney'; Porter, *Reformation and Reaction*, 44-9; Greg Walker, *Persuasive Fictions* (London: Scolar Press, 1996), 143-65.

1527 trial before Tunstall and Wolsey, 'Whether they do think all true Christians to be by like right priests' and thereby receive the Holy Spirit and the keys directly from Christ? Arthur was accused of preaching on Trinity Sunday that 'every man, yea every layman is a priest'. He defused the sharpness of the question by affirming 'every christian man is a priest, offering up the sacrifice of prayer', and yet, 'if they did murmur against the order of priesthood, they did murmur against themselves'. Arthur subsequently abjured this opinion. On his part, Bilney apparently left the question unanswered.[229] Bilney was more interested in promoting the sole sufficiency of Christ by opposing idolatrous pilgrimages and images than in defining universal priesthood. He died for his beliefs in 1531.

Robert Barnes, an evangelical clergyman with connections to Wittenberg, never directly affirmed the doctrine. He came close when praying for 'all true christian men' rather than the three estates of the church, when denying auricular confession as necessary, and when finding monks no holier than laymen. However, he was more interested in promoting presbyters and kings over bishops than in advocating universal priesthood.[230] In his first *Supplication* of 1534, Barnes said the king was absolute in temporal affairs; in spiritual affairs, God committed authority to those learned in Scripture. In his second *Supplication* of 1534, Barnes brought nearly all spiritual matters under Henry's purview.[231] Edward Crome and Hugh Latimer were forced by Tunstall to affirm the keys of binding and loosing were given to Peter and his successors and 'not at all to the laity'.[232] George Joye was accused by John Ashwell, prior of Newnham in Bedford, of teaching that every layman may hear confession. Joye did not remember advocating this doctrine but believed confession should be made to the one sinned against.[233]

Thomas Garrett, or Garrarde, curate at Honey Lane in London, moved to Oxford to take up a position at Wolsey's new Cardinal College. Ironically, rather than reinforcing Wolsey's orthodoxy, he provided a fledgling Lutheran group in the university with heretical books. These 'brethren' were led by Master Clark, a canon at St Frideswide's, an Augustinian monastery that eventually became Christ Church Cathedral. Wolsey and Tunstall began a search for Garrett in 1528 to prevent his selling Lutheran works. Garrett's

---

[229] *A&M*, IV, 623–6, 755.

[230] Barnes, *A supplication unto the most gracious prince King Henry VIII* (London, 1534), arts. 6, 25. Cf. Barnes, *A Supplicatyon . . . vnto . . . Henry VIII* (n.p., 1534), fols xxiii–xxxvi; Clebsch, *England's Earliest Protestants*, 50.

[231] *England's Earliest Protestants*, 63–4.

[232] Burnet, II, i, 165. On Cranmer's praise for Crome, see Cox, II, 397. Cf. Susan Wabuda, 'Equivocation and Recantation During the English Reformation: The "Subtle Shadows" of Dr Edward Crome', *JEH*, 44 (1993), 224–42.

[233] Charles G. Butterworth and Allan G. Chester, *George Joye, 1495?–1553* (Norwich: Fletcher, 1962), 39, 81.

capture led to the suppression of the Oxford 'brethren'. Among the beliefs confessed by one of the brethren, Anthony Dalaber, was that 'indifferently to a man or woman confession may be made and that *mulier habet potestatem clauium*,' a woman has the power of the keys.[234] Garrett recanted his belief 'that every man may preache the word of God, and that no law to the contrary can be made'.[235] Escaping further harassment for the time, Garrett received a preaching license from Cranmer in 1535, making tours through Yorkshire and Lincolnshire.[236]

Sir Francis Bigod was possibly introduced to Garrett and his doctrine of common proclamation in Oxford; later, he used Garrett to spread evangelicalism and flush out opponents of Henry's royal supremacy. Bigod asked Cromwell to help him enter the priesthood as a married man or give him leave to preach while 'beyng no preiste'.[237] Bigod both affirmed common proclamation, and practiced it, informing a priest and a monk of the error of their ways. He found himself caught up in the Pilgrimage of Grace, but during that time was able to practice the election and discipline of clergy by representative government, and oppose Henry's pretension to practice a 'cure of souls'.[238]

John Lambert, or Nicholson, a Cambridge convert of Bilney's, also ministered to Tyndale in Antwerp. Archbishop Warham placed forty-five articles against Lambert in 1532. Lambert provided detailed answers to each article. His conclusions were unorthodox, but Warham's death and Cranmer's promotion delayed his prosecution. Asked whether he believed in the sacrament of orders, Lambert says the apostolic polity included priests and deacons but not the minor orders. Moreover, although episcopal election is acceptable, popular election has been unnecessarily omitted. When asked whether auricular confession was necessary and must be made to priests only, he denied its necessity and affirmed common confession, in cases where the priest is untrustworthy.[239]

Article 23 enquired, 'Whether thou beleuest that it bee laufull for laie men of bothe kyndes, that is to wytt, both men and women, to sacrifice and preache the worde of God?'[240] Lambert considers these activities separately. As for public preaching, only those chosen by God or men may normally do so. But 'in time of great necessity lay people may preach, & that of both kindes both men & women.' To buttress his opinion he quotes Scripture, canon law, and a dialogue by Erasmus.[241] As for sacrifices, he carefully lays aside the idea that

---

[234] Dr London to John Longland, 24 February 1528; *A&M*, V, appendix vi.

[235] Tunstall's Register, fols 137–8; *A&M*, V, 421–9.

[236] Susan Wabuda, 'Setting Forth the Word of God', in *C&S*, 85.

[237] Dickens, *Lollards and Protestants*, 58–9, 77.

[238] *Lollards and Protestants*, 82, 90–9.

[239] Foxe, *Ecclesiastical History* (1563), III, 591, 597–9.

[240] *Ecclesiastical History*, 591.   [241] *Ecclesiastical History*, 610.

laypeople should 'saye masse, as priestes vseth to do thervnto apoynted'. Yet, Christian people are 'sacerdotes, that is to saye, sacrificers' and ought to offer spiritual sacrifices. There are two manner of spiritual sacrifices: the living sacrifice, wherein one mortifies the flesh and alters the mind, according to Romans 12; and, the sacrifice of praise, which includes both 'the fruits of our lips' and doing good to our neighbors, according to Hosea 14. However, both activities are limited to emergencies.[242] Although Lambert escaped punishment in 1532, and left the priesthood to become a teacher, he was brought before Cranmer for his sacramentarian views in 1538. He denied Christ's body could be simultaneously in heaven and in the eucharist. Unwisely appealing to Henry, his case became a show-trial for Henry's orthodoxy. Foxe described Lambert's burning as a self-offering, 'vnto the Lord a sacrifice of swete sauor', in spite of the involvement of evangelicals like Barnes, Cromwell, and Cranmer.[243]

Other than Lambert, William Tyndale was the only English priest to give the doctrine extended treatment. In *Obedience*, an earlier Erastian tract apparently read and appreciated by Henry,[244] he encouraged people to follow their traditional vocations and obey their superiors. Children, wives, and servants are to obey, respectively, their fathers, husbands, and masters. All the people, including the clergy, must obey the king. Although assigning the king sweeping powers over the temporal regiment, Tyndale reminds him the people are God's, not his. In the kingdom of God, the lowest person of the realm is 'the king's brother, and fellow-member with him, and equal with him'.[245] During his discussion of the sacraments, Tyndale considered the biblical doctrine of priesthood. Agreeing with Luther's redefinition of order, he says the various clerical positions 'be names of offices and service, or should be, and not sacraments'. Any talk of an essential mark conveyed by ordination is demonic: 'that character' is 'the mark of the beast'. Traditionalists themselves betray the inadequacy of their doctrine of ordination since they cannot agree on exactly what part of the ceremony makes a man into a priest.[246]

Tyndale then offered a linguistics lesson. 'There is a word called in Latin *sacerdos*, in Greek *hiereus*, in Hebrew *cohan*, that is, a minister, an officer, a sacrificer or a priest.' The priest has a twofold task: to sacrifice for the people and to be a mediator between God and man. Under this definition of priest, only Christ is the true priest and he is such eternally. Since all are, derivatively, priests through him, we 'need no more of any such priest on earth, to be a mean for us to God'. Radically, Tyndale denies any mediatorial role for anyone other than Christ. Although Christians still need officers to teach them God's

---

[242] *Ecclesiastical History*, 611.   [243] *Ecclesiastical History*, 625.
[244] Daniell, *Tyndale*, 242–6.
[245] *Obedience of a Christian Man* (1528), in Walter, I, 202.
[246] *Obedience of a Christian Man*, 254–5, 258–9.

Word, teaching is not mediation and the teacher is not a mediator.[247] In his haste to deny the traditional sacrificial role of the priesthood in the ceremony of the mass, Tyndale thus emasculates the concept of mediation. Classical communication theory affirms the messenger is the bearer of a message from a sender to a receiver—that is, the messenger is a mediator—but Tyndale denies that teaching is mediation.[248] Tyndale's logical blunder has contributed to a long-standing Protestant dilemma where, on the one hand, universal priesthood is equated with unmediated access to God, yet on the other hand, mediating the Word by proclamation is deemed necessary for salvation.[249]

Tyndale's positive definition of universal priesthood also suffers from an inadequate anthropology. Although he elsewhere affirms the need for communal support and love, even going so far as to say, 'Every Christian man to another is Christ himself',[250] he here places every Christian on his own. Christ has brought the Christian into the inner temple before God, 'where we offer, every man for himself'. This individualism is of a different type from that expounded by Fisher, whose individualism was limited by the clerical monopoly over communal power. In his attack on clerical monopoly, Tyndale downplays the community, separating man before God from all other humans. At the deepest relational level, that of creature worshipping Creator, man is now isolated. Universal priesthood has, for the first time, become supremely atomistic.

A number of sacrifices may be offered by the individual at this point: 'the desires and petitions of his heart', 'the lusts and appetites of his flesh', and 'prayer, fasting, and all manner godly living'. Because of his personal access to the divine presence, the individual is empowered to baptize in time of need. And, in limited ways, people may teach the gospel. Every man may teach his wife and household; the wife may teach her children.[251] Although Tyndale restricted common teaching, he does allow it, and in terms not antithetical to traditionalists.[252] Where Tyndale really departs from tradition is in his isolation of individuals before God (though the medieval mystics may be said to encourage such a departure) and in his thoroughgoing ontological egalitarianism. (Egalitarianism must be distinguished from atomistic individualism: Wyclif was both egalitarian and

---

[247] *Obedience of a Christian Man*, 255–6.

[248] David S. Cunningham, *Faithful Persuasion: In Aid of a Rhetoric of Christian Theology* (Notre Dame, Indiana: University of Notre Dame Press, 1991).

[249] 'God worketh with his word, and in his word: and when his word is preached, faith rooteth herself in the hearts of the elect.' *The Parable of the Wicked Mammon* (1528), in Walter, I, 54. In the first English evangelistic tract, Tyndale denies the need for mediation yet acts as a literary mediator. He leads the sinner in prayer and speaks on God's behalf. *A compendious introduccion vnto the pistle to the Romayns* (1526). Yarnell, 'The First Evangelical Sinner's Prayer Published in English', *Southwestern Journal of Theology*, 47 (2004), 27–43.

[250] Walter, I, 98. Tyndale's community is presented as individual opposition—one 'man to another'.

[251] Walter, 256.   [252] Haigh, *English Reformations*, 27.

communal; Tyndale was simultaneously egalitarian and individualistic.) Tyndale believes traditionalist clergy 'make themselves holier than the lay-people' although they are really false priests in their sinfulness and pride. 'Nevertheless the truth is, that we are all equally beloved in Christ, and God hath sworn to all indifferently.' Based on his personal faith, every man may have his prayer heard and fulfilled by God, whether he is 'cobbler', 'butcher', or 'baker', or 'cardinal', 'bishop', or 'pope'.[253] Conservatives found Tyndale's doctrine objectionable enough to include it in the heresy charges against him: 'Every man is a priest, and we need no other priest to be a mean for us unto God.'[254] Betrayed by a confidant, Tyndale was strangled and burned at the stake near Brussels on 6 October 1536.

Tyndale's denial of all human mediation, except for that of Christ, and his resulting atomistic anthropology caused problems for evangelicals. This became evident with the October 1530 will of William Tracy. Tracy's will was refused probate in the Prerogative Court of Canterbury and condemned by Convocation in 1531. His body was removed from consecrated soil and burned.[255] Evangelicals were outraged. Tyndale and John Frith, an evangelical priest burned in 1533 for denying purgatory and transubstantiation, penned defenses of Tracy's will.[256] Since Tracy excluded funerary endowments, Frith assumes the driving force behind the backlash was clerical anger over lost wealth.[257] Tracy testified 'there is but one God and one mediatour betwene God and man, whiche is Jesus Christ. So that I doe except none in heaven nor in earth to be my mediatour between me and God but onely Jesus Christ.' He then added a small caveat: 'all other be but petitioners in receyvyng of grace, but none able to geve influence of grace'.[258]

Both Tyndale and Frith strengthened Tracy's caveat because traditionalists assumed 'that he held that none should pray for him save Christ, and that we be not bound to pray for one another, nor ought to desire the prayers of another man'. Tyndale says 'we may and ought to desire other to pray for; but [Tracy] meaneth that we may not put our trust and confidence in their prayer'. Their prayers are effective only through Christ and not of themselves.[259] Frith solves the evangelical dilemma by distinguishing mediators from petitioners: 'He only deserveth the name of a mid-dealer, which being God, became men to make men gods. And who can by right be called a mid-dealer between God

---

[253] Walter, I, 257–8.   [254] Walter, 255n.

[255] John Craig and Caroline Litzenberger, 'Wills as Religious Propaganda: The Testament of William Tracy', *JEH*, 44 (1993), 423.

[256] *The Testament of master Wylliam Tracie esquier expounded both by William Tindall and Ihon Frith* (Antwerp, 1535). For modern editions, see Walter, III, 271–83; *The Work of John Frith*, ed. by N.T. Wright (Oxford: Sutton Courtenay Press, 1978), 243–55.

[257] *The Work of John Frith*, 250.

[258] Craig and Litzenberger, 'Wills', 424.   [259] Walter, III, 277–8.

and man, but he that is both God and man?' All others are called 'petitioners which receive grace, but are not able to impress and pour [or power] thereof into any other man, for that doth only God distribute with his finger'.[260]

Evangelicals created difficulty for themselves, when emphasizing the uniqueness of Christ's mediation, through effectively excluding all other forms of mediation. If Christ is the only mediator, then why should humans preach to others and pray for others? William Shepherd, a yeoman of Mendlesham, Suffolk, adopted Tracy's will as a model for his own in 1537 but strengthened the caveat: 'Here I wold not that men shuld say that I dyspyset other holsome sacramentes or good sermonys'.[261] Similarly, John Dennys of Cirencester wrote in 1538 that his works resulted from 'my ynward fayth, takyng Jesu Cryst for a full and hole savyour nedyng no other helpe of man, not denyyng the decent and cumly ordre taken by man and so alowyd'.[262] Tracy's will was published and used as a model throughout the sixteenth century, some adopting it wholesale, others dropping the reference to Christ's sole mediation, but it did not appeal to many, 'even among strong Protestants'.[263] This was probably due to the difficulties raised by its confused language of mediation. The evangelical desire to emphasize Christ while attacking the abuses of traditional priesthood complicated the evangelical understanding of mediation.

ANTICLERICALISM

Various types of anticlericalism were at work in the 1520s, both reformist and radical. The reformist anticlericalism of humanists and of many evangelicals was mild compared to the radical brand promoted by Simon Fish. Fish, a bookseller connected with Gray's Inn, fled England in 1526 after acting the part of Wolsey in a play critical of the Cardinal.[264] He spent some time with Tyndale at Worms and saw his *Supplicacyon for the Beggers* published in Antwerp in late 1528.[265] Foxe says Henry read *Supplicacyon*, enjoyed it, and gave Fish immunity from More's rigorous persecution of opponents of the clergy. Fish died of the plague soon after, and his wife married James Bainham, the son of William Tracy's sister. More grouped Tyndale and Fish as co-conspirators, but Fish and Tyndale had different concerns. Fish learned

---

[260] *Work of Frith*, 249.   [261] Craig and Litzenberger, 'Wills', 425.
[262] Litzenberger, *The English Reformation and the Laity* (CUP, 1997), 41.
[263] Craig and Litzenberger, 'Wills', 427–30.
[264] Clebsch, *England's Earliest Protestants*, 241–5; *A&M*, IV, 656–8.
[265] *A Supplicacyon for the Beggers*, ed. by J.M. Cowper, EETS extra series, 13 (London: Trübner, 1871), 1–18; *A&M*, IV, 659–64.

some theology from Tyndale and both beat the drum of 'obedience' to win over Henry, but Tyndale carefully distinguished his works from Fish's *Supplicacyon*.[266]

Supplicacyon's concern is economic and political; theology plays a supporting role. Fish attacks all types of clergy: prelatic, religious, and secular. They are economic parasites, controlling a third of the land and consuming half the realm's income. What do they contribute? Nothing, unless one takes into account the priests chasing after every man's wife, daughter, and maid. Their only duty is to pray for the people in purgatory, yet 'many men of great literature and judgment' say there is no purgatory.[267] On the political front, addressing Henry, Fish accuses the clergy of separating the spiritual and temporal kingdoms so they can eventually dominate both. Their accusations of heresy and opposition to vernacular Bibles are designed to oppress the people and withdraw obedience from the king. Fish promises Henry that, if he will remove the clergy from the realm's highest offices and set the monks to work, the people will prosper and give him full obedience.

Tyndale retained a reformed clergy in his doctrine, but Fish made no room for a separate ministerial class, even in his systematic theology. *Summe of the holye Scripture* is his translation of a Dutch work that appropriates both Lutheran and Reformed sources, giving preference to the latter in sacramental, ecclesiological, and political matters.[268] Fish says the Bible was not intended only for priests; Christ died equally 'for the comon housholder as for the priests'. Parents should teach their children to read the Bible and disregard priestly 'fables and lyes'.[269] Monks, who are all now evil, are worse than laypeople. Moreover, God hears laymen's prayers, too.[270] Fish elevates the spiritual value of secular vocations while denigrating all priests. He transfers their teaching function to male householders, the bedrock of society.[271] There are two governments, 'goostly and secular', but spiritual government is actually unnecessary since Christ rules his people directly and the Gospel 'teacheth, governeth and kepeth the same'. Only the secular government should be obeyed.[272] The clergy should seek more productive employment. Ultimately, Fish leaves no room for ordained ministry and he addresses neither royal priesthood nor eucharist. In spite of its author's dubious

---

[266] Steven W. Haas, 'Simon Fish, William Tyndale, and Sir Thomas More's "Lutheran Conspiracy"', *JEH*, 23 (1972), 130–1.

[267] *A&M*, IV, 662.

[268] Clebsch, *England's Earliest Protestants*, 245–7; Fish, *The Summe of the holy Scripture* (London, 1529).

[269] *The Summe of the holy Scripture*, ch. 3.

[270] *The Summe of the holy Scripture*, chs. 16, 17, 19.

[271] *The Summe of the holy Scripture*, chs. 23–24.

[272] *The Summe of the holy Scripture*, ch. 26.

evangelical credentials, *Summe* has incorrectly been considered 'the most complete compend of Protestant theology' written in English.[273]

Christopher Haigh's denial of a sharp rise in Fish-like anticlericalism during the early Reformation is affirmed, though modified, by a number of studies. Margaret Bowker concludes 'few Tudor parishioners were as anticlerical as Simon Fish'; rather, hostility was occasional and limited to certain issues, such as extended non-residence without a deputy, incontinence, abuse of benefit of clergy, tithes, and mortuary fees. Anticlericalism was 'a smouldering rather than a blazing fire' dormant in many parishes until stirred up by king and Parliament.[274] Peter Heath says Fish's *Supplicacyon* marks the transition to a tighter anticlericalism fueled by inflation and fed by religious ideas.[275] Peter Marshall agrees anticlericalism did not cause the Reformation, but neither was it a result; rather, anticlericalism was 'in an unremitting dialectic' with it.[276]

Citing the case of Hayes, Middlesex in 1530, G.R. Elton showed how anti-clericalism could even be conservative in religious temper. The parishioners were outraged by their lay rector, Thomas Gold, a lawyer of Middle Temple, and his brother and vicar, Henry. When Warham sent his officials to enforce tithes, they started by serving warrant to the Hayes congregation during the mass. After three such impositions, the conservative parishioners of Hayes claimed the privilege to serve God without sacrilegious intervention. They denied Gold's chaplain his vestments and were brought before the Star Chamber by Warham for violating his spiritual authority.[277] In light of these facts, Haigh is mistaken to categorize the evangelical doctrine of universal priesthood as a branch of anticlericalism.[278] On the one hand, Simon Fish was the most radical anticler-ical of the early Reformation, but he never advanced the doctrine of universal priesthood. On the other hand, the Hayes parishioners were religiously conser-vative, but they disciplined their clergy.

In summary, most evangelical clergy either ignored the doctrine or proffered a moderate version. Tyndale limited its functions and suggested a problematic individualist definition, but no major evangelical equated universal priesthood with the abolition of clergy. Some evangelical laypeople, such as Bigod and the later Lollards, challenged the clerical monopoly on preaching and the trad-itional doctrine of the mass. However, their views are available to us primarily through hostile sources. Whether they wished to abolish all clergy or simply redefine their functions is unknown. There were probably representatives of

---

[273] Clebsch, *England's Earliest Protestants*, 245.

[274] *The Secular Clergy in the Diocese of Lincoln 1495–1520* (CUP, 1968), 105, 117–24, 147–52, 180.

[275] *English Parish Clergy*, 192–3. Cf. Michael L. Zell, 'The Personnel of the Clergy in Kent, in the Reformation Period', *EHR*, 89 (1974), 513–33; Bowker, 'The Henrician Reformation and the Parish Clergy', *BIHR*, 50 (1977), 30–47.

[276] *Catholic Priesthood*, 212–13.

[277] *Star Chamber Stories*, 2d edn (London: Methuen, 1974), 174–220.

[278] 'Anticlericalism', 392.

both positions among the laity. Fish was obviously a radical anticlerical; how pervasive his views were among lay evangelicals is beyond the extant evidence.

Ironically, only one aspect of the doctrine of royal priesthood really mattered after Henry's bolt from Rome. The king was adamant that his supremacy in both the temporal and spiritual realms never be challenged by anyone, cleric or layman, conservative or evangelical. Henry executed the greatest opponents of the radical doctrine of universal priesthood, Fisher and More, in 1535. Evangelicals suffered similar fates. Tyndale was dispatched in 1536, most likely at Henry's insistence. At the conclusion of *Practice of Prelates*, momentarily forgetting the assertions of *Obedience*, Tyndale threatened Henry with rebellion if he would not cease persecuting evangelicals.[279] This crass threat— conveniently deleted from the Edwardian and Elizabethan editions—has received scant attention within modern scholarship. David Daniell believes Cromwell, an otherwise efficient administrator, repeatedly mishandled opportunities to save Tyndale. He accuses Stokesley and excuses Henry, but Daniell's assessment lacks credibility.[280] Cromwell was Tyndale's protector and only one hand could have kept him from saving Tyndale: Henry's. Henry also persecuted the evangelical Lambert,[281] but was even-handed in his murderous treatment of theologians. The traditionalist Powell was killed simultaneously with the evangelical Garrett in 1540; two others from each camp joining them in a fellowship of death. Henry no longer cared for either the conservative or the evangelical versions of the doctrine. He had something different in mind. To his royal priesthood we now turn.

---

[279] Walter, II, 344. Cf. Bruce Boehrer, 'Tyndale's *The Practyse of Prelates*: Reformation Doctrine and the Royal Supremacy', *Renaissance and Reformation* 3 (1986), 257–76.

[280] *Tyndale*, 367–73; Ralph S. Werrell, *The Theology of William Tyndale* (Cambridge: James Clarke, 2006), 159–65.

[281] G.W. Bernard, 'The Making of Religious Policy, 1533–1546', *HJ*, 41 (1998), 325.

4

Royal Priests: Henry VIII and Edward VI

To understand how the theology of priesthood developed during the English Reformation, one must pay attention to that pivotal spiritual figure, Thomas Cranmer, Archbishop of Canterbury (1533–1553). And yet, to understand Cranmer, one must consider his temporal lords, Henry VIII, who pictured himself a sacral king with supreme authority over the church and the state in England, and Henry's son, Edward VI, whom Cranmer described as a 'second Josiah' and 'God's vice-gerent and Christ's vicar'.[1] With all the emphasis on popular religion in recent years, it behooves us to remember, as Sir Maurice Powicke famously put it, 'The one definite thing which can be said about the Reformation in England is that it was an act of State.'[2] From the central government of England, ecclesiastical dogma was determined and disseminated, even as it was variously received in the life of the local church.

Considering Henry's absolute insistence on 'obedience', 'quietness', and 'unity', his disgust for the revolutionary consequences of our subject doctrine in peasant Germany in 1524–1525 and in the city of Münster a decade later, and his penchant for editing his bishops' doctrinal formulations, it should be no surprise the priesthood of all believers, as conceived by Luther, had limited prospects in the official English Reformation. Finding an elaborate formulation of the doctrine in Henry's reign is frustratingly akin to looking for the proverbial needle in a haystack; most affirmations are limited to the radical fringes. However, Henry embraced the doctrine in some sense in his own person. Moreover, the doctrine was widely discussed within the governing circles.

Thomas Cranmer was instrumental in furthering the monarch's 'royal supremacy', one of the most important ideas in Tudor political philosophy. Royal supremacy included an appeal to the sacred position of the king, a position we shall refer to as 'royal priesthood'.[3] Royal priesthood had deep

---

[1] Cox, II, 127.   [2] *The Reformation in England* (OUP, 1941), 1.
[3] Although the term was not applied to Henry, Martin Bucer repeatedly referred to Edward VI's realm as a 'royal priesthood' or 'priestly kingdom'. *De Regno Christi* (1550); *LCC*, XIX, 189, 191, 206–7.

ramifications for English ecclesiology. Soon after its promulgation as an antipapal weapon, it challenged the privileged status of the English clergy and forced numerous questions to be answered. If England is to retain a spiritual order, what is its relationship to the temporal order, especially the temporal lords? Moreover, since England was moving, though haltingly, in an evangelical direction, how could she incorporate the evangelical doctrine of common priesthood into her structure and practices? As we shall see, Thomas Cranmer helped define each of these priesthoods: royal, ministerial, and popular. We begin with the king's priesthood in this chapter.

The separation from Rome and domination of the English church by the crown had its legal basis in the Reformation Parliament (1529–1536), but in the intellectual background were both ancient and novel conceptions granting Henry sacerdotal status. His well-known claim for juridical dominion, royal supremacy, was accompanied by an oft-denied claim for spiritual power, the royal priesthood. It will be our purpose here to show in what sense the king is a priest, especially that understanding held by Cranmer. First, we will consider the historical context in which Henry VIII might have learned of divine kingship. Then we will examine Cranmer's more novel opinions, composed of orthodox concepts but strengthened in an Erastian direction. These concepts were: the royal 'conscience' as arbiter of truth; the king as 'vicar of God' possessing a 'cure of souls'; royal ordination as the basis of episcopal vocation and discipline; 'obedience' to the royal will; and, the king's judgment of doctrine.

Many scholars have uncritically accepted Franklin le van Baumer's assertion that Henry 'consistently' denied personal sacerdotal powers. Geoffrey R. Elton agreed, citing a 1531 distinction between *potestas ordinis* and *postestas iurisdictionis*, the king claiming the latter while rejecting the former. In his discussion of Henry's celebrated response to Bishop Tunstall, Scarisbrick concurs with an early definition of *potestas ordinis*.[4] More recently, Christopher Haigh denied that Henry claimed priestly powers, moreover making Henry's 'fundamental conservatism' integral to his historiography of a reluctant Reformation.[5] However, a careful reading shows Henry never denied himself sacerdotal power in his 1531 correspondence. The first official distinction of the *potestates* appears in the working papers for the *Bishops' Book* of 1537. Moreover, the *Bishops' Book* never received Henry's sanction and the *potestates* distinctions were excised from the approved *King's Book* of 1543. The terms under debate in the 1531 correspondence are *temporalia* and *spiritualia*, and, as we shall discover, Henry was careful to leave those definitions quite vague.

---

[4] Baumer, *The Early Tudor Theory of Kingship* (YUP, 1940), 82–3; Elton, *Tudor Constitution*, (CUP, 1960), 333n; Scarisbrick, *Henry VIII*, 279. Cf. Richard Rex, 'The Crisis of Obedience: God's Word and Henry's Reformation', *HJ*, 39 (1996), 875; Dickens, *Thomas Cromwell and the English Reformation* (London: Hodder and Stoughton, 1959), 67–8.
[5] *English Reformations*, 156.

TRADITIONAL DIVINE KINGSHIP

Henry and his advisors drew upon some ancient traditions to support his claims for supremacy over church as well as state. Both civil and canon law gave prominent place to the maxim of Ulpian, the Roman jurist, that public law is grounded in the sacred, which sacred includes priesthood and civil magisterium. At the Council of Nicaea, Constantine the Great applied this to his relationship to church and state, and the tradition of caesaro-episcopacy— in which the emperor was *episkopos ton ektos*, bishop of external, as opposed to internal, matters—began.[6] As we saw in our discussion of the medieval royal priesthood, these concepts were appropriated not only by continental monarchs, but also by English kings. Henrician apologists believed England had a special claim to the Constantinian succession by virtue of the emperor's British background.[7] The comparison with Constantine was not only made with regard to Henry VIII, but also Edward VI and Elizabeth I.[8]

The concept of sacerdotal kingship was supremely embodied in the coronation *ordines*, including the rite used in the consecration of Henry VIII. The prayer of the metropolitan while placing the crown on his new monarch's head affirms the king's participation in 'our ministry', especially through the external defense of the faith. The ceremony concluded with a prayer for he who is *mediator Dei et hominum* as well as *mediator cleri et plebis*.[9] Afterwards, both temporal and spiritual lords took oaths of fealty and homage. Henry was concerned enough about the meaning of coronation to rewrite the coronation oath. In an incredible display of prerogative, he strengthened the monarch's position against both clergy and people. He promised to defend the rights of the church, but only insofar as it was 'not preiudyciall to hys Jurysdiccion and dignite royall'. Moreover, he promised to deliver justice, but only 'according to hys consienc', a reminder of the juridical self-sufficiency that was, as we shall see, promoted by Cranmer.[10]

When only ten, Henry took part in the ceremonies arranged for the marriage of Arthur, his older brother and heir-apparent to England's throne. These pageants, recently described in detail by Sydney Anglo, are a study in

---

[6] Claudia Rapp, 'Imperial Ideology in the Making: Eusebius of Caesarea on Constantine as "Bishop"', *JTS*, 49 (1998), 685–95.

[7] Walter Ullmann, 'This Realm of England is an Empire', *JEH*, 30 (1979), 175–203. Cf. John N. Figgis, *The Divine Right of Kings*, 2d edn (1914; reprint, Bristol: Thoemmes Press, 1994); and appreciation and correction of Figgis by G.R. Elton, 'The Divine Right of Kings', in *Studies in Tudor and Stuart Politics and Government*, 4 vols (CUP, 1974–1992), II, 193–214.

[8] *Literary Remains of King Edward the Sixth*, ed. by John Gough Nichols, 2 vols (London: Roxburghe Club, 1857), cxlv, ccclii; King, *Tudor Royal Iconography*, 155, 241.

[9] Ullmann, 'Realm of England' 179–83. A better reading is found in the seventeenth century translation for Charles I, where Jesus is the 'Mediator of God and Man' who establishes the king who is 'mediator betwixt the Cleargie and the layetie'. *English Coronation Records*, 264.

[10] *English Coronation Records*, 240–1.

divine kingship. In the third pageant, 'The Sphere of the Moon', four characters 'Declare such heavenly mysteries to man': the Archangel Raphael, the Prophet Job, the Philosopher Boethius, and the Astronomer-King. Priests are conspicuous in their absence.[11] In the fourth pageant, 'The Sphere of the Sun', Prince Arthur is pictured as the sun, the center of the whirling cosmos. Anglo says this is 'a refulgent, and shameless, identification of Prince Arthur both with Christ the Redeemer and Christ the Sun of Justice'.[12] In case the analogy was overlooked, it was repeated in the fifth pageant, 'The Temple of God', when the Father of Heaven who rules the Catholic Church is equated with Henry VII and Arthur with the Son of God.[13] With such ideals in the background, one may surmise what went through Henry's mind when he became king in 1509, or what went through Edward VI's mind when he played a prelate in the pageants following his own coronation.[14]

In *Education of a Christian Prince* (1516), in part originally dedicated to Henry, Erasmus praises monarchy. A number of sacred motifs reappear throughout the work. The perfect ruler is a philosopher–prince in the Platonic tradition.[15] Of course, being a philosopher, according to Erasmus, is no different from being a Christian. Being a Christian means belonging to the order of Christ, which order exceeds any monastic order, even if the Christian king may not administer sacraments or teach.[16] Yet, the king is not without divine attributes, for 'you are the likeness of God and his vicar', who must master the divine qualities of power, wisdom, and goodness. In an Erastian rendition of Dionysian hierarchies, Erasmus says 'the prince in the state' is the third hierarchy through which 'all his goodness flows from him to other men as from a spring'. This earthly prince is an image of the Eternal Prince.[17] He may, therefore, claim the divine titles of 'your Highness', 'your Majesty', and 'the Divine'.[18]

The prince's special relationship with God was not based only on law, history, and philosophy, but also Scripture. English *ordines* had long made the comparison between the English king and biblical kings. A litany of exemplars could be drawn upon as the need arose. Dunstan reminded Edgar in 973 that he stood in the tradition of Abraham, Moses, Joshua, David, and Solomon, and was thereby to teach and defend the church against its spiritual

---

[11] *Spectacle, Pageantry and Early Tudor Policy*, 68–76.
[12] *Spectacle, Pageantry and Early Tudor Policy*, 82.
[13] *Spectacle, Pageantry and Early Tudor Policy*, 86–9.
[14] *Spectacle, Pageantry and Early Tudor Policy*, 296; *Documents Relating to the Revels at the Court in the Time of King Edward VI and Queen Mary*, ed. by Albert Feuillerat (Louvain, 1914), 20, 22–3, 194.
[15] *The Education of a Christian Prince*, ed. by Lisa Jardine (CUP, 1997), 2, 15, 48.
[16] *The Education of a Christian Prince*, 19.
[17] *The Education of a Christian Prince*, 22–3.
[18] *The Education of a Christian Prince*, 60.

and physical enemies. Like Zadok the Priest and Nathan the Prophet, Solomon the King was anointed, rendering him special before God and man. This portion of the *ordo* remained fairly intact through the centuries.[19] Apologists for royal power—under Henry VIII,[20] Edward VI,[21] and Elizabeth I,[22] and even under Mary I[23]—drew on these biblical traditions in order to justify their monarch's particular ecclesiastical policies.

With such a longstanding tradition behind divine kingship, Henry did not have to go far to assert 'the kings of England in times past never had any superior but God' during the Hun–Standish affair ending in 1515. However, he did not, at the time, encroach upon Roman papacy or English prelacy, but the 'high clerical arrogance' of the prelates was thereby given a warning it failed to heed.[24] Henry's effort to secure the succession by divorcing Catherine of Aragon, Arthur's widow, came to light in early 1527. The divorce proceedings in the ecclesiastical courts, hopelessly complicated by international politics, resulted in the downfall of Wolsey in 1529 and the eventual elevation of the Boleyns. Ironically, Wolsey himself played a part in the development of the royal supremacy. As chancellor, the keeper of the court of the king's conscience, he attempted and largely succeeded in dominating common law, and as papal legate *a latere*, Wolsey ruled the English church. This monopolizing combination of the jurisdictions of church and state meant that, 'In fact, though not in form, he was the first who wielded sovereignty in England because he ruled both church and state.'[25]

In 1528 and 1529, Henry warned the pope he might break away from Roman jurisdiction by appealing to the true vicar of Christ.[26] In September 1530, the dukes of Suffolk and Norfolk informed the papal nuncio 'the king was absolute both as emperor and pope in his own kingdom'.[27] In spite of these warnings, it was quite some time before the break that began with Wolsey's prosecution was complete. Moreover, it took the incisive intellectual skills of Cranmer, Edward Foxe, and Thomas Cromwell to formulate a complete separation. These ministers helped craft the rupture with Rome

---

[19] Duckett, *Dunstan*, 102–4; *Coronation Order of James*, 26.

[20] King, *Tudor Royal Iconography*, 59, 72–83.

[21] MacCulloch, *Tudor Church Militant* (London: Penguin, 1999), 14–15; Christopher Bradshaw, 'David or Josiah? Old Testament Kings as Exemplars in Edwardian Religious Polemic', in *Protestant History and Identity in Sixteenth-Century Europe*, ed. by Bruce Gordon, 2 vols (Hampshire: Scolar Press, 1996), II, 77–90; *Literary Remains of Edward*, cxlv, cxlix, cclxxxvii–cclxxxviii.

[22] King, *Tudor Royal Iconography*, 255–61.

[23] *Tudor Royal Iconography*, 195–219.

[24] Elton, *Reform and Reformation: England 1509-1558* (London: Edward Arnold, 1977), 50–8.

[25] A.F. Pollard, *Wolsey* (London: Longmans, 1953), 372.

[26] *L&P*, IV, 4897, 5476, 5650. Cf. *CSPS*, III, ii, 661; Scarisbrick, *Henry VIII*, 216, 222; Ullmann 'Realm of England', 196–7.

[27] *CSPS*, IV, 445. However, Henry later denied a 'nouvelle papalité' in England. *CSPS*, IV, 641.

and subsequent religious policies, but as G.W. Bernard argued persuasively Henry controlled religious change and 'was not the plaything of factions'.[28]

HENRY'S CONSCIENCE

When Thomas More, the new chancellor, and a layman at that,[29] opened Parliament in 1529, he compared Henry to a 'sheaperd, ruler, and governour of his realme', who must 'preserve and defende' his flock. More was not announcing any new titles in ruler, governor, or defender, but 'sheaperd' certainly carried pastoral overtones that More might later regret.[30] Events in the Commons show a vivid anticlericalism at work, with, inter alia, detailed complaints against heresy trials. In response, John Fisher made a controversial blanket accusation of heresy and lack of faith. Decrying the heretical succession, he claimed if the lay Lords did not resist the Commons' mischief, they would 'shortly see all obedience withdrawn, first from the clergie, and after from yourselves'. Following a protest by the Commons, Fisher was called before Henry. The bishop assured the king that he was complaining about heretics in Bohemia and Germany, not England.[31] Whatever Rochester's real meaning, he temporarily preempted any anticlerical legislation.

From early on, Henry displayed a care for souls which went far beyond the late medieval ruler's responsibility to defend the ecclesiastically defined faith with the temporal sword, at least according to the clerical definition. In the previously discussed *Assertio Septem Sacramentorum*, Henry stepped into the ecclesiastical arena to wage a theological battle with Luther, with pen instead of sword. Although he defended orthodoxy at the time, both Luther and the papal court noted the unusual nature of this layman's theological activity. Even more radically, in 1529 and 1530, he adopted language expressing his concern for the welfare of his subjects' souls. The prompting for this may have come from William Tyndale. Tyndale's *Obedience of a Christian Man* defended evangelical theology against charges of insurrection. Tyndale turned the charges of insurrection against the prelates, accusing them of civil

---

[28] Bernard, 'The Making of Religious Policy, 1533–1546', *HJ*, 41 (1998), 321–49. Cf. Bernard, *The King's Reformation: Henry VIII and the Remaking of the English Church* (YUP, 2005); Joseph D. Ban, 'English Reformation: Product of King or Minister?' *CH*, 41 (1972), 186–97.

[29] Since its inception in the Norman Conquest, this office was normally held by a cleric. Following More, it was normally held by a layman. *Handbook of British Chronology*, 3rd edn, ed. by E.B. Fryde (CUP, 1986), 82–92.

[30] Edward Hall, *Chronicle* (London: J. Johnson, 1809), 764. Cf. More, *Utopia*, transl. by Paul Turner (London: Penguin, 1965), 61. Ironically, this 'anticlerical' Parliament was opened at Blackfriars, the same place where Wyclif was condemned in 1382.

[31] Stanford E. Lehmberg, *The Reformation Parliament 1529–1536* (CUP, 1970), 81–9.

disobedience. He exalted the king's power, demanding obedience even to wicked kings and called on Henry to approve the vernacular Bible for the wealth of the commons. Henry is rumored to have liked the book yet allowed its addition to a list of prohibited works.[32]

Although Henry exclaimed, 'This is a book for me and all kings to read,' due perhaps to its exaltation of monarchy, he considered other parts inappropriate. *Obedience* was set before a gathering of some twenty clerics in early 1530. One of the agreed errors and heresies was that 'Every man is a preest, and we nede noon other preest to be a meane'. Tyndale had some appealing ideas but others were too radical for the king's taste. As we shall see, however, Cranmer helped successfully repackage the obedience teaching.[33] Tyndale's call for vernacular Scripture was put off for the time being but the prelates were ordered to prepare a translation for the day when the king felt he might release it.[34] Scarisbrick calls Henry's concern for the welfare of his subjects' souls in this proclamation, 'an interesting statement of royal responsibility'.[35] But Henry was yet careful to distinguish between the prelates' need to compel the people as a result of their 'cure and charge of your sowles' and the prince's responsibility 'to punysshe and correcte you not doing of the same'.[36] This old distinction between temporal and spiritual was soon threatened.[37]

In August 1529, Stephen Gardiner and Edward Foxe brought Thomas Cranmer (at the time a Cambridge tutor) to Henry with an intriguing suggestion. Cranmer believed the appeal to canon law in the king's great matter would never bear fruit. The matter should be referred to theologians as the problem is really theological not legal. After all the convoluted historical and legal arguments, the crux of Cranmer's theology was a novel concept of 'conscience'. Theologians and universities should be consulted, 'Whose sentence maie be sone knowne and brought so to passe with litle industrie, that the king's conscience therby maie be quieted and pacified, whiche we all cheiflie ought to consider.... And than his highnes in conscience quieted maie determen with himself that whiche shall seme good before God, and lett theis tumultuary processes give place unto a certeyne trueth.' Such optimistic personal access to God, apart from and opposed to the church hierarchy, was

---

[32] Walter, I, 127–344. Daniell, *Tyndale*, 242–7; Steven W. Haas, 'Henry VIII's *Glasse of Truthe*', *History*, 64 (1979), 360–2.

[33] E.W. Ives, *Anne Boleyn* (Oxford: Blackwell, 1986), 161–6. For Anne's reformed faith, see ch. 14.

[34] *TRP*, nos. 122, 129; *Concilia*, III, 728–9.

[35] *Henry VIII*, 253.

[36] *Concilia*, III, 736.

[37] There were three medieval theories of the relation between church and state: hierarchic, dualist, and cooperative. Each recognized the papal powers that Henry VIII vanquished. Stanley Chodorow, *Christian Political Theory and Church Politics in the Mid-Twelfth Century* (London: University of California Press, 1972), ch. 9.

an evangelical principle often related to universal priesthood.[38] Here, however, access to the deity is located in the king's conscience.

Henry was intrigued and set Cranmer and a team of scholars immediately to work. In the resulting *Gravissimae... Censurae* (April 1531), and Cranmer's translation, *The Determinations* (November 1531), the king was accorded supreme jurisdiction within his realm. The new emphasis on 'conscience' emerges in Chapter 7. The novelty in Cranmer's doctrine lay not in its internal focus, nor even in its secular juridical usage,[39] but in its opposition to and triumph over ecclesiastical law. According to *Oxford English Dictionary*, 'conscience' denoted a shared consciousness in Middle English. It eventually came to signify the opposing internal judgments of individuals. Cranmer strengthened this definition of conscience from a private opinion to an authoritative reflection of the mind of God.

Determinations announces that church law may not reflect divine law at all while 'private law' may give an accurate reflection. 'The private lawe is the lawe that is written in mennes hartes by the inspiration of the holye goste'.[40] When their conscience is moved, bishops and priests must decide against the bishop of Rome. The king, too, has a conscience that, when moved by the Holy Spirit, is above the mere human law of the church.[41] Cranmer and his co-author, Edward Foxe, meant only to apply the powers of such a conscience to the case of king and bishops against pope, but their language was broader.

> For if the Pope wolde by any manner of power determyne any thynge other wyse than lernyng, that is the cnowledge of goddis lawe wolde haue it be determyned, other in our fayth, or in good maners: his determinacion shulde be vtterly nothinge worthe at al. Yea it shuld be lefull for euery christian man, that knoweth this to crie out ageinst it and all to be spyt & bespue it and to reproue and damne it as hereticall.[42]

Earlier, during his divorce proceedings before the papal legate, Henry had appealed to his conscience as an important but indefinite arbiter of truth. This definition was echoed by Lorenzo Campeggio, the papal legate, and by Fisher, Catherine's counsel, reflecting the orthodox belief that personal conscience may not legitimately oppose canon law.[43] But Cranmer and Foxe then raised

---

[38] Ralph Morice, 'Anecdotes and Character of Archbishop Cranmer', in *Narratives of the Reformation*, ed. by John Gough Nichols ([N.p.]: Camden Society, 1859), 242.

[39] Wolsey referred to the court of Chancery as 'the court of conscience'. Pollard, *Wolsey*, 96–8. Cf. Sharon K. Dobbins, 'Equity: The Court of Conscience or the King's Command, the Dialogues of St German and Hobbes Compared', *Journal of Law & Religion*, 9 (1991), 113–49.

[40] *The Divorce Tracts of Henry VIII*, ed. by Edward Surtz and Virginia Murphy (Angers: Moreana, 1988), 267–9.

[41] *Cranmer*, 45–56.

[42] *Divorce Tracts*, 253.

[43] *Life of Fisher*, 60–5. Christopher St German places conscience under the rule of law. When law is changed 'by the competent authority', then conscience must also change. *St German's Doctor and Student*, ed. by T.F.T. Plucknett and J.L. Barton (London: Selden Society, 1974), 111.

the concept of conscience to a new level by giving it a superior role to church law in determining divine truth. Henry embraced and gave form to this new matter of conscience by bucking the papacy with the annulment of his marriage to Catherine and bringing the English church under his control.[44]

In *Articles Devisid by the holle consent of the Kynges most honourable counsayle*, written immediately after Cranmer approved Henry's divorce, the new archbishop is defended for having acted 'in discharge also of his conscience'. Henry, of course, could not be expected to act 'contrary to his conscience, directed by God's law'. As for the pope's disapproval, he has acted 'contrary to all right and conscience' and bishops are 'bound more to obey God than man'.[45] In spite of its potential service to the king, this elevation and opposition of conscience over public law was a double-edged sword. Henry used 'conscience' to defy the papacy, but More and Fisher relied on conscience to defy king and Parliament.[46] England was thereafter filled with appeals to conscience as indicative of a higher law.[47] Cranmer did not, however, view his doctrine of conscience as simply utilitarian. The appeal to conscience played a great part in the major crises of his life.[48]

---

[44] He added the statement 'according to hys consiene' in the section of the coronation oath affirming his ministry of justice. *English Coronation Records*, 241. 'Henry VIII once described "the law of every man's conscience" to be "the highest and supreme court for judgement or justice".' MacCulloch, 'Henry and Reform', 178.

[45] *Records of the Reformation: The Divorce 1527–1533*, ed. by Nicholas Pocock, 2 vols (OUP, 1870), II, 523–31.

[46] *Records of the Reformation: The Divorce 1527–1533*, 70–1, 106, 109, 115–19; Ackroyd, *Life of Thomas More*, 377, 382–9.

[47] Bishop Ridley used the concept to rebut Protector Somerset's criticism concerning the closing of a Cambridge college in 1549. *Works of Nicholas Ridley*, ed. by Henry Christmas (PS, 1851), 329. The early Baptist, Thomas Helwys, used it to refute governmental control over religion in 1612. *A Short Declaration of the Mystery of Iniquity*, ed. by Richard Groves (Macon, Georgia: Mercer University Press, 1998), 53. Helen Costigane, 'A History of the Western Idea of Conscience', in *Conscience in World Religions*, ed. by Jayne Hoose (Herefordshire: Gracewing, 1999), 3–20.

[48] As an executor of Henry's will in 1547, Cranmer agreed they were 'bound in conscience' to perform their lord's will. *Acts of the Privy Council of England*, vol. 2, ed. by John Roche Dasent (London: Stationery Office, 1890), 15. When asked by the council in 1553 to subscribe to Edward's will abrogating Henry's will for the succession, Cranmer balked. The council indignantly replied 'they had consciences as well as he'. Cranmer answered, 'I am not judge over any mannes conscience but myne own only; for, as I wyll not condempn your fact, no more wyll I stay my fact upon your conscience, seing that every man shall answer to God for his own dedes and not for other mennes.' Only after speaking with Edward and a number of judges did he acquiesce and virtually assure his own destruction on Mary's accession. After all of his recantations of Protestantism, on the day of his death, Cranmer proclaimed at St Mary's Church, Oxford, 'And nowe I come to the greate thynge that so much troublethe my conscience more than anye other thynge that ever I dyd or sayd in my lyfe. And that ys settynge abrode in wrytynge contrarye to my conscience and the truthe; which nowe I here renounce and refuse as thynges wrytten with my hand contrarye to the truthe which I thought in my harte, and wrytten for feare of deathe, to save my lyfe yf yt myght be.' Anonymous, 'The Life and Death of Archbishop Cranmer', in *Narratives of the Reformation*, 225, 232–3.

VICAR OF GOD

At one point in his authoritative biography, Scarisbrick notes Henry appealed against the papacy to the vicar of Christ. In puzzled amazement, Scarisbrick responds 'whatever that meant'.[49] Scarisbrick's query requires a response. What did Henry mean, and where did he get the idea?

The working document upon which *Gravissimae Censurae* was based is *Collectanea Satis Copiosa*, compiled about 1530 by Henry's divorce scholars. Although Cromwell has been credited with formulating the new doctrines contained in the preamble to the 1533 Act of Appeals, those doctrines were already contained in this document in which Cranmer played a leading role.[50] *Collectanea* dwelt on the difference between royal and ecclesiastical power and saw all power in the kingdom, including ecclesiastical power, as descending through the king. The authors built on a long tradition with its roots in the mythical second-century correspondence from Pope Eleutherius to King Lucius I, the first Christian ruler of Britain. The pope's letter stated, 'For you are vicar of God in your kingdom' with powers over both *regnum* and *sacerdotium*.[51] The early church father known as Ambrosiaster similarly considered the king to be 'the vicar of God', who 'has the image of God as the Bishop has that of Christ'.[52]

As noted in Chapter 1 (see 'Dominion and Grace', pp. 24–6), this definition was adopted by Wyclif, who himself drew on a vibrant medieval tradition. Whatever its immediate origin, the concept of royal vicarage was available to Cranmer through a number of sources, including the legal theorist, Bracton;[53] Wyclif, as mediated through the Lollards;[54] and the history of the dialogue over authority between pope and emperor. The idea was appreciated by Henry and promoted by his apologists. One section in an early draft of the Act of Appeals began with an appeal to English kings as 'vicars of God'.[55] Richard Sampson asked, 'What else is it to condemn God's Word than to disobey the king, the

---

[49] *Henry VIII*, 222.

[50] 'Cranmer is a better candidate than Cromwell as agent of the research team's new direction.' John Guy, 'Thomas Cromwell and the Intellectual Origins of the Henrician revolution', in *Tudor Monarchy*, ed. by Guy (London: Arnold, 1997), 217. Guy is answering Elton's confinement of the ideological reformation to Cromwell. Elton, 'King or Minister? The Man Behind the Henrician Reformation', *Studies*, II, 173–88.

[51] Felicity Heal, *Reformation in Britain and Ireland* (OUP, 2003), 120–1, 389–93.

[52] E.G. Rupp, *Studies in the Making of the English Protestant Tradition* (CUP, 1947), 83.

[53] Cromwell cited Bracton to that effect. *L&P*, XIII, i, 120; Fritz Schulz, 'Bracton on Kingship', *EHR*, 60 (1945), 136–76.

[54] A contemporary Lollard tract, *A Compendious Old Treatise*, cites Augustine as a source. *A&M*, IV, 674.

[55] Graham Nicholson, 'The Act of Appeals and the English Reformation', in *Law and Government under the Tudors*, 19–30.

minister of God, the vicar of God?'[56] In a translation of Edward Foxe's *De Vera Differentia* made for and owned by Edward VI, it was affirmed that England's king is 'the vicar of God in that realm'.[57] Not to be outdone, the Bishop of Winchester, Stephen Gardiner, in a tract composed after the Bishop of Rochester's execution, proclaimed Fisher erred for not obeying 'his prince beyng the vicar of god, for the catholike religion'.[58] Thus, Cranmer was appropriating long-standing language when he referred to Edward VI as the vicar of God in the 1547 coronation speech. Scarisbrick may marvel at the royal claim, but Henry believed he could legitimately use the idea.

THE KING'S CURE OF SOULS

The monumental efforts of the international team of scholars under the direction of Foxe and Cranmer established an intellectual precedent that Henry turned upon the clergy in early 1531. To empower the royal claim, the ancient statute of Praemunire was brought out and laid against the whole clergy of England, ostensibly on account of Wolsey's legatine activities.[59] When Convocation balked, Henry sent five articles to be added to the prologue of the subsidy. The first claimed Henry as the 'sole protector and supreme head of the English church and clergy', to which the saving phrase *quantum per legem Dei licet*, 'as far as the law of God allows', was added at Fisher's behest. The second article concerned the king's incredible claim to have a 'cure of souls' committed to himself. However, as Scarisbrick notes, 'by altering a case-ending and shuffling the word-order of the second article, the clergy obliterated the royal claim to a cure of souls and, instead, accorded the king a platitudinous care for subjects whose souls were committed to their, the clergy's, charge.'[60] Three lesser claims were ignored or sidestepped.

---

[56] *Quid aliud est quam contemnere verbum Dei, non obedire regi, ministro dei, vicario Dei?* Strype, V, 488.

[57] Edward Foxe, *The true dyfferes betwen the regall power and the Ecclesiastical power*, transl. by Henry Lord Stafforde (London, 1548), fol. lxxxiii; *Literary Remains of Edward*, cccxxxii.

[58] *Obedience in Church and State: Three Political Tracts by Stephen Gardiner*, ed. by Pierre Janelle (CUP, 1930), 31.

[59] *Documents Illustrative of English Church History*, ed. by Henry Gee and William John Hardy (London: Macmillan, 1896), 103–4, 122–5. Prior to his own appearance before the King's Bench, Wolsey himself employed *praemunire* repeatedly against the clergy. Pollard, *Wolsey*, 248–50.

[60] Scarisbrick, *Henry VIII*, 275–6; Scarisbrick, 'The Pardon of the Clergy, 1531', *HJ*, 12 (1956), 34–5; Lehmberg, *Reformation Parliament*, 112–15. The articles demanded and conceded are listed in *Concilia*, III, 725, 742–4. Guy argues the clerical subsidy was the primary motive for Henry's activities, but Bernard disputes this interpretation. J.A. Guy, 'Henry VIII and the *Praemunire* Manoeuvres of 1530–31', *EHR*, 97 (1982), 481–503; G.W. Bernard, 'The Pardon of the Clergy Reconsidered', *JEH*, 37 (1986), 258–87.

When the smaller Northern Convocation convened to discuss the royal supremacy, the concept met with more resistance. Scarisbrick cites three separate protests, but there is direct evidence only of two.[61] The most important protest came in May 1531, when Cuthbert Tunstall, Bishop of Durham, defended a traditional theory that the king's temporal overlordship may not invade spiritual jurisdiction. If there are any doubts about the matter, such must be left to the judgment of mother church.[62] However, like the Southern Convocation, the Northern quickly capitulated. Thus, in 1531, the English clergy submitted to a vaguely defined royal supremacy in juridical matters, thereby receiving a royal pardon,[63] but nonetheless tried to maintain an ancient and crucial distinction between spiritualty and temporalty: the preserve of the clergy known as the cure of souls.

In his 1531 response to Tunstall and the Northern Convocation, Henry warned them to conform to the Southern Convocation. He claimed 'all spiritual things, by reason whereof may arise bodily trouble and inquietation, be necessarily included in a prince's power'.[64] The order and government of the church is, therefore, within the prince's prerogative. Against Tunstall's effort to distinguish the temporal and spiritual powers, Henry moved the goalposts of what was defined by the terms spiritual and temporal in his favor but he never firmly planted them elsewhere. Previously, *spiritualia* included preaching and the sacraments, as well as jurisdiction and government. Now, jurisdiction and government come under the heading of *temporalia*, which belong to the king as *supremum caput*, who in the tradition of Justinian has *cura ecclesiae* committed to him.[65]

As supreme head, Henry claimed he had a threefold power: first, the king licenses and assents to the election of bishops, but even after installation, they are still the king's subjects. Although he listens to their message from Christ, as soon as they cease speaking, the clergy immediately return to the status of private people. Second, all clerical goods are under his 'occasion and order'. Third, the church courts are delegated their jurisdiction by the king and he may 'punish adultery and insolence in priests as emperors have done'. Henry agreed that *spiritualia* include the sacraments and that Christ is the head of the clergy who minister them, but he refused to make a final distinction between *spiritualia* and *temporalia*. One may neither unduly separate nor conflate the

---

[61] The first protest is Tunstall's letter, the second is an unknown 'formal' complaint of the northern clergy, while the third is a document signed by a minority in the lower house. The third document, now residing in the Vienna archives, resulted in a series of *praemunire* charges and subsequent abject surrender. Scarisbrick, *Henry VIII*, 276–81.

[62] *Records of the Northern Convocation*, ed. by Dean Kitchin, Surtees Society 113 (Durham: Andrews, 1907), 217–18, 218–20; *Concilia*, III, 745.

[63] 22 Henry VIII, ch. 15.

[64] *Records of the Northern Convocation*, 225.

[65] *Records of the Northern Convocation*, 226.

terms. He ended his letter with a refusal to confine his headship *temporalibus,* reminding Tunstall the clergy had recently submitted to never assembling Convocation without his call.[66]

Henry probably had some help in formulating his theological response to Tunstall. Considering the rising star of the common lawyers, especially of Thomas Cromwell and Christopher St German, they seem likely candidates. Common lawyers often used the early Christological controversies to distinguish king from realm,[67] and Henry's response twice refers to the two natures of Christ. Earlier, he said 'subtile wit' has often used the indefinition of Scripture concerning Christ's *humanitas, substantia,* and *primogenitum* to trip up the orthodox. Later, Henry warned Tunstall not to forget that many words have two senses—for instance, *ecclesiam,* which can mean either universal church or Church of England—for such omissions led to the Arian heresy.[68] Moreover, in the same year in which Henry wrote to Tunstall, St German definitively affirmed that God gave Henry 'not only charge on the bodies, but also on the souls of his subjects'.[69] The royal theologian was reflecting the theology of the lawyers.

Against the scholarly consensus rooted in le van Baumer, it has now been shown that Henry rejected the attempts of the clergy to limit his sacerdotal powers or boost their own powers in 1531. Moreover, Henry affirmed the royal cure of souls to the very end of his reign. The preface to the 1536 *Ten Articles* speaks of 'cures appertaining unto this our princely office'.[70] In his offer of a pardon to the rebels involved in the Pilgrimage of Grace, Henry claimed to have 'the chief charge of you under God, both of your sowles and bodies'. Francis Bigod, an evangelical leader of the rebellion, denied this assertion as vehemently as his Romanist compatriots.[71] Henry reminded the bishops in a circular letter that 'it appertains especially to our office and vocation, unto whose order, cure and government it hath pleased almighty God to commit this part of his flock'.[72] In his 1538 corrections to the 1537 *Bishops' Book,* Henry amended the statement asserting the people are committed to the charge of bishops and preachers to read 'committed to our and their spiritual charge'.[73] Walter Ullmann tried to solve the dilemma of Henry's

---

[66] *Records of the Northern Convocation,* 231–2.

[67] Kantorowicz, *King's Two Bodies,* 14–19.

[68] Henry says Arius erred by not understanding that *Pater major me est* referred to Christ's *humanitas* while *Ego et Pater unum sumus* referred to Christ's *substantia. Records of the Northern Convocation,* 222, 230. Cf. Rowan Williams, *Arius: Heresy and Tradition* (London: Darton, Longman & Todd, 1987).

[69] *Doctor and Student,* 327.

[70] *Documents,* 163.

[71] Dickens, *Lollards and Protestants,* 92–108.

[72] PRO SP 1/101, fols 33–4; *L&P,* X, 45; Elton, *Policy & Police,* 244.

[73] Scarisbrick, *Henry VIII,* 414.

cure of souls by separating the priestly 'cure' from the royal 'care' for souls, but this distinction is anachronistic.[74]

Many scholars retrospectively apply a rigid division between temporal and spiritual, church and state to the early modern period, but such a separation is difficult to maintain. The king may not have administered the sacraments, but then again he did not need to do so, for he appointed others to these tasks. The crucial issue was whether he could claim divine approbation for his policies and act as he deemed best, whether or not this violated traditional sacramental theology. In a brilliant essay, Max Weber shows that natural leaders in turbulent situations often take on the attributes of a divine 'arbiter', in other words, a 'priest' or 'priestly lord'.[75] According to this Weberian thesis, Reformation England could be defined as being in a turbulent state, and Henry could be seen pushing his claim for charismatic authority to its limits. David Starkey says it was common belief that the king's very presence possessed a religious aura, a numinous metaphysical power that demanded reverence and could even be delegated. Henry, a strong opponent of what he considered superstitions and idolatries, never seems to have disputed this belief.[76] Gardiner said Henry continued blessing cramp rings to the end of his reign. Gardiner explicitly compared such royal invocations to the grace conferred on holy water blessed by the clergy.[77] Henry, like Richard II before him, used religious imagery to bolster his position. Richard II sang a collect before going to Ireland.[78] Henry, more than once, apparently in the role of a sub-deacon, helped offer the sacrament of the altar: at his coronation, after the example of Melchisedek, king and priest, and in Holy Week in 1539.[79] From early on, it appears that Henry was questioned about the sacramental consequences of his revolt against Rome. If not the pope, 'Who shall presume to give Orders, or Administer the Sacraments of the Church?'[80] Henry's answer to the first part of the question would have been himself; his answer to the second was whomever he delegated. Henry was a new David, a shepherd–king embodying both sacerdotal and regal powers.[81]

[74] Ullmann, 'Realm of England', 192.

[75] 'The Sociology of Charismatic Authority', in *From Max Weber: Essays in Sociology*, transl. by H.H. Gerth and C. Wright Mills (London: Routledge & Kegan Paul, 1948), 245–52.

[76] David Starkey, 'Representation through intimacy', in *Tudor Monarchy*, 47–51.

[77] Gardiner to Ridley, February 1547. *The Letters of Stephen Gardiner*, ed. by James Arthur Muller (CUP, 1933), 259–62.

[78] *Coronation Order of James*, xli.

[79] 'I was told by those of the King's chapel and by Kellegrew that upon Good Friday last the King crept to the cross from the chapel door upwards devoutly *and served the priest to mass that same day*, his own person kneeling on his Grace's knees' (my italics). John Worth to Lord Lisle, May 1539; *L&P*, XIV, i, 967.

[80] 'A Speech made at the Council-Board, on King Henry the Eight, taking upon him the Supremacy in Ecclesiastical Affairs', in *A Third Collection of Scarce and Valuable Tracts*, ed. by Lord Somers (London, 1751), 6–7.

[81] King, *Tudor Royal Iconography*, 59.

A series of seventeen questions put to some prelates in 1540 shows a continuing interest in royal priesthood. The origin of these questions has been debated but it seems that Henry, Cranmer, and Cromwell participated in their origination, distribution, and collation.[82] They indicate a royal search for emergency sacerdotal power. The questions begin with the general definition of a sacrament and move into the king's power to ordain or preach. Cranmer's answers blend both evangelical and Erastian elements. In answer to question nine, Cranmer responds, 'All Christian princes have committed unto them immediately of God the whole cure of all their subjects, as well concerning the administration of God's word for the cure of souls, as concerning the ministration of things political and civil governance.' Answering the thirteenth, Cranmer not only allowed the king to preach but made it a requirement.[83] In his own rejoinder to a response that confirmation, the laying on of hands by the bishop after baptism, is grounded in Scripture, Henry, always suspicious of any power he could not exercise, retorted, 'Laying on of hands being an old ceremony, is but a small proof of confirmation'.[84]

In the 1543 *King's Book*, kings are given 'the cure and oversight of all the people'. In his famous 1545 oration to Parliament, Henry claimed God appointed him 'vicar and high minister' over both clergy and laity. He is the 'soul of the whole kingdom' and must 'animate, rule and save' his people. All powers, sacerdotal and juridical, flow down through himself and are only 'lent' to the clergy and the lay magistrates.[85] This new understanding of the monopolization of authority within the crown was represented visually through royal portraiture created for governmental circles, and through woodcuts in the Coverdale Bible and the Great Bible intended for widespread distribution. The title page for the Great Bible presented Henry, in the words of one scholar, 'as a second Christ', who passes the divine authoritative word 'down to preachers and magistrates who call upon all to seek peace and obey rulers' [see Plate 5]. Kevin Sharpe describes this change in the representation of the king as a 'revolution in royal portraiture' that was intended to meet 'the need to sacralize secular authority and the person of the monarch'.[86] The royal

---

[82] The final answers to these questions can be fixed to somewhere between 17 September and 29 December 1540 as Thirlby is 'elect of Westminster'. A rumor attributes the questions to Henry VIII, who replied to the respondents. *The Work of Thomas Cranmer*, ed. by G.E. Duffield (Appleford: Sutton Courtenay Press, 1964), 24n. Strype, Cox, and Duffield attribute the drafts to Cranmer. Cox, II, 115n. The Spanish Ambassador said Cromwell summoned certain bishops before the council to question them on the king's ability to make and break bishops. *L&P*, VIII, 121.

[83] Cox, II, 116–17.

[84] Burnet, III, Records, 167.

[85] *Formularies*, 286; Scarisbrick, *Henry VIII*, 386; *Journals of the House of Lords*, 10 vols (London: 1771?), I, 128–9; *A&M*, V, 535; Guy, 'Tudor Monarchy', 83.

[86] Kevin Sharpe, *Selling the Tudor Monarchy: Authority and Image in Sixteenth-Century England* (YUP, 2009), xxviii, 131, 141.

priest, exercising his cure of all the souls in England, was thenceforth alive and well to the end of Henry's days.

Cranmer and other reformers carried the concept into Edward's reign. Like Cranmer in Edward's coronation sermon, Latimer referred to Edward as 'God's high Vicar in earth' and 'God's high minister'.[87] Edward, Cranmer's godson, believed he should advance the Protestant faith with the sword, 'For there is nothing better nor more excellent nor more just in the cause of war than when religion itself is involved'.[88] Yet, Edward's interests were not confined to the merely temporal. MacCulloch has demonstrated the young king's lively interest in religious matters.[89] In a French-language tract, Edward attacked the pope for being *vicare de Belzebub, lieutenant de Lucifer, et le diable terreste*.[90] Christ did not send a great bishop to rule in his stead; rather, he appointed *ses lieutenans*, the kings, to whom he gave all spiritual and temporal authority on earth.[91]

THE REFORMATION PARLIAMENT

The anticlerical complaints noted by Hall in the 1529 session of Parliament constituted only the first act in a dramatic battle between the House of Commons and Convocation, which witnessed its second act in the 1532 session. There were two legislative fronts concerning religion in the 1532 session, against the Pope through his revenues, and against the English church through its jurisdiction. In relation to the latter, Henry arbitrated between lay reformers in the Commons and conservative clergy in Convocation, wresting power from both.[92] Igniting this conflict were concerns about the burning of heretics. Although heresy trials continued during the early Reformation, there were no burnings between 1518 and 1531.[93] But a series of burnings surrounded the parliamentary session that began in January 1532. Thomas More orchestrated these events and, considering his infamous distaste for the

---

[87] *Sermons by Hugh Latimer*, ed. by George Elwes Corrie (PS, 1844), 204.

[88] *Nulla enim est melior nec praestantior nec magis legitimas causa belli, quam ipsa religio existit. Literary Remains of Edward*, 125.

[89] *Tudor Church Militant*, 21–3.

[90] *Literary Remains of Edward*, 194–6.

[91] *Literary Remains of Edward,*, 192–3.

[92] G.R. Elton, 'The Commons' Supplication of 1532', in *Studies*, II, 107–36. Elton was corrected for ascribing too much initiative to 'the government' in these proceedings. J.P. Cooper, 'The Supplication against the Ordinaries Reconsidered', *EHR*, 72 (1957), 616–41; and M.J. Kelly, 'The Submission of the Clergy', *TRHS*, 5th series, 15 (1965), 97–119. Elton narrowed his ascription of initiative to the rising, though not yet ascendant, star of Cromwell in *Reform and Reformation*, 150–5.

[93] Cooper, 'Supplication Reconsidered', 622; *A&M*, IV, 623.

doctrine, it is instructive that he claimed Henry was keen to persecute the heretics, and this as late as June 1533.[94] This led to the 'Supplication of the Commons' of 18 March 1532.[95]

The preamble of 'Supplication' claims the battle between spiritualty and temporalty is being caused on the one hand by 'new fantastical and erroneous opinions' in various books and on the other hand by the 'uncharitable behaviour and dealing' of the clergy. This led to a great 'inquietation, vexation, and breach' of the king's peace. The Commons, therefore, beseeched the king to curb the church's ability to make laws without the knowledge and assent of king and laity. There are other complaints, for instance against 'parsons, vicars, curates, parish priests, and other spiritual persons having cure of souls', who exact money for dispensation of the sacraments. But their most vehement criticism concerns the heresy proceedings geared to obtaining a confession of heresy that may never have occurred, and this without the presentation of witnesses. In conclusion, the Commons requested Henry, as 'the only head, sovereign lord, protector, and defender of both the said parties', to formulate a remedy. The king is the one 'in whom and by whom the only sole redress, reformation, and remedy herein absolutely rests and remains'. Rome is completely ignored and the Commons assume the clergy must submit themselves to Henry's jurisdiction.

Henry passed 'Supplication' to the prelates. The clergy, however, were not in a receptive mood and William Warham, the ageing Archbishop of Canterbury, led a series of counter-moves, culminating in a bold verbal assault against the king in the House of Lords. Henry vowed revenge and Warham was charged with *praemunire*, but his death stalled any further retaliation.[96] 'Reply of the Ordinaries', partially crafted by Stephen Gardiner, was received by Henry on 27 April.[97] It claims the clergy are at peace with the laity as a whole but not with 'certain evil-disposed persons infected and utterly corrupt with the pestilent poison of heresy'. The clergy assure Henry their authority for making laws is 'grounded upon the Scripture and the determination of Holy Church', which must also be the basis of the king's temporal laws. They are willing to reform their laws if he will 'temper' his accordingly. While

---

[94] *Rex videtur adversus haereticos acrior quam Episcopi ipsi.* 'The king is seen to be keener against the heretics than the Bishops themselves.' *Opus Epistolarum Des. Erasmi Roterodami*, ed. by P.S. Allen *et al*, 12 vols (OUP, 1906–1958), X, 259.

[95] *Documents*, 51–6.

[96] Lehmberg, *Reformation Parliament*, 142–5.

[97] *Documents*, 57–70. Kelly believes Gardiner's opposition probably cost him Canterbury. Kelly, 'Submission of the Clergy', 111. The same has been said for John Longland. Margaret Bowker, *The Henrician Reformation* (CUP, 1981), 14. For a sampling of the clerical theology, see, 'That the bishops have immediate authority to make such laws as they shall think expedient for the weal of men's souls', and '*Clerici sunt exempti de jurisdictione laicorum, etiam de jure divino*'. *L&P*, V, 1020–1. Warham, Fisher, and Tunstall registered similar statements. *L&P*, V, 1247; VIII, 887.6; VIII, 819.

treating Henry courteously, they assert that granting him their juridical power 'dependeth not upon our will and liberty', and they 'may not submit the execution of our charges and duty, certainly prescribed by God, to your Highness's assent'. It is Henry's duty 'to maintain and defend such laws and ordinances as we, according to our calling and by the authority of God shall, for his honour, make'. As for the heresy trials, the problem is not with the spiritual courts but with 'abominable and erroneous opinions lately sprung up in Germany'.

As is widely known by Hall's report and the declaration of the clergy themselves, 'Reply of the Ordinaries' displeased the king. He called representatives from the Commons to appear before him on 11 May. To their surprise, Henry delivered the two oaths that the clergy swore, one to the king and one to the pope. He claimed the clergy were thereby only half his subjects and demanded the Commons 'invent some ordre, that we bee not thus deluded of our spirituall subjectes'.[98] Simultaneously, Henry delivered an ultimatum through prominent lay lords to Convocation in the form of three articles requiring the clergy to acknowledge his supreme jurisdiction over spiritual matters, submit all future canons to his assent, and agree to a committee of thirty-two for reforming the realm's ecclesiastical laws.[99] Finally, Henry claimed the power to call and prorogue Convocation at will. This elicited the comment of Chapuys, the Spanish ambassador, that the clergy were now lower than shoemakers, for the latter could at least convene at will and make their own laws.[100] On 15 May, *in verbo sacerdotii*, 'by the word of the priesthood', the clergy submitted their jurisdiction to the king. It is noteworthy that the clergy submitted their juridical power to the king alone, not to the king in Parliament. Though substantially buttressing the king's power, they omitted any mention of the Commons. Priests retained a vague spiritual power but it was shorn of any independent temporal teeth. One day after the submission of the clergy, Thomas More resigned and returned the Great Seal to Henry.

The 1533 Parliament opened with both crisis and opportunity at hand for Henry. Anne Boleyn was found with child and the king needed an immediate divorce from Catherine to assure his succession. With More's resignation and Warham's death, the way was open to bring in a more compliant leadership. More was replaced by Thomas Audley, and Thomas Cranmer was chosen as Warham's successor. Thomas Cromwell also rose to prominence, for it was his work to concisely summarize the concepts that were foreseen in the legal activities of Wolsey, then explored further by Cranmer and Foxe. Cromwell thus crafted for the English people that clear declaration of English

---

[98] Hall, *Chronicle*, 788; *Concilia*, III, 753–4.

[99] *Concilia*, III, 749; *The Anglican Canons 1529–1947*, ed. by Gerald Bray (Woodbridge: Boydell Press, 1998), xl.

[100] *L&P*, V, 1013; *CSPS*, IV, ii, 951.

independence from Rome, the Act of Appeals. Through at least eight drafts and four fragments, the Act of Appeals took shape under Cromwell's able leadership but with Cranmer's input as well.[101] In its final form, it made three great claims: the division of clergy and laity, the supreme headship of king over both, and the self-contained imperial nature of the English nation. In other words, 'the see of Rome', no longer styled 'the apostolic see', was robbed of any jurisdiction in England. As Scarisbrick notes, however, there was still an opportunity at this time for the papacy to retain some vague spiritual leadership in the midst of this 'English Gallicanism of a thorough kind'.[102] Through emphasizing clerical 'obedience' to the crown, the laity, as a consequence, claimed the power to authorize the clergy to administer the sacraments.[103] This last point became even more relevant in the consecration of Cranmer as Archbishop of Canterbury.

ROYAL ORDINATION

In medieval England, the pope, the cathedral chapter, and the crown shared responsibility for filling vacant episcopal sees. The crown normally nominated the bishop, the chapter voted on the candidate, and the pope approved or disapproved by issuing bulls for confirmation, or translation, and provision. In the latter part of the fifteenth century, the crown's desire was so taken for granted that it normally bestowed the temporalities of the see upon the candidate before confirmation or translation was approved by the papacy.[104] The new bishop or archbishop swore a comprehensive oath of fidelity to the pope at his consecration. Cranmer swore such an oath at his elevation to the see of Canterbury, an oath that became a major issue at his trial during the reign of Mary.[105] Although early moderns took such oaths extremely seriously, the claim of royal supremacy was also at play in Cranmer's elevation and he had to step carefully.

Cranmer himself was instrumental in the decline of papal supremacy and rise of the royal supremacy. Not only did he personally elevate the king's conscience above papal law in *Determinations*, as mentioned previously (see 'Henry's Conscience', pp. 128–31) but he probably had a hand in the preparation of *A Glasse of the Truthe* (1531), a popular summation of the unpublished *Collectanea Satis Copiosa*, which vaulted the doctrine of 'obedience' to the forefront of discussion. In this dialogue

---

[101] *Documents*, 78–83; Elton, *Studies*, II, 99–106; Lehmberg, *Reformation Parliament*, 161–81.
[102] The language slowly transitioned from 'Pope' to 'bishop of Rome' to 'Antichrist'. Scarisbrick, *Henry VIII*, 295.
[103] *Documents*, 80.
[104] Thompson, *English Clergy*, 15, 30, 38.
[105] Cox, II, 559–62. Summarized in Paul Ayris, 'God's Vicegerent and Christ's Vicar', in *C&S*, 119.

between a lawyer and a theologian, the ancient tradition of the Scriptures, the early fathers, the councils, and of 'most ancient popes', supported by certain 'blessed men' of today, was set against the 'private appetites, mixed with too much headiness and obstinacy' of more recent traditions. (Interestingly, the two condemnations of Wyclif at Constance are cited for support but only on the issue of the Levitical prohibition that stood at the center of Henry's theological case.)[106] The pope is still 'the Vicar of Christe', but he is capable of heresy, and if he issues commands and excommunications against the king, who has the support of God, then 'both the king, his spiritual and lay subjects also, should manfully in God withstand them'. Competing confessional themes are evident in this treatise. From the evangelical side comes the higher authority of Scripture against tradition and the placing of God's law above papal law. From the conservative side comes the authority of councils and popes. From the royalist side comes the due obedience owed by subjects to their prince and, according to Nicaea, the self-contained 'special jurisdiction or power within every province in ecclesiastical observations and deciding of causes'.[107]

Cranmer also probably helped in the 1531 reissue of an old French anticlerical tract, *Disputatio inter Clericum et Militem*. Translated by John Trevisa in the fourteenth century and circulated by the Lollards in the fifteenth, it was now retooled at the behest of Cromwell to propagandize royal power. The debate reveals the arguments used by either side for the spiritual invasion of temporal jurisdiction and the temporal invasion of the spiritual. When it became clear he was losing his argument, the character of 'Cleric' opted for a complete separation of jurisdictions, but 'Soldier' triumphantly ordered Cleric to 'aknowlege the kynge by his royall power to be aboue your lawes, customes, priuileges, and liberties'. Moreover, 'kynges ordeyned who shulde be priestes; but priests dyd not ordeyne who shuld be kynges'. Henry would soon embrace this tenet of royal ordination.[108] Soldier argued for disendowment of the clergy on the basis of the needs of the commonwealth. The church includes both clergy and laity, and the property of the church is for the needs of both. The king's will is explicitly claimed as always being intended for the profit of the commonwealth. The old dualism vividly gives way to an Erastian royal priesthood in this Cranmerian tract.[109] This doctrine of obedience, first

---

[106] Oxford University was ordered by Henry VIII to surrender the articles by which the University and the Council of Constance had condemned Wyclif. Edward Leighton presented these letters on 31 July 1530. *L&P*, IV, iii, 6546. If surrendered in their totality, they would contain the article on marriage and articles on the king as vicar of Christ and universal priesthood. For more on the condemnations, see Chapter 1, n. 101 of this book.

[107] *Records of the Reformation*, II, 385–421; Haas, 'Henry VIII's *Glasse of Truthe*', 358–60.

[108] Wyclif, *De Officio Regis*, 144–5.

[109] *Trevisa's Dialogus inter Militem et Clericum*, ed. by Aaron Jenkins Perry, EETS 167 (OUP, 1925), 36, 18–19, 28–9, 35; S.W. Haas, 'The *Disputatio inter Clericum et Militem*', *Moreana*, 14 (1977), 66–9.

introduced by Tyndale, became the characteristic theme of much government propaganda in the mid-1530s. Cranmer was knee-deep in the development of this new doctrine, the Henrician doctrine of obedience, by which he was careful to live until Mary's reign. As we shall see, in *De Vera Obedientia*, Gardiner joined with Cranmer to craft a clerical apologetic for obedience to the king, while Thomas Starkey and Richard Morison, humanist scholars in the employ of Thomas Cromwell, contributed lay apologetics.

At his consecration as Archbishop on 30 March 1533, Cranmer took what MacCulloch deemed a 'morally dubious' course in swearing papal obedience and then claiming such oaths did not override the law of God and loyalty to the crown. Apparently, the oath was formulated by a group of lawyers whose task was to appease Cranmer's conscience in receiving approbation from pope and king, rather than from king alone.[110] No doubt, this was the reason for his reluctance to occupy the office, but once convinced, he gave the king full credit for his calling.[111]

> I, Thomas Cranmer, renounce and utterly forsake all such clauses, words, sentences, and grants, which I have of the pope's holiness in his bulls of the archbishoprick of Canterbury, that in any manner was, is, or may be hurtful, or prejudicial to your highness, your heirs, successors, estate, or dignity royal: knowledging myself to take and hold the said archbishoprick immediately, and only, of your highness, and of none other. Most lowly beseeching the same for restitution of the temporalities of the said archbishoprick; promising to be faithful, true, and obedient subject to your said highness, your heirs and successors, during my life. So help me God and the holy evangelists![112]

Less than two weeks after that statement, Cranmer had the messy task of rendering judgment in favor of Henry's divorce. He wrote two letters seeking the king's permission for jurisdiction. The former letter, perhaps originally prepared by Cromwell, was amended by the king to make Cranmer even more subservient, but this was, in the opinion of Ridley, more for policy than for pride.[113] What was this royal policy? Amazingly, in both letters, Cranmer claimed his 'call' to the high office of primate and archbishop was given by 'Almighty God, and your grace'. Moreover, it is the king who defines the juridical duties of that office: 'that where the office and duty of the archbishop of Canterbury, by your and your progenitors' sufferance and grants, is to direct, order, judge, and determine causes spiritual in this your grace's realm.'

---

[110] *Cranmer*, 88–9.

[111] Cox, II, 216. Moreover, Henry, apparently under the influence of Anne Boleyn, was so keen on elevating Cranmer, a dark horse candidate with no previous high ecclesiastical office, that he lent him the substantial sum of £1000 on easy terms in order to bear the initial expenses and harried the papacy with threats in order to obtain the necessary bulls *post haste*. Jasper Ridley, *Thomas Cranmer* (OUP, 1962), 54–5.

[112] Cox, II, 460.   [113] Ridley, *Cranmer*, 59–60; *Cranmer*, 90–1. Cox, II, 237–9.

Finally, he may not exercise his office 'in the said weighty cause touching your highness, without your grace's favour and licence obtained in that behalf'. Henry added, significantly, 'and licence' to this clause.

The distinction between the continental reformed understanding of vocation to ministry and Cranmer's understanding of his vocation to Canterbury must be pointed out. Martin Luther maintained the calling to preach comes from above and below; that is, from God and the congregation. Although he later allocated this power to the superintendents appointed by those emergency bishops, the nobles (in reaction to the radical 'self-made preachers'), these ordered authorities acted on behalf of the congregation. The community was still the entity responsible for calling its ministers and might conceivably withdraw that calling.[114] John Calvin ascribed vocation to the ministry to the internal call of the Holy Spirit and to an external call. While there is 'no sure rule in this matter' of external call, the people must have a vote. Only after such a call should a minister be ordained; then other pastors must ordain him.[115] As opposed to the continental reformist understanding, Cranmer seems to be assigning his 'external call' or 'calling from below' to the king alone! Although this may sound strange, the early modern distinction between 'public' and 'private' allowed for one person to act on behalf of the whole community. The king's person, in a real sense, represented the realm as a whole. Reflecting this exalted view of royalty, Robert Barnes informed Luther, *Rex meus, regem meum*, Henry was his king from beginning to end.[116]

Cranmer received the pallium, that important symbol of archiepiscopal authority, from the papacy, and was consecrated by the Bishops of Lincoln, Exeter, and St Asaph. Thus, in one sense he was consecrated to his office by the ordained ministry of the church. But, in another sense, he was consecrated in St Stephen's, the royal chapel and a peculiar exempt from episcopal authority, and it was Henry's machinations that elevated him. To give definition to his claim over Cranmer, Henry, in his reply to Cranmer's submissive request, boldly declared, 'God and we have ordained [you] archbishop of Canterbury'. Henry was very clear in his assertion of calling and jurisdiction; indeed his response was strengthened to read that the Archbishop was allowed by the king to determine 'mere' spiritual causes, an adjectival reinforcement of the continually constricting scope of meaning applied to the word 'spiritual'.[117]

---

[114] *LW*, XL, 3–43, 263–320; XLIV, 129; XXX, 55. Brian A. Gerrish, 'Priesthood and Ministry in the Theology of Martin Luther', *CH*, 34 (1965), 404; Haendler, *Luther on Ministerial Office and Congregational Function*, 79–80.

[115] *Institutes of the Christian Religion* (1559), IV, iii, 13–15.

[116] This reference comes in Luther's preface to Barnes' *Articles of Faith*. Doernberg, *Henry and Luther*, 125.

[117] *Cranmer*, 91. 'Mere spiritual things' was a favorite of Christopher St German, which phrase is reputedly synonymous with the later definition of *potestas ordinis*. Baumer, *Early Tudor Theory of Kingship*, 78n.

Henry concluded, in consideration of the need to quieten the realm, 'albeit we, being your king and sovereign, do recognise no superior in earth, but only God, and not being subject to the laws of any other earthly creature; yet, because ye be under us, by God's calling and ours, the most principal minister of our spiritual jurisdiction, within this our realm', we 'do license you to proceed in the said cause'. Henry soon received his long-awaited divorce from Catherine, by Cranmer; had his marriage to Anne legally approved, by Cranmer; witnessed the coronation of his new queen, by Cranmer; and, acquired a conditional papal excommunication for himself, and Cranmer, whom he had just 'ordained'.

Four of the questions put forward by the trio of Cranmer, Cromwell, and Henry in 1540 concern the power of the king to 'make' or 'appoint' priests and bishops. Henry understood these questions in the sense of 'ordering'. Henry refused to distinguish between election and ordination, considering himself capable of exercising the sacramental power of orders. Drs Redmayn and Edgeworth[118] separated the king's power of 'Appoyntment' of a priest from the bishop's power of 'ordering wherin grace is conferred ... *per manuum impositionem cum oratione*'. Henry hotly retorted, 'Wer is thys distinction founde now sins you confesse that the appostyllys did occupate the won part, whych now you confesse belongyth to prynces, how can you prove that orderyng is only commyttyd to yon bysshoppes?'[119]

Cranmer agrees that the king can ordain priests and bishops but follows the evangelical line that denies an indelible character for the priesthood. 'And there is no more promise of God, that grace is given in the committing of the ecclesiastical office, than it is in the committing of the civil office.'[120] Romanist orders were traditionally understood as conferring 'powers' essential to the exercise of a 'cure', whilst Lutheran orders conferred the 'authority' to exercise powers already possessed as a result of the priesthood received at baptism.[121] In his annotation of Henry's 1538 corrections to the *Bishops' Book*, Cranmer adopted an evangelical definition. 'It is small difference between "cure" and "charge", but that the one is plain English, and the other is deducted out of the Latin'.[122] In his twelfth answer of 1540, the archbishop responded, 'In the new Testament, he that is appointed to be a bishop or a priest, needeth no consecration by the scripture; for election or appointing thereto is sufficient.'

---

[118] In a sermon preached in Mary's reign, Roger Edgeworth confined visible priesthood to the clergy and spiritualized the universal priesthood, according to the patristic hermeneutical rule, *de specie et genere*. *Sermons Very Fruitfull, Godly and Learned*, ed. by Janet Wilson (Cambridge: Brewer, 1993), 245–50.

[119] BL Cotton MS Cleopatra E, V, fol. 42ʳ; Burnet, III, Records, 168.

[120] Cox, II, 116.

[121] Ernest C. Messenger, *The Reformation, the Mass and the Priesthood*, 2 vols (London: Longmans, 1936–1937), I, 151.

[122] Cox, II, 94.

In this evangelical sense, the king certainly has the power to 'make' and 'appoint' bishops. If Henry is a medieval Erastian, Cranmer is an evangelical Erastian.[123]

Cranmer's eleventh answer must be carefully analyzed. 'A bishop may make a priest by the scripture, and so may princes and governors also, and that by the authority of God committed to them, and the people also by their election.' The people, 'before Christian princes were', commonly did 'elect' or 'choose' their priests. Is he saying anyone may make priests? Two interpretations have been put forward. First, MacCulloch says Cranmer believed the lack of proper authority in the early church was remedied by the appearance of Christian rulers. Cranmer denied a doctrine of apostolic succession, because the first Christians were in a transitional period, 'casting round to create makeshift structures of authority'.[124] The second interpretation says that Cranmer could have been saying that any of these methods might be followed. The determinative factor was the custom of the time or region, whatever the practice of the early church. The *Bishops' Book*, in which Cranmer took a great part and of which he approved, takes this second approach.[125]

It must be remembered that Cranmer was gently searching out the possibilities as an independent thinker for he stresses 'this is mine opinion and sentence at this present, which I do not temerariously define'. Later, after encountering some radical Anabaptists, he declared no man may minister publicly unless he is 'lawfully called and sent' by those 'who have public authority given unto them in the congregation' to do so. The focus is not on royal supremacy, apostolic succession, or congregationalism, but 'public authority'.[126] This public authority is supremely embodied in the king or the king's delegate, for he may both install and discipline bishops. Henry's public authority was used to justify his deprivation and execution of Fisher, in spite of the latter's indelible character.[127] After the promulgation of the *Six Articles* in 1539, Latimer and Shaxton resigned under pressure but were not deprived.[128]

This royal authority was even more baldly asserted to the English bishops at the beginning of Edward's reign. At the apparent request of Cranmer, the bishops were issued new commissions to exercise their powers, in a move parallel to the issuance of new letters patent to all temporal officials. The

---

[123] The other respondents were more conservative. Burnet, I, *Records*, 201–44.

[124] *Cranmer*, 278–9; MacCulloch, 'Archbishop Cranmer: Concord and Tolerance in a Changing Church', in *Tolerance and Intolerance in the European Reformation*, ed. by Ole Peter Grell and Robert Scribner (CUP, 1996), 201–2.

[125] *Formularies*, 112, 278.

[126] *Forty-Two Articles* (1553), art. 24; *Documents*, 298.

[127] 'A Declaration of the Faith, and a Justification of the Proceedings of King Henry VIII in matters of Religion', in Jeremy Collier, *An Ecclesiastical History of Great Britain*, new edn, ed. by Francis Barham, 9 vols (London: Straker, 1840–1841), IX, 172.

[128] David Loades, *The Oxford Martyrs* (Bangor: Headstart History, 1992), 49.

reasoning was that all authority, ecclesiastical and secular, originally flows from the king as supreme head.[129] The Privy Council decided this course on 6 February 1547 and Cranmer's commission was issued the next day, but Gardiner was kept on hold for over a month. Part of the problem was Gardiner's attitude towards the novelty of a commission with every new king. He complained in a letter to one of his former students and current representative of the council, William Paget, that he was called as an 'ordinary' (i.e. given his powers by reason of his consecration), but with the 'construction of a commission' he had been made 'but a delegate'. To add salt to the wound, the Protector restrained bishops from preaching.[130]

THE ROYAL JUDGMENT OF DOCTRINE

It is generally agreed that the Act in Restraint of Appeals was the legal watershed for the royal supremacy in the English church's separation from Rome and its juridical subordination to the king. What remained for Cromwell and Parliament in the 1534 sessions was the complicated task of enforcing it by statute and oath.[131] The Act in Restraint of Annates followed an earlier conditional restraint of the payment of English annates to the papacy, but this one reserved those payments for the crown. It also provided for a new method of episcopal and archiepiscopal election. The cathedral chapters are still required to hold elections, but they will now be served 'with a letter missive containing the name of the person which they shall elect and choose'. Thus, the crown received 'the initiative and the last word in appointments', the papacy no longer made provisions, and the cathedral chapter became a rubberstamp.[132] In Edward's reign, even the rubberstamp of *congé d'élire* was dispensed.[133] Whereas Luther in the early 1520s reserved election to the congregation in his discussions of universal priesthood, Parliament turned that power over to the king alone.

The Dispensations Act of 1534 abolished the lay payment of Peter's Pence to the papacy, assured Christendom of the English realm's Catholic faith, and assigned to the crown the authority to conduct monastic visitations.[134]

---

[129] *Acts of the Privy Council*, 6–7, 13–14; '*Commissio regia archiepiscopo Cantuar. ad exercendam suam jurisdictionem*', in *Documentary Annals of the Reformed Church of England*, ed. by Edward Carnell, 2 vols (OUP, 1844), 1–4.

[130] J.A. Muller, *Stephen Gardiner and the Tudor Reaction* (London: Macmillan, 1926), 145–51.

[131] Lehmberg, *Reformation Parliament*, 175.

[132] 25 Henry VIII, ch. 20, section 3; 23 Henry VIII, ch. 20; Elton, *Tudor Constitution*, 331. Cf. *L&P*, XII, ii, 408.

[133] 1 Edward VI, ch. 2.   [134] 25 Henry VIII, ch. 21.

A second Act for the Submission of the Clergy slightly redefined the commission for the revision of canon law.[135] A bill of attainder against Elizabeth Barton, the Holy Maid of Kent, and her conspirators put their executions on the fast track. Fisher and More were implicated but dropped from the bill; however, this did not prevent their prosecution under the newly passed Succession and Treasons Acts. This first Act on succession required an oath to be sworn, but when Fisher and More were called before Cranmer to do so, they refused. Cranmer wanted to let them swear by the Act apart from its preamble, which rejected papal supremacy and affirmed the divorce, but his request was denied and Fisher and More, the two most prominent English opponents of the Lutheran common priesthood, eventually became martyrs against the royal supremacy.[136]

The 1534 Act of Supremacy was the icing on the cake of royal supremacy and gave a lofty definition to the king's relation to the church. Not only is he 'Supreme Head of the Church of England', he is also 'the only Supreme Head on earth of the Church of England'. The theological precisionists are thereby assured that Christ is still celestial head of the church, but he is conveniently removed one step from the complex workings of time. Moreover, Henry is the head of the Church of England, not the universal church. In approbation, Cranmer issued an order affirming the new style and altering the traditional order in the bidding of the bedes. Previously, the worshipper repeatedly prayed in the order: church—pope—clergy—king—lords—commons. Now, the chain of supplication was altered to elevate the king above the clergy: Catholic Church—king—clergy—temporalty. Significantly, a layman had replaced the pope in the tradition of prayer. This was not the only liturgical change made by Cranmer, but it was a visible portent of future activity.[137]

The Act of Supremacy gave further definition to the king's juridical powers. The king 'shall have full power and authority from time to time to visit, repress, redress, reform, order, correct, restrain, and amend all such errors, heresies, abuses, offences, contempts, and enormities, whatsoever they be, which by any manner spiritual authority or jurisdiction ought or may lawfully be reformed, repressed, ordered, redressed, corrected, restrained, or amended'. Where Luther reserved the judgment of doctrine to the congregation, Parliament reserved such judgment to the King of England. Thus, one of Luther's most important defining characteristics of common priesthood, the last of the seven, judgment—which includes discernment, election, and discipline—was transferred by Parliament to the one lay-priest that really mattered, 'the

---

[135] 25 Henry VIII, ch. 19.

[136] 25 Henry VIII, ch. 22 and 26 Henry VIII, ch. 16; Cox, II, 285-6. *Cranmer*, 124-5; Lehmberg, *Reformation Parliament*, 194-6, 204-6; Ackroyd, *Life of More*, 350-4; Rex, *Theology of John Fisher*, 8-11.

[137] *Lay Folks Mass Book*, 61-80; Cox, II, 460; Duffy, *Stripping*, 124, 475. The royal chain came into the Litany without the purgatorial trappings of the bedes. *Liturgies*, 101-2, 233-4.

spiritual authority' in England, Henry VIII.[138] Cranmer, however, never gave Henry unmitigated freedom to determine doctrine. After refusing the monarchy's prerogative to determine conciliar doctrine in 1537, Cranmer boldly corrected Henry's marginal notes to the *Bishops' Book*.[139] And though he would eventually acquiesce to the king's decisions embodied in the *Six Articles* and the *King's Book*, he crafted careful responses to sway the king to his position, preserving his conscience on such issues as confession and transubstantiation.[140]

As we have seen, by reconfiguring the ancient doctrines of conscience, cure of souls, vicar of God, obedience, and ordination, Henry and Cranmer assigned to the king sacerdotal and juridical powers formerly reserved to the clergy. In only one arena, but in one very dear to the Archbishop, the judgment of doctrine, did Cranmer limit the king's priestly prerogative. It must now be examined how Henry's new priesthood could be related to the ministerial priesthood. Where are the limits of the king's priesthood? More importantly, can sacerdotal power also be claimed by magistrates under Henry? Are there any distinctions remaining between the lay and clerical priesthoods?

---

[138] 26 Henry VIII, ch. 1.
[139] Cox, II, 83–114. Chapter 6 of this book.
[140] Glyn Redworth, 'A Study in the Formulation of Policy', *JEH*, 37 (1986), 58–63.

5

Priestly Magistrates: Thomas Cromwell's Faction

Henry's invasion of clerical prerogative in the early 1530s has often been classified as concerned exclusively with juridical as opposed to spiritual matters. We have seen such a distinction is difficult to maintain; Henry distrusted any limitation of his powers. The fight against the papacy broke down old walls between clergy and laity, but Henry hesitated before constructing new ones. This royal equivocation engendered confusion concerning the proper relationship between the temporal and spiritual orders, and led to some interesting debates over the nature of priesthood. These debates were brought to a climax in the persons of Thomas Cromwell and Thomas Cranmer. Cranmer tried to forge a new position for the clergy in the midst of this theological turmoil. On the one hand, he affirmed the ministerial priesthood as necessary. On the other, he redefined it in terms of evangelical vocation.

Before considering Cranmer's theology of ministerial priesthood, the pressure put on the clergy by the lay faction affiliated with Cromwell must be considered. In Reformation historiography, it is typical to speak of two factions operating in the royal court: evangelicals and conservatives. It is assumed that Cranmer was the junior partner in a fairly amicable relationship with Cromwell.[1] The relationship between Cranmer and Cromwell was, however, strained at points. Ralph Morice reports that Cromwell told Cranmer that Henry would never hear a complaint against the Archbishop, even when those complaints originated with Cromwell himself.[2] We are never told the nature of those complaints, but, considering Cromwell's 'grudge against the clergy',[3] it may have been simply because of his prelatical status, or perhaps Cromwell knew Cranmer was not as committed an Erastian as he appeared, especially when it

---

[1] Dickens, *English Reformation*, 192–221; Joseph S. Block, *Factional Politics and the English Reformation 1520–1540* (Woodbridge: Boydell Press, 1993); Rory McEntegart, *Henry VIII, The League of Schmalkalden and the English Reformation* (Woodbridge: Boydell Press, 2002).

[2] *Narratives of the Reformation*, 258–9.

[3] B.W. Beckingsale, *Thomas Cromwell: Tudor Minister* (London: Macmillan, 1978), 20. Elton said Beckingsale's biography was judicious but lacks original research.

came to the definition of doctrine. Moreover, Cranmer was not above refusing Cromwell's attempts at disendowment and preferment.[4] As we shall see, the debate over the definition of doctrine became acrimonious when the clergy around Cranmer and the magistrates[5] around Cromwell weighed in with their views. Among Cromwell's manuscripts are various works prepared for the 1536 session of the Reformation Parliament. These manuscripts questioned the very necessity for a distinct class of clergy, and the clergy were forced to respond to that query.

LAY HEADS OF THE ENGLISH CHURCH

Although Henry was now head of the English church by name, in statute, oath, and popular prayer, with powers of jurisdiction, election, doctrine, and visitation, his headship lacked implementation. It was Cromwell's privilege to enforce the powers of the royal priest. In January 1535, Cromwell was given the office of vicegerent or vicar-general—the titles are synonymous, but the latter borrows directly from a recognized ecclesiastical office. Bishops appointed vicars-general to run day-to-day affairs in the diocese in the former's absence; Henry, 'lay-bishop', appointed his own national representative, also a layman, to handle ecclesiastical affairs.[6] Cromwell's fullest title was *vicegerens vicarius generalis ac commissarius specialis et principalis*,[7] and as is well-known, he zealously shepherded the church's doctrinal synods, dissolved the monasteries, and policed the clergy. Joseph Block demonstrates how he also created a subservient shadow episcopate through appointing at least thirteen suffragan bishops.[8]

As vicegerent, Cromwell freely appointed his representative, Dr William Petre, a layman of less than thirty years, to oversee the bishops in his absence. A doctor of civil law, Petre submitted early proposals for a reorganization of ecclesiastical jurisdiction.[9] Then, in June 1536, Petre successfully defended his right to sit in Cranmer's place during Convocation, due to his derivative charge to office through Cromwell. Petre also managed probate for larger estates in the ecclesiastical courts. Although the official vicegerency ceased

---

[4] Cranmer to Cromwell, 7 May 1533 and 21 January 1539; Cox, II, 240–1, 388–9.

[5] 'Magistrates' were the mediating officials between king and people. Erasmus, *Education of a Christian Prince*, 91–3.

[6] Hamilton, *English Clergy*, 46–8; Elton, *Tudor Constitution*, 333. Cromwell's office has been divided between a 'visitational vicegerency', January 1535–July 1536, and a 'full vicegerency', July 1536–June 1540. F. Donald Logan, 'Thomas Cromwell and the Vicegerency in Spirituals: A Revisitation', *EHR*, 103 (1988), 658–67.

[7] BL Cotton MS Cleopatra F, II, fol. 132[r].

[8] *Factional Politics*, 117–25.   [9] C.S. Knighton, 'Sir William Petre,' ODNB.

with Cromwell's death in 1540, Petre retained the seal *ad causas ecclesiasticas* for the Privy Council during Edward's reign, wielding powers of visitation.[10] Petre, though not vicegerent in name, was vicegerent in deed.

Cranmer encountered great difficulties during his first metropolitical visitations in 1534 and 1535. Normally, when an archbishop visited a diocese within his province, episcopal powers were inhibited. John Stokesley of London, Richard Nix of Norwich, John Longland of Lincoln, and Stephen Gardiner of Winchester protested Cranmer's visitation and refused his inhibitions, alleging that Canterbury's relationship to the royal supremacy was not defined. Cranmer, exasperated by his encounter with Gardiner's *realpolitik*, complained in Tyndalian terms when he wrote, 'But I would that I, and all my brethren the bishops, would leave all our styles, and write the style of our offices, calling ourselves *apostolos Jesu Christi*: so that we took not upon us the name vainly, but were so even indeed.' Cranmer, however, unlike Tyndale, was not denying the office of bishop but unworthy occupancy, especially by non-preachers, of that office.[11]

To settle the conflict, Cromwell intervened, issuing letters of inhibition to both archbishops and their respective provincial bishops. The episcopal powers of ordination and confirmation, inter alia, were immediately suspended. These inhibitions preempted the bishops from reckoning they received their jurisdiction 'from elsewhere, than from the kings highnes'.[12] Licenses were then issued by Cromwell or Henry to reinstate those powers. This maneuver left little doubt as to where ultimate authority resided in the new ecclesiastical structure.[13] Margaret Bowker says of the bishops, 'All their powers had, during this period, been demonstrated as emanating from the king alone to be given or taken away according to his pleasure.' Bishops were henceforth 'civil servants'. Weakened by the inability to appeal outside the realm by the break with Rome, the clergy succumbed to temporal power.[14] In effect, a leading cleric, the Primate of All England, was superseded by three laymen: king, vicegerent, and vicegerential representative.

Although Henry was nigh impossible to refuse, the vicegerent was another matter. Cromwell's practice of sitting at the highest place in synod certainly raised the ire of conservative clergy[15] and he was not above wrangling with

---

[10] F.G. Emmison, *Tudor Secretary: Sir William Petre at Court and Home* (London: Phillimore, 1961), 8–9; C.J. Kitching, 'The Probate Jurisdiction of Thomas Cromwell as Vicegerent', *BIHR*, 46 (1973), 102–6. *Acts of the Privy Council*, II, 33, 114–15, 148.

[11] Cranmer to Cromwell, 12 May 1535; Cox, II, 304–6.

[12] Thomas Legh and John ap Rice to Cromwell, 24 September 1535; Strype, V, 540.

[13] Ayris, 'God's Vicegerent and Christ's Vicar', 122–30; *Cranmer*, 130–5.

[14] Bowker, 'The Supremacy and the Episcopate: The Struggle for Control, 1534–1540', *HJ*, 18 (1975), 227–43. *Concilia*, III, 797; Cox, II, 463. Cf. Bonner's 'strange commission'. Burnet, I, I, 267; I, ii, 184–6.

[15] 'But this is true that of certain of the Clergie he was detestably hated ... for in ded he was a man that in all his doynges semed not to fauor any kynde of Popery, nor could not abide the

evangelicals either. By his very position,[16] Cromwell was at the forefront of a decline in ecclesiastical jurisdiction and the partial but substantial disendowment of the English church. What drove Cromwell to his task? Was he thoroughly anticlerical? Did he embrace a Lollard or Lutheran conception of universal priesthood?[17] The 1540 Act of Attainder resulting in his execution charged him with several instances of disobedience, even treason, against Henry. Religiously, the most damaging articles concerned his dispersing heretical books, licensing heretical preachers, and claiming 'It was as Lawful for every Christian man to be the Minister of that Sacrament, as a Priest'.[18] This otherwise unsupported accusation must be received skeptically, yet there may be some truth behind the accusation of common priesthood. The related, if spurious, charge of sacramentarianism was thrown in for its guttural appeal to one of Henry's few remaining orthodoxies.

It is difficult to pinpoint Cromwell's religious beliefs since he kept relatively mum about them. This has led to diverse scholarly opinions: Merriman said he believed 'absolutely nothing when disconnected from political ends'.[19] Elton disagreed. At first, he classified Cromwell as neither atheist nor agnostic but firm adherent of 'logical Erastianism'. Later, he conceded that Cromwell might have embraced evangelicalism.[20] McConica ranks him among the proponents of Erasmian humanism.[21] Brigden cites his connections with radical preachers but concludes Henry 'wrongly' believed he was a sacramentary.[22] After reviewing Cromwell's personal documents and the literature of associates, Lehmberg concludes he was neither Anabaptist, Lutheran, nor sacramentarian, but an 'eclectic and pragmatic' proponent of reformation and above all 'the doctrine of "the mean"', a reference to the much-vaunted conceptions of

---

snoffyng pride of some prelates, wiche vndoubtedly, whatsoeuer els was the cause of his death, did shorten his life and procured the end that he was brought vnto.' Hall, *Chronicle*, 838–9.

[16] In 1536, 'also Mr Secretorye, Lord Prevaye Seale, was made High Vycar over the Spiritualtye under the Kinge, and satt diverse tymes in the Convocation howse amonge the byshopps as headd over them.' Charles Wriothesley, *A Chronicle of England During the Reigns of the Tudors*, ed. by William Douglas Hamilton, 2 vols (London: Camden Society, 1875–1877), I, 52.

[17] For detailed treatment of Cromwell's career, see Elton, *Studies, passim*; Elton, *Policy and Police*; Elton, *Reform and Renewal: Thomas Cromwell and the Common Weal* (CUP, 1973); Block, *Factional Politics*. The better biographies include Dickens, *Thomas Cromwell and the English Reformation*; Beckingsale, *Thomas Cromwell*; Elton, *Thomas Cromwell* (Bangor: Headstart History, 1991).

[18] Burnet, I, ii, 187–92.

[19] Roger Bigelow Merriman, *Life and Letters of Thomas Cromwell*, 2 vols (OUP, 1902), I, 86–8, 301.

[20] Elton, *Studies*, I, 206; Elton, *Reform and Renewal*, 36; Elton, *Reform and Reformation: England 1509–1558* (London: Edward Arnold, 1977), 171.

[21] McConica, *English Humanists*, 150–99.

[22] Susan Brigden, 'Popular Disturbance and the Fall of Thomas Cromwell, 1539–1540', *HJ*, 24 (1981), 257–78.

via media and *adiaphora*.[23] Most recently, McEntegart, carefully reviewing the ample diplomatic archives on both sides of the channel, pictured Cromwell as a careful politician driven primarily by a sincere evangelical faith.[24]

This writer believes Cromwell's religious affiliation combined aspects of humanism, Lutheranism, and Erastianism; he is definitely more Lutheran than has often been acknowledged. Aside from McEntegart's research into the diplomatic evidence, this can be seen in Cromwell's support for vernacular Scripture and the dissolution of the monasteries, and in his views of orders, vocations, and sacraments. First, through his various injunctions, and his personal efforts at publication, the Vicegerent did more to promote the availability of an English Bible than any other individual.[25] Cranmer, stymied by episcopal foot-dragging, assured Cromwell he would have 'a perpetual laud and memory' among the saints for his diligence to set forth God's Word in a form the people might understand.[26] Vernacular Scripture was a major tenet of Lollardy, humanism, and Lutheranism. Henry approved it because he believed, perhaps naively, it would bring obedience.[27]

Second, the dissolution of monasteries, friaries, and nunneries that began in 1536 and culminated in 1540 was ably managed by Cromwell.[28] On the continent, Huldrych Zwingli made the brotherhood of all believers, as opposed to the brotherhood of the few, a major platform in Zurich's Reformation. Luther, too, complained against these cloistered violators of common priesthood.[29] In England, Cromwell's theological attack against monasticism was soldiered by preachers such as Hugh Latimer. Latimer equated monk and mass with 'purgatory pick-purse'. Christians are justified by faith, not masses.[30] Through the dissolutions Cromwell and his faction rid England of this ancient life of perfection, a form of life that, according to the reformation world view, robbed the laity of true faith by denying evangelical perfection to the people.

---

[23] Lehmberg, 'The Religious Beliefs of Thomas Cromwell', in *Leaders of the Reformation*, ed. by Richard L. DeMolen (London: Associated University Presses, 1984), 134–52.

[24] McEntegart, *Henry VIII and the League of Schmalkalden*, 223.

[25] *Documents*, 175–83.

[26] Cranmer to Cromwell, 4, 13, and 28 August 1537; Cox, II, 344–7.

[27] Rex, *Henry and the Reformation*, 104–32.

[28] G.W.O. Woodward, *The Dissolution of the Monasteries* (Andover, Hampshire: Pitkin, 1975).

[29] 'Sixty-seven Articles', in Huldrych Zwingli, *Writings*, ed. by E.J. Furcha (Allison Park, Pennsylvania: Pickwick, 1984), art. 27. Monks 'divide the Christian life into a state of perfection and imperfection. To the common people they ascribe a life of imperfection; to themselves, a life of perfection.' 'They not only think that their obedience, poverty and chastity are certain roads to salvation, but that their ways are more perfect and better than those of the rest of the faithful. This is an open, obvious lie, and an error and sin against the faith.' 'Judgment of Martin Luther on Monastic Vows' (1521), in *LW*, XLIV, 262, 285.

[30] Blench, *Preaching in England*, 264, 266–7; Kreider, *English Chantries*, chs 4–5.

Third, Cromwell's doctrine of vocation was both Henrician and Lutheran. He received his office from Henry and never lost sight of that fact.[31] The Lutheran delegation of 1538 noted his sympathy with them but also that he would move no faster than Henry.[32] In a cover letter to Henry's 1536 circular, Cromwell reminded the bishops of his 'office' to implement reformation as 'eye to the prince'.[33] In his argument with Nicholas Shaxton, evangelical Bishop of Salisbury, Cromwell defended his decision to overrule the latter in a case of ecclesiastical preferment by employing Lutheran terminology. Decrying Shaxton's inappropriate interpretation of Scripture, Cromwell consistently compares 'my calling' and 'myn office' with 'your call', 'your office', and 'your duetie'. He believes his office is a direct gift of God; as a divine instrument, he uses his office for 'edification' rather than destruction. He concludes, 'To take a controuersie owt of your handes into myne, I do but myn office, yow meddle farder then youres woll bear yow, thus ruffely to handle me for vsing of myne.'[34] That he compares his calling with, even elevating it above, that of a bishop suggests a Lutheran view of vocation.[35] Luther alleged God gave a vocation to all Christians, and that whatever office one fulfilled it had the same dignity in the sight of God as any other.[36] Cromwell agreed.

PROPAGANDA THROUGH PULPIT AND PAMPHLET

Part of Cromwell's task in reforming the church involved setting the new ideas before the public. It is through such propaganda and corroborating statements from contemporaries that the laity's two-pronged strategy—to promote the king's supremacy and to corner the clergy—may be discerned. The first part of his propaganda strategy was to coordinate preaching in support of royal supremacy, through elevating reform-minded clerics. Block notes that Cromwell's patronage of quiescent preachers and administrators within the church was so powerful that 'No man before or after enjoyed such control over ecclesiastical appointments'.[37] But the clergy also needed direction in what to proclaim from their pulpits. In Cromwell's papers are found four copies of

---

[31] Bernard, 'Making of Religious Policy', 339–47.

[32] *Life and Letters*, I, 279.

[33] *Life and Letters*, II, 111–13.

[34] *Life and Letters*, II, 128–31. Cf. Shaxton to Cromwell. Strype, V, 546–53.

[35] Cromwell also retained his rights as the Dean of Wells. Lehmberg, *The Later Parliaments of Henry VIII 1536–1547* (CUP, 1977), 109.

[36] Gustav Wingren, *The Christian's Calling*, transl. by Carl C. Rasmussen (London: Oliver and Boyd, 1957).

[37] *Factional Politics*, 83, 94–106.

one exemplary sermon for the royal supremacy, described as 'By the king', which such clergy were to preach.[38] The author remains anonymous but the title may indicate a royal provenance.

The sermon begins by praising the means of preaching, and by affirming the power of kings to choose and appoint who will fill the preaching offices of priest and bishop. Princes 'may put oute the olde and make new, for where ought princes to be more vigilant then here, in the chosing of the good and the desposing of the evell'. The prince appoints and deposes bishops just as he appoints and deposes judges. The parallel between bishops and priests on the one hand, and judges and common lawyers on the other, is developed. 'They bothe are the ministers of a Christen king.' Bishops and priests are as much the king's 'deputies' as are judges.[39] The king is comparable to Moses, Saul, and Solomon, who appointed priests and lawyers as his deputies. Appealing to Matthew 18, the writer says laymen may bring their neighbors before the congregation for discipline. And yet, 'seeyng the damiges that myght folow if it shulde be Lawfull for every brabeling ffelow accuse openly whome he Lusted', kings have restrained this liberty and appointed priests to that task.[40] Yet, the priests need to beware that the king, through his magistrates, monitors their preaching. Whoever reads the Bible will discover all good kings were thus 'greate teachers of the people'.[41] Through sermons such as these, through his detailed injunctions, and through his policing activities, Cromwell turned the local parish into a governmental unit in which preachers disseminated the court's official policy and local magistrates monitored preachers.[42]

The second part of Cromwell's propaganda strategy was to patronize lay scholars to further the supremacy, assuring the availability of carefully crafted works, in both sermonic and prose form and providing a legal and moral basis for lay headship.[43] Many of the propagandists in Cromwell's employ or of his acquaintance demonstrated expertise in either common law or civil law, and this non-canonical legal expertise supported their defense of royal supremacy alongside lay leadership within that supremacy. Among these scholars, as among Henrician government leaders generally, there was a spectrum of religious opinion. Some scholars were more conservative in their outlook, such as Thomas Starkey, Sir Thomas Elyot, Christopher St German, and Jasper Fyloll; others were more evangelical, including Sir Richard Morison, Richard Taverner, and Christopher Mont; yet others, including Sir Thomas Audley and Sir William Paget, were, like Cromwell and Petre, governmental

---

[38] 'As ther be many things whiche at the begynnyng war well instituted'. PRO SP 6/7, fols 159–63; SP 6/8, fols 100–8; SP 6/8, fols 153–5; SP 6/8, fols 157–9. *L&P*, VII, 1384.

[39] PRO SP 6/8, fol. 157.

[40] PRO SP 6/8, fols 158ᵛ–159ʳ.

[41] PRO SP 6/8, fol. 159ᵛ.

[42] Block, *Factional Politics*, 115–17, 136; Elton, *Policy and Police*, 239–43.

[43] Elton, *Policy and Police*, 171–210; 233–5.

movers and shakers rather than scholars. All were laymen within Cromwell's reforming circle and all possessed keen legal minds.

Some of the scholars patronized by Cromwell in the 1530s first garnered attention in the events surrounding the foundation of Wolsey's college at Oxford in the 1520s. Starkey, Morison, and Taverner probably first came to Cromwell's notice at this time, and later were instrumental in Cromwell's print campaign. More radical clerical scholars in the 1520s, including John Frith, Thomas Garrett, and John Clerk, though preserved through the moderate policies of Wolsey, failed to merit Cromwell's patronage in the next decade.[44] The pool of scholars who wrote pamphlets under Cromwell's direction consisted of conservatives and evangelicals, laity and clergy. The common factor for such high patronage was utility in the promotion of the royal supremacy,[45] but the subtext was Cromwell's lay and evangelical preferences, as demonstrated in the propaganda he gathered and disseminated. While Henry's clerical supporters merit our consideration, of equal importance are the highly competent laypeople within Cromwell's circle.

Thomas Starkey, a well-known recipient of Cromwell's largesse, has been credited with laying 'the foundations of English polity'.[46] Educated in Oxford and on the continent, where he studied civil law and humanities, Starkey's primary contribution was to formulate a restrictive doctrine of 'thinges indifferent' that granted the government authority to define religious matters. Starkey pursued the overarching goal of 'unitie' through 'obedience' to the government, a government that would seek 'the meane' between the 'sedition' of the papists on the one hand and 'heresie' on the other. Warning against the problem of lack of unity, Starkey raised the specter of events in Germany, where 'all turned up so downe'.[47] What makes Starkey's doctrine of *adiaphora* different from that of Martin Luther and Philip Melanchthon is that the latter emphasized the freedom of the Christian man.[48] Departing from the Lutheran emphasis, Starkey insists throughout his government-approved pamphlet on unity and obedience that things indifferent are within the freedom of the government, for Henry is 'the chyefe offycer and mynyster here under Christe'.[49] After his friend Reginald Pole rounded violently upon

---

[44] W. Gordon Zeeveld, *Foundations of Tudor Policy* (London: Methuen, 1969), 22–38. On Wolsey's policy of charity toward errant scholars, see Craig W. D'Alton, 'The Suppression of Lutheran Heretics in England, 1526–1529', *JEH*, 54 (2003), 228–53.

[45] Elton, *Policy and Police*, 182.

[46] Zeeveld, *Foundations of Tudor Policy*, 90.

[47] Thomas Starkey, *An Exhortation to the people, instructynge theym to Unitie and Obedience* (London: Thomas Berthelet, 1536), 'To the Reders.'

[48] Thomas F. Mayer, 'Starkey and Melanchthon on Adiaphora: A Critique of W. Gordon Zeeveld', *SCJ* 11 (1980), 39–50.

[49] Starkey, *An Exhortation to the people*, fol. Ii^r.

Henry, Starkey fell from favor and turned to emphasizing the consent of the nobility.[50]

Mirroring Starkey, Cromwell's common law colleagues in the government likewise utilized the language of 'the mean'. Thomas Audley, a common lawyer from the Inner Temple and a serjeant-at-law, became Lord Chancellor after More's surrender of the office in 1532. In 1540, Audley exhorted parliament to work for concord, 'declining neither to the right nor the left, but with one unified viewpoint sincerely prescribing according to the pure Word of God and the gospel'. Unity would be found in the vernacular Bible, as interpreted officially by the government, which was competent to deny 'impious and irreverent' interpretations.[51] Although not religiously radical himself, against Gardiner, who advocated clerical jurisdiction, Audley defended the priority of the common law and parliament over the church. Audley warned the Bishop of Winchester in a private conversation that *praemunire* would continually be maintained as a means of restricting clerical authority.[52] Similarly, Gardiner once noted that Sir William Paget, a friend of Cromwell's from Gray's Inn and later a member of Henry's Privy Council and secretary to three queens, said he loved 'noe extremites and the meane is best'. The controversy, therefore, between the clergy and leading laity was not over the doctrine of the mean but its definition.[53]

The educated laity's ability to oppose clerical pretensions was firmly rooted in the common law tradition advocated within the Inns of Court. The stages of the lawyers reinforced these controversial views, as glimpsed when Simon Fish was compelled to flee the country after he mocked Wolsey at Gray's Inn. 'The masques of the Inns of Court prolonged the myth of a sacred, mystical body by presenting lawyers as "Heroes Deified for their Vertues" and the judiciary as "Jupiters Priests".' The mythical status of a lawyerly priesthood, rooted in medieval sacerdotal metaphors, began to wane only in the seventeenth century,[54] by which time the Enlightenment was diminishing the power of the sacred anyway. Cromwell inhabited a thought world alongside governmental and radical lawyers, who were not intimidated in the least by the opposition of even the staunchest cleric like Fisher, Gardiner, or Tunstall. Bainham, Fish, and Bartholomew Green (an Inner Temple barrister who suffered under

---

[50] Mayer, 'Thomas Starkey, an Unknown Conciliarist at the Court of Henry VIII', *JHI* 49 (1988), 217; Mayer, *Thomas Starkey and the Commonweal: Humanist Politics and Religion in the Reign of Henry VIII* (CUP, 1989).

[51] *Journal of the House of Lords*, I, 128–9.

[52] L.L. Ford, 'Thomas Audley', ODNB; Elton, *Tudor Constitution*, 25.

[53] Sybil M. Jack, 'William Paget, first Baron Paget', ODNB.

[54] Paul Raffield, 'A Discredited Priesthood: The Failings of Common Lawyers and Their Representation in Seventeenth Century Satirical Drama', *Law & Literature*, 17 (2005), 389.

Edmund Bonner) were more radical lawyers,[55] but even the more conservative Audley, Petre, and Paget demonstrated independence in thought and deed.

Another traditionalist, Sir Thomas Elyot, clerk at the Middle Temple and son of a serjeant-at-law, eschewed an earlier friendship with Thomas More in a deferential letter to Cromwell.[56] In his 1531 *The Boke Named the Gouernour*, Elyot compared the king's reign within his realm to that of God over creation. Through what has been described as a 'great chain of meaning' all of society was drawn into obedience to the royal hierarchy.[57] Lehmberg believes Elyot's exaltation of kingship was 'added at the request of Thomas Cromwell.'[58] Jasper Fyloll, another Middle Templar, served both Henry VII and Henry VIII and was 'Cromwell's servant' during the monastic visitations. Rex argues Fyloll was 'invited by his master to turn his talents to propaganda with the general aim of undermining the status and self-esteem of the clergy', an activity pursued with considerable success. In his pamphlets of 1532–1533, Fyloll exhibited traces of evangelicalism alongside numerous traditional religious references. In spite of his generally conservative religious outlook, Fyloll wrote two highly polemical tracts that made 'sweeping denunciations of the entire clerical body'. Fyloll's conservative anticlericalism, published under royal protection, provided cover for traditionalist laity to join in undermining clerical power.[59]

Christopher St German, yet another conservative Middle Templar, proposed legislative reforms 'in tune with Cromwell's policies.'[60] His writings probed the relation between authority in law and conscience. For instance, his *Newe addicions*, issued by the king's printer in 1531, considered the relation of the spiritual jurisdiction to parliament. Following the principle that common law was founded, alongside canon law, in divine law through conscience, St German argued that wherever 'the welthe of the realme' was involved, parliament should legislate.[61] In this way, the 'common wele' might be expanded into almost every realm of English life,[62] effectively bringing parliament and common law into preeminence over the church. St German drew upon the canonical distinction between *potestas ordinis* and *potestas iurisdictionis*, transferring the latter to the temporal power, which according to St German acted in behalf of 'the hole

[55] Wilfrid Priest, 'Heterodox and Radical Lawyers in England, 1500–1800', ODNB.

[56] BL, Cotton MS Cleopatra E, IV, fol. 260; cited in Stanford Lehmberg, 'Sir Thomas Elyot', ODNB.

[57] David Rollison, *A Commonwealth of the People: Popular Politics and England's Long Social Revolution, 1066–1649* (CUP, 2010), 181–4.

[58] Lehmberg, 'Sir Thomas Elyot'.

[59] Richard Rex, 'Jasper Fyloll and the Enormities of the Clergy: Two Tracts Written during the Reformation Parliament', *SCJ*, 31 (2000), 1043–62.

[60] J.H. Baker, 'Christopher St German', ODNB.

[61] Christopher St German, *Here after foloweth a lytell treatise called the newe addicions* (London: Berthelet, 1531), Av.

[62] On the definitions of 'commonwealth', see Rollison, *A Commonwealth of the People*, 13–21.

congregation of Christen people'.[63] St German did not dismiss the clergy entirely, preferring the 'preesthode be holle and sounde' so the people's faith might be preserved.[64] In 1531, he did not grant parliament authority over the 'mere spiritual', but parliament decided what is spiritual and what temporal.[65]

Among the evangelical lay scholars in Cromwell's circle, the most prominent was Sir Richard Morison. Part of the group investigated at Cardinal's College, Morison removed to Padua where he joined the law faculty, then resided with Pole in Venice before entering Cromwell's service in 1536. The government published eight of Morison's pamphlets at critical junctures in the nation's political history. Morison translated two evangelical works into English, including Martin Luther's *The Freedom of a Christian*, and pursued a policy of promoting evangelical thought whenever judiciously possible.[66] In his published writings, Morison not only argued for obedience to the government hierarchy, but also redefined nobility as a matter of 'vertue' rather than birth. He sought to increase lay literacy and make available vernacular Scripture, as a means of social order, even before the 1538 Injunctions allowed individual ownership.[67] In an unpublished treatise on the seven sacraments, prepared for the discussions leading to *Bishop's Book*, Morison opined, 'pristes regal, be all they that ar membres of the churche'.[68] Morison's affirmation of universal royal priesthood was intended as a means of denying the necessity of personal confession to a priest.

Another evangelical scholar in Cromwell's employ was Richard Taverner. Taverner also was accused of heresy at Cardinal's College in 1529 but survived unmolested. He then studied law at one of the inns of chancery before joining the Inner Temple. Taverner's greatest contributions were in the areas of translation and editing, publishing works by continental evangelicals, such as the *Augsburg Confession* and Melanchthon's *Apology*, dedicated to Cromwell; Erasmus Sarcerius' *Commonplaces of Scripture*, dedicated to Henry and translated for Cromwell; and, Wolfgang Capito's commentary on the Psalms, given to him by Cromwell.[69] Taverner also translated several works by Erasmus of Rotterdam, but with an evangelical edge. His revised edition of

---

[63] Francis Oakley, 'Conciliarism in England: St German, Starkey and the Marsiglian Myth', in *Reform and Renewal in the Middle Ages and the Renaissance*, ed. by Thomas M. Izbicki and Christopher Bellitto (Leiden: E.J. Brill, 2000), 235–7; cf. Mayer, 'Thomas Starkey', 214.

[64] R.J. Schoeck, 'The Use of St John Chrysostom in Sixteenth-Century Controversy: Christopher St German and Sir Thomas More in 1533', *HTR*, 54 (1961), 22.

[65] St German, *Newe addicions*, Cv^v.

[66] Tracey A. Sowerby, *Renaissance and Reform in Tudor England: The Careers of Sir Richard Morison c.1513–1556* (OUP, 2010), 22, 31, 36.

[67] *Renaissance and Reform in Tudor England*, 50–3, 82–3.

[68] SP 6/2, fol. 148^r, cited in *Renaissance and Reform in Tudor England*, 163.

[69] James H. Pragman, 'The Augsburg Confession in the English Reformation: Richard Taverner's Contribution', *SCJ*, 11 (1980), 77, 80, 82.

the vernacular Bibles of Tyndale and Rogers was published in 1539 but was soon replaced by the Great Bible. Although some of his works were later burned, and Gardiner imprisoned him for short periods after Cromwell's fall, portions of his banned translations found their way into the *King's Primer* and he went on to serve as a Member of Parliament, prospering under both Edward and Elizabeth. While never ordained, he was both licensed to preach[70] and gathered various homilies into four volumes, portions of which later appeared in the official Elizabethan homilies. Taverner edited his sermons to draw a compelling picture of the reformed parishes as filled with preaching priests, who submitted to royal supremacy and competently presented Scripture to 'intelligent, engaged, and cooperative Christians.'[71]

RADICAL EVANGELICALS IN CROMWELL'S CIRCLE

Among the 'helpers and furthers' of the gospel who came alongside that 'valiant soldier and captain of Christ', as John Foxe describes Cromwell, were a number of truly radical evangelicals. One of these was an evangelical lawyer and minor royal official, William Marshall. Marshall's 1534 letters to Cromwell indicate the Vicegerent's affirmation of translations of Marsiglio's *Defensor Pacis*, Valla's *Donation of Constantine*, and an Erasmian text on the creed. Ten of the eleven titles Marshall published appeared between 1534 and 1535, some of which furthered the royal supremacy, others of which furthered the evangelical movement more audaciously than attempted later by Morison or Taverner. Essential to undermining the papacy were the translations of Valla and Marsiglio, but alongside these approved texts, Marshall published numerous evangelical translations, including treatises by Girolamo Savonarola, on justification; Joachim von Watt, on *sola scriptura*; Martin Bucer, for iconoclasm and against the sacrifice of the mass; and, Martin Luther, on clerical marriage. A number of Marshall's books were subsequently banned and burned, and Marshall may have been culpable in Cromwell's condemnation. Although William Underwood concludes 'Cromwell shared the radical views in Marshall's texts', primarily because Cromwell did not suppress Bucer's work though encouraged by Audley, it is telling that Cromwell was not affiliated with any of Marshall's translations after 1536.[72]

---

[70] Andrew W. Taylor, 'Richard Taverner', ODNB.

[71] Margaret Christian, '"I knowe not howe to preache": The Role of the Preacher in Taverner's Postils', *SCJ*, 24 (1998), 397.

[72] William Underwood, 'Thomas Cromwell and William Marshall's Protestant Books', *HJ*, 47 (2004), 517–39. Underwood also concludes, incredibly, that 'Cromwell's support for conservative writers has never been reliably demonstrated'. 'Thomas Cromwell and William Marshall's Protestant Books', 536.

A second instance of Cromwell's circumspect treatment of radical writers is found in his relationship with Clement Armstrong. This 'grocer-turned-theologian', who was active among London evangelicals, advocated that lay Christians be granted licensure to preach, a view not far from Cromwell's own. However, unlike Cromwell, this 'fringe member' of his circle even appears to grant sacramental powers to Henry, appealing to the king's two bodies: 'the king in form of son of man must minister the body of Christ in form of bread to all men'. Ethan Shagan interprets this as sacramental power, but Armstrong more likely uses the supper as a metaphor for the national economy, the commonwealth. Armstrong undoubtedly questioned the necessity of a separate priesthood within the church, for 'priests needeth not where every man is a priest, and the person of a priest is no matter'. According to Shagan, Armstrong imagined a world 'where the Protestant mantra of a "priesthood of all believers" is actually put into practice and the institutional basis of the worldly Church is stripped away.' It is noteworthy that Cromwell never brought Armstrong's works to print.[73]

A third instance of radical theology within Cromwell's circle is evident in the manuscript translations of Robert Trueman made by Thomas Derby. Derby, an active clerk in the king's council and a Member of Parliament, advocated a sizeable sum be paid to Trueman, and soon after, Trueman's treatises, in Derby's hand, appeared in Cromwell's papers. In addition to peculiar citations of a so-called Scythian code, Trueman and Derby correlated the royal supremacy with their evangelical theology. In 'The thre maners of preisthod', they argue that the first two tabernacles, those of Moses and of Christ in his first appearance, are now supplanted by a third. The third tabernacle is entered through faith in Jesus Christ, whose perfect priesthood perfects those who believe his Word. In turn, the 'sede of faith' in believers grows into full obedience in the believer. The only sacrifice now available to men in the third tabernacle is a spiritual sacrifice, 'the sacrifice of due obedience of mans heart'. Derby and Trueman proceed to identify three types of priesthood in Scripture, all of which are 'without any mass'. The first priesthood is of the law of Moses and merely prepares for the second. The second priesthood is the perfect priesthood of Christ that perfects believers. 'The third presthode is the most damnable presthode of Ball [Bael], which is neither obeidient to observe the lawe neither is not under obedience of any man, but unto vayne imaginacions, & to the worshyping of images turnyng the due obedience due unto god to such & other like vanities.' The authors leave the contemporary identification of 'the most damnable presthode of Ball' to

---

[73] Karl Gunther and Ethan H. Shagan, 'Protestant Radicalism and Political Thought in the Reign of Henry VIII', *P&P*, 194 (2007), 39–43; Shagan, 'Clement Armstrong and the Godly Commonwealth: Radical Religion in Early Tudor England', in *The Beginnings of English Protestantism*, ed. by Peter Marshall and Alec Ryrie (CUP, 2002), 60–5, 77.

the reader but hint that the third priesthood refuses to come '*under the lawe*' and cannot abide the '*word of the othe*', intentionally pregnant allusions to both the oath of God in Hebrews 7 and the oath to the royal supremacy.[74] Though 'The thre maners of preisthod' strikes points for the royal supremacy, it leaves no reason for the continued existence of the clergy in the English church. Cromwell paid for this anticlerical manuscript but never brought it to publication.

It has often been noted that the Hans Holbein woodcut adorning the Great Bible of 1539 placed Henry between God and people. Less noticed is that Henry is passing *Verbum Dei* not only to Cranmer, who gives it to the priests, but also to Cromwell, who in turn instructs the magistrates on their task in enforcing the word of God [see Plate 5]. The two orders, of priesthood and magistracy, were equated and integrated by Cromwell, patron of the 1539 Bible and of Hans Holbein.[75] The more Lutheran definition of orders put forward by the *Bishops' Book* committee carried Cromwell's signature but the final version, which contains Tunstall's strong delineation of powers, did not. Chapuys reported Cromwell's summons to several bishops to answer whether the king could make and unmake bishops.[76] He was, therefore, partially responsible for the 1540 questions concerning the royal powers put to the bishops. In 1539, he submitted a parliamentary bill concerning ordination, but it was referred to Gardiner and Tunstall.[77] Both of these conservative bishops have been fingered as candidates for engineering the downfall of Cromwell,[78] and this bill, no longer extant, may have been similar to the draft bills of 1536 (for discussion see 'Radical Maneuvers In Parliament', pp. 171–5). If so, it is easy to see why conservatives, who made little distinction between reformers, accused Cromwell of sacramentarianism.

The traditionalist accusation that Cromwell was personally sacramentarian lacks merit. He was rather faithful to his former benefactor, Cardinal Wolsey, even after the latter's political demise. At the time, he turned to an orthodox primer for comfort and was moved by orthodox worship. Cromwell also left money for purgatorial prayers in his 1529 will.[79] In 1538, he proclaimed the death sentence against the sacramentarian John Lambert. In the same year, when a row broke out in Calais over radical preaching, he urged Lord Lisle to examine the antagonists on both sides but was adamant that those who denied the Real Presence be punished. If Adam Damplip denied transubstantiation,

[74] Gunther and Shagan, 'Protestant Radicalism', 48–54; PRO SP 6/2, fols 23^r–29^v.

[75] Rex, *Henry and the Reformation*, 132. Dickens, *Cromwell and the Reformation*, 120–1; Stephanie Buck, *Hans Holbein 1497/98–1543* (Cologne: Könemann, 1999), 112–13.

[76] Dickens, *Cromwell and the Reformation*, 87.

[77] *Journals of the House of Lords*, I, 115, 117.

[78] Elton, *Studies*, I, 189–230; Glyn Redworth, *In Defence of the Church Catholic: The Life of Stephen Gardiner* (Oxford: Blackwell, 1990), 105–27.

[79] Beckingsale, *Cromwell*, ch. 2.

Plate 1. Reflecting a royal claim to authority, without a priestly intermediary and in the presence of biblical and royal saints, Richard II, the King of England, kneels to communicate directly with Jesus Christ, the King of Heaven, and receive the banner of resurrected kingship. The Wilton Diptych, late fourteenth century. Used by permission of the National Gallery.

Plate 2. Reflecting a clerical claim to authority, a priest distributes the consecrated host, the body of God with its attendant soteriological and apotropaic power, to the receptive laity. Illuminated manuscript, *Omne Bonum*, late fourteenth century. Used by permission of the British Library Board, Royal MS 6E, VI, fol. 337ᵛ.

Plate 3. Reflecting a popular claim to authority, John Ball addresses the 1381 Peasants' Revolt. Ball queried in an egalitarian manner, 'Whan Adam dalf, and Eve span, Wo was thanne a gentilman?' Illuminated manuscript, Jean Froissart, *Chroniques de France et d'Angleterre*, Book II, late fifteenth century. Used by permission of the British Library Board, Royal MS 18E, I, fol. 165ᵛ.

Plate 4. The King of Heaven invests spiritual authority in the church through the granting of the tiara to a pope attended by a cardinal and other clergy before a church (at left) and temporal authority in the state through the granting of the crown to a king attended by nobles and knights before a castle (at right). Illuminated manuscript, *Concordantia Discordantium Canonum*, twelfth century. Used by permission of the British Library Board/De Agostini.

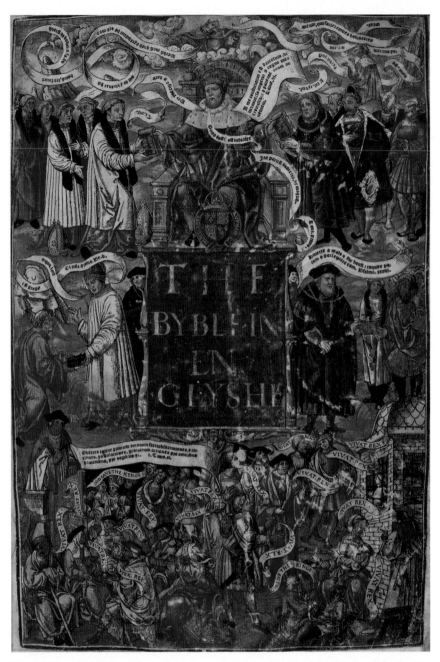

Plate 5. The King of England, Henry VIII, authorized by heaven, distributes authority through the Word of God to Thomas Cranmer at the head of the clergy (at left) and to Thomas Cromwell at the head of the magistrates (at right). Title page of the second 'Great Bible', also known as 'Cranmer's Bible'. *The Byble in Englyshe, that is to saye the content of all the holy scrypture, both of ye olde and newe testament, truly translated after the veryte of the Hebrue and Greke textes* (London: Rychard Grafton and Edward Whitchurch, 1539). Used by permission of the British Library Board, C18, d.1.

Plate 6. This popular woodcut demonstrates some of the royal, clerical, and popular aspects of the English evangelical doctrine of royal priesthood. Drawing upon Josiah's lettered reformation of Israel's worship through Solomon's Temple, in the higher part of England's temple, Edward VI grants the submissively kneeling reformed clergy the Bible while the magistrates triumphantly stand (at bottom left). The new Josiah suppressed the 'Romish Church' through destroying her images and expelling her clergy (at top). The reformed vision of the church included people of both genders and all ages entering the house of common prayer, the clergy preaching God's Word and the laity reflecting upon it, and true worship through the two reformation sacraments, including a centered table for communion as opposed to an eastern altar for the sacrifice of the mass (at bottom right). John Foxe, *The second volume of the ecclesiasticall history, conteynyng the actes and monumentes of martyrs* (London: John Day, 1570), 1521. Used by permission of the Bodleian Library, University of Oxford.

Plate 7A. The Blessing of Cramp Rings, an illuminated miniature from 'Queen Mary's Manual', owned by the Roman Catholic Cathedral of Westminster and currently on loan to Westminster Abbey Library. The Cathedral Administrator currently notes, 'Although the word "Consecration" is used in the manual, that action is reserved to a bishop or priest and is not used in relation to this ritual.' Used by permission of the Administrator, Westminster Cathedral.

Plate 7B. Standing between Heaven and England, a majestic Elizabeth I dispenses the blessings and judgments of God upon the nation. Sir Henry Lee, the patron of this imposing portrait, likely indicated hereby his thanksgiving for Elizabeth's forgiveness in a 1592 visit. The Ditchley Portrait. Used by permission of the National Portrait Gallery.

Of Enuie.

{ Where Gods word preached is in place : vnto the people willingly :
  Woe be to them that would deface : for if such ceafe,the stones will crie.

¶ The fignification.

HE which preacheth in the pulpit,fignifieth godly zeale,&
a furtherer of the gofpel:and the two which are plucking
him out of his place, are the enemies of Gods word, threat-
ning by fire to cófume the profeffors of the fame : and that
company which fitteth ftill,are *Nullifidians*,fuch as are of no
religion,not regarding any doctrine, fo they may bee quiet
to liue after their owne willes and mindes.

uoho

Plate 8. Reflecting the rivalry of competing clergies, a reformed preacher with an open
Bible battles a bishop, on the one hand, and a Roman friar with a closed text, on the
other, around the pulpit, with the disconcerted yet quiescent laity observing. 'Of Enuie,'
in Stephen Bateman, *A Christall glasse of christian reformation* (London: John Day,
1569), sig. G4ᵛ. Used by permission of the Bodleian Library, University of Oxford.

then Cromwell deemed it a 'most detestable and cancered heresy'.[80] It was only when Cranmer wrote in defense of Damplip's denial that Cromwell relented. Cromwell warned his alleged co-conspirator, Robert Barnes, himself not a sacramentarian, to be circumspect in his teachings. Again, he supported the temperamental Barnes only after Cranmer's request.[81] In his last letter to Henry, now badly damaged, Cromwell appears to deny being a '[sacra]men-tarye'.[82] At his execution, he affirmed the Trinity and the sacraments, denying his detractors. In his final speech and prayer, his recognition of personal sin and reliance on Christ alone sounds Lutheran in tone.[83] Significantly, Cromwell was not burned as a heretic; rather, he lost his head to the axe, the punishment for treason. Cromwell was not a sacramentarian and was careful to keep public distance from radical evangelicals, but he also pursued a vision of the church as a lay-led institution.

THREE AGENDAS FOR RELATING LAY AND CLERICAL POWERS

As we have seen, Henry violated the ancient boundaries between clergy and laity, especially in the arena of jurisdiction, but also in the sacrament of orders and the definition of doctrine. Cromwell, as Henry's vicegerent, also crossed those boundaries. If king and vicegerent, both laymen, could exercise some aspects of priesthood, could his magistrates, as his deputies, also exercise a priesthood? Where were the boundaries to be redrawn, or were they to be redrawn? Henry's 1531 refusal to delineate *spiritualia* from *temporalia* preserved Henry's claim to divine approbation and allowed him to pressure the clergy at whim. (The definition of what constituted *praemunire* was similarly left unresolved, most likely as a weapon with which to threaten the clergy. Perhaps the inability of the Tudor regime to reform its ecclesiastical laws could be attributed to the same reasoning.) Henry's invasion of the priestly realm raised many questions, questions that took years to answer.

The most important issue, providing some definition of lay–clerical relationships, especially the relationship of magistrates to prelates, had to be given.

---

[80] *Life and Letters*, II, 139–40, 142, 148–9, 222–4, 226–8.

[81] Cox, II, 375–6, 380–1. In his first trial, Barnes was not accused of being a sacramentarian. *A Supplicatyon*, fols xxiii–xxxvi.

[82] '...oche grevyd me, That I sholde be notyd...e I hadde your lawse in my brest, and...mentarye god he knowythe the...he ton and the other gyltles, I a...ful Crysten man and so will I...e and Conscyens your highness tre...wooll, but gracyous'. *Life and Letters*, II, 273–6.

[83] Hall, *Chronicle*, 839; *A&M*, V, 402–3. Neville Williams, *The Cardinal & the Secretary* (London: Weidenfeld and Nicolson, 1975), 262–3.

Three separate agendas arose in the 1530s in an attempt to provide a new formula. These agendas are typified in the thought of Stephen Gardiner, Edward Foxe, and William Tyndale. Gardiner envisioned a conservative hierarchical structure with the clergy dominating the laity under the cure of the king. Foxe opted for a more Lutheran cooperation between laity and clergy below the king. Tyndale was the respectable face of those radical elements who desired an elimination of lay–clerical distinctions, even flirting with rebellion to obtain it. We shall treat each of these agendas.

Edward Foxe, a leading proponent of the king's divorce, was also an architect of the new supremacy. Bishop of Hereford (1535–1538), he became the king's ambassador in the new attempt to forge an alliance with the German Lutherans as a counterbalance to France and the Empire in the winter of 1535–1536. During the theological negotiations resulting in the *Wittenberg Articles*, Foxe approached a Lutheran position. The *Wittenberg Articles* were based on the Lutheran *Augsburg Confession* (1530) and in turn became a basis for England's *Ten Articles* (1536).[84] However, even before his trip to Germany, Foxe displayed a tendency towards a less than conservative position. Foxe's beliefs seem to have been close to those of Cranmer. In *De Vera Differentia* (1534), for example, Foxe limits the claims of ecclesiastical, especially papal, power. Their position has grown into a 'tyrannical' power with ambiguous limits.[85] Foxe's polemic against the papacy clouds his effort to clarify the distinction between regal and ecclesiastical power. He even excoriates the papacy for daring to discriminate between the powers and jurisdictions of temporalty and spiritualty. It is easy to see how a reader might be confused about the exact boundaries between laity and clergy; nonetheless, Foxe makes a distinction.[86]

Foxe elevates the powers of the king. He has 'the supreme authority of spiritual and temporal things'. He may 'make', 'ordain', and 'consecrate' bishops.[87] Concurrent with the royal elevation is an episcopal demythologization. Bishops were formerly included in the priestly order. Since Christ gave the keys to all the apostles, all priests share the authority of Peter. Bishops were only raised in order to put away schism, and their elevation has the force of human custom, not divine law. A bishop's office is to pray and preach the

---

[84] Tjernegal, *Henry and the Lutherans*, 153–66; 255–86.

[85] Edward Foxe, *Opus Eximium, De Vera Differentia Regiae Potestatis et Ecclesiasticae, Et Quae Sit Ipsa Veritas Ac Virtus Utriusque* (London: Berthelet, 1534), fols 4ʳ–5ᵛ; *The true dyfferes*, fols iiᵛ–iiiiʳ. Harking back to *Collectanea*, Foxe subverts the papal claim to fashion public law by appealing to a higher private law, the conscience inspired by the Holy Spirit. *De Vera Differentia*, fols 30ᵛ–31ᵛ; *True dyfferes*, fols liᵛ–liiʳ.

[86] *De Vera Differentia*, fol. 26; *True dyfferes*, fols xliʳ–xliiʳ.

[87] Although in his explanation Foxe says the king causes the bishops to be ordained, it is easy to see how Henry might be persuaded that he held the power directly. *True dyfferes*, fols lxxxiiiᵛ–lxxxvʳ.

Word of God, and to offer gifts and sacrifices for sin. He cannot claim the temporal sword and must obey his prince.[88] The Bishop of Hereford retains a distinction between priest and laity. This division is based on property, similar in some ways to Wyclif's vision of a disendowed priesthood. Etymologically, the Greek κλῆρος, lot, means clerks are chosen by God and given a kingship. The kingship of priests is now expressed only in virtue, being reserved for full expression in future. The λαός, people, hold temporal possessions by which they should materially support clergy. Their works will save them.[89] In the end, Foxe's Wyclif-like poor priests are totally subservient to the king and he apparently exercises some of their sacerdotal powers. Clerical position was at the same time reconceived as an 'office' closer to the reformed understanding as opposed to an 'order' in the Roman understanding.

Foxe was neither Romanist nor egalitarian. In his mind, the truth-standard of Scripture excludes two groups: those who exalt ecclesiastical power and those who deny it. Some so enlarge and extend the limits of ecclesiastical power that they submit to that power everything, holy and profane, earthly and heavenly. They make the Bishop of Rome not a servant of the Word but the overweening vicar of God. The opposing error is just as great: 'Som other make al christen men equal and ye was spoken unto ye apostles with small dyscretion, they applye to all Christen men, Confounding al orders of Christen people being cleane repugnant unto the othere sorte and as the other without al measure dyd attribut to the byshoppes of Rome al power, so these with no lyke faute seme too take al power awey.'[90] Cranmer had a close working relationship with Foxe, both in the divorce team and in formulating *Bishops' Book*. Considering Cranmer's attraction to Lutheran principles during his Nuremberg stay and his continuing Lutheran contacts,[91] there is little doubt Cranmer agreed with Foxe's solution. He would not, however, have agreed with Gardiner's scheme.

The Bishop of Winchester, though initially surprised by Henry's newfound feistiness towards clerical prerogative, speedily made amends. His apology for his part in crafting 'Reply of the Ordinaries' is a careful dance of assertion and submission. He only held those opinions, he says, because of the doctrine of so

---

[88] *True dyfferes*, fols xii^r–xiii^r, xv^r, xxvi, xxxv^r, ci^r.

[89] 'These surelye be the kynges that rule themselues and other in vertue and so they haue theyr kyngdome in god and that betokeneth the crowne upon theyr heddes this crowne they haue by the ordinaunces of ye church of rome in the token of kindome which is loked for in christe and the shauige of theyr heddes betokenyth ye forsakinge of al temporal thinges for they beinge contented with meate drynke and cloth shulde haaue nothynge proper amongest them but althinges shulde be comon.' *True dyfferes*, fols xliii^r–xlv^r.

[90] *True dyfferes*, fols iiii^r–v^r. *Alii omnes christianos pares faciunt, et quod apostolis dictum est ridicule ad omnes detorquent christianos, omnes christianorum ordines confundentes, illis aliis ueluti ex diametro pugnantes. Et quemadmodum illi omnia sine modo triuere pontificibus: sic isti pari uitio omnia adimere uidentur. De Vera Differentia*, fol. 6^r.

[91] Basil Hall, 'Cranmer's Relations with Erasmianism and Lutheranism', in *C&S*, 3–38.

many learned men, apparently Warham, Fisher, and Tunstall. He also points to the implied high clericalism in the king's own book against Luther, to the English book in support of the king's great cause (perhaps Cranmer's *Determinations*), and to the Council of Constance whose articles against Wyclif manifestly decreed his former opinion. However, he will submit to Henry's contrary evidence.[92]

If Foxe compressed the ecclesiastical hierarchy under a sacerdotal king, Gardiner glorified the royal priest while simultaneously strengthening the old hierarchy. Gardiner begins *De Vera Obedientia* with acknowledgement of his slackness in coming to the truth of obedience. The realm consists of all Christians, lay and clerical; the king as supreme head of the realm is, therefore, supreme head of the church in England, since it is one and the same congregation.[93] Everyone owes obedience to the king, *sine exceptione*, laity and clergy without caveat. Gardiner's interpretation of obedience begins with a refutation of the passages applied so often to the papal doctrine of obedience. The 'obey your rulers' of Romans 13 and Hebrews 13.7, and Paul's ascription of authority to the elders and bishops in Acts 20.28 apply not to pope but king. He says that although Peter's 'royal priesthood' is exegetically geared to another purpose, it is a legitimate prooftext for the king. 'Let us not pass over and omit this, although it has another sense, that godly Peter speaks of the *regali sacerdotio*.'[94] As for John 20.23,[95] an old prooftext for papal authority over the keys, it applies to royal government of the church. In this church, there is no major separation between spiritual and temporal government.

But Winchester was no egalitarian. The conflation of temporal and spiritual government applies only at the top. Everything centers in the prince. From God comes a procession of jurisdiction through the king. The very real degrees of clergy—archbishop, bishop, and curate—cooperate in the offices of teaching and ministry of the sacraments. The king holds a cure, which cure is to see the laity do not oppress 'good men', i.e. clergy.[96] Henry also has a cure to correct the customs or morals of the church.[97] This cure is effected by deploying the parallel swords of prince and clergy. His cure is comparable to that of Solomon, who ordained priests to their ministry. And like Hezekiah, he is responsible for disciplining priests. In sum, a king is constituted by God with a cure for spiritual and eternal affairs before he is ever charged with corporal

---

[92] Gardiner to Henry VIII, 1532; *Concilia*, III, 752.

[93] *De Vera Obedientia* (1535), in *Obedience in Church & State*, 72, 94.

[94] *Ac ne quid praetermittamus, etiam illud non ommittamus, quanquam alium sensum habet, quod diuus Petrus de regali sacerdotio loquitur. Obedience in Church & State*, 100.

[95] 'Whose soever sins ye remit, they are remitted unto them; and whose soever sins ye retain, they are retained.' (Authorized Version)

[96] *Itaque ne furentur, ne occidant, ne uim bonis inferant laici, id uero curet rex. Obedience in Church & State*, 104.

[97] *Obedience in Church & State*, 106.

matters.[98] Gardiner even allows the king broad power to define basic doctrines.[99]

There is a rigid hierarchical structure to Gardiner's scheme. Government flows from king to clergy to laity, and obedience returns from laity to clergy to king. Both king and clergy gain their power from God, but the king like Moses is above even the highest priests of all. Princes represent God's image to men; they inhabit the highest room above all other men. In a direct refutation of constitutional monarchy, he says, 'A Prince's mighty power is not gotten by flattery or by privilege from the people but it is given by God.'[100] If anything, Gardiner's conception of the Henrician church is more clerical, if possible, than the medieval church. The pope is ejected but a powerful priest–king has taken his place.

Many have interpreted Gardiner's maneuver in this tract as an effort to return to Henry's favor.[101] This was part of Gardiner's purpose but not his only one. He also offered a constitutional arrangement for increasing the power of prelates over the lower clergy and the laity, all the laity except one. Although he slavishly submits to the king and jettisons the pope, there is no room for power sharing with nobility, commons, or lower clergy. King and bishop are united in a rigid ecclesiocracy. Winchester's scheme no doubt raised hackles among those parliamentarians who fought so hard to raise common law above canon law, once they realized what he was saying. Indeed, there was a backlash against Winchester's line among the more forward lay magistrates. While disagreeing with Gardiner, they did not embrace Foxe's interpretation either. They toyed with something a bit more radical, something learned from Tyndale.

It is widely acknowledged that the sacrament of orders was a hot issue in the mid-1530s but the material has apparently never been drawn together in an effort to summarize that debate. Two problems are confronted in analyzing this material. First, the papers are often anonymous, although their inclusion in Cromwell's papers shows his and his colleagues' interest in them. Second,

---

[98] *Obedience in Church & State*, 108–12. *Vt uidelicet rex a deo constitutus, qui spiritus est aeternus, spiritualia, et aeterna potius, ac priori loco curaret, quam corporalia, et tempore peritura? Obedience in Church & State*, 108. 'Is there no doubt that the king constituted by God, who is spirit and eternal, should have cure of spiritual and eternal things before particular corporal and temporal things which perish?'

[99] *Obedience in Church & State*, 116–18.

[100] *Obedience in Church & State*, 130, 88, 128. In answer to whether the people and Parliament correctly call Henry the supreme head of the Church of England, Gardiner concurs. Bale's tendentious translation of Gardiner says the supremacy is 'grounded upon' the decision of Parliament. Bale, however, relies on a later Hamburg edition that altered *imitatur* of the earlier Berthelet and Strasbourg editions to read *innitatur*. The change in lettering is significant. It altered Gardiner's meaning from parliamentary approbation or consent to initiation. *Obedience in Church & State*, 92n.

[101] Bucer mistook Gardiner for a converted evangelical. *Cranmer*, 174–6.

they are often undated, causing them to be haphazardly scattered from 1531 to 1537 by the editors of *Letters and Papers*. As many of the same issues were under discussion in the Parliament of 1536, discussions which prompted the synod of 1537, we offer a tentative dating of 1536 for most of them. These problems of anonymity and dating have resulted in the debate's unfortunate classification as 'behind-the-scenes'.[102] On the contrary, as we shall see, this debate was public and was incorporated in the *Bishops' Book*.

The debate centers on the conflict between universal priesthood and clerical priesthood, specifically the interpretation of such passages as Acts 20 and John 20. Medieval ordinals and theologians used the commission of Christ to the apostles in John 20.22—'Receive the Holy Spirit, whoever's sins you remit are remitted unto them, and whoever's sin you retain, they are retained'—as a prooftext for episcopal dispensation of the Holy Spirit and the power of the keys. Paul's commission to the Ephesian priests in Acts 20.28—'Attend to yourselves and to the whole flock over which the Holy Ghost has made you rulers'—fed the same interpretation.[103] This hierarchical hermeneutic was challenged by the new vernacular translations coming forth from Tyndale. He translated the Greek πρεσβύτερος as 'elder', not as the traditional English 'priest', which was equated with the Latin *sacerdos*. The implication was that all elders, temporal as well as spiritual, are to rule the church.

In his discussion on the sacrament of orders in *Obedience*, Tyndale denies the New Testament word for priest indicates a particular order in the church. 'Of that manner is Christ a priest for ever; and all we priests through him, and need no more of any such priest on earth, to be a mean for us unto God.' Although we previously discussed this passage, it should be noted that immediately after his self-sufficient definition of universal priesthood, Tyndale affirms a ministerial office, but one almost devoid of any uniqueness in relation to the laity. An elder 'is nothing but an officer to teach, and not to be a mediator between God and us'. This elder does not need episcopal ordination. His authority to teach, baptize, and wield the keys may conditionally be taken up by any man or woman.[104] To the medieval mind, Tyndale's less-than-clear distinction between offices—a distinction that Luther painstakingly spelled out following the German Peasants' Wars—could only be seen as a call for the dissolution of sacramental orders.

In *A Dialogue Concerning Heresies*, Thomas More registered his concerns about Tyndale's doctrine of priesthood. Tyndale rebutted in 1529 with a murky denial that the laity could hold the office of elder, but his extended treatment again cast opprobrium on priestly orders. Elder indicates 'age, gravity, and sadness'. Bishop only indicates a governor of the congregation.

---

[102] Rex, 'Obedience', 876.
[103] Messenger, *Reformation, Mass and Priesthood*, I, 92–3.
[104] Walter, I, 254–9.

In Acts 20, Paul sent for 'the elders *in birth* of the congregation or church' and made them bishops or overseers (italics mine).[105] More responded with an even more detailed accusation that Tyndale was doing away with all order in church and society by confusing and flattening the clerical estate.[106] As we have seen, Tyndale's next tract, *Practice of Prelates*, made some threats which could only be taken as radical, if not downright rebellious. Of three competing agendas—those of Foxe, Gardiner, and Tyndale—some of Cromwell's associates took Tyndale's to heart.

RADICAL MANEUVERS IN PARLIAMENT

The Reformation Parliament met for the last time in 1536 and was quite busy about its business of economic, social, and religious reformation. One of its tasks, which Lehmberg fails to note, was to decide whose job it is to interpret Scripture.[107] In 1535, Christopher St German issued a treatise calling king and parliament to define doctrine. The church consists of 'emperours, kynges and princes with their people as well of the clergye as of the lay fee'. Since the king in parliament represents all the people, it may, therefore, determine doctrine. The clergy have violated their trust with their worldly ambitions and they cannot be trusted. 'Why shuld nat the parlyament than whiche representeth the whole catholyke churche of Englande expounde scrypture?'[108] St German's treatise augured a novel attempt by the laity in the subsequent 1536 session of parliament to formulate an official interpretation of a number of passages of Scripture previously used to buttress the clerical position.[109]

The British Library has a memo asking, 'Whether your lordshyp thinke convenyent that we shold endevor ourself to prove these articles foloyng'. Strype identifies it as the hand of Stephen Gardiner, but this is doubtful as Gardiner was then in France. It is more likely a memo used by Cromwell or Cranmer in preparation for the synod of 1537.[110] The first three articles concern the dependence of spiritual jurisdiction upon the king. The fourth questions whether 'the king's majesty hath aswell the care of the soules of his subjects as is their Bodyes and may by the lawe of God by his parlyament make

---

[105] Walter, III, 16–20. [106] *CWM*, VIII, 112–15, 259–62, 594–5.

[107] Lehmberg, *Reformation Parliament*, 217–48.

[108] Christopher St German, *An Answer to a Letter* (1535), ch. 7; quoted in John Guy, 'Scripture as Authority: Problems of Interpretation in the 1530s', in *Reassessing the Henrician Age*, ed. by Alistair Fox and John Guy (Oxford: Blackwell, 1986), 207–10.

[109] A 1538 treatise proved that the idea of parliament interpreting biblical doctrine had not disappeared. *A Treatise proving by the king's lawes*, cited in Sowerby, *Renaissance and Reform in Tudor England*, 72.

[110] BL Cotton MS Cleopatra E, VI, fols 232–3; Strype, I, 214–15; *L&P*, XI, 84.

laws touching and concernyng as well to the one as the other'. The fifth asks whether Christ's commission to the apostles in Matthew 16 ceased once a number of laity were converted. Matthew 18 came into effect at that time so that power was given 'to the hole church to make lawes and restrayned the peculiar authority of the appostells on that behalf'. The sixth concerns the power of calling councils: Does it belong to the apostles' successors or to kings and princes? The eighth concerns whether Acts 20.28 'was not ment of such bysshops only as be now of clergye but was aswell ment and spoken to every ruler and governor of the christian people'.

'Whether your lordshyp' was probably prompted by the following papers found in Cromwell's files. First, an anonymous writer versed in common law deposited a manuscript with Cromwell which begins 'Of dyvers heresies which haue not ben taken for heresies in tyme paste'.[111] The lawyer furthers Tyndale's attacks on a distinct priesthood. He says Psalm 105.15—'touch ye not myn annoynted'—cannot be confined to priests but is said of 'them that have believed or shall belieue in Christe'.[112] For priests to say 'the clergye onely haue cuer of soules and noon but they is heresie'. Ecclesiasticus 17 and the 'texte of fraternall correction, Matthew 16 [*sic*, 18]', prove 'cure and charge is severally in Rulers and gouernouers of *comynalties*, fathers, mothers, heades of house-holdes and in especialle in kyngs and prynces'.[113] A priest's benedictions are no more effective than a layman's, a contention with which Cranmer agreed.[114] All of the texts that the anonymous lawyer addresses concern the transmission of power. He pleads for a return to Scripture and dismisses clerical appeals to 'unwritten verities'. The clergy appeal to tradition so that 'they myght fasshon themself a power as by the wordes of Christe that he neuer spake, and yet all men shuld be bounden under payne of damnation to belieue their waye'.[115] In answer to the question, 'who shuld have power & auctorite to iudge and determyn what thyng is heresie and what not', he gives a twofold answer. With 'playne texts of scripture', the king or his commissioners may determine. With doubtful texts, only a general council legitimately called by kings may determine. In the interim, 'the kyng and his parliament' may determine. 'Of dyvers heresies' concludes by asking Parliament to determine the definition and punishment for heresy since *De Haeretico Comburendo* is now expired.[116]

Another radical government paper is the anonymous 'The question moved'.[117] The writer uses Tyndalian terminology (e.g. 'minister' rather

---

[111] PRO SP 6/1, fols 105–21; *L&P*, XI, 85. Rex endorses *L&P*'s date of 1536. Rex, 'Obedience', 876.
[112] PRO SP 6/1, fol. 114.
[113] PRO SP 6/1, fol. 115^v.
[114] PRO SP 6/1, fol. 116^r; Cox, II, 333–4.
[115] PRO SP 6/1, fol. 117^v.
[116] PRO SP 6/1, fols 119–20.
[117] PRO SP 6/2, fols 94–6; *L&P*, V, 1022. The editors of *L&P* date this to 1532; Lehmberg and Haas to 1531; Rex redated it to 1536 on internal evidence. Lehmberg, *Reformation Parliament*, 114; Haas, 'Divine Right', 318n; Rex, 'Obedience', 874–6.

than 'priest' to denote clergy) and constantly condemns presumptuous prelates. He declares that all Christians are priests. Moreover, bishops and elders in John 20.21 and Acts 20.28 must be equated with temporal rulers as much as clergy. Christ's spiritual kingdom 'resteth in no presumptuous preste used authoritie, in no idle usurped names, nor within presacred titles, but in effecatious vertue'. Finally, the king is the proper recipient of these texts. Josiah is the exemplar temporal prince who executes 'spirituall administracion'. 'Nor no impedimente ys knowen by scripture why that a temporall prince maye not be a ministre: yee a head over the church the spirituall kyngedome of Christe.'[118] The climax is reached with an affirmation of universal priesthood as the basis of royal priesthood: 'Melchisedech King of Jerusalem, *qui erat rex et sacerdos*, by whom all christen people are made *sacerdos*, now maye be esteemed so moch in the spirituall kingdome of Christe which is the churche. *Aduersas quam, ni inferiorum porte, possint prenatere*, to be christ, ruler and supreme lord, as a christen prince.'[119]

In a subtle but extremely important move, royal priesthood is now rooted in universal priesthood rather than sacramental coronation by the archbishop. The king is royal priest on the basis of his participation in common priesthood. The intervention of a Gardiner-type mediating priesthood between king and people is eliminated and the king derives his power from the people. As a safeguard against rebellion, however, obedience is promoted. Common priesthood cannot be the basis for any type of egalitarian revolt against monarchy, even if a monarch were to turn tyrannical. Christian rulers and heathen tyrants are 'in no wise to be disobeyed'.[120]

Building on this extensive manuscript literature, sometime in the early 1536 session of parliament, two drafts of a bill were prepared. The first, of some thirty-two pages, calls for a declaration by king and parliament concerning the true interpretation of certain texts of Scripture.[121] The second, of some eighteen pages, corrects the former.[122] The first begins, 'The kyng our soueraigne Lorde intending as he hathe begone to sett fourth to the honor of God and to the welthe of all people being under his governince.' The act maintains 'the true understandyng of certayne textes of scripture'. With each text is provided (1) a refutation of the clericalist interpretation; (2) the determination of Parliament, sitting in the place of a general council, on the true meaning;

---

[118] PRO SP 6/2, fol. 95ʳ.
[119] 'Melchisedek King of Jerusalem, who was king and priest, by whom all Christian people are made priests, may now be esteemed so much in the spiritual kingdom, which is the church. According to which, if not carried to inferiors, these passages could apply the interpretation of christ, ruler and supreme lord to a Christian prince.' PRO SP 6/2, fol. 96.
[120] PRO SP 6/2, fol. 94ʳ.
[121] PRO SP 6/4, fols 106–22; *L&P*, XII, ii, 1313.1.
[122] PRO SP 6/4, fols 123–32; *L&P*, XII, ii, 1313.2.

and, (3) a proclamation of the penalty for believing otherwise, which penalty is left blank for future insertion.

For instance, the rock on which Christ will build his church in Matthew 16 is the confession of Peter. The words granting the keys to Peter were not meant of Peter's successors, nor of all the bishops and priests together, but 'of all the disciples and of the universale churche'.[123] Similarly, by commanding all the apostles to teach, Christ commanded all Christians to teach.[124] Several texts from Matthew 18 are dealt with. The power of binding and loosing is given to the universal church, not just the clergy. Before Christian kings existed, apostles could gather councils, but after Christian kings appeared, only they could gather them. When Christ said two or three gathered in prayer is effective, he was calling for Christians to reconcile with each other before their prayers could be heard. Christ also said he would be present where two or three are gathered. The clergy say, therefore, that where the clergy gather, Christ is there with his authority, but the clergy are not the principal members of the church and their gathering does not monopolize Christ's authority.[125] In Matthew 28, Christ said he would be in the midst of the universal church, so that even if the apostles' successors were to fall away, he is still with the church.[126] A number of other texts are dealt with, but one of the most interesting is the controversial text of Acts 20. According to the draft, 'busshops' signify 'gouernours and others whether they wer of the temporaltie or of the clergie', because 'bishop' signifies 'elder' or 'senyours of the people'.[127]

The cumulative effect of these interpretations was to deny the clergy any special distinction. The act apparently kept a clergy, but it could not claim any real distinction from the magistracy. This was radical Lutheranism with a vengeance. Felicity Heal's contention, that the 1530s were 'the decade when all seemed possible' for rearranging the clerical system,[128] is given added force in the parliamentary drafts. However, the radicals were overplaying their hand. The monasteries might be easy targets, but Henry needed bishops and priests to enforce discipline. Moreover, with Anne Boleyn's fall accomplished and William Tyndale's execution imminent, evangelicals of all stripes were weakened. The bills were judiciously shelved. Within a few years, Cromwell himself was removed from the scene, but he fostered a fundamental and enduring transformation of the English church into a lay-led institution. As the dean of Cromwellian scholarship noted, 'the Henrician Reformation signalled the triumph of the laity in the realm of religion. . . . By making himself supreme head, King Henry, that enemy of Luther, testified strikingly

---

[123] PRO SP 6/4, fols 107–8.   [124] PRO SP 6/4, fols 108ᵛ–9.
[125] PRO SP 6/4, fols 109ᵛ–11.   [126] PRO SP 6/4, fols 111ᵛ–12.
[127] PRO SP 6/4, fols 115ᵛ–16.   [128] *Of Prelates and Princes* (CUP, 1980), 100.

to a belief in the priesthood of all believers.' Thenceforth, sovereignty 'rested exclusively, as Audley said, with the King-in-Parliament.'[129] With the additional factors of the abolition of the study of canon law in the universities to crown the triumph of the common law[130] and the steady growth of the prerogative of parliament, Cromwell's faction ensured an independent clergy would never again challenge lay sovereignty.

CROMWELL AND CRANMER OPEN A SYNOD TO CONFRONT THE ISSUES

After the 1536 session of the Reformation Parliament was completed, the lower house of Convocation, still in session in June, sent sixty-seven articles to the upper house. Their complaints regarding erroneous opinions were aimed at the radical beliefs of lay magistrates and common lawyers. The first three articles concern the eucharist, the third complaining 'that priests have no more authority to minister sacraments than the laymen have'. Articles 26 to 30 decry the loss of sacramental power in confession, including 'that it is sufficient for a man or woman to make their confession to God alone' and 'that it is as lawful at all times to confess to a layman as to a priest'.[131] The lower clergy thus condemned the parliamentary lay radicals.

The debate between conservatives and radicals over the interpretation of those texts traditionally used to support a separate and powerful clergy was still very alive in 1536. Two papers were drawn up with the same title, 'Thinges necessary as it semeth to be remembered Before the brekyng of the parliament'. One was prepared for, if not directly by, Cromwell.[132] The other has been assigned to Cranmer.[133] One may only surmise the origin of these memoranda. Perhaps before Parliament was dismissed, both Cromwell and Cranmer were called before the king, told to take notes on the king's mind and ordered to find a solution to the conflict over jurisdiction between laity and clergy. Perhaps Henry ordered them to use one of his favorite methods, the organization of a theological committee, and report their findings back to him. We do know that, at that time, Henry had two related concerns: the powers of the clergy and the calling of a council.

---

[129] Elton, *Reform and Reformation*, 199.
[130] Sowerby, *Renaissance and Reform in Tudor England*, 183.
[131] *Concilia*, III, 804–7. Burnet dates the complaints to 23 June 1536. Burnet, I, i, 213.
[132] PRO SP 1/105, fol. 56; *L&P*, XI, 83.
[133] BL Cotton MS Cleopatra E, VI, fol. 330. P.A. Sawada, 'Two Anonymous Tudor Treatises on the General Council', *JEH*, 12 (1961), 208n. The two memoranda are virtually identical in the first paragraph. The British Library memorandum has three additional paragraphs.

Essential and juridical distinctions between laity and clergy were simultaneously bound up with the discussion concerning the convocation of councils. Henry was nervous about the pope's proposed council at Mantua. If the Holy Roman Empire and France were to reconcile and pass judgment on England's Reformation, Henry would be isolated from any power other than the German Protestants, who themselves occupied a precarious position. Since the pope was convoking the council, the issue of lay involvement had to be addressed. Henry Cole and Alexander Alesius prepared tracts on this very issue. Alesius, a Scottish evangelical, treats the issue as one of *regnum* versus pretentious *sacerdotium*. According to him, the laity should be involved in all aspects of a council, including the definition of doctrine, for the infallible church includes both laity and clergy. The Byzantine emperor was ἱερεύς καί βασιλεύς and European princes can claim the same prerogative in councils.[134] With such thoughts, it seems little wonder that Cromwell invited Alesius to the resulting synod. Alesius' claim that it was 'bi chance' seems doubtful.[135] The external struggle between pope and king was conflated with the ongoing internal struggle between laity and clergy in England.

The first and longest paragraph, basically Cromwell's entire memorandum, concentrates on the lay–clerical distinction. Many clerics take the texts of John 20 and Acts 20 to prove the power of bishops to be above that of kings and princes. 'It is expedient that the question be demanded of such of the clergy as be most like by their authority and learning to be disposed to declare the truth therein.' After the committee's conclusion is reached, everyone is to declare his mind openly on the matter. The tone of the memorandum reflects both Cromwell's pragmatic desire to reach a middle way in religious issues and his suspicion of priests. Priests claim the Holy Spirit gave them the rule and government of the church. They also say there is no higher power than sacramental power. Cromwell concludes the true meaning of the texts is 'little to that effect'.

Cranmer's memorandum adds a further three paragraphs, and treats the issue as a problem of conciliar definition, an attitude commensurate with his fascination for councils. He suggests 'that it be secretly enquyred of the most notable lerned men in thys Realme who shuld haue auctorite to gather a generall counceill, for what cause it ought to be gathered, and who ought to have voyce in the generall counceill, and that their opynyons therin be only certefyed to the kyng and his counceill'.[136] The pope claimed *ius concilium*

---

[134] Sawada, 'Two Tudor Treatises', 204, 210, 213.
[135] Alexander Alane [Alesius], *Of the auctorite of the word of god*, ([n.p.], [n.d.]), sig. Av. *A&M*, V, 378.
[136] BL Cotton MS Cleopatra E, VI, fol. 330ᵛ.

convocandi, the right to call councils, on his own, apart from other bishops and the princes. Henry and Cranmer wanted to dispute that issue. Another concern was 'who ought to have voyce'. It is at this crucial juncture that Cranmer would diverge from the radical laity around Cromwell, and from Henry. We now turn to the synod called for by these memoranda to discover how Cranmer defended the necessity of a ministerial priesthood even while redefining its role.

6

Thomas Cranmer: The Ministerial Priesthood is 'Necessary'[1]

When the London synod began meeting in late February 1537, its primary task was the status of the sacraments.[2] *Ten Articles* included only the three sacraments approved by Luther. Marriage, unction, confirmation, and orders were silently excluded, to the ire of the conservatives. In his tirade against John Stokesley, Alexander Alesius recounts the opening session he attended at Cromwell's invitation.[3] After receiving obeisance from the assembled prelates and doctors, Cromwell, speaking for the king, called for certain controversies to be determined. These controversies were to be settled in the synod then approved by Parliament. Striking for the evangelical agenda, Cromwell warned the prelates to conclude all things by God's Word, eschewing 'unwritten verities'.

Cranmer then delivered an oration concerning the principal points of religion to be discussed. Cranmer's speech, as related by Alesius, exhibits commonalities with a list of fifteen questions attributed to Cranmer, though the attribution is debatable. Both the speech and the list end with a question about the four missing sacraments.[4] The list includes questions on the mechanical power of the clergy to forgive sins, on whether laity may sit in general councils, and on the relationship of lay to clerical jurisdictions. The list consistently refers the final decision to king and Parliament. A debate ensued between Cromwell's man, Alesius, and Stokesley, the Bishop of London, over the definition of sacrament, dependence on the Word of God alone, and vernacular Scripture. Cranmer subsequently asked Cromwell to withdraw Alesius from the debates. After the opening sessions, Cromwell also departed to attend to other business. He signed some declarations while merely

---

[1] *Formularies*, 103.
[2] P. Holmes, 'The Last Tudor Great Councils', *HJ*, 33 (1990), 10–13.
[3] *Of the auctorite of the word of god*, sigs Av–Bviii.
[4] Speech is in *A&M*, V, 380. List is in Burnet, I, ii, 316–18. *L&P*, XII, ii, 409; X, 241.

receiving others, and was eventually reduced to receiving reports from Cranmer on the synod's progress.[5]

In spite of the hopes expressed in the radical bills, the bishops opted for a rigid distinction between laity and clergy. This was, moreover, one of their first decisions.[6] Indeed, evangelical clergy dominated the subcommittee responsible for the first crucial document asserting this distinction. Did Cromwell stack this subcommittee with evangelicals hoping for a determination in favor of a lay interpretation of Acts 20 and John 20? Was Cromwell outmaneuvered by Cranmer and the evangelicals in league with the conservatives? If Cromwell, in the name of the king and on behalf of rising temporal rulers, was behind the assertions of lay eldership in the first place, it certainly suggests such a scenario.

As the basis for subsequent definitions of priesthood and as an indicator of the limit to which even evangelical bishops were willing to go with universal priesthood, 'Judgment of some Bishops' is quoted here in full:

> The words of St. John in his 20th Chap. *Sicut misit me Pater, & ego mitto vos, &c.* hath no respect to a King's or a Princes Power, but only to shew how that the Ministers of the Word of God, chosen and sent for that intent, are the Messengers of Christ, to teach the Truth of his Gospel, and to loose and bind sin, &c as Christ was the Messenger of his Father. The words also of St. Paul, in the 20th Chap. of the Acts; *Attendite vobis & universo gregi, in quo vos Spiritus Sanctus posuit Episcopos regere Ecclesiam Dei,* were spoken to the Bishops and Priests, to be diligent Pastors of the People, both to teach them diligently, and also to be circumspect that false Preachers should not seduce the People, as followeth immediately after in that same place. Other places of Scripture declare the highness and excellency of Christian Princes Authority and Power; the which of a truth is most high, for he hath power and charge generally over all, as well Bishops, and Priests, as other. The Bishops and Priests have charge of Souls within their own Cures, power to minister Sacraments, and to teach the Word of God; to the which Word of God Christian Princes knowledge themselves subject; and in case the Bishops be negligent, it is the Christian Princes Office to see them do their duty.

To help the reader see the theological importance of this statement, the signatories are listed in the footnote, along with their dates of occupancy and reputed confessional persuasion in 1537. Not only were conservative

---

[5] Cox, II, 334–8.

[6] All eight bishops signing the document were among the eleven that Alesius cited as being present at the synod's opening. BL Stowe MS 141, fol. 36; Burnet, I, ii, 177. This is dated between September 1535, the consecration of Hilsey to Rochester, and July 1539, when Shaxton and Latimer resigned. MacCulloch shows that a document composed after this one must be dated before mid-1537. See chart in note 7.

bishops willing to limit the royal and universal priesthoods, so were evangelicals. Cranmer himself took the lead.[7] Why were the bishops so bold? What necessity drove them to define where Henry preferred ambiguity? In short, the bishops were concerned with the very survival of ministerial priesthood. The dissolution of the monasteries and the radical threats in Parliament called into question the need for the clergy. It is no coincidence that the number of men offering themselves for ordination experienced a sharp decline in 1536 and that levels stayed low for years.[8] The ministry was under siege from king and laity. In a stand of unity, the bishops concluded kings have a general charge but not a sacerdotal cure. Bishops and priests are the objects of Acts 20 and John 20. They are to teach and determine doctrine, and loosen and bind sin. Kings are subject to them in these matters. On their part kings are to ensure that bishops and priests do their duty.

How would Henry take such a bold statement excluding him from priestly office and forcing him to submit to the Word preached by the priest? Cromwell was a serious obstacle but Henry was quite another. Henry often revealed his own dislike for exclusive priestly and episcopal powers in confirmation and orders, even striking the word 'holy' from 'holy orders'.[9] The bishops knew this and found a diplomatic way to present their message to him. Henry was still worried about the pope's summoning of a general council to Mantua in May 1537. He did not want a council without his approval and input, and he called on his bishops to provide him theological justification. They previously raised questions regarding the relationship of princes to general councils in the 1536 Convocation,[10] but they now gave him much of what he wanted in this respect, indeed allowing for kings to convene or veto the calling of a council. On the other hand, they refuted the positions of Alesius and St German by asserting, 'In all the auncyent Counsailles of the Churche, in matiers of the

---

7

Signature	Name	See Occupied	Persuasion in 1537
T. Cantuarien	Thomas Cranmer	1533–1553	Evangelical
Joannes London	John Stokesley	1530–1539	Conservative
Cuthbertus Dunelmen	Cuthbert Tunstall	1530–1559	Conservative
Jo. Batwellen	John Clerk	1523–1541	Conservative
Thomas Elien	Thomas Goodrich	1534–1554	Evangelical
Nicolaus Sarisburien	Nicholas Shaxton	1535–1539	Evangelical
Hugo Wygorn	Hugh Latimer	1535–1539	Evangelical
J. Roffen	John Hilsey	1535–1539	Evangelical

[8] Bowker, 'The Henrician Reformation and the Parish Clergy', *BIHR*, 50 (1977), 33–4.
[9] Scarisbrick, *Henry VIII*, 411–12, 416–18.
[10] Burnet, I, ii, 155–7. Cf. Cranmer's statement on royal convocation of councils. Cox, II, 76–8.

Faith and interpretacion of Scripture, no man made diffinitive subscription, but busshopes and preistes; for somoche as the declaration of the Wourde of Godde perteignyth unto them.' They judiciously attached their defense of clerical priesthood, 'Judgment of some Bishops', to the end of their new statement on councils and addressed the combined statement to the Lord Keeper of the Privy Seal, Cromwell.[11]

'SACRAMENT' OF ORDERS

There must have been some discussion between Cromwell and the bishops on the inadequacy of the combined statement. The bishops might vaguely win on general principle at this point but a fuller treatment was necessary. In the papers assigned to Cranmer is a document entitled '*De Ordine et Ministerio Sacerdotum et Episcoporum*'.[12] Modern scholars have followed *Letters and Papers* in assigning this document to the 1538 Anglo-Lutheran summit, but this is unlikely. Messenger believes the paper was written to bring English reformed theology into line with Lutheranism, but he overstates his case.[13] First, there was no need to convince Lutherans of the viability of priesthood or episcopate. Lutherans retained a priesthood although they redefined it in favor of a ministry of Word and sacraments as opposed to the sacrifice of the mass. They were also perfectly willing to allow affiliated churches to retain bishops, as seen in Denmark and Sweden and in Melanchthon's *Apology*.[14] Second, the preamble of the document defines its purpose as arguing for the retention of orders and is thus a direct response to the radical attack on orders in the 1536 Parliament. Third, much of its wording is translated into English and taken directly into another synodal working paper, 'As touching', which became the basis for the article, 'The sacrament of Orders', in *Bishops' Book*. Fourth, the basic outline of 'As touching' and 'The sacrament of Orders' is strikingly similar to '*De Ordine*'. Since both 'As touching' and 'The sacrament of Orders'

---

[11] MacCulloch dates the combined document before 10 July 1537 on the basis of Robert Aldrich's signature without episcopal designation. The draft on the councils is in the hand of Ralph Morice, with corrections by Cranmer. Lambeth MS 1107, fol. 163. Combined version of opinion on councils and of judgment on Acts 20 and John 20 is in PRO SP 1/105, fols 78–9; *State Papers Published under the Authority of His Majesty's Commission, King Henry VIII*, 11 vols (London, 1830–1852), I, 543–4; *L&P*, XI, 124.2.

[12] Cox, II, 484–9.

[13] *L&P*, XIII, I, 1307.19. Messenger, *Reformation, Mass and Priesthood*, I, 269–70; Paul Bradshaw, *The Anglican Ordinal* (London: SPCK, 1971), 12–13; Evans, *Problems of Authority*, 222n; *Cranmer*, 221n.

[14] Heal, *Of Prelates and Princes*, 17–19; *The confessyon of the fayth of the Germaynes exhibited to the most victorious Emperour Charles the V, To which is added the Apologie of Melanchthon*, transl. by Richard Taverner (London: Robert Redman, 1536), 'Faith', art. 15, 'Abuses', art. 7.

are much fuller than '*De Ordine*', '*De Ordine*' deserves temporal priority. We conclude, therefore, that this document was a preliminary outline for the 1537 synod's discussion of orders, most likely originating in Cranmer's household.

'*De Ordine*' was written to show that the ministry 'is certainly necessary for the church, however long we battle in the earth against the flesh, the world and Satan, and should not be abolished for any reason'. Its reasoning is more evangelical than most conservatives would allow but more conservative than radical evangelicals would allow, reflecting Cranmer's position at the time. In 1535, he intimated the primary duty of a bishop was to preach the Word. Immediately before the synod, he downplayed the mechanical power of priests over salvation, favoring personal volition instead.[15] On the conservative side, '*De Ordine*' retains both priesthood and episcopacy: 'Scripture plainly teaches the order and ministry of priests and bishops is not by human authority but divine institution.' Deacons and the minor orders are never mentioned. On the evangelical side, it does not consider orders a sacrament, referring instead to an office or function: priests and bishops have a stewardship of the divine mysteries, a ministry of Word and sacraments.[16]

The document falls thematically into three parts. Chapters 1–13 defend the existence and nature of priests and bishops; Chapters 14–32 refute papal primacy; the remainder exalt the royal cure over all people, laity, and clergy. The first part divides thematically and linguistically into three sections, the final chapter of each section beginning with a Latin conjunction for 'accordingly', *proinde* or *itaque*. Chapters 1–5 refute the radical universal priesthood; Chapters 6–9 sketch the superintending power of bishops in ordination and discipline; and Chapters 10–13 place limits on priestly power. A comparison of medieval lists of priestly duties with the list in '*De Ordine*' reveals a partial but definite shift in sacerdotal thought. Modern scholars of sixteenth-century clergy note the transition from a traditional emphasis on the priest's power to mediate grace through sacraments to an evangelical emphasis on the priestly functions of preaching and administering sacraments with primary stress on proclamation.[17] This document is the first clear sign of that change in official English theology. The medieval *Sarum Pontifical* exalted the ritual sacrificial

---

[15] 'For I pray God never be merciful unto me at the general judgment, if I perceive in my heart that I set more by any title, name, or style that I write, than I do by the paring of an apple, farther than it shall be to the setting forth of God's word and will.' Cranmer to Cromwell, 12 May 1535. Concerning a conservative cleric he wants investigated, Cranmer says, 'He taught openly in the pulpit there, that one paternoster, said by the injunction of a priest, was worth a million paternosters said of a man's mere voluntary mind: by this you may soon savour what judgment this man is of, and how sincerely he would instruct the people.' Cranmer to Cromwell, 28 January 1537; Cox, II, 305, 333. Cf. *Formularies*, 109.

[16] '*De Ordine*', chs 1, 5.

[17] Claire Cross, 'Priests into Ministers', in *Reformation Principle and Practice*, ed. by Peter Newman Brooks (London: Scolar Press, 1980), 203–25; Marshall, *Catholic Priesthood*, 1–2; O'Day, *English Clergy*, 27, 126, 134.

duties of priests, referring more than once to eucharistic function: 'It behooves the priest to offer, bless, preside, preach, confect, and baptize.' The medieval bishop granted the priest power to offer sacrifice to God for the sins and offenses of the people, living and dead.[18] The sacrificial power of the priest in the mass, put into doubt but still allowed by *Ten Articles*, is completely absent in '*De Ordine*'. The duty list here includes teaching, virtuous living, ministry of sacraments, protection of doctrine, and binding and loosing, summarized as a ministry of Word and sacraments.

In response to the radicals, '*De Ordine*' denies the elimination of holy orders is a result of universal priesthood. 'Accordingly, the power or function to minister the Word of God and the sacraments . . . , Christ himself gave to his apostles, and in them and through them he delivered the same, by no means indeed to all in common [*promiscue quidem omnibus*], but only to certain humans, without a doubt to bishops and presbyters, who to that duty are initiated and admitted.' Why is a particular priesthood necessary? Three reasons are cited. First, God has commanded it. Second, God has established 'no other certain and constituted reason or manner' by which He reconciles us in Christ and imparts spiritual gifts than through Word and sacraments.[19] Third, the Holy Spirit is conferred through the exercise of their office. The radical and indiscriminate universal priesthood is effectively denied, yet the traditional priesthood has also been significantly altered.

With '*De Ordine*' as a foundation, the synod constructed a statement that begins, 'As touching the sacrament of holy orders we wool[d] that all by-sshoppes and preachers shall instructe and teache our people comytted by us unto their spirituall chardge'.[20] Written in the hand of Ralph Morice, with a corrected line by Cranmer,[21] 'As touching' is a careful apology for the exist-ence of clergy. Drawing on a medieval distinction previously discredited by Edward Foxe,[22] it finds two major *potestates* instituted by God in the New Testament: *potestas gladii*, the power of the sword, and *potestas clavium*, the power of the keys. *Potestas gladii* concerns the civil powers and governance of kings. Following '*De Ordine*', the bishops collectively reject the radical univer-sal priesthood. The *potestas clavium* is a spiritual office, power, authority, and function committed 'unto certen persones onely' by Christ and his apostles. These 'certen persones' with their exclusive office are variously entitled priests and bishops, pastors and rectors, officers and ministers. Their duty list is quite similar to that of '*De Ordine*'. They 'shuld also be continually in the churche

---

[18] *Monumenta Ritualia Ecclesiae Anglicanae*, ed. by William Maskell, 3 vols (London: Pick-ering, 1846–1847), III, 202–22.

[19] Cf. *Fayth of the Germaynes*, 'Faith', art. 5.

[20] BL Cotton MS Cleopatra E, V, fols 48–50ʳ; Burnet, I, ii, 321–4.

[21] *Cranmer*, 190n.   [22] *De Vera Differentia*, fol. 26; *True dyfferes*, fols xliʳ–xliiʳ.

militant', the purpose for which the three reasons of '*De Ordine*' are translated and inserted.[23]

The issue in these early synodal discussions is power, pure and simple. Henry wanted to exalt his while denying the pope's. Radical gentry wished to exalt theirs at the expense of the clergy. Conservative clergy sought to maintain as much of the old religious power as possible under the new system. Evangelical clergy desired to retain the uniqueness of their office while transforming its nature. Each faction appealed to Scripture and tradition to buttress their position. The division of power between Henry and clergy had been decided in his favor, although he was still wary. Now, Henry wanted a consensus among the other groups; powers and offices needed a workable definition.

The division of power between gentry and clergy was based on a twofold definition. To satisfy the clergy (see "'Sacrament' of Orders', pp. 182–9) clerical orders are affirmed. To satisfy the radical gentry, represented in the presence of Cromwell, clerical powers are limited. The clerical office 'is no Turannical power, havyng no certein lawes or limytes, . . . nor yet an absolut power, but it is a moderate power subject, determyned, and restrayned unto those certein limittes and ends for the which the same was appoynted by godis ordenances'. According to Romans 1, I Timothy 4, and Ephesians 4 this power and office is counted among the 'proper and special' gifts of the Spirit. However, it is 'a certayn lymytted office restrayned unto the execution of a special function or ministracion', the ministry of Word and sacraments.[24] Henry's goal of making the priesthood 'little more than a trade union of confessors' was incrementally being realized.[25]

'As touching' also seeks to satisfy both evangelical and conservative sensibilities among the clergy. As a bone to the conservatives, they are assured 'the sacrament of ordre may worthily be called a sacrament' on the Augustinian basis of its twofold nature as a spiritual and invisible grace, and an outward and visible sign. Evangelicals, who tended to deny the existence of an indelible character, are assured 'the invisible gyfte or grace conferryed in that Sacrament, is nothyn else but the power thoffice and the auctorite before mentyoned'. Episcopal prayer and imposition of hands are retained in the conferment of orders. The minor orders were established by the Fathers to 'beautifie and ornate' the church but have no basis in the New Testament.[26]

With the brooding presence of a king desiring quietness in matters of religion and society, Cromwell and the bishops and theologians, evangelical and conservative, signed 'As touching'. (The positioning of the signatures is

---

[23] BL Cotton MS Cleopatra E, V, fols 48ʳ, 49ᵛ.
[24] BL Cotton MS Cleopatra E, V, fol. 48. Cf. '*De Ordine*', ch. 11.
[25] MacCulloch, 'Henry VIII and Reform', 167. Cf. *CSPS*, IV, I, 224.
[26] BL Cotton MS Cleopatra E, V, fol. 49ᵛ.

interesting. At top center is Cromwell, 'Vgrint'; below and left is Cranmer under which are three columns of his provincial bishops and theologians; below and right is Edward Lee of York under which is the signature of his lone provincial bishop, Cuthbert Tunstall.) 'As touching' is a quintessential English theological statement. Compiled by a diverse committee, it includes something to make everyone happy, and unhappy. It is thus a formula for concord and discord. Although Cromwell signed this statement, he was soon occupied elsewhere. Contemporary letters from Cranmer to Cromwell included one dated 21 July, informing him they have 'almost made an end of our determin-ations'.[27] Cromwell never approved the final synodal document, *The Insti-tution of a Christian Man*, otherwise known as the *Bishops' Book*.

The sacrament receiving the greatest attention in *Bishops' Book* is 'The sacrament of Orders', numbering some twenty-four folio pages in the first edition. The first section of this article is a close rewrite of 'As touching'. Rupp gives credit to Tunstall for the second section due to its distinction between *potestas ordinis* and *potestas iurisdictionis*. Considering the controversial nature of this article, its Janus-like alternation between conservative and evangelical sentiments, and Foxe's editorial role, it is doubtful Tunstall was entirely responsible.[28] The first new topic raised concerns Donatism, the belief that a priest's sinfulness might hinder the efficacy of a sacrament. This is denied since 'God is the only principal, sufficient, and perfect cause of all the efficacy of his word and sacraments'.[29] A common belief of the time, Cranmer later condemned Donatism in *Forty-Two Articles*.[30]

The second new topic concerns the *ordo–iurisdictio* distinction created by the canon lawyers. Here, both powers are assigned to clergy alone. Of the two, *iurisdictio* is manifestly the controversial issue. Clerical jurisdiction 'consisteth in three special points'. First is the power to rebuke, excommunicate, and absolve. This power is restricted to verbal, as opposed to physical, constraint and must be sparingly used. The second juridical power involves the approval or rejection of clerical nominees. The third juridical power concerns ceremo-nial order in the church. Ceremonial order is necessary since Scripture commands all Christian people to gather themselves together for invocation, hearing, reception of the sacraments, giving 'laud and praise', and honoring God. Though necessary, gathering brings with it the danger of 'great trouble, unquietness, and tumult'. The remedy to this danger is the suppression of individualist tendencies; it is 'not suffered to do every man after his own fashion or appetite'. Priests and bishops, like fathers, are there for governance,

---

[27] Foxe, too, lamented Cromwell's absence. Cox, II, 333–8, 337n.
[28] Rupp, *English Protestant Tradition*, 141; *L&P*, XII, ii, 401. Some drafts concerning juris-diction are in Tunstall's hand. Messenger, *Reformation, Mass and Priesthood*, I, 269.
[29] *Formularies*, 106.
[30] Marshall, *Catholic Priesthood*, 47–54. *Forty-Two Articles*, art. 27; *Documents*, 300.

which tends to the people's profit and tranquility and God's honor. Spiritual fatherhood, which requires obedience and the provision of sustenance on the part of the people, is affirmed here and amplified later in the article on the fifth commandment.[31]

Several pages are then devoted to two doctrines that temper the juridical powers just delineated. The first, a doctrine of variable jurisdiction, moderates the still controversial exposition of Acts 20. The passage commits rule to the clergy only 'in general words'. The 'particular' form of governance was not authorized through Scripture, 'but was and is left to be declared from time to time, and from age to age, by certain positive rules and ordinances'. Scripture witnesses to the variable nature of *potestas iurisdictionis*. Interestingly, both ceremonial rites and the diversity of degrees among ministers are subject to variable jurisdiction. (Another variable scriptural rule is 'that women should keep silence, and not take upon them to teach in the church'.) Two ages in church history are normative for how rules are determined. Before the conversion of princes, rules were made 'by the ministers of the church, with the consent of the people'. Since their conversion, kings, 'with the consent of their parliaments', have decided juridical matters and may restrict clerical jurisdiction as needed.[32]

Cranmer espoused this variable jurisdiction doctrine in a series of antipapal sermons in summer 1535. He differentiated human laws from divine law. Human laws, such as the pope's, do not 'remit sin' but are made for 'good order' and 'remembrances'. Canon law is thus reduced to the level of common law. These laws, though not soteriologically necessary, must be obeyed, unless changed by the proper authority; i.e. kings. Periodic changes in ecclesial jurisdiction are necessary since the church is prone to err. In the 1540 questions, Cranmer went so far as to make the three degrees of ministry variable. Cranmer's adamant defense of the necessity of ministry coupled with a relaxed view towards an exact polity was a characteristic view of English reformers through most of the sixteenth century.[33]

Corollary to variable jurisdiction is a second moderating doctrine, that of 'things indifferent', *adiaphora*, which the humanists under Cromwell also advocated. Although priests must temper their decisions and people must humbly obey, outward ceremonies are 'but mean and indifferent things' subject to magisterial definition. *Adiaphora* are defined as practices 'neither commanded expressly in scripture, nor necessarily contained or implied therein, nor yet expressly repugnant or contrary thereunto'. Of a ceremonial

---

[31] *Formularies*, 107–11, 151–2. On the theologically significant renumbering of the Ten Commandments to a Swiss format, and Cranmer's hand in it, see *Cranmer*, 192.

[32] *Formularies*, 110–14.

[33] Cranmer to Henry, 26 August 1536; Cox, II, 325–8. Burnet, I, ii, 220–3. H.F. Woodhouse, *The Doctrine of the Church in Anglican Theology 1547–1603* (London: SPCK, 1954), 109, 163–4.

nature, 'indifferent things' must be held by the people in order to maintain 'common order and tranquility'. On the other hand, Christian liberty may not be jeopardized and 'reasonable' omissions are allowed. The *Bishops' Book* does not define what 'reasonable' means. *Adiaphora* was also an important concept in the Lutheran *Augsburg Confession*, a possible source for the Anglican formulary.[34]

Summarizing the second part of *'De Ordine'*, 'Of the sacrament of Orders' then addresses the issue of papal primacy. Papal primacy is an historical development with no basis in Scripture and dubious basis in tradition. The most presumptuous claim of the papacy, next to the denial of an egalitarian episcopate, is dominion over princely realms. This leads into the final topic broached by *'De Ordine'*, royal power. The wording of *'De Ordine'* is incorporated in the discussion but a new and rather stringent qualification of royal power is introduced. 'We may not think that it doth appertain unto the office of kings and princes to preach and teach, to administer the sacraments, to absoyle, to excommunicate, and such other things belonging to the office and administration of bishops and priests.' This denial of certain aspects of royal priesthood is preceded and followed by strong affirmations that clergy must be held accountable for the performance of offices by the king. Clergy must obey princely laws 'not only *propter iram*, but also *propter conscientiam*', on account of wrath and conscience. In exercising his jurisdiction, the king restores the liberty the clergy lost under the pope.[35]

Other than Cromwell, and he left early, temporal lords had been excluded from the synod. Upon reviewing the synod's decrees, the magistrates feared exclusion from the divine power structure being erected under Henry. While Lord Cromwell's implicit disapproval was expressed in his lack of signature, certain of his comrades explicitly expressed their disappointment. After examining *Bishops' Book* at Henry's behest (a summary of his annotations is extant), St German wrote an unpublished manuscript, 'A Dyalogue shewinge what we be bounde to byleve as thinges necessary to Salvacion, and what not'. 'A Dyalogue' rejects the biased clerical interpretations of the 1537 synod and calls for a council. This council will be 'gathered and kepte by auctoritie of kinges and princes, and wherin notable men of the temporaltie, as they be callede, shulde have voices'.[36] In the 1530s, St German had moved inexorably toward granting authority for defining doctrine to the crown in Parliament[37] on the theological basis that 'the universall church is the congregation of all

---

[34] *Formularies*, 114–16. *Fayth of the Germaynes*, 'Faith' art. 15, 'Abuses' art. 7.
[35] *Formularies*, 121–2.
[36] PRO SP 6/2, fol. 122. Guy, 'Scripture as Authority', 210–20.
[37] Daniel Eppley, *Defending Royal Supremacy and Discerning God's Will in Tudor England* (Aldershot: Ashgate, 2007), ch. 7.

faithefull people, and not only of the byshops and priestes.'[38] He decried the idea that the clergy could define doctrine on their own, while advocating the laity, especially the king, shared a 'cure' or 'charge' over souls: 'And why shuld nat the parlyament than whiche representeth the whole catholyke churche of Englande expounde upon scrypture rather than the convocacyon whiche representeth onely the state of the clergy[?]'[39] St German's conciliar appeal yielded nothing immediately, but his criticisms, including lengthy references to orders, influenced the king.[40]

CRITICIZING THE CRITIC

The bishops withdrew from London in August, leaving the final editing to Foxe. He finished the work, procured the necessary signatures, sent it to the printer, and died soon after. Although issued in early autumn, Henry did not review the book until late November due to the birth of Edward and death of Jane Seymour. Reflecting humanist assumptions—that the overarching Henrician goals of unity and quietness could be reached through the elimination of superstition and the spread of personal, therefore vernacular, knowledge of the truth—the preface calls on Henry to read and approve the finished product:

> yet we do most humbly submit it to the most excellent wisdom and exact judgment of your majesty, to be recognised, overseen, and corrected, if your grace shall find any word or sentence in it meet to be changed, qualified, or further expounded, for the plain setting forth of your highness' most virtuous desire and purpose in that behalf. Whereunto we shall in that case conform ourselves, as to our most bounden duties to God and to your highness appertaineth.[41]

The bishops should not have been surprised that Henry did what they suggested and expected what they promised. The royal priest withdrew to render royal judgment on his bishops' doctrine; Henry's personal copy warns, on both flyleaves, that the book should not be taken from his Privy Chamber. The king's editing shows his primary concern was power, specifically its derivation and transmission. His first correction localized God's power with the addition of 'by hys ordinat poure' in the commentary on the creed. Thereafter, Henry habitually refers to the exercise of all human powers as being 'by his grace'. His first large deletion softens the denunciation of a fellow

---

[38] *A Treatise concernynge generall councilles, the Byshoppes of Rome, and the Clergy* (London: Berthelet, 1538), sig. C5ᵛ.
[39] *Answer*, sig. G6ᵛ, cited in Eppley, *Defending Royal Supremacy*, 118.
[40] BL Royal MS 7C, XVI, fols 204ʳ, 205ʳ. Kreider, *English Chantries*, 132.
[41] *Formularies*, 23–7.

magistrate, Pontius Pilate.[42] Though comments are found throughout Henry's copy, the heaviest markings occur in the section on orders. Henry apparently read through this section twice: first, accepting some parts with heavy amendments; later, marking whole paragraphs and pages with various spellings of *nihil*, delete. Both readings begin with vigor but diminish two-thirds of the way through the section, an indicator perhaps of the extent to which the royal interest could be held. In the second reading, some sixty per cent of the attended portion is deleted, with the last four folio pages, on jurisdiction, completely eradicated.[43]

Though the deletions are instructive, Henry's amendments and Cranmer's subsequent responses are most enlightening. The archbishop acknowledged receipt of Henry's amendments on 14 January 1538 and returned his responses in less than a fortnight.[44] MacCulloch maintains Cranmer's responses are the first 'unambiguous' statements of his new evangelical theology.[45] The fourth and longest response, frequently cited by Cranmer, is an extended sermon refuting Henry's soteriological reliance on works. Cranmer coolly employs the humanist emphasis on internal disposition as a bridge to the evangelical doctrine of justification by faith. The mind and the will must have a firm intent and purpose of love towards God and people. God knows the inward disposition; therefore, faith is the only possible remedy for sin. As for good works, external action without internal faith is hypocrisy. However, good works follow rather than precede faith.[46] Cranmer's concern, an exposition of evangelical faith, is stated clearly, but Henry's concern, a clarification of ecclesiastical and regal powers, is woefully ambiguous.

In his critique of the section on orders, Henry disparaged the bishops' construal of ecclesiastical order but offered no coherent alternative. His confusion is most apparent in his treatment of key terms. At first, cure, authority, power, and administration are synonyms describing priestly action. But he soon shows consternation over the relationship of order to power, and function to office. Later, jurisdiction is equated with power, and cure is distinguished from jurisdiction. Cure becomes the catchall term for the duties of priesthood, which include authority to preach, dispense sacraments, consecrate the sacrament of the altar, loose and absolve sins in confession, bind and

---

[42] Bodleian Quarto Rawlinson 245, fols 2^r, 6^r.

[43] Bodleian Quarto Rawlinson 245, fols 39^v–46^v. Another critic, likely the evangelical bishop of Ely, Thomas Goodrich, similarly excised the section on jurisdiction in his private copy. Dunstan C.D. Roberts, 'An Annotated and Revised Copy of *The Institution of a Christen Man* (1537)', *BIHR*, 84 (2011), 41–2.

[44] Cranmer to Cromwell; Cox, II, 358–60.

[45] *Cranmer*, 209.

[46] Cox, II, 84–7, 113–14. On the unique shape of Cranmer's evangelical doctrine of salvation, see Ashley Null's definitive thesis, *Thomas Cranmer's Doctrine of Repentance: Renewing the Power to Love* (OUP, 2000).

excommunicate, and ordain priests. Consistent with this use of cure, Henry separates the priest's 'cure' from the layman's 'charge' or 'care'. But in a telling inconsistency, he approves his own 'cure and oversight' and commits 'spiritual charge' for the people to himself along with priests. Henry wanted to buttress his own position as mediator in the divine dispensation of power or 'grace', but failed to recognize his claims still subverted traditional lay–clerical distinctions.[47] He vacillates between the traditional assignment of spiritual cure to priests alone and the reformers' emphasis on vocation or calling to an office or function.

Cranmer, sensing Henry's confusion, pushed him towards the Lutheran doctrine of vocation to office. Cranmer believes God grants a calling or vocation unto an office or function to a person through some authority, by birth or 'degree' or as assigned by a social superior. The individual is called in one sense to salvation, but in another sense to fulfill an office or function. Vocation itself is not a gift of God, 'but the operation of God toward us'. The office or function to which one is called has an accompanying set of responsibilities described synonymously as a cure, charge, custody, or care. In fulfilling their divinely ordained vocations, persons benefit the whole community. When Henry opposed spiritual cure to temporal charge, Cranmer would have none of it. 'It is small difference between "cure" and "charge", but that the one is plain English, and the other is deducted out of the Latin.'[48] In short, priestly office is comparable to, though distinct from, civil office. This helps explain what Cranmer meant when he responded to the ninth question in 1540, 'And there is no more promise of God, that grace is given in the committing of the ecclesiastical office, than it is in the committing of the civil office.' He was not denying the transmission of grace to recipients of ecclesiastical office; he was affirming the necessity of divine gift in the holding of any office. Although the priest was still necessary, his indelible character was fictional.

In the Middle Ages, it appears that only monks used the term *vocatio* to indicate their role in life, a role that was specifically bound up with society's spiritual redemption.[49] For the more mundane roles in life, the preferred term was *status*. Aquinas used *vocatio* to indicate 'God's help moving and exciting our mind to give up sin'.[50] *Status*, for Aquinas, meant the estates and offices

---

[47] Cox, II, 96–8, 102, 109.

[48] Cox, II, 91, 94, 108–9. The editor of Cranmer's works incorrectly located annotation xxxv. It refers to Henry's correction to the fifth petition of *Paternoster*. However, the phrase, 'we think it convenient, that all bishops and preachers shall instruct and teach the people committed unto their spiritual charge', was a frequent formula indicating the homiletic nature of *Bishops' Book*. Bodleian Quarto Rawlinson 245, fol. 88; Cox, II, 94n.

[49] *Medieval Callings*, ed. by Jacques Le Goff, transl. by Lydia G. Cochrane (London: University of Chicago Press, 1990), 64–5.

[50] *Summa Theologica*, I-II, qn. 113, art. 1.

that members of the church filled. State, grade, and office were intimately related. 'The order of ecclesiastical beauty' required that when a person is appointed to a higher duty, 'he attains thereby both office and grade and at the same time a certain state of perfection, . . . as in the case of a bishop.'[51] Luther turned Aquinas' distinction on its head. For Luther, *vocatio* includes both the call to salvation and the secular role to which God calls the Christian. All Christians have a vocation and none is better than the other. Though the calling to ministry was special, Luther envisioned no essential distinction between clergy and laity, just a functional distinction. The Wittenberg theologian used *status* to indicate various roles in ministry, marriage, and magistracy. The Christian could claim a *vocatio* when he recognized God had put him in his particular *status*. *Status* in no way implies perfection; again, it is a functional distinction, not an essential one.[52]

Cranmer also used this Lutheran doctrine of vocation to help Henry develop his doctrine of forgiveness. Reflecting a dilemma common to Christian magistrates, Henry deleted sections from the fifth petition of *Paternoster* calling him to literally forgive his brother's sins. How could he forgive others and still be the dispenser of justice? Cranmer perceived Henry's predicament and, in his second-longest response, distinguished public office from private spirituality. The doctrine Cranmer teaches here is surprisingly similar to that found in Luther's *Temporal Authority* (1523). The officeholder has been deputed by God to administer public justice and must be faithful in its execution, but he must also inwardly, or privately, forgive sins committed against him.[53] 'Now, these things well considered, these two may stand both well together; that we, as private persons, may forgive all such as have trespassed against us, with all our heart; and yet that the public ministers of God may see a redress of the same trespasses that we have forgiven.'[54] To other Lutheran influences upon Cranmer's developing evangelical theology we now turn.

CRANMER'S LUTHERAN THEOLOGY

As noted previously, as a result of the Peasants' Wars, Luther and his allies on the continent reconfigured their ecclesial framework. The common priesthood received in baptism—with its authority to preach, baptize, administer the eucharist, hear confession, judge doctrine, and excommunicate and elect

---

[51] *Summa Theologica*, II-II, qn. 183, art. 3.
[52] Paul Althaus, *The Ethics of Martin Luther*, transl. by Robert C. Schultz (Philadelphia: Fortress Press, 1972), 36–42; Wingren, *The Christian's Calling*, 1–10.
[53] *LW*, XLV, 95–6, 100–3, 117, 123–4; Althaus, *Ethics of Luther*, 70–5.
[54] Cox, II, 110–12.

clergy—was an excellent foil against the papal hierarchy, but its social implications were unforeseen. When the peasants stressed their communal prerogative, the Lutherans learned a harsh lesson in the relationship between religious
doctrine and social stability. Subsequently, they stressed order and magisterial
rule. People must stay within their natural states or God-given vocations. The
doctrine of vocation applied calming oil to the troubled waters of evangelical
society.

At the same time, vocation allowed the reformers to retain the anti-papal
teachings connected with common priesthood. The sacramental priest
offering sacrifices for the people due to an indelible character given in ordination was denied on the basis of baptism as ordination and of the people's
ability to receive grace through faith and offer spiritual sacrifices on their own.
The sacrificing, papally approved priest was replaced by the minister, who
followed his own vocation of preaching and administering sacraments as the
result of being publicly called and authorized. Only ministers may publicly
preach the Word to the people; in turn, householders must instruct their
dependents.[55] Although the people no longer needed a sacrificing priest to
apply the benefits of Christ's sacrifice, administration of the sacraments, still
necessary for common welfare, was restricted to clergy. Election, ostensibly
still in the hands of the people, was confined to representatives appointed by,
or at least agreeable to, the magistrates. Confession could still be heard by
anyone and congregational music arose as an expression of popular worship,
but there was minimal social danger in the reformers' construal of confession
or hymnody.

Radical and Anabaptist conventicles, who reified congregational priesthood,
were anathematized by evangelicals and conservatives alike. Self-sufficient
spiritualists and rationalists, who atomized common priesthood in the manner
of Sebastian Franck and Caspar Schwenckfeld, were just as vehemently
condemned. In evangelical areas, the rigid hierarchical structure of the pre-
Reformation church was replaced by attenuated structures tethered to temporal authorities, not by self-governing congregations, nor by free-thinking
spiritualists. Indeed, it has been argued the Reformation was 'successful' only
where it enjoyed the support of secular authorities.[56] The evangelical weapon of
common priesthood was tamed by the doctrine of 'vocation' but retained its
anti-papal teeth with the doctrine of 'spiritual sacrifices'. Of these two major
loci in Cranmer's doctrine of royal priesthood, vocation is discussed in this
chapter while spiritual sacrifices is treated in Chapter 7.

---

[55] Cf. *Documents*, 179–80.
[56] Hans R. Guggisberg, 'The Secular State of the Reformation Period and the Beginnings of
the Debate on Religious Toleration', in *The Individual in Political Theory and Practice*, ed. by
Janet Coleman (OUP, 1996), 79.

Henry's disdain for Luther was apparent throughout the 1520s. However, after his serpentine efforts to obtain a papal divorce repeatedly met failure, he fixed on the final plan promoted by Cranmer, appealing to the academy over the papacy. Surprisingly, Henry also sought Luther's opinion, not only once but twice. Thus began a tortured courtship.[57] The first sign of Henry's changed attitude towards Luther was his statement to Eustace Chapuys on 28 November 1529 that Luther uncovered some truths in spite of his heresy.[58] Throughout the 1530s there were various official embassies between the evangelical princes of the Schmalkaldic League and Henry. These embassies were part of Henry's effort to protect himself in international affairs, and the accompanying English–German theological negotiations were subject to his policy changes,[59] the most spectacular reversal being his failed marriage with Anne of Cleves and the precipitous fall of Cromwell. Henry never accepted Lutheranism fully, perhaps for fear of social upheaval. Although Luther had modified his views on priesthood, justification by faith alone might encourage disobedience. However, Lutheran theology helped Henry defeat Roman jurisdiction. It also provided the rationale for dissolving purgatorial institutions.[60] During the king's flirtation with Lutheranism, Cranmer's sympathy for the movement became apparent.

Philip Melanchthon dedicated his 1535 edition of *Loci Communes* to Henry.[61] Where Luther was still difficult to stomach, Melanchthon was acceptable, perhaps even malleable. Henry and Melanchthon shared a common interest in humanism. More importantly, Melanchthon strongly affirmed civil obedience and refused to give a prominent place to common priesthood.[62] Shortly after his *Augsburg Confession* passed over the doctrine in silence, Melanchthon verbally relegated it to the 'odious and unessential articles which are commonly debated in the schools'.[63] This was a brilliant move, for it demonstrated that 1530s Lutheranism was not as radical as in the

---

[57] Like others, including the pope, Luther endorsed bigamy as less evil than divorce. Doernberg, *Henry and Luther*, 63–93.

[58] *L&P*, VII, 152.

[59] Doernberg, *Henry and Luther*, 97–120; Rupp, *English Protestant Tradition*, 89–127; Tjernegal, *Henry and the Lutherans*; McEntegart, *Henry VIII, The League of Schmalkalden and the English Reformation*.

[60] *L&P*, V, appendix 7; Kreider, *English Chantries*, chs 4–5.

[61] 'Epistola Nuncupatoria Mel. ad Henricum VIII. Angliae Regem', in *Corpus Reformatorum*, ed. by Henry Ernest Bindseil *et al*, 101 vols (1834–), XXI, 333–9.

[62] In the commonplace titled '*De Magistratibus Civilibus et Dignitate Rerum Politicarum*', Melanchthon sets out five rules. First, against the fanatics, a civil officer has dignity. Second, all of life, political and economic, is a vocation and a good work. Third, the magistrate's office is fully approved by Christians. Fourth, the gospel is not revolutionary and requires no new civil order. Fifth, it is a mortal sin to disobey the commands of the magistrate. *Loci Communes* (1535), in *Corpus Reformatorum*, XXI, 542–4.

[63] Gerrish, 'Priesthood and Ministry', 404.

1520s.[64] Impressed, Henry repeatedly called for Melanchthon to visit his realm. Cranmer, too, sought Melanchthon's presence, even after Henry's death, but this never occurred.

Melanchthon's *Loci Communes* were presented to Henry in 1535 and *Augsburg Confession*, along with Melanchthon's *Apology*, was translated into English and published *cum privilegio regali* in 1536.[65] Luther believed Henry might accept *Apology* as a confessional basis and the impact of the Augsburg documents is seen in the 1536 *Wittenberg Articles* agreed by Lutheran and English delegates and in the *Ten Articles* approved soon after in England's Parliament.[66] After a hiatus in 1537, the English again approached the Lutherans in 1538. This resulted in the arrival of a Lutheran delegation on 31 May, composed of Franz Burchard, George Boyneburg, and Friedrich Myconius, but without the coveted Melanchthon.

During this conference, Cranmer came out in support of Adam Damplip's Calais preaching, agreeing that Real Presence could be held while transubstantiation is an opinion worthy of confutation.[67] However, the impact of Lutheranism upon Cranmer's thought was even greater than his denial of transubstantiation. Indeed, this whole period may be characterized as a deepening evangelicalization in Cranmer's theology of priesthood: in the summer of 1532, he rejected priestly celibacy by secretly marrying Margarete, a relative of Andreas Osiander, the Nuremberg reformer.[68] Ashley Null speculates that Cranmer adopted the Lutheran doctrine of justification at this time. Whatever Cranmer's personal view of Lutheran solafideism, he obviously at the least adopted the associated doctrine of common priesthood in Nuremberg: 'Moreover, the Lutheran commitment to the priesthood of all believers would have removed the need for Cranmer to have maintained his priestly celibacy as a godly manner of living which was separate from and morally superior to the less spiritually demanding lives of the married laity.'[69]

This shift in personal doctrine is glimpsed in subsequent events. In a 1533 letter to Master Stapleton, schoolmaster-parson of Byngham, Cranmer commended him on filling his cure with teaching and exemplary living. Sacramental functions are conspicuous by their absence.[70] In 1538, Cranmer assured Cromwell that a priest could 'renounce his priesthood' and still make an excellent schoolmaster.[71] In 1540, he allowed his chaplain,

---

[64] Yet, Lutheranism developed two theories of imperial rebellion in the 1530s and 1540s. Skinner, *Foundations of Modern Political Thought*, II, 189–206.
[65] *Fayth of the Germaynes.*
[66] Doernberg, *Henry and Luther*, 103.
[67] Cranmer to Cromwell, 15 August 1538; Cox, II, 375.
[68] *Cranmer*, 71–2.　　[69] Null, *Thomas Cranmer's Doctrine of Repentance*, 111.
[70] 12 October 1533; Cox, II, 262.　　[71] 25 August 1538; Cox, II, 380.

Humphrey Darell, to hold two cures, without taking orders.[72] In practice, clerical vows and indelible characters no longer mattered. The priest was ontologically and juridically indistinct from a lay magistrate. As he told Mary, it was not 'for private subjects' such as himself to attempt reform without royal approbation, even though he was still Archbishop of Canterbury at the time.[73]

Gordon Jeanes attributes a Lambeth manuscript, '*De Sacramentis*', to Cranmer, dating it to the 1538 conference. '*De Sacramentis*' confirms Cranmer's careful appropriation of Melanchthon's theology.[74] Cranmer agreed that, according to the restricted definition of institution by Christ and signification of the remission of sins, only three of the seven original sacraments are truly sacraments: baptism, eucharist, and penance. Others, such as orders, are allowed as sacraments but only in a secondary sense. 'Holy order, which is given through the imposition of hands by the authority of the priesthood, confers the power to preach the Gospel and minister the sacraments, rather than the remission of sins.'[75] Consent and election by the people is required before orders are given by the imposition of hands. The laying on of hands was originally a task performed by priests but *postea*, at some indefinite time afterwards, the church transferred it to bishops.[76]

Citing Paul's admonition to Timothy, Cranmer says, 'a gift of God is given by the imposition of hands and priestly authority'. He suspends, however, the high view of medieval orders, which gave priests the power to remit sins, with vague and shifting qualifications. Cranmer retains the transmission of a grace or gift to the ordinand but classes it with other spiritual gifts. This gift is simply 'fortitude in preaching the Gospel' and is one among many gifts of the Spirit that edify the church, 'such as prophecy, understanding of scripture, gifts of miracles, and the like'. Since ordination is one of the gifts and is unnecessary for the remission of sins, 'it should not be numbered with the sacraments'.[77]

Cranmer's vocation doctrine appeared in a working document resulting from the 1538 conference, *Thirteen Articles*. 'Moreover, Christians in general may enter upon and exercise such offices and duties as this mortal life either stands in need of or is adorned or preserved with, according to the station and rank which each has individually received and in accordance with the laws of

---

[72] Maria Dowling, 'Cranmer as Humanist Reformer', in *C&S*, 106.

[73] Cranmer to Mary, Late 1553; Cox, II, 444.

[74] Lambeth MS 1107, fols 84ʳ–93ᵛ; Jeanes, 'A Reformation Treatise on the Sacraments', *JTS*, 46 (1995), 151–4. Cranmer also quoted liberally from Melanchthon in his *Commonplace Books*. Jeanes, 165–7.

[75] Jeanes, 169, 182–3.

[76] 'And unto the *priests or bishops* belongeth, by the authority of the gospel, to approve and confirm the person which shall be, by the king's highness or the other patrons, so nominated, elected, and presented unto them to have the cure of these certain people, within this certain parish or diocese' (my italics). *Formularies*, 109.

[77] Jeanes, 'Reformation Treatise', 178–9, 189.

God and of princes and the noble custom of the respective realms.' This statement encapsulates the common social doctrine of Henrician England and Lutheran Germany in 1538. Since Rome is not preeminent, regional variations in 'traditions, rites, and ceremonies' are perfectly normal. However, dissidents might take heart in the rejection of Roman obedience, so it is asserted that 'without ecclesiastical rites and traditions church order cannot be preserved'. Who, then, determines right order? The prince, a 'minister', governs by divine authority and is 'to compel all, priests as well as common people, properly and diligently to do their duties'. Although all Christians have gifts, everyone must respect their publicly authorized vocation. 'Concerning the ministers of the church, we teach that nobody should publicly teach or administer the sacraments unless he is regularly called, that is, called by those in the church into whose hands the laws and customs of each region, in keeping with the Word of God, have placed the right of calling and admitting people into the ministry.'[78] The necessity for public authorization subsequently became a hallmark of Cranmer's theology.[79]

Vocation, with its characteristic emphasis on magisterial obedience, was accompanied by a loosened sacrament of penance. Penance is not considered according to the old threefold distinction of confession, satisfaction, and absolution. Rather, the motions of the Holy Spirit provide an *ordo salutis*, a structured plan of personal salvation. The focus is on God's Spirit and Word, and human conscience and faith. Referring to the power given in John 20 to remit sins, the minister becomes an important, but purely instrumental, tool. 'For it is the voice of the Gospel by which, in spoken word, not in his own name or authority but in Christ's, the minister announces and offers the remission of sins to him who confesses.' The critical confession occurs in a person's conscience and heart. Cranmer read through this section carefully but was still worried by the belief that the priest possesses divine power to 'supersede inwardly'.[80] Thrice, he struck the words *necessariam* or *summe necessariam*, necessary or most necessary, replacing them with *commodam* or *commodissimam*, appropriate or very appropriate. Moreover, 'although not commanded by scripture, nevertheless [auricular confession] is allowed'. Aquinas believed absolution was effective only if the sinner was contrite. John Duns Scotus believed the priest could shape inward contrition, provided

---

[78] '*De Unitate Dei et Trinitate Personarum, de Peccato Originalie*', in Cox, II, 477, 480. Translation in Tjernegal, *Henry VIII and the Lutherans*, 299, 305.

[79] *Forty-Two Articles*, art. 24; *Documents*, 298. *The Reformation of the Ecclesiastical Laws of England*, 1552, transl. by James C. Spalding (Kirksville: Sixteenth Century Journal Publishers, 1992), 87–90; *The Reformation of the Ecclesiastical Laws*, ed. by Edward Cardwell (OUP, 1850), 35–9. Spalding translated a 1552 working draft of *Reformatio Legum Ecclesiasticarum*, while Cardwell's edition represents Cranmer's completed 1553 version. MacCulloch, review of Spalding edn, *JEH*, 44 (1993), 308–10.

[80] '*De Ordine*', ch. 11.

no obstacle was placed in the way. Both Aquinas and Scotus believed, however, that auricular confession was necessary. Concerned by the abuses of the medieval confessional, Cranmer redefined private confession as instruction and made it voluntary—'provided they find a learned and pious confessor'.[81] The sinner's internal disposition was also stressed in the article on sacraments. Sacraments are 'clear witnesses and efficacious signs of grace and of God's goodwill toward us, through which God works invisibly in us and invisibly pours His grace into us if indeed we receive them rightly'. On the one hand, it is recognized that the sacrament offers some tangible gift to the recipient. On the other, there is a clear rejection of the teaching that sacraments confer grace *ex opere operato*, by virtue of the work performed; the faith of the recipient is necessary.[82]

The 1538 English–German conference went nowhere. Cromwell did not attend to the conference, the German delegates were unhappy with the progress, and Henry was under the conservative influence of Tunstall all summer. In an effort to address their most crucial concerns, the so-called abuses—private mass, communion in one kind, and clerical celibacy—the Germans addressed a pointed letter to the king. Tunstall, on behalf of Henry, composed a conservative rebuttal, and the evangelical archbishop saw all progress cease. The conservative bishops, recognizing Henry's intransigence, championed the four sacraments and the conference dispersed without agreement.[83] Thenceforth, English evangelicals weakened. Eventually, under pressure from Henry, the 1539 Parliament passed *Six Articles*, codifying the very abuses despised by the Lutherans. Although Cranmer was able to sway Henry to his commodious view of confession, he was otherwise forced into a defensive position.[84] Further reformation was, for the moment, forestalled.

The last major theological statement of Henry's reign, the *King's Book*, in many ways reinterpreted the *Bishops' Book* in a conservative direction. In the sacrament of orders, however, the traditional *potestates* distinctions disappear, as does the limitation of Henry's sacerdotal powers. This was not the only change in favor of sacerdotal kingship. The fifth commandment under the Swiss numbering, concerning obedience to parents, was altered. In the fifth commandment, the *Bishops' Book* stressed the clergy's spiritual fatherhood, giving second place to the king's national fatherhood. The *King's Book* reversed the sequence. Henry's 'new-found conservatism' in theology most definitely did not include the recovery of an orthodox sacrament of orders.[85]

---

[81] Cox, II, 475–7; Tjernegal, *Henry and the Lutherans*, 294–8. Tentler, 'Summa', 109–11.

[82] Cox, II, 477; Tjernegal, *Henry and the Lutherans*, 298–9; Null, *Thomas Cranmer's Doctrine of Repentance*, 133–56.

[83] Cranmer to Cromwell, letters of 18 and 23 August 1538; Cox, II, 377–80.

[84] Glyn Redworth, 'A Study in the Formulation of Policy', 58–63.

[85] *Formularies*, 277–89, 311–20, 148–57. *Pace* Haigh's contention that Henry was returning to his theological moorings. *English Reformations*, 155.

Moreover, on the issue of auricular confession and the power of the keys, 'Cranmer carried the day', and it was defined as 'expedient'.[86] In 1545, 'An acte that the Doctors of the Civill Lawe may exercise Ecclesiastical Jurisdiction' was passed with Henry's approval. Its preface blasted lay–clergy distinctions.[87] To the end of his days, Henry was the royal priest.[88]

REFORMED ORDINAL

With the accession of Edward, Cranmer exerted his greatest influence, and his evangelical understanding of the ministry, characterized by the doctrine of vocation, was solemnized in the English liturgy. The first part of the foregoing statement will probably not be disputed. The second part will be controversial. The Oxford or Anglo-Catholic Movement of the nineteenth century radically reoriented many Anglicans to a Catholic interpretation of the Reformation. Cranmer's Reformation came to be viewed more as myth or accident than reality.[89] Encouraging an Anglican rapprochement with Catholicism, Abbé Fernand Portal and Viscount Halifax prompted a papal review of the validity of Anglican orders.[90] The result was disheartening for Anglo-Catholics. Following a theological evaluation of the history of the Anglican Ordinal, Pope Leo XIII issued an encyclical in 1896, *Apostolicae Curae*, in which he condemned the Anglican Ordinal as 'null and void' due to defects in both 'form' and 'intention'. The central issue was the omission of language granting the priest the power to consecrate the mass as a sacrifice.[91] The Archbishops of Canterbury and York responded with *Saepius Officio*, basically conceding the necessity of conveying the power to offer the sacrifice of the mass.[92] Since then, Anglo-Catholics and sympathetic Roman Catholics have sought to

---

[86] Null, *Thomas Cranmer's Doctrine of Repentance*, 154–5.

[87] 37 Henry VIII, ch. 17. Thanks to Alec Ryrie for this reference. NB that though passed in 1545, it originally failed in 1542. *Concilia*, III, 862.

[88] As to the objection that Henry accepted orthodox priesthood because he defended clerical celibacy, we note Felicity Heal's argument that Henry was more concerned to avoid the concentration of wealth in clerical dynasties. *Of Prelates and Princes*, 121.

[89] MacCulloch, 'The Myth of the English Reformation', *JBS*, 30 (1991), 1–19.

[90] Viscount Halifax, *Leo XIII and Anglican Orders* (London: Longmans Green, 1912); R.C. Moberly, *Ministerial Priesthood* (London: Murray, 1897), Appendix.

[91] *Anglican Orders: The Documents in the Debate*, ed. by Christopher Hill and Edward Yarnold (Norwich: Canterbury Press, 1997), 265–80. Leo XIII's position is perhaps most vulnerable when compared to Augustine's condemnation of Donatism. Augustine argued for the validity of even heretical orders.

[92] In particular, ch. XI of *Saepius Officio* supports the 'intention' of the English bishops to convey the authority to offer sacrifice. *Saepius Officio*, 281–318. Colin Buchanan, 'Anglican Ordination Rites', in *Visible Unity and the Ministry of Oversight* (London: Church House Publishing, 1997), 126–7.

overcome these 'defects' in the ARCIC process, often by stressing the 'moment of ordination' and 'consecration by formula'. Paul Bradshaw has demonstrated that such a stress on the moment has distorted modern reviews of Cranmer's *Ordinal*.[93]

In his treatment of the English ordinal, Edward Echlin has complicated the historiographical problem. Echlin seeks to validate Anglican orders from a Catholic perspective by stretching the principle *lex orandi est lex credendi*, the law of prayer is the law of faith. Although Cranmer embraced the principle in practice—the very fact that he expended so much time and effort in revising the liturgies of the church is sufficient proof of this—Echlin has, in practice, overstated Cranmer's use of this principle. Echlin is also scandalized by Cranmer's intimations of a doctrine of variability in ceremonies.[94] On his part, Cranmer would have been mystified by the modern project of establishing continuity between his work and the medieval rites by examining every jot and tittle of his liturgical project.[95] Cranmer's efforts were pointed in the opposite direction. He was more than willing to alter the form of common worship, *lex orandi*, in order to correct abuses and restore true doctrine, *lex credendi*. As his preface to the 1549 *Book of Common Prayer* (*BCP*) states, 'There was never any thing by the wit of man so well devised, or so surely established, which in continuance of time hath not been corrupted. . . . These inconveniences therefore considered, here is set forth such an order, whereby the same shall be redressed.'[96]

The medieval rites served as examples, but they were the only such models. The case has been forcefully made that Cranmer relied on Protestant rites from the continent as much as traditional medieval rites. Cranmer was quite comfortable with the idea of a continuing liturgical reformation, in a 'Reformed' direction.[97] While Cranmer did rely on medieval forerunners, such as the *Sarum Missal*, this was a stealth tactic, an 'opportunist adoption of medieval forms for new purposes'.[98] The continuities between medieval forms and the 1549 *BCP* were only a 'stopgap' measure to further reformation in the

---

[93] Bradshaw, 'The Liturgical Consequences of *Apostolicae Curae* for Anglican Ordination Rites', in *Anglican Orders: Essays on the Centenary of Apostolicae Curae, 1896–1996*, ed. by R. William Franklin (London: Mowbray, 1996), 75–86.

[94] Echlin, *Story of Anglican Ministry*, 97.

[95] Cf. Francis Aidan Gasquet and Edmund Bishop, *Edward VI and the Book of Common Prayer* (London: Hodges, 1890); F.E. Brightman, *The English Rite*, 2nd edn, 2 vols (London: Rivingtons, 1921); Francis Procter and Walter Howard Frere, *A New History of the Book of Common Prayer* (London: Macmillan, 1941); R.T. Beckwith, 'Thomas Cranmer and the Prayer Book', in *Study of Liturgy*, 101–5.

[96] *Liturgies*, 17–19.

[97] G.J. Cuming, *A History of Anglican Liturgy* (London: Macmillan, 1969), 66–116; Colin Buchanan, *What Did Cranmer Think He Was Doing?* (Bramcote: Grove Books, 1976).

[98] *Cranmer*, 461.

1552 *BCP*, and if the Protestant regime had survived, perhaps beyond.[99] A further indication of Cranmer's intent here is found in the structure of his *Commonplace Books*. These manuscripts arranged authoritative sources under various theological topics. In his extended research into ecclesiastical orders,[100] Cranmer characteristically began with references to Scripture followed by references to theological authorities. The theological authorities cited were primarily the early church Fathers, but interspersed among the Fathers were extensive quotations from Henry's *Assertio* and Calvin's *Institutes*.[101] The only authorities cited from the Middle Ages were Bede and Bernard of Clairvaux, both dead before Lateran IV.[102] For Cranmer, continuity with medieval doctrine was not a priority, even if continuity with liturgical form was a temporary necessity.

Cranmer's 1550 *Ordinal* exemplifies his willingness to infuse medieval forms with new meaning. Most famously, the ordinal retains the basic three-fold structure of the medieval church—bishop, priest, and deacon—giving each 'order' a separate rite. However, these orders are not understood in the traditional sense; they are treated in terms of Protestant vocation as opposed to Roman sacerdotalism. The ardent and ecumenical reformer, Martin Bucer of Strassburg, provided the formative influence in the *Ordinal*. After Charles V defeated the Protestant armies, Bucer was forced into exile. Cranmer invited him to England and a close friendship resulted. Bucer became Regius Professor of Divinity at Cambridge and gave advice to Cranmer on both revising *Book of Common Prayer* and formulating the 1550 *Ordinal*. During his English period, Bucer's works show an intense concern for the form and purpose of ministry.[103]

Bucer promoted at least four different ecclesial disciplines in his career: (1) the *Kirchenpfleger* system, in which wardens were appointed by a city council to oversee ministers in their parishes; (2) a presbyterian system, wherein elders provided discipline in tandem with their ministers; (3) the *Gemeinschaften*, a type of *ecclesiola in ecclesia* offering a more committed fellowship than the wider parish, in response to, and in reflection of, Anabaptism; and (4) the 'priestly kingdom' of England.[104] When this variability in form is compared

---

[99] MacCulloch, *Tudor Church Militant*, 74, 81, 91.

[100] BL Royal MS 7B, XI, fols 178–206.

[101] BL Royal MS 7B, XI, fols 190–3. Cranmer owned either a 1536 or 1543 edition of *Institutes*, but it is now lost. D.G. Selwyn, 'Cranmer's Library', in *C&S*, 53n. The section quoted here was available in 1536.

[102] BL Royal MS 7B, XI, fols 189, 196ᵛ.

[103] Bucer, *Scripta Anglicana Fere Omnia* (Basil, 1577), 220–355, 370–538, 553–610.

[104] Yarnell, 'Reformation Development', 56–8; Amy Nelson Burnett, 'Confirmation and Christian Fellowship: Martin Bucer on Commitment to the Church', *CH*, 64 (1995), 202–17; James Kittelson, 'Martin Bucer and the Ministry of the Church', in *Martin Bucer: Reforming Church and Community*, ed. by D.F. Wright (CUP, 1994), 83–94.

with his contention that discipline is important enough to be ranked a third mark of the church, in addition to the two marks—right preaching of the Word and right administration of the sacraments—held by the Lutherans, it is obvious Bucer considered discipline to be necessary in fact but variable in form.[105] In the English situation, he was careful to contextualize the discipline, or government, of the church to the monarchic–episcopal system already in existence. Bucer's reflection on the English system is recorded in a treatise written in thankfulness for his invitation by Cranmer and the young king. Edward, impressed, summarized it in his journal.[106] Bucer's *De Regno Christi* (1550) was composed after consultation with Cranmer and his advisers concerning the state of England's Reformation.[107]

De Regno Christi sets England's king over a *respublica Christiana*, Christian commonwealth, which establishes laws to secure Christian discipline in every area of social and private life. Reflecting Cranmer's Erastian views, the king is encouraged to develop a system whereby each person 'keeps his place in the body of Christ'. God has called every individual to a certain task and graced them with the appropriate spiritual gifts. 'Prefects' are to oversee office-holders, including priests, ensuring their diligence. If anyone is lazy or inadequate to the task, he is to be reassigned to another vocation. This reflects the evangelical view of ministerial vocations: clerical priesthood is temporary, reassignable without the loss of an indelible character.[108]

Bucer uses the metaphor of royal priesthood variously. Christ is king and has a spiritual kingdom. Yet, England may be compared to a 'priestly kingdom' since Christ has set over the people kings and priests who are concerned first and foremost with establishing *regnum Christi*. The people of Christ are a 'royal priesthood' but are rightly ruled by 'true kings and princes', even by 'savage tyrants'. In one passage, he ties universal priesthood directly to the doctrine of vocation: 'those who are truly its citizens are all likewise true priests of God, i.e. by confession of their lips and of their whole life' as practiced in their vocations. Although some do not have the ability to publicly teach, they can render service in 'external ways' to those who have that ability. 'For in the Church of Christ, men ought to be so ordered and distributed that those who are better at spiritual things should not be much occupied with temporal things, and those who are less instructed in and inclined toward

---

[105] Calvin waffled on the third mark of discipline, opting out of its necessity in debate with Anabaptists.

[106] 'Discourse on the Reform of Abuses in Church and State'; *The Chronicle and Political Papers of King Edward VI*, ed. by W.K. Jordan (London: Allen and Unwin, 1966), 159–67.

[107] *LCC*, XIX, 160.

[108] *LCC*, XIX, 182, 346. Cf. his fourth law, in which he calls for the removal of *aposkopous*, false bishops, an Erasmian-like word-play on *episkopos*, bishop. Priests who are wolves are likewise removable.

spiritual matters proper to the Kingdom of Christ should be of service to them in the provision of the necessities of life.'[109]

As for ecclesial orders, Bucer believes, on the basis of John 20, inter alia, that Christ has given ministers to the church and entrusted them with soteriological power. He also approves of a distinction between bishops and presbyters. First among elders, '*one* exercises singular care for the churches and the sacred ministries and in that care and solicitude presides over all others (Acts 20.28). For this reason, the name of bishop has been especially attributed to these chief administrators.' Although he distinguishes bishops from presbyters, he adds that bishops 'should decide nothing without the consultation of the other presbyters, who are also called bishops in the Scriptures because of this common ministry'. Bishops are 'first among the elders'. While elders administer all three marks of the church, bishops have a unique responsibility for discipline and doctrine. Thus, while agreeing with the traditional role of bishops as responsible for ecclesial discipline, Bucer goes one step further and stresses their duty of teaching and preaching the Word of God. Not only are they the focus of unity in the church, bishops must 'devote themselves totally to the reading and teaching of the Holy Scriptures'. Failure to teach and monitor doctrine is grounds for dismissal.[110]

Another work from Bucer's English period is *De Ordinatione Legitima Ministrorum Ecclesiae*,[111] attributed to a request by Cranmer for Bucer's help in constructing a new English ordinal. On the basis of this probable request, it has been dated specifically to Bucer's stay with Cranmer at Croydon in May and June 1549. The compilation of the *Ordinal* occurred sometime between the early summer of 1549 and February 1550. Although the Privy Council appointed an unnamed bishop and other learned men 'to devise Orders for the creation of bishops and priests' on 2 February 1550, there is nothing to preclude Cranmer having a working copy available beforehand. The council accepted the *Ordinal* sometime in February, as Nicholas Heath was imprisoned on 4 March for refusing it.[112] Messenger concludes from an exhaustive comparison with Cranmer's *Ordinal* of 1550 that '*Bucer wrote this work in response to a request from Cranmer, and with a view to providing a model for the proposed Anglican Ordinal*', that '*Cranmer definitely copied from Bucer*' and that 'there was *no real difference between Cranmer and Bucer*' (italics in original). While there is room for debate over when and why this

[109] *LCC*, XIX, 189, 191, 206–7.

[110] *LCC*, XIX, 225–32, 283–95. Cf. Cox, II, 305; *Martin Bucer and the Book of Common Prayer*, ed. by E.C. Whitaker (Chester: Alcuin Club, 1974), 86–9, 124–7.

[111] *Scripta Anglicana*, 238–64. Partial English translation in *Common Places of Martin Bucer*, ed. by David F. Wright (Abingdon: Sutton Courtenay Press, 1972), 253–83.

[112] *Troubles Connected with the Prayer Book of 1549*, ed. by Nicholas Pocock (London: Camden Society, 1884), 136–8.

treatise was written, most modern commentators agree that Cranmer's *Ordinal* is heavily dependent on Bucer's *De Ordinatione Legitima*.[113]

Perhaps the greatest distinction that can be made between Cranmer and Bucer is that Bucer provides one rite to be used by all three orders while Cranmer provides three separate rites, one for each order. Without Cranmer's own comments, the theological significance of Cranmer's liturgical digression is debatable. Using a rigid *lex orandi, lex credendi* hermeneutic, it could be interpreted that Cranmer had a higher view of episcopal order than Bucer. However, both Bucer's already-discussed acceptance of episcopacy and Cranmer's distinction between the 'ordering' of priests and deacons versus the 'consecrating' of bishops mediate against such an interpretation. Cranmer may have simply been offering a user-friendly format to standardize ordinations throughout the realm.[114]

While recognizing a parallel between Bucer and Cranmer, the English archbishop was reconsidering the foundation of ecclesiastical order *before* Bucer's coming to England. In his *Commonplace Books*, Cranmer began his discussion of orders by quoting Scripture. He begins with the royal priesthood texts from I Peter 2 and Revelation 1 before moving to the pastoral epistles and ordinations from the book of Acts.[115] Was Cranmer making universal priesthood the basis for ministerial priesthood? It is difficult to support such a thesis on a short list of Scripture passages. When his other notes are taken into account, the thesis may gain credibility; however, a commonplace quotation alone may not be taken as personal affirmation. The three passages quoted from Bede all emphasize universal priesthood.[116] The passage quoted from Calvin concerns Christ's unique priesthood. Calvin says Roman priests do wrong to Christ by offering a sacrifice of expiation. Rather, 'In him we are all priests but to offer praises and thanksgiving, in short to offer ourselves and ours to God. It was his office alone to appease God and atone for sins by his offering.'[117] Afterwards, Cranmer lists the medieval orders, and their functions, which orders Calvin was previously quoted as condemning.[118] Cranmer then questions whether Moses, the archetypal secular *dux*, was a priest; after all, Moses 'tonsured priests', just as Samuel 'made priests'. He lists the things that Christ did which are not required today. He finally notes that episcopal

---

[113] E.C. Messenger, *The Lutheran Origin of the Anglican Ordinal* (London: Burns, Oates & Washbourne, 1934), 7–8, 14, 28–9, 34–5. Constantine Hopf, *Martin Bucer and the English Reformation* (Oxford: Blackwell, 1956), 88–94; Procter and Frere, *New History*, 662; Brightman, *English Rite*, I, cxxxi; *Cranmer*, 460–1.

[114] *Liturgies*, 162, 172, 181.

[115] BL Royal MS 7B, XI, fol. 178^r.

[116] BL Royal MS 7B, XI, fol. 189.

[117] BL Royal MS 7B, XI, fol. 193^v. Calvin, *Institutes*, IV, xix, 25.

[118] BL Royal MS 7B, XI, 196^v.

consecration is not necessary for many priestly dignities, and wonders whether orders is a sacrament.[119]

But did Cranmer ever explicitly correlate Christian baptism with the ordination of all Christians to the royal priesthood? When Cranmer and Bucer were together at Croydon in 1549, they may have collaborated on a commentary on Matthew. The modern editor ascribes the first three chapters to Cranmer and the next five to Bucer.[120] While commenting on John's baptismal practices in Matthew 3.9, Cranmer cites Exodus 19.6: 'And you will be to me a royal priesthood and a holy nation.' The Archbishop argues that 'this kingdom' was first found 'among' (Latin *in* with the ablative) the nation of Israel alone, and after Christ, it is found among all the nations. The key to personal presence in the kingdom is, however, not baptism; rather, the kingdom 'has grown strong among all those who also received this promise of God with true faith'.[121] In a committee manuscript to which Cranmer contributed in the early 1540s, a commentary on liturgical ceremonies, baptismal anointing was retained and explained. However, the commentary likewise fails to correlate baptism with ordination to the royal priesthood.[122] Similarly, during the Oxford disputations, Cranmer argued for a spiritual change in the person being baptized but without referencing the royal priesthood.[123] In summary, it may be concluded that while Cranmer might have considered baptism an anointing into the royal priesthood, he never made an explicit claim for such, preferring to emphasize faith instead.

Leaving the matter of Cranmer's indefinite comments on the relation of baptism with royal priesthood, and turning to *Ordinal*, we notice Cranmer's stress on the doctrine of vocation to ministry. Ministerial calling has a twofold source: personally, from Christ; publicly, from an authorized entity. In the public examination, the first question for the priest-candidate asks, 'Do you think in

---

[119] BL Royal MS 7B, XI fols 197ʳ–198ʳ, 203ᵛ–204ʳ, 204ᵛ, 205–6.

[120] *Martin Bucer und Thomas Cranmer: Annotationes in Octo Priora Capita Evangelii secundum Matthaeum, Croydon 1549*, ed. Herbert Vogt (Frankfurt: Athenäum, 1972), 12–16. Vogt notes where the writing and corrections are in Cranmer's own hand.

[121] *Hoc regnum datum fuit veteri populo, viguitque in omnibus iis, quicumque hanc dei promissionem vera fide, receperunt, Et vos eritis mihi regium sacerdotium, et gens sancta.* 'This kingdom was given to the ancient people, and it has grown strong among all those who also received this promise of God with true faith, "And you will be to me a royal priesthood and a holy nation."' *Martin Bucer und Thomas Cranmer*, 46. Cf. Gordon P. Jeanes, *Signs of God's Promise: Thomas Cranmer's Sacramental Theology and the Book of Common Prayer* (London: T&T Clark, 2008), 182.

[122] The anointing of the baptizand is for 'faith in his mercy' and strength 'to bear the yoke' the Lord lays on the believer, as well as being 'made an Christian man' by Christ and anointed with the Holy Spirit. *The Rationale of Ceremonial, 1540–1543: With Notes and Appendices and an Essay on the Regulation of Ceremonial during the Reign of King Henry VIII*, ed. by Cyril S. Cobb (London: Longmans, Green and Co, 1910), 11–12. In the comments upon the Lord's Supper and the consecration of holy oil, Christians are said to receive their name from Christ's anointing. *The Rationale of Ceremonial*, 14–15, 36.

[123] Cox, I, 417.

your heart, that you be truly called, according to the will of our Lord Jesus Christ, and the order of this Church of England, to the ministry of Priesthood?'[124] The favourite evangelical terms connected with vocation—function, ministry, office, and calling—abound and are significant pointers to Cranmer's intent.

In a letter received in September 1540, Cranmer was rebuked by John Dantiscus, an old acquaintance from the emperor's court and now pluralist bishop in Poland, for his personal style, *ecclesiae Cantuariensis, ministrum*, minister of Canterbury church. Dantiscus snorted, the 'title [is] very different from that of former days'. The Polish papist conceded that bishops are ministers but they have a peculiar calling to oversight or government that must be placed first. Cranmer defended himself as simply following God's Word.[125] In the form for consecrating bishops, Cranmer refers repeatedly to the 'office', 'work', 'ministry', 'administration', or 'ministration' to which a bishop is called, stressing the bishop's teaching office in particular, though his governmental function remains. Against Echlin's finding government to be the primary task of episcopacy in *Ordinal*, we note Cranmer put questions concerning Scripture and doctrine first in the examination. Moreover, the Bible was laid on the Bishop's neck before the staff signifying oversight was given. The staff was even omitted from the 1552 *Ordinal*.[126]

Turning to the rite for priests, we notice that, like Bucer's presbyter in *De Ordinatione Legitima*, Cranmer's minister must live 'by word and good example'. His duties include the ministry of Bucer's three marks: 'doctrine, and Sacraments, and the discipline of Christ'.[127] The stress is ever on the Word as constitutive of priesthood; the medieval emphasis on the power to sacrifice is conspicuous in its absence. He also altered the highly symbolic *porrectio instrumentorum*, which traditionally included the paten and chalice along with the instruction to offer sacrifice. In the 1550 *Ordinal*, the bishop handed over a cup, the bread, and a Bible, and the instruction to sacrifice was replaced by an instruction to preach the Word and administer the sacraments. In the 1552 *Ordinal*, only the Bible was handed over.[128] Moreover, harking back to his debate with Henry, Cranmer treats the priest's 'cure and charge' synonymously.[129]

Much speculation has been offered concerning the episcopal imposition of hands in the form for ordering priests. Does the bishop confer the Holy Spirit *ex opere operato* by imposing hands?[130] In the context of the entire ordination

---

[124] *Liturgies*, 176–7; *Common Places of Bucer*, 255, 274.

[125] Cranmer to Wriothesley, 21 September 1540; Cox, II, 401–4.

[126] *Liturgies*, 183–5, 353–4. Echlin, *Story of Anglican Ministry*, 100.

[127] *Liturgies*, 174, 177; *Common Places of Bucer*, 273, 275.

[128] *Liturgies*, 179, 349. Buchanan, 'Anglican Ordination Rites', 123.

[129] *Liturgies*, 177, 346.

[130] Cranmer said consecration involved a change in use not nature. On baptism and eucharist, see E.C. Ratcliff, 'The English Usage of Eucharistic Consecration', *Theology*, 60 (1957), 233–4. On

service, Cranmer speaks much about the Spirit and spiritual gifts. The Spirit is called down by the entire congregation in the hymn, 'Come Holy Ghost'. The Holy Spirit is himself a gift and yet he offers 'manifold' gifts. He is invited to the whole congregation, into 'our wits' and 'our hearts' to strengthen 'our weakness'.[131] Concluding the examination, the bishop, who has already examined the candidate 'in the name of the Congregation', prays for God to give the candidate 'strength and power' to perform his office; the people are to join in with their prayers. The next prayer, immediately preceding the imposition of hands, beseeches the Spirit of God 'to grant unto all us'. The final prayer beseeches for grace to come on all. Vocation and reception of the Spirit are, thereby, corporately focussed. He is called down *through* bishop, priest, and entire congregation. He is called down *upon* bishop, priest, and entire congregation. In using the vernacular, Cranmer came to include the people in a formerly mysterious rite.[132]

The episcopal statement accompanying the imposition of hands includes a direct quote from John 20—'Receive the Holy Ghost: whose sins thou dost forgive, they are forgiven'. This statement might be interpreted as an *ex opere operato* conferral, or at least a unique conferral of some type, of the Holy Spirit by the bishop; however, this is highly unlikely. First, though he did not include it in the prayer of imposition, Bucer was comfortable including this passage in the ordination service and it is doubtful he would make such a connection. Second, Cranmer was relying on what he saw as scriptural precedent in the words of Christ. Christ was still the only one capable of mediating between God and human.[133] Third, when John Hooper, the most radical English bishop, objected to the 1550 *Ordinal*, Hooper never referred to this prayer. This is important, because he characteristically objected to that which detracted from the Word and assigned more power to creation than Scripture allowed. Fourth, in the sermon before the examination, the priest is specifically warned that only God gives the spiritual power needed to perform his ministry of the Word. 'Therefore ye see how ye ought and have need, earnestly to pray for his Holy Spirit [who assists us] by the mediation of our only Mediator and Saviour Jesus Christ.' Finally, in the 1540 questions, Cranmer denies the

---

confirmation, see Cox, II, 80. On the progressive eradication of consecration in communion, see Buchanan, *What Did Cranmer Think?*; Jeanes, *Signs of God's Promise*, 102–10, 197–204.

[131] Based on the Sarum rite's '*Veni Creator Spiritus*', Cranmer takes some liberty by offering a communal translation. Brightman, *English Rite*, II, 974–9.

[132] *Liturgies*, 172–80; Bradshaw, *Anglican Ordinal*, 25–36. Bradshaw is confused about the vocational relationship of universal and clerical priesthoods. *Anglican Ordinal*, 30–1.

[133] 'This is the honour and glory of this our high priest, wherein he admitteth neither partner nor successor.' Cox, I, 346. The imposition of hands should be retained 'since it is mentioned in the sacred scriptures and has been the consistent practice of the church.' *Reformation of the Ecclesiastical Laws*; Spalding edn, 127–8; Cardwell edn, 32.

necessity of episcopal consecration.[134] It is only with the next generation, in Elizabeth's reign, that the debate over whether the conferral of the Spirit in John 20 applies to ordination again becomes contentious.[135]

Yes, grace must be given to the priest, and it is prayed for in the ordination rite. However, this is a grace for understanding Scripture so that it might be preached to the people. Bradshaw says Cranmer believed he was not bound 'of necessity' by anything the apostolic church did in appointing ministers. There are many actions that Christ and the apostles performed that we do not. Consecration is thus subject to his doctrine of variability.[136] It is interesting to compare Cranmer's treatment of the other liturgical events in which grace was considered to transmit through anointing. In his 1547 coronation speech, Cranmer denied that external unction was necessary for a divinely approved king. 'The oil, if added, is but a ceremony; if it be wanting, that king is yet a perfect monarch notwithstanding, and God's anointed, as well as if he was anoiled.'[137] In the 1549 *BCP*, he allowed external unction in the rites of baptism, confirmation, and visitation of the sick to remain. However, the stress was placed on a prayer for internal anointing by the Holy Spirit.[138] Bucer, in his comments on the first prayer book, notes the superstition engendered by such activity, and preferred 'to see these signs abolished rather than maintained'.[139] In the 1552 *BCP*, all three unctions, with their requests for internal anointing, are excluded.[140] Similarly, the ancient anointing of a priest's hands with oil was excluded from the *Ordinal*.[141] Cranmer no longer believed anointing of any type, including that of priests, effectively transmitted grace.

Cranmer believed the clerical priesthood was an office of 'dignity' and 'importance' that deserves respect. It was part of the divine plan. Indeed, a certain obedience was due to the teaching of those called to 'serve' this body of Christ, the church or congregation.[142] However, the clerical priesthood was but one of many vocations and, if anything, secondary to the magistrate. Cranmer's officially approved homilies summarize priesthood among the vocations:

[134] 'Third Sermon upon Jonas', 5 March 1550, in *Early Writings of John Hooper*, ed. by Samuel Carr (PS, 1843), 479; Bradshaw, *Anglican Ordinal*, 37–8; *Common Places of Bucer*, 272; *Liturgies*, 176; Cox, II, 117.

[135] John Field and Thomas Wilcox deemed it a 'blasphemous saying'. *Puritan Manifestoes*, ed. by W.H. Frere and C.E. Douglas (London: SPCK, 1954), 10. Cf. *The Seconde Parte of a Register*, ed. by Albert Peel, 2 vols (CUP, 1915), I, 127, 216–7, 259.

[136] Bradshaw, *Anglican Ordinal*, 14–17.

[137] Cox, II, 126.

[138] *Liturgies*, 112, 125, 139.

[139] *Bucer and the Book of Common Prayer*, 86–9, 124–7.

[140] *Liturgies*, 289, 300, 315.

[141] *Monumenta Ritualia Ecclesiae Anglicanae*, III, 12–13; *Liturgies*, 179, 348–9.

[142] *Liturgies*, 175.

Every degre of people, in their vocacion, callyng and office, hath appoynted to them their duetie and ordre. Some are in high degre, some in lowe, some kynges and princes, some inferiors and subjectes, priestes and laimen, masters and servauntes, fathers and chyldren, husbandes and wifes, riche and poore, and every one have nede of other: so that in all thinges is to be lauded and praysed the goodly ordre of God, without the whiche, no house, no citie, no common wealth can continue and endure.[143]

In spite of the wishes of some Anglo-Catholics, Cranmer was not interested in promoting theories of apostolic succession or moments of consecration. He was ultimately hostile to any suggestion the priest was given power to offer a propitiatory sacrifice in the mass. Rather, Cranmer sought to establish a publicly authorized reformed ministry that saw its vocation as preaching the Word and administering the sacraments.

Thomas Cranmer carefully weaved his way between the extremes. First, he protected the very existence of the clerical office against the assault of the radicals affiliated with Thomas Cromwell. Second, he inserted Lutheranism directly into the English church's rites of ordination, codifying the nation's formal shift from a traditional sacrificing priesthood to an evangelical ministry of the Word. However, his liturgical–theological reformation, especially with regard to the priesthood of the people, was not yet complete.

---

[143] *Certain Sermons or Homilies (1547) and A Homily against Disobedience and Wilful Rebellion (1570)*, ed. by Ronald Bond (London: University of Toronto Press, 1987), 161.

7

Thomas Cranmer: The People's Priesthood

As we have seen, Thomas Cranmer allowed his monarch wide latitude in ecclesiastical affairs, including powers of jurisdiction and order. The archbishop concurrently defended ministerial priesthood as a necessary part of the divine plan against radical parliamentarian views. His clerical priesthood incorporated certain aspects of evangelical ministry and denied certain aspects of traditional priesthood. At this point, Cranmer's theology of the people's priesthood must be addressed. Our method will now change from the previous chronological format to a more topical approach, keeping in mind, as always, the historical context. After surveying his theology of the laity in both its personal and social spheres, we will analyze Cranmer's view of the priestliness of the people.

THEOLOGY OF THE LAITY

Like other reformers, Cranmer de-emphasized external observances and excoriated ceremonies he considered abusive and superstitious. What especially galled him were traditional rites that either bolstered papal supremacy, such as Thomas Becket's shrine at Canterbury, or kept the people in ignorance of fundamentals of the faith. Not all extra-canonical rites were rejected, however, for some might be retained in the interests of orderly instruction. Like other English humanists,[1] Cranmer believed personal instruction and social order were intertwined. Moreover, personal instruction must begin with God's Word, since it is in relationship with God that a person is brought to salvation and social harmony is produced. As he explained to Edward VI in the dedicatory epistle to his 1548 *Catechism*,

---

[1] More, *Utopia*, 123–4, 127–8; Thomas Starkey, *A Dialogue between Pole and Lupset*, ed. by T.F. Mayer, Camden Society 4th series, 37 (London: Royal Historical Society, 1989), 37, 140–1.

For by thys lytle treatyse, not only the youth of your graces realme, may lerne to know God, and howe they maye mooste purelye and syncerelye honoure glorifie and serue hym, and may also learne their office and dewtie, howe they oughte to behaue themselfes, first towarde God, secondly towardes your Magestie, and so towardes all ministers vnder the same, towardes theyre fathers and mothers, and all other persones of what sorte or degree soeuer they be.[2]

Although Cranmer assumed an interconnection between the personal and the social, we shall, strictly for the purpose of analysis, separately consider both aspects in Cranmer's theology of the laity.

People as Persons[3]

The issue of the individual's direct access to God often dominates modern discussions of universal priesthood.[4] Cranmer agreed that human beings have direct communication with God and that this communion is transformative. In the first place, God has immediate knowledge of human minds and what he finds there determines the divine–human relationship. As Cranmer explained to Henry in his first exposition of justification by faith, the mind and will are open to God. Hypocrites, those who conform outwardly but do not believe inwardly, cannot fool him. 'For, as for the other feigned, pretended, hypocritical, and adulterate faith in the mouth, it is but only a painted visor before men; but before God it is hollow within, dead, rotten, and nothing worth.' The intent and purpose of our mind, heart, and will must be faith in, and love towards, God: 'let no man deceive his own mind [for] God loveth and favoureth them that be thus minded.' As he explained in his homily on Scripture, 'For without a single iye, pure intent, and good mynde, nothyng is allowed for good before God.'[5]

Not only does God have knowledge of us but our salvation is dependent on our personal knowledge of him. Under the guidance of the Spirit, this knowledge becomes faith, thus bringing salvation. 'And as the body is but dead that lacketh a soul, even so is that faith but dead that is but in the mouth, and doth not enter effectuously into the heart, and work accordingly.'[6] This humanist emphasis on personal 'knowledge', based in Erasmus' *philosophia Christi*,[7] was

---

[2] Justus Jonas, *A Short Instruction into Christian Religion Being a Catechism Set Forth by Archbishop Cranmer* (OUP, 1829), xxxiii–xxxiv.

[3] 'Person' indicates the necessity of relationship with others for self-definition, as opposed to 'individual', which often connotes the disconnected self. Zizioulas, *Being as Communion*, 27–65.

[4] Calvin taught this doctrine. However, he was adamant that access through prayer to God always occurred through the mediation of Christ. *Institutes*, III, xx, 17–20.

[5] Cox, II, 86; *Certain Sermons*, 63.

[6] Cox, II, 85.

[7] For Erasmus, the two weapons every Christian needs are 'prayer and knowledge'; one is impossible without the other. *LCC*, XIV, 302; McConica, *English Humanists*, 26–7.

transformed by evangelicals into a weapon against the traditional doctrine of 'intention'.

Under the old penitential regime, the priest granted absolution to the penitent on the basis of contrition and sincere intention to amend. Intention was what mattered, for the church could supply any knowledge the layperson lacked. The sacrament of penance in itself was endowed with soteriological power. Defects in individual conscience were overcome through priestly power.[8] Under Cranmer's new system of repentance, forgiveness was granted on the basis of personal knowledge of God. Intellectual knowledge, however, was not enough, for heartfelt trust, or faith, is also required. As Cranmer said concerning the creed, 'And all these things even the devils also believe, and tremble for fear and grievousness of God's indignation and torments, which they endure and ever shall do.' What is required is personal trust in the deliverance from God's wrath through the unique sacrifice of Christ.[9] Luther went behind the Vulgate's *poenitentia*, which stressed works and sacrament, and reclaimed the Greek μετάνοια, 'repentance', which considered a change in internal disposition. Cranmer's diffidence concerning confession as *necessariam* (see "'Sacrament' of Orders', pp. 182–9) is a further indication that he embraced the personal focus in Luther's theology.[10] Where penance traditionally restored the individual for sins after baptism, Cranmer ascribed restoration to personal repentance and faith. 'And thei whiche actually synne after their baptisme, when they turn converte and turn unfainedly, thei are likewise washed by this sacrifice [of Christ] from their synnes.'[11]

Moreover, Cranmer explained that 'heavenly knowledge' or 'clear understanding' is vital to godly reception of the eucharist's benefits. Indeed, this need for understanding launches him into an extended discussion on the psychological process of salvation.[12] Ever mindful of the practical dimension in theology, he explained this knowledge comes through Scripture, whether preached or read.[13] Holy Scripture is the means of knowledge and, without it, the eucharist becomes a papistical mass that, in turn, leads to popular magic and 'superstition'.[14]

Cranmer denies any *ex opere operato* efficacy for the sacraments, especially the eucharist. God is not bound to work in them. However, Cranmer does not

---

[8] Marshall, *Catholic Priesthood*, 30; R.N. Swanson, *Religion and Devotion in Europe, c.1215–c.1515* (CUP, 1995), 26–7, 62. On the difference between Aquinas and Scotus on priestly power, see Tentler, 'Summa', 117–19.

[9] Cox, II, 85; Null, *Thomas Cranmer's Doctrine of Repentance*, 165–71, 186.

[10] Evans, *Problems of Authority*, 151–3.

[11] *Problems of Authority*, 147–8; *Certain Sermons*, 79.

[12] *Defence*, 11–15; Cox, I, 38–9.

[13] *Certain Sermons*, 66.

[14] *Defence*, 255–6; Cox, I, 353–4; Thomas, *Religion and the Decline of Magic*, 60–1.

totally decouple the offering of grace from the sacraments. He believes Christ comes spiritually to the faithful when they receive the eucharist in faith. While drawing on the well-known Augustinian definition of the visible and invisible dimensions of the sacrament, the pre-existing condition of faith is ever a necessity for receiving its benefits:

> And doth not the nature of sacraments require that the sensible elements should remain in their proper nature, to signify an higher mystery and secret working of God inwardly, as the sensible elements be ministered outwardly? And is not the visible and corporal feeding upon bread and wine a convenient and apt figure and similitude to put us in remembrance, and to admonish us how we be fed invisibly and spiritually by the flesh and blood of Christ, God and man?[15]

Although Cranmer freely uses the image of eating the body and drinking the blood of Christ, he has in mind a spiritual meaning divorced from any gross physical consumption. *Eating is faith.* 'The spiritual eating of his flesh, and drinking of his blood by faith, by digesting his death in our minds [is] our only price, ransom, and redemption from eternal damnation.' This spiritual eating is not confined to eucharistic celebration. 'And if Christ had never ordained the sacrament, yet should we have eaten his flesh, and drunken his blood, and have had thereby everlasting life; as all the faithful did before the sacrament was ordained, and do daily when they receive not the sacrament.' Of the three ways of eating, the eating of faith is most important, whether in eucharistic worship or not.[16]

The personal approach to God was also expressed in his interpretation of *sursum corda*, the ancient liturgical call for the people to lift up their hearts and call on God.[17] Traditionally, with the doctrine of transubstantiation, it was believed that the host actually became the body of God and should be worshipped. Cranmer, having dismissed transubstantiation and having localized Christ's physical body in heaven, taught that we should not 'direct our minds downward to the bread and cup, but lift them up to Christ by faith'. The movement of the eyes must not hinder the movement of the heart; the mind is directed heavenward, wherein there is a direct entrance into God's very presence. As he eloquently put it in his second Oxford explication, 'Lifting up our minds, we should look up to the blood of Christ with our faith, should touch him with our mind, and receive him with our inward man; and that, being like eagles in this life, we should fly up into heaven in our hearts, where that Lamb is resident at the right hand of his Father, which taketh away the sins of the world.' Or as he summarized it

---

[15] Cox, I, 37.   [16] Cox, I, 25–6, 205.

[17] Brightman, *English Rite*, II, 682–3; *Liturgies*, 85, 277. *Sarum Missal*, however, apparently reserved *sursum corda* for the choir, effectively excluding the people. *Sarum Missal*, 28, 40.

in his homily on salvation, 'faythe doth directely sende us to Christe for remission of our synnes.'[18]

Every person, for himself or herself, must receive the benefit of salvation that Christ wrought in his unique sacrifice on the cross. 'And the benefit hereof is in no man's power to give unto any other, but every man must receive it at Christ's hands himself, by his own faith and belief, as the prophet saith.'[19] While rejecting the traditional application of Christ's sacrifice by the priest to both living and dead, the necessity of self-application is repeatedly and forcefully advocated by Cranmer: 'by his own faith every man may apply the same unto himself, and not take it at the appointment of popish priests, by the merit of sacrifices and oblations!' '[E]very man should receive them for himself', for the priest 'can apply the benefit of Christ's passion to no man, being of age and discretion, but only to such as by their own faith do apply the same unto themselves'. However, although this is a personal faith, it is not by personal fiat. 'If we be indeed, as we profess, christian men, we may ascribe this honour and glory to no man, but to Christ alone.'[20]

Through his doctrine of predestination, Cranmer effectively excluded personal initiative on the part of human beings.[21] He did not believe that, once justified, a person had a 'right' to enter God's presence, in the modern sense of the term. Evangelical conversion is not merely a punctiliar affair,[22] but a complex event comprised of our external justification by Christ through faith and internal renovation by the Holy Spirit, which issues forth in good works.[23] Therefore, when considering access to God, he emphasized the

---

[18] Cox, I, 356, 398; *Certain Sermons*, 85. Cf. Cox, I, 183, 235–6, 317. Peter Newman Brooks says this is a common Swiss doctrine, citing Oecolampadius at the 1529 Marburg Colloquy. Brooks, *Thomas Cranmer's Doctrine of the Eucharist*, 2nd edn (London: Macmillan, 1992), 101n.

[19] *Defence*, 33; Cox, I, 47.

[20] Cox, I, 349–53. Cf. Cox, II, 150, 152.

[21] *Cranmer*, 30–1, 211–12, 346, 615–16; Null, *Thomas Cranmer's Doctrine of Repentance*, 195–204.

[22] Alister E. McGrath's modern evangelical bias is evidenced by his concern with one obscure text by the old Luther. He seeks the exact moment of Luther's 'radical alteration' or 'theological breakthrough' in his 'tower experience'. While recognizing Luther considered justification an 'all-embracing process'—*semper peccator, semper penitens, semper iustus*—McGrath focusses on a supposed punctiliar experience. Moreover, he unfortunately contends that Luther's doctrine of justification caused him to break with Rome, rejecting any ecclesiastical motives. A distinction between Luther's leading doctrine temporally, common priesthood, and his leading doctrine thematically, justification, is the solution to McGrath's confusion over the timing between *initia Reformationis*, the ecclesiological break with Rome, and *initia theologiae Lutheri*, the theology of the cross. McGrath, *Luther's Theology of the Cross: Martin Luther's Theological Breakthrough* (Oxford: Blackwell, 1985), 95–100, 141–7; McGrath, *Iustitia Dei: A History of the Christian Doctrine of Justification*, 2nd edn (CUP, 1998), 188–207.

[23] Cranmer's three homilies on salvation, faith, and good works were apparently written as a connected series and commanded to be read in that order. *Certain Sermons*, 56, 79–87, 91–100, 103–13; Cox, II, 504. E.C.E. Bourne, 'Cranmer and the Liturgy of 1552', *CQR*, 155 (1954), 384–5. For Null, justification and renovation are 'concomitant' in the 'moment' of conversion. *Thomas Cranmer's Doctrine of Repentance*, 178–9.

continual mediation of Christ and assigned a much higher role to Christ's mediation than to the experience of human decision. We enter heaven as 'the guests of Christ', even 'having him dwelling in us though the grace of his true nature, and through the virtue and efficacy of his whole passion'. Thus, the language of 'incorporation' into Christ and continuing 'participation' in his life took on a deeper meaning than post-Enlightenment minds often conceive.[24]

Christ's mediatorial role is further defined in Cranmer's critique of Henry's *Bishops' Book* annotations. The 1537 formula taught that, in his priestly office of mediation, Christ continually intercedes for his church. Excluding all other mediators,

> whensoever I do invoke and call upon him in right faith and hope with full intent and purpose to amend and return from my naughty life, he presenteth and exhibiteth unto the sight of his Father his most blessed body, as it was wounded, crucified, and offered up in sacrifice for the redemption of mankind, and so from time to time maketh continual request and intercession unto God his Father for the remission of all my sins, and for my reconciliation unto his favour.

Again, it affirms he 'is now our continual and perpetual advocate, our patron and defender before the throne of his Father, and maketh continual intercession and prayer for the remission of all our sins.' Cranmer agreed, upbraiding Henry for removing 'made due satisfaction and propitiation' from a section extolling Christ's sacrifice. As far as Cranmer was concerned, Christ's sacrifice invalidated Roman doctrines and practices, including 'satisfactory masses' and the intercession of saints. The mediation and prayers of holy saints are unnecessary, for 'by Christ we have also access unto the Father.' Any human effort, our own or another's, is completely set aside by the unique and continuing work of Christ.[25]

Christ's mediation is unique and continually necessary, but Word and sacrament have an instrumental role in generating faith.[26] 'We cannot attain to the true and perfect knowledge and feeling of [spiritual generation], but only by faith, which must be grounded upon God's most holy word and sacraments.' As the Word is the auditory agent, so sacraments are visible and physical agents. 'For as the word of God preached putteth Christ into our ears, so likewise these elements of water, bread, and wine, joined to God's word, do after a sacramental manner put Christ into our eyes, mouths, hands, and all our senses.' For the reformers, Christ's mediation is unique but the

---

[24] Cox, I, 398. Daniel A. Keating provides an excellent primer regarding the contemporary recovery of deification. *Deification and Grace* (Naples, FL: Sapientia Press, 2007).

[25] Cox, II, 90, 93.

[26] 'He worketh with his word, using the voice of the speaker, as his instrument to work by; as he useth also his sacraments, whereby he worketh, and therefore is said to be present in them.' Cox, I, 11.

instrumental means of preaching and sacraments are also necessary. The Word is, moreover, more important than the sacraments, for the sacraments depend upon the Word for their effectiveness.[27] For Cranmer, Word and sacrament work outwardly as the Spirit works inwardly through faith.[28]

The minister also plays a role in this process. The role is derivative, however, for the stress is normally on the Word rather than the minister of the Word. 'The minister of the church speaketh unto us God's own words, which we must take as spoken from God's own mouth, because that from his mouth it came, and his word it is, and not the minister's.' Likewise, sacraments come from God through the minister. However, although publicly approved ministers have a monopoly on public proclamation, they do not have a monopoly on the Word, for the Bible must be available to all in the vernacular. Cranmer expended much effort making sure the vernacular Bible was not only published but available in the parishes. His encouragement of Cromwell in 1537 has already been noted, and after parish provision of vernacular Bibles became legally required, Cranmer made sure his diocese and cathedral had them freely available.[29] He believed not only that private reading is necessary to prepare for hearing public proclamation of the gospel by approved ministers, but the laity may be taught directly by God when a minister is not available.[30] Faith comes by hearing (or reading) God's Word, and personal faith in Christ enables access to God.

In spite of an accusation by Richard Smith, Cranmer distinguishes between reason and faith, giving preference to the latter. According to Smith, untiring enemy of Cranmer and his ally, Peter Martyr Vermigli,[31] Cranmer put reason before faith, his own ruminations before church tradition. Cranmer answered Smith's accusation in an appendix to his 1551 *An Answer to a Crafty and Sophistical Cavillation devised by Stephen Gardiner*. 'I set not reason before faith, but, as an hand-maiden, have appointed her to do service unto faith, and to wait upon her.'[32] In his controversy with Smith, reason and faith, and Scripture and tradition were bound together. Traditionalists accused evangelicals of following innovations conceived in their own minds. Smith looked back to a long tradition begun in Scripture and extending through the centuries as codified in the writings of the Fathers and canon law. The argument was somewhat effective: traditionalists appealed to the corporate faith embodied

---

[27] Cox, I, 41, 366; *Cranmer*, 616. Cf. Philip E. Hughes, *Theology of the English Reformers* (Grand Rapids: Baker, 1980), 161–2.

[28] Jeanes, *Signs of God's Promise*, 142.

[29] Cox, II, 155, 161.

[30] *Homilies*, 5.

[31] Ellen A. Macek, 'Richard Smith: Tudor Cleric in Defense of Traditional Belief and Practice', *The Catholic Historical Review*, 72 (1986), 383–402.

[32] Cox, I, 371.

in Scripture and tradition and accused evangelicals of depending on recent, private readings of Scripture; i.e. 'new learning'.[33]

Cranmer's answer subtly but effectively identified the traditionalist fallacy. His first principle is to ground theology upon God's Word. This foundation is then fortified 'by the authority of all the best learned and most holy authors and martyrs.' Smith could agree up to this point, but Cranmer makes further qualifications. First, he distinguishes between the earlier Fathers and the later 'Antichrist of Rome'. Where Cranmer may safely, in the anti-papal atmosphere generated by royal supremacy, dismiss the eucharistic doctrines conceived 'within these four or five hundred years',[34] Smith is forced to appeal to the relatively recent pope, 'Innocentius anno 1200', which recent event becomes painfully obvious in his own chronological table.[35] Second, Cranmer makes a distinction between true and false councils. The visible church has both true and errant members, amongst clergy as well as laity. Since 'the holy church of Christ is but a small herd or flock, in comparison to the great multitude of them that follow Satan and Antichrist', the decisions of all councils, especially later ones, are thrown into doubt. Although the church may not 'wholly err', 'the open face of the church' may be 'miserably deformed'. The problem is to discern between the teaching of 'the holy church of Christ' and the teaching of 'Antichrist', which is obvious since later Rome is the seat of Antichrist.[36] Thirdly, since earlier and later fathers wrote so much, it is nigh impossible to correlate all their 'unwritten verities'. Some of what they wrote is obviously false. The fathers and more recent theologians thus require scriptural judgment. The church may not judge Scripture. Revelation is above reason but not everything that goes by the name of revelation truly is.[37] Finally, like so many other papists, Smith is himself guilty, according to Cranmer, of the logical fallacy of *petitio principii*, circular reasoning. He 'taketh that thing for a supposition and an approved truth, which is in controversy'.[38] Of course, Cranmer failed to see he might likewise be accused of circular reasoning, for, according to him, Scripture is self-referential. Scripture interprets Scripture by 'conferring of places'.[39]

---

[33] Rex, 'The New Learning', *JEH*, 44 (1993), 26–44.

[34] *Defence*, 2; Cox, I, 23. Rex, 'New Learning', 39.

[35] Smith, *A Defence of the Sacrifice of the masse* (London, 1547), fols i^v–ii^r.

[36] Cox, I, 377–9. Cf. *Forty-Two Articles*, art. 22.

[37] Cox, I, 34.

[38] Cox, I, 371. Cf. the posthumous publication of a portion of Cranmer's *Commonplace Books*. The preface and editorial material, which sharpens these arguments against Smith, was most likely written by Steven Nevinson. *A Confutation of Unwritten Verities* (London, 1558); Cox, II, 1–67; *Cranmer*, 608–9, 633–6; Macek, 'Richard Smith', 399. Cf. Cox, II, 514–17.

[39] Cox, I, 423.

People as Community

At the conclusion of his essay on the social aspects of the mass, John Bossy, in a not-so-apparent continuation of one-half of Gregory Dix's thesis,[40] says Cranmer utterly failed to retain the social value of the mass. In spite of Cranmer's promotion of vernacular worship and communion in both kinds, Bossy believes the reformer's emphasis on frequent communion was 'asocial mysticism'. The exclusion of the *Pax* ultimately doomed the reformed eucharist as a social institution.[41] Bossy's conclusions are disputable, especially his unsupported and counter-intuitive identification of frequent communion as asocial.[42] Noting the divisive and temporary nature of the *Pax*, Miri Rubin effectively criticized Bossy's naive use of 'ideal-types'.[43] Bossy aside, a rebuttal to an essay by Eamon Duffy will serve as a catalyst for a recovery of Cranmer's communal theology.

Duffy believes Cranmer destroyed community in two ways. First, by ridding parishes of traditional ceremonies and symbols, charity and peacemaking were lost. Second, by rejecting purgatory and its institutions, interpreted as 'excommunicating the dead', the Christian community was significantly narrowed.

> For in repudiating the religious framework of late medieval English Christianity, Cranmer was not replacing superstition, error and magic with Gospel truth. He was turning from a profoundly communal understanding of the Gospel to something more individualistic, more stark. It is not clear to me, at least, that the exchange was wholly for the better.[44]

Duffy's critique is based on a twofold misunderstanding of Cranmer. First, Cranmer was not dispensing with community, much less 'excommunicating' the dead. He was trying to build community through stronger personal attachments. According to his humanist tenets, instruction facilitates personal understanding, which in turn facilitates social harmony. Cranmer believed people were intellectually capable and culpable and that traditionalists, who prefer popular ignorance as a guarantee for popular acquiescence, only further

---

[40] Dix considers Cranmer's emphasis on personal remembrance hopelessly individualistic. On the other hand, he also laments the atomistic individualism of the late medieval liturgy. *Shape of the Liturgy*, 615–25, 638–9, 670–1.

[41] Bossy, 'Mass as a Social Institution', 57–61.

[42] Burnett demonstrates the social dimensions of communion were not nearly as discontinuous as Bossy argues, but retains the idea that infrequent communion fostered community. However, Brilioth contends sacrifice so dominated late medieval eucharistic thought that thanksgiving, communion, commemoration, and mystery gave way. The reformers restored these, especially *communio*. Amy Nelson Burnett, 'The Social History of Communion and the Reformation of the Eucharist', *P&P*, 211 (2011), 77–119; Yngve Brilioth, *Eucharistic Faith and Practice*, transl. by A.G. Hebert (London: SPCK, 1961), 78–90, 95.

[43] Rubin, *Corpus Christi: The Eucharist in Late Medieval Culture* (CUP, 1991), 2, 76.

[44] Duffy, 'Cranmer and Popular Religion', in *C&S*, 199–215.

disobedience. Social disharmony results from popular ignorance. Reading Scripture is a bulwark against social sin; ignorance threatens good order.[45] Second, Cranmer did recognize the value of symbol and sacrament. His liturgical work is more than adequate proof of that. But he was adamant that symbol and sacrament must conform to God's Word; human innovations that detract from the Christocentric gospel must be improved or abolished.[46] The following consideration of Cranmer's theological, liturgical, political, and philosophical views help recapture his theology of a unified people.

First, theologically, Cranmer has a real sense of believers being incorporated into Christ. His doctrine of deification synthesized the incarnation of Christ with personal faith. By his incarnation, Christ has taken into his person our human nature and, in turn, communicated to us his divine nature. 'And yet the same body joined unto his divinity, is not only the beginning, but also the continuance and consummation of our eternal life.' Incorporation is moral and spiritual as well as substantial and essential: 'we be united together and with Christ, not only in will, but also in nature'. This participation in the divine nature, however, is limited to the immortality of God and does not extend to his other attributes: 'we are partakers of their [the Trinity's] nature, which is eternity, or everlastingness'. Participation in Christ also means being united with his body, the church. He draws here on the Pauline metaphors of body and marriage. 'We have fellowship with Christ, when we are united in the unity of the church, when we are made flesh of his flesh, and bones of his bones; and so we are united in the communion, in baptism, and in faith.'[47] Cyril Richardson comments, 'there is a mystical union of the believer with the substance of Christ's body by reason of the incarnation; but the Eucharist is not a medium of such a participation.' Cranmer's repudiation of transubstantiation and the corporeal eating of Christ's body will not allow him to do otherwise.[48] And yet, in the twenty-sixth of *Forty-Two Articles*, Cranmer says the sacraments were given to create community: 'Our Lord Jesus Christ hath knit together a company of new people with sacraments.'[49]

Second, in his liturgical emphases and rubrics, as with his polemical work, Cranmer unalterably places people and priest together in worship. The one cannot be considered without the other. After quoting Christ and the Fathers, he concludes, 'Whereby we may plainly see, howe that the holy fathers in those

---

[45] Cox, II, 121; *Certain Sermons*, 64.   [46] *Liturgies*, 197–9.

[47] Cox, I, 19, 150, 165, 169, 410, 413. 'As the bread and wine become our flesh and blood, even so be all faithful Christians'. C.W. Dugmore, *The Mass and the English Reformers* (London: Macmillan, 1958), 192n.

[48] Richardson, *Zwingli and Cranmer on the Eucharist: Cranmer Dixit et Contradixit* (Evanston, Illinois: Seabury-Western Theological Seminary, 1949), 36–44.

[49] O'Donovan, *On the Thirty-Nine Articles: A Conversation with Tudor Christianity* (Exeter: Paternoster Press, 1986), 128–46.

dayes, dyd take the communicatyng of the folke with the sacramente, to be the chiefest, parte, effecte, and substaunce of the messe.' The need for communion, the people worshiping together, informed his argument against the private mass. 'Beholde, he called it not the eating of the lordes souper, when every man eateth a souper for himselfe'. The rule for right worship is one priest to represent and show Christ, one altar, one mass, and all the prayers of the congregation 'together as out of one mouth and herte'. This holistic rule is summarized as 'one at ones',[50] and is expressed in the continual use of the first person plural pronoun in *BCP*. On the other hand, *Sarum Missal* interchangeably used the singular with the plural, even speaking of the priest alone being incorporated into Christ's mystical body.[51] The rubrics for communion, too, emphasize corporate communion by priest with people. 'And there shall be no celebration of the Lord's Supper, except there be a good number to communicate with the Priest, according to his discretion.' Corporate communion was fortified by calls for frequent communion.[52]

A series of analogies are used to describe the eucharist as a corporate sacrament. Persons are to the church what branches are to a tree, members to a body, grains to a loaf, and grapes to wine. The eucharist is a meal of friendship and a sacrament of unity and concord.[53] He invited Calvin, Melanchthon, and Bullinger in March 1552 to make the eucharist a 'sacrament of unity' rather than 'food for disagreement'. Indeed, Cranmer's proposed pan-evangelical council was meant to remove internal dissensions, thereby enabling an effective response to the Council of Trent.[54] 'Christ ordained the sacrament to move and stir all men to friendship, love, and concord, and to put away all hatred, variance, and discord, and to testify a brotherly and unfeigned love between all them that be members of Christ.' Those coming to the eucharist must come not only with a lively faith in Christ but 'an unfeigned love to all Christ's members'.[55] Neighborly charity as necessary for lay participation in communion was enforced in his 1548 visitation of Canterbury.[56] Communion, of course, entails excommunion and restored communion; the disciplinary function serves as a rough representation of

---

[50] The clearest exposition of his theology of corporate worship is found in the pseudonymous treatise of 1548 built on Martin Bucer's *Constans Defensio*. Richard Bonner, *A treatyse of the ryght honourynge and wourshyppyng of our sauiour Jesus Christe in the sacrament of breade and wyne* (London, 1548), sigs Ivii^r–Ki^r, Kiii, Kv. Note that Jeanes questions MacCulloch's identification of Bonner with Cranmer. *Signs of God's Promise*, 101, n. 14.

[51] *Liturgies*, 87–9, 218, 278–80; *Sarum Missal*, 19, 31–8.

[52] *Liturgies*, 97–8, 282–3.

[53] Cox, I, 42–3.

[54] *Original Letters Relative to the English Reformation*, ed. by Hastings Robinson, 2 vols (PS, 1846–1847), I, 22–6.

[55] *Defence*, 10–11; Cox, I, 30.   [56] Cox, II, 157.

divine reconciliation and preserves human community.[57] This is joined by calls for a 'common table' as opposed to 'private masses'.[58]

Christ knits the church together in love during other times of worship, too. On Trinity Sunday,[59] as on other holy days, the collects speak in a corporate voice. The collect for All Saints Day prays, 'Almighty God, which hast knit together thy elect in one communion and fellowship in the mystical body of thy Son Christ our Lord; grant us grace so to follow thy holy Saints in all virtues, and godly living, that we may come to those unspeakable joys, which thou hast prepared for all them that unfeignedly love thee; through Jesus Christ.' The collect for Simon and Jude beseeches, 'Almighty God, which hast builded the congregation upon the foundation of the Apostles and prophets, Jesu Christ himself being the head corner-stone: grant us so to be joined together in unity of spirit by their doctrine.' This love is to be promoted by priest and people. In the *Ordinal*, the people sing, 'Of all strife and dissension, O Lord, dissolve the bands, And make the knots of peace and love throughout all Christian lands.' And the bishop examines the priest, 'Will you maintain and set forwards quietness, peace, and love amongst all Christian people, and specially amongst them that are or shall be committed to your charge?'[60]

When Cranmer considers the church at worship, he dwells upon 'the whole church', with participation by 'all'. Divine worship is a unified corporate activity.

> But the very supper was by Christ instituted and given to the whole church, not to be offered and eaten of the priest for other men, but by him to be delivered to all that would duly ask it.... The priests and ministers prepare the Lord's supper, read the gospel, and rehearse Christ's words, but all the people say thereto, Amen. All remember..., all give thanks..., all repent and offer..., all take him for their Lord....[61]

But when it comes to the historical development of satisfactory masses and private communion, Cranmer is not willing to place the blame on all. At this point, an underlying 'anticlericalism', especially pointed towards the papists, is at work. Masses arose 'partly through the ignorance and superstition of unlearned monks and friars,... but chiefly they sprang of lucre and gain'. Clerical greed created or fed upon the people's superstitions. And as for the princes, they followed along only because they were 'blinded by papistical doctrine' and did not want to offend their clergy and subjects.[62]

[57] *Defence*, 239; Cox, I, 347; Null, *Thomas Cranmer's Doctrine of Repentance*, 191.

[58] Cox, I, 352; Jeanes, *Signs of God's Promise*, 237.

[59] Cranmer rarely discusses the Trinity at any length, though he apparently added the pseudo-Athanasian creed to the Evening Prayers in order to combat Antitrinitarianism. *Liturgies*, 38–40, 229–31.

[60] *Liturgies*, 74–5, 173, 178, 263–4, 343, 347.

[61] *Defence*, 246; Cox, I, 350.

[62] *Defence*, 253–5; Cox, I, 353. Cf. Cox, II, 514–15.

Perhaps the strongest statement Cranmer made concerning the corporate nature of worship involved his interpretation of Matthew 18.20. The gathering of two or three, whether it be for eucharist or prayer, brings the presence of Christ. Traditionalists employed this passage to defend the inerrancy of councils.[63] Cranmer redeployed it in favor of 'common' worship against the restriction of the presence of Christ to the consecrated host. 'I say that Christ is spiritually and by grace in his supper, as he is when two or three be gathered together in his name, meaning that with both he is spiritually, and with neither corporally.' Cranmer considered this passage important enough to conclude his *Litany* with a prayer originating from Chrysostom dwelling on it.[64] His later language is stronger:

> And yet I know this to be true, that Christ is present with his holy church, which is his holy elected people, and shall be with them to the world's end, leading and governing them with his holy Spirit, and teaching them all truth necessary for their salvation. And whensoever any such be gathered together in his name, there is he among them, and he shall not suffer the gates of hell to prevail against them.[65]

Although Cranmer meant no such thing, when Elizabethan separatists combined Cranmer's ideas of a small remnant and Christ's presence in gathered fellowship with the Calvinist threefold office of Christ as Prophet, King, and Priest, the potential result was covenanted, self-governing congregations.[66]

Third, in political terms, Cranmer was an Erastian, at least until his execution in 1556. But he also taught Henry that, before God, all men are equal. 'Christ testifieth that all that be elect shall of God be equally and indifferently regarded of him in every condition, concerning not only the soul but also the body.' What truly matters is not one's estate but the disposition of one's heart.[67] However, Cranmer equally insisted this was no excuse for political disobedience or rebellion. Like others in the Tudor period, in both the lower and higher classes, he was horrified by the possibilities for disorder in rebellions,[68] and thus opposed both traditionalist rebels and radical Anabaptists. Following the traditionalist Western Rebellion of 1549, Cranmer received example sermons against rebellion from both Vermigli and Bucer, subsequently compiling his own. He also devised answers to the *Fifteen Articles* put forth by the Devon rebels.[69] With an eye on the German Peasants' Revolt, he excoriates the audacity of the rebels: 'First, to begin with the manner of your phrase. Is this the fashion of subjects to speak unto their prince, "We will have?"'[70] He does lay blame on the governors of the realm but only for being

---

[63] Cox, II, 53.   [64] Cox, I, 92; *Liturgies*, 105, 238. Cf. Cox, I, 89.
[65] Cox, I, 376.   [66] See Chapter 8.
[67] Cox, II, 106. Cf. Latimer, *Sermons*, 249.
[68] Anthony Fletcher and Diarmaid MacCulloch, *Tudor Rebellions*, 4th edn (London: Longman, 1997), 118–21.
[69] Cox, II, 188–9, 190–202, 163–87.   [70] Cox, II, 189, 164.

'too remiss in punishing offenders'. The ruler's task is to preserve the body of the commonwealth by wielding the sword like a scalpel against an infectious disease. 'For whensoever any member of our body is diseased or sore, if we suffer it long to continue and fester, do we not see that at length it doth infect the whole body, and in process of time utterly corrupteth the same?'[71] Private individuals are to amend their personal lives; public reformation is the preserve of public authority. 'Is it the office of subjects, to take upon them the reformation of the commonwealth, without the commandment of common authority?' No, for God 'hath forbidden all private persons to presume to take any such thing upon them'.[72]

Cranmer also recognized the dangers on his left. Both papists and Anabaptists were classified as 'sects' due to their asocial characteristics. According to Cranmer, radical evangelicals did more harm to the divine purpose than traditionalists, on account of their disdain for proper vocations.[73] Cranmer's register contains a number of processes, in Edward's reign, against those who professed anabaptism and the related doctrine of the celestial flesh of Christ, and against antitrinitarians. Two of these processes ended in death for the recalcitrant radicals, Joan Bocher and George van Parris.[74] In the section of the *Reformatio* entitled 'Concerning Heresies', sandwiched between a number of articles condemning Roman doctrines are several articles condemning Anabaptist tenets such as soul sleep, community of goods and wives, oaths, and the magistracy. Chapter 15 excoriates the Anabaptist tendency to sectarianism:

> Then they separate themselves from the body of the church and refuse to come to the Lord's holy table with others, and claim that they are held back either because of the wickedness of the ministers or because of other brethren, as if excommunication could be perceived in someone before the church has pronounced against him a sentence of excommunication in which it is declared that he is to be avoided like a heathen and a publican.[75]

The community may have been redefined away from the dead, but any further definition towards particular self-defined communities was intolerable. Public authority and individual vocations must be honored.

However, Cranmer was not thoroughly Erastian, for as we have seen, he would not let Henry arbitrarily define doctrine. He taught the young that although rebellion should never be committed, this is no excuse for an undiscerning obedience. 'Notwithstandyng yf the commen officer do byd

---

[71] Cox, II, 191.   [72] Cox, II, 192–3.

[73] MacCulloch, 'Archbishop Cranmer: Concord and Tolerance', 202–3, 214; *Narratives of the Reformation*, 246–7.

[74] Wilkins records five such processes, all in Edward's reign, from Cranmer's register. *Concilia*, IV, 40–5. On Bocher, see John Davis, 'Joan of Kent, Lollardy and the English Reformation', *JEH*, 33 (1982), 225–33.

[75] *Reformation of the Ecclesiastical Laws*; Spalding edn, 71–2; Cardwell edn, 15–16.

you do any thinge expressely agaynst God, then you may not obey him, but say with the apostle Peter, we must obey God rather then men.'[76] Bromiley reminds us that when confronted with conflict between civil obedience and divine obedience in his final arraignment and martyrdom,[77] Cranmer realized that both the 'powers that be'[78] and the gospel ministry 'are ordained by God, and in a Christian land their responsibilities necessarily overlap'. Thus, his struggle between obedience to divinely ordained magistrates and his own understanding of divine truth came to its dramatic conclusion.[79]

Neither did Cranmer have a rigid understanding of estates, or vocations. Both the very structure of estates and the movement of individuals within that structure could and often did change. This is seen most clearly in Cranmer's efforts to reestablish Canterbury Cathedral. As for structure, he wanted to alter the prebendaries 'to a more expedient use'. Like the religious estate, the estate of prebendaries began with a good purpose but, since it has no scriptural basis and is now offensive, 'it maketh no great matter if they perish together'.[80] As for movement within the structure, he contended with the gentry who wished to restrict entrance to the planned grammar school. They argued on the basis of paternal vocation that only the sons of gentlemen should be admitted. Cranmer disagreed, calling on the doctrine of spiritual gifts to argue for open admission. The natural gifts by which one is able to exercise a vocation are gifts of the Holy Spirit. And he 'giveth his gifts, both of learning and other perfections in all sciences, unto all kinds and states of people indifferently.' He reminded the assembled gentry that each of them began of 'low and base parentage' and ascended to their current estate.[81]

Finally, in philosophical terms, Cranmer was undoubtedly a nominalist. In contrast to Wyclif, he normally began with linguistic units rather than ontological universals. Eugene McGee has persuasively demonstrated Cranmer's nominalist training and continuing penchant for linguistic analysis.[82] But did this necessarily mean, as McGee concludes, that Cranmer lost sight of community and embraced atomistic individualism? Our discussion should have dispelled such a contention by this time. Moreover, McGee's article has been harshly criticized for relying on secondary sources and confusing medieval nominalism with early modern views. Neither should nominalism be confused with complete voluntarism.[83] Richardson reminds us that even if Cranmer was a nominalist, he did not take the hair-splitting philosophy to its 'logical' conclusion of 'sharp and irreconcilable'

---

[76] *Catechism*, 54.   [77] Cox, II, 214–15, 219, 224.

[78] The classic Erastian prooftexts include Romans 13 and I Peter 2.

[79] G.W. Bromiley, *Thomas Cranmer Theologian* (London: Lutterworth Press, 1956), 54.

[80] Cranmer to Cromwell, 29 November 1539; Cox, II, 396–7.

[81] Narratives of the Reformation, 273–5.

[82] McGee, 'Cranmer and Nominalism', *HTR*, 57 (1964), 189–95.

[83] William J. Courtenay, 'Cranmer as a Nominalist *Sed Contra*', *HTR*, 57 (1964), 367–80; McGee, 'Cranmer's Nominalism Reaffirmed', *HTR*, 59 (1966), 192–6.

contrasts between Christ, church, and eucharist. This was to be the achievement of Descartes. Cranmer was still a realist when it came to the incarnation of Christ and the believer's union with Christ.[84] This answers Francis Clark's contention that Catholic 'incarnational' theology was overthrown by the reformers, whose 'pristine' theology he grossly caricatures as promoting individualism and denying mediation and participation.[85] Cranmer, in his theology of incarnation, retained the ontological unity of the people of God.

Moreover, 'mutually exclusive dichotomies'[86] and individualism are not restricted to medieval nominalists and their early modern and modern successors. Traditional realists divided and categorized just as much. The strong medieval division between laity and clergy was held by both realists and nominalists, as was the monopolization of sacramental distribution to the clergy alone, or the fifteenth-century English restriction of lay Bible ownership. The quasi-arithmetical terms McGee unearths in Cranmer—'only', 'alone', 'but', 'after', and 'until'—are certainly there, but the same terms may also be discovered in any medieval text.[87] The crucial point is not *that* a division was made, but *where* it was made. Cranmer accused Gardiner of heedlessly separating the body and spirit of Christ between baptism and the mass. In defense of the universal faith, Cranmer proclaimed, 'The catholic church acknowledgeth no such division between Christ's holy flesh and his Spirit, that life is renewed in us by his holy Spirit, and increased by his holy flesh'. Thus, he could accuse Gardiner of filling his book with logical 'crafts, sleights, shifts, obliquities, and manifest untruths'.[88] Theological hair-splitting was not the sole preserve of the reformers.[89]

In summary, from the perspectives of theology, liturgy, politics, and philosophy, the first evangelical Archbishop of Canterbury exhibited a strong sense of community, even as he maintained a humanist personalism. With Cranmer's personal–communal theology adequately established, we now examine his theology of popular priesthood.

A PRIESTLY PEOPLE

It will be remembered that Luther extended unprecedented authority to all Christians on the basis of their baptismal ordination to priesthood. In his

---

[84] Richardson, *Zwingli and Cranmer*, 47–8.
[85] Clark, *Eucharistic Sacrifice and the Reformation* (London: Darton, Longman & Todd, 1960), 103–7.
[86] McGee, 'Cranmer and Nominalism', 209.
[87] 'Cranmer and Nominalism', 208.
[88] Cox, I, 34, 19. Cf. Cox, I, 25, 31.
[89] See 'Kingly Priests' (pp. 54–68) and 'Three English Conservatives' (pp. 101–9).

treatise to the Bohemians, he offered a functional definition of universal priesthood. We shall follow Luther's septemic structure to analyze how Cranmer incorporated the concept into his theology. First, it must be noted that by no means was the English reformer willing to open the doors to any radical understanding of the concept. Chapter 16 of the *Reformatio* section entitled 'Concerning Heresies' says:

> Similar is the madness of those who separate the ordination of ministers from the church, denying that certain doctors, pastors and ministers ought to be stationed in certain places. They do not allow lawful vocations, or the solemn imposition of hands, but spread the power of publicly teaching to all who, whenever they have a smattering of sacred letters, claim to possess the Holy Spirit; and they employ them not only for teaching but also for governing the church and administering the sacraments. Indeed, all of these practices are clearly contrary to the writings of the apostles.[90]

This was not a denial of universal priesthood, but it was a denial of the radical application of universal priesthood. Cranmer understood the priesthoods of people, ministers, kings, and Christ to function in a cooperative harmony: Christ's eternal priesthood entailed his constant intercession on our behalf. The kings' priesthood coordinated and defended the harmony of church and society. The ministers' priesthood was to teach, lead an exemplary life, and administer sacraments. The people's priesthood was to labor within their distinct vocations and offer spiritual sacrifices both in worship and at other times.

Common Proclamation[91]

Cranmer agreed with Luther but, like Luther (especially after the Peasants' Wars), he limited the scope of lay preaching. Prerequisite to lay proclamation is the availability of Scripture to the people in the vernacular. Cranmer's efforts in this cause have been discussed. The reasoning behind these efforts is revealed in the preface to *The Great Bible* (1539), which became known as *Cranmer's Bible,*[92] and in the 1547 homily on the reading and knowledge of Scripture.[93] In the preface, he sets himself against two sundry sorts of people.[94] 'For truly some there are that be too slow and need the spur; some other seem too quick and need more of the bridle.' The first sort are given four reasons for reading Scripture: sermon preparation, household teaching,

---

[90] *Reformation of the Ecclesiastical Laws*; Spalding edn, 72; Cardwell edn, 16.
[91] *Concerning the Ministry* (1523), in *LW*, XL, 21.
[92] Cox, II, 118–25.
[93] *Homilies*, 1–6.
[94] Cf. Cranmer to Cromwell, 14 November 1539; Cox, II, 396.

private discussions, and readiness for spiritual battle. Cranmer believes interpretation operates on two levels: at the lower level, the Bible can be understood
by anyone needing comfort and salvation; at a higher level, difficult passages
need skilled exposition. One must read contextually and repeatedly. If difficulty remains, then a 'curate or preacher' should be humbly approached for
explanation. Through this teacher, the Spirit will illumine the teachable heart.
Cranmer is adamant that Bible reading is 'for every man'.[95]

The second sort, those requiring the bridle, were a constant source of worry
for Cranmer. They endangered the success of vernacular Bible distribution by
engaging in frivolous disputation in 'every marketplace, every alehouse and
tavern, every feast house, briefly every company of men, every assembly of
women', even disrupting worship. Such 'idle babblers' endangered the Reformation by disturbing the peace and abusing Henry's permissive injunctions of
1536 and 1538.[96] Cranmer's solution was a fourfold restraint. First, those who
read Scripture must be spiritually clean. Second, it should be read at times of
leisure. Third, the audience must be kept in mind. Fourth, limited personal
capacity to consider the deeper matters must be remembered. With such
limitations, Cranmer did not want to discourage Bible-reading. He believed
it was 'as necessary for the life of man's soul, as for the body to breathe'.
Considering again the problem of idle babblers, Cranmer assures the people
that, although they might want to teach and should be enabled, he prefers the
layperson teach 'not only with his mouth, yet with his living and good
example, which is sure the most lively and effectuous form and manner of
teaching'.[97]

The root distinction between the common ministry of all believers and the
office of the ordained is a function of the division between private and public.
The *Oxford English Dictionary* notes that 'private' in the early modern period
meant 'withdrawn or separated from the public body'. A private person does
not hold a public office, or if holding a public office, functions at particular
times in a nonofficial capacity. The conscience is the possession of a private
person, though the conscience displays itself in public obedience. 'Public', the
opposite of private, refers to an activity done on behalf of the whole or to a
person who is 'authorized by, acting for, or representing the community'.[98]
The minister, according to Cranmer, has public authorization. Private individuals must not arrogate to themselves a public office.[99] Thus, preaching

---

[95] Cox, II, 118–21. Cf. *Certain Sermons*, 64–7.

[96] Cranmer to Lord Lisle, 13 July 1539; Cox, II, 391.

[97] Cox, II, 121–5, 180.

[98] Public entities are not restricted to private use; e.g, a prostitute or a public house. However,
even the premier public person, the king, has his 'privy chamber', but this 'privy chamber' was
the ground for the 'privy council' that had highly public functions. Starkey, 'Representation
through intimacy', 55, 61.

[99] *Liturgies*, 161, 331.

licenses, originating with the diocesan, are necessary for any extraparochial clergy. Cranmer was fairly consistent in his call for preaching licenses,[100] and in denouncing contentious lay discussions.[101]

In the Lutheran summer of 1538, Cranmer examined John Harrydaunce, or Henry Daunce, forerunner of the tub-preachers who became so numerous in the seventeenth century.[102] Perhaps because of the bricklayer's popularity, Cranmer did not prosecute him, but instead inhibited him from preaching.[103] In 1539, Cranmer condemned George Wishart, a gentleman from Scotland, for preaching heresy in Bristol. The nature of Wishart's heresy is difficult to ascertain, for it was reported by the town clerk of Bristol as 'openly declaring that Christ neither had nor could merit for him nor yet for us'.[104] Back in Scotland, Wishart subsequently defended his right to preach on the basis of I Peter 2 and Revelation 1, going so far as to preside over the eucharist.[105] During his trial, Wishart was accused of maintaining 'every layman was a priest.' His response: 'On the authority of the Word, I taught that believers are "a holy priesthood" and that those ignorant of the Scriptures, whatever their rank or degree, cannot instruct others; without the key of knowledge, they cannot bind or loose.' The Scottish bishops reportedly 'smiled derisively', then condemned Wishart as a heretic.[106]

Lay Baptism and Lay Presidency[107]

Like Luther, Cranmer believed that a change in status of sonship occurs to the individual in baptism, but, unlike Luther, Cranmer never explicitly connected baptism with ordination to common priesthood, as noted previously.[108] Due to their common baptism, Luther argued that the sacraments might, conceivably, be ministered by anyone. The key to understanding the reformers here is that the Word is the critical issue, not the sacraments themselves. Salvation

---

[100] Cranmer to Latimer, 1534; Cranmer to Lord Lisle, 13 July 1539; Cox, II, 296–7, 391. Royal Proclamations of 6 February, 13 May, and 23 September 1548; Cox, II, 508–9, 512–13.

[101] Royal Proclamation, 27 December 1547; Cox, II, 505–6.

[102] Christopher Hill, *The World Turned Upside Down* (London: Maurice Temple Smith, 1972), 296–300. Hill's understanding of universal priesthood deserves correction.

[103] Wriothesly, *Chronicle*, I, 83.

[104] Robert Ricart, *The Maire of Bristowe is Kalendar*, ed. by Lucy Toulmin Smith (Westminster: Camden Society, 1872), 55; Skeeters, *Community and Clergy*, 51–6. Charles Rogers argues 'nother' (i.e. 'neither') was a misspelling of 'mother', making Wishart's heresy a denial of Marian piety. *Life of George Wishart, the Scottish Martyr, with his Translation of the Helvetian Confession* (Edinburgh: Paterson, 1876), 10–12.

[105] Collier, *Ecclesiastical History*, V, 142–6. Rogers denies this event on the thin basis that John Knox did not explicitly affirm it. Rogers, *Life of George Wishart*, 50–1.

[106] *Life of George Wishart*, 44. Wishart's burning before the bejeweled and cushioned bishops helped ignite the early Scottish Reformation and inspire John Knox.

[107] *LW*, XL, 23–4.   [108] See Chapter 6.

comes by the Word, which is to be preached publicly only through authorized ministers, and privately through everyone. Eucharist and baptism no longer convey grace *ex opere operato*; rather, the Word is the agent and vehicle of grace. Nevertheless, the eucharist is only to be administered publicly by authorized ministers. Baptism may be ministered privately, but only in emergency situations, and even here not everyone agreed.[109]

Cranmer allowed emergency baptism to be administered even by women,[110] but he never considered lay presidency. He saw the eucharist as a public matter, which requires publicly authorized ministers.[111] However, by redefining the role of ministers, Cranmer brought the sacraments into closer relationship with the people. The difference between priest and layman is only one of ministration. The whole church participates in the eucharist. 'Private' masses are abolished due to their privacy.[112] The priest serves instrumentally as a vernacular 'trumpet' of God's Word, so that the people's hearts might comprehend and draw close to God.[113] Interestingly, in spite of his liturgical efforts to make both baptism and eucharist sacraments of incorporation, Cranmer retained the rite of private baptism, even as he gave prominence to the role of communal faith in public baptism.[114] This is an anomaly when compared with his rejection of private masses. It was up to the Elizabethan puritans to turn baptism into an entirely visible and communal initiation rite.

Binding and Loosing[115]

The keys were traditionally understood as localizing soteriological and juridical powers in the hierarchy. Luther objected they were not juridical but proclamatory in nature, and since all may proclaim the gospel, all thereby bind and loose. The most enduring legacy of Luther's common priesthood, in Lutheranism, is the hearing of confession by any Christian.[116] Cranmer followed Luther, to an extent.[117]

According to Peter Marshall, after the break with Rome private confession increasingly came under official suspicion as 'the privy chamber of treason'. Conservative priests were accused of utilizing the privacy of the confessional

---

[109] Robert C. Doyle, '"Lay Administration" and the Sixteenth Century', *Churchman*, 113 (1999), 328.

[110] Cox, II, 58.

[111] *Thirteen Articles*, art. 10; *Forty-Two Articles*, art. 24; *Documents*, 199, 298.

[112] Cox, I, 350.

[113] Cox, II, 169–70.

[114] Cuming, *History of Anglican Liturgy*, 111; *Liturgies*, 114–19, 291–4; Jeanes, *Signs of God's Promise*, 243–4.

[115] *LW*, XL, 25.   [116] Althaus, *Theology of Luther*, 315–18.

[117] *Catechism*, 193–7.

to encourage opposition to religious changes.[118] Cromwell, in the 1538 injunctions, turned the tables by transforming the confessional into an institution for vernacular instruction. We have already noted Cranmer's suspicion of inward supercession by overbearing priests in *'De Ordine'* and his downgrading of confession from necessary to beneficial in the *Thirteen Articles*.[119] The only major victory for Cranmer during the evangelical debacle of the *Six Articles* was convincing Henry of the dispensability of confession.[120] In his liturgical work, he went one step further. Although private confession before a priest is an express option, it is not a necessity. Only a general confession of sins to the church is required. Personal confession is strongly encouraged, but this should be directed to God. The sacrifice of Christ on the cross is the only necessary satisfaction. As for the third aspect of medieval penance, although the priest still pronounces absolution, it is a public pronouncement applicable to faithful consciences.[121] Whether by liturgical change, official suspicion, or general apathy, private confession to a priest underwent a popular decline.[122]

Spiritual Sacrifices[123]

Other than Cranmer, early modern theologians tended to debate presence rather than sacrifice. For most, eucharistic sacrifice was important, but secondary. Modern theologians, especially since the Oxford Movement, have furthered this trend. Much ink was and has been spilled on presence, less on sacrifice. Contrary to this later tendency, Cranmer considered the propitiatory sacrifice of the mass, not presence, to be 'the greatest blasphemy and injury that can be against Christ'.[124] Cranmer saved his discussion of sacrifice for the last book in his *Defence* because it delivered the crowning blow to medieval eucharistic theology, and he treated the interconnected doctrine of transubstantiation first since traditionalists were relatively weak there. Gardiner, a brilliant strategist, rearranged his rebuttal of Cranmer's *Defence* in order to strike first where his enemies were divided, on presence. In his *Answer* to Gardiner, Cranmer noted the strategy and more than doubled the material devoted to presence. As for sacrifice, Gardiner recognized it as his weakest point and wisely saved it for last,[125] making little response other than to affirm

---

[118] Marshall, *Catholic Priesthood*, 28–9.   [119] See Chapter 6.
[120] Redworth, 'A Study in the Formulation of Policy', 60–2. Cf. *Formularies*, 261.
[121] *Liturgies*, 4–6, 82, 218–19.
[122] Marshall, *Catholic Priesthood*, 33.
[123] *LW*, XL, 28.
[124] *Defence*, 232; Cox, I, 345.
[125] There was already a strong undercurrent against sacrifice as seen in humanist discussions that ignored the issue or even decried it. Colet, *Opus de Sacramentis*; More, *Utopia*, 126. None of the Henrician formularies affirm the doctrine.

traditional doctrine.[126] The resulting arrangement and bulk in *Answer* has influenced modern emphasis on presence, as has the anachronistic expedition for a Roman doctrine in Cranmer's work.[127]

Peter Brooks helped settle the issue of Cranmer's changing views on presence. He established that Cranmer moved from traditional transubstantiation to a definite Lutheran presence in 1538; he then proceeded to a Swiss 'true' or 'spiritual' presence by 1548.[128] Cranmer, however, in his famous 1555 argument with Thomas Martin, asserted he only held 'two contrary doctrines' of the eucharist.[129] While various explanations have been offered as to Cranmer's meaning here, none have been satisfactory.[130] The solution may be that Cranmer was not thinking of two contrary doctrines of *presence*, as is usually presumed, but of two contrary doctrines of *sacrifice*. He previously explained that sacrifice was the most crucial issue. In rejecting transubstantiation in 1538, he also came into the evangelical orbit, and across the board, evangelicals agreed to discard the sacrifice of the mass. Although the Marburg Colloquy is remembered for the fatal disagreement over presence, Zwingli and Luther agreed the eucharist was definitely not a propitiatory sacrifice.[131] Moreover, in a draft paper on the private mass from the 1538 Lutheran–Anglican dialogue, applying the sacrifice to the living and the dead for the remission of sins is condemned.[132] Following Martin's accusation of twice changing his mind and Cranmer's saying he changed once, Cranmer attributed another change in his eucharistic doctrine to a conference in 1546 with Nicholas Ridley, who 'drew me quite from my opinion'. By this time, however, Cranmer's conversation with Martin had moved on to the issue of presence.[133] In the earlier question

---

[126] In Wace's edition of *Defence*, the order and number of pages devoted to each topic are: transubstantiation (62), presence (68), reception (31), sacrifice (29). In Cox's edition of *Answer*, which is in much smaller print: presence (150), reception (38), transubstantiation (105), sacrifice (24). Cox, I, 50.

[127] Such efforts were fostered by the Oxford Movement. More recently, C.W. Dugmore and Fred Cate have championed a 'Ratramnian' or 'Reformed Catholic' view in Cranmer. They pin the changes from a basically orthodox 1549 to a radical 1552 on a reluctant but weak Cranmer being cornered by radicals. This is an unlikely hypothesis with little evidence. Cranmer might relent to a king on doctrinal definition but was rarely cowed by peers or underlings. Dugmore, *Mass and English Reformers*, 129, 171, 182; Fred H. Cate, 'Thomas Cranmer's Eucharistic Doctrine and the Prayer Books of Edward VI', *Historical Magazine of the Protestant Episcopal Church*, 55 (1986), 95–111.

[128] Peter Brooks, *Cranmer's Doctrine of the Eucharist*. MacCulloch corrects Brooks' terminology, using 'true' to describe his Lutheran phase and 'spiritual' to describe his Swiss phase. *Cranmer*, 182, 392.

[129] Cox, II, 217–18. The accusation concerns editorial changes in his *Catechism*. D.G. Selwyn, 'A Neglected Edition of Cranmer's Catechism', *JTS*, 15 (1964), 76–91.

[130] Buchanan emphasizes 'contrary' rather than 'two'. *What Did Cranmer Think?*, 3n. Brooks places the blame on 'anxieties'. *Cranmer's Doctrine of the Eucharist*, 12. Dix assigns it to a 'flicker of inconsistency'. *Shape of the Liturgy*, 646.

[131] 'The Marburg Colloquy and the Marburg Articles', in *LW*, XXXVIII, xv, 51, 88; Clark, *Eucharistic Sacrifice*, 171.

[132] Cox, II, 482.

[133] Cox, II, 218. Ridley was convinced the mass was no sacrifice. *Works of Ridley*, 206.

about 'contrary doctrines', Cranmer was thinking of sacrifice while Martin was thinking of presence; in the latter, they both were thinking of presence. Therefore, Cranmer held *two* doctrines concerning *sacrifice*, and *three* concerning *presence*. The archbishop was not being inconsistent in his argument with Martin.

Transubstantiation and sacrifice fell simultaneously for most reformers, while the issue of presence could bring profound disagreement. Cranmer, although finally embracing a spiritual presence position, did not consider evangelical disagreements over presence to be insurmountable.[134] The paramount issue was 'the greatest blasphemy and injury that can be against Christ', the papal dogma of the propitiatory sacrifice of the mass. That Cranmer considered the issue of sacrifice paramount is also evident in his liturgies. It is generally agreed that the communion services of 1549 and 1552 removed any possibility of interpreting the eucharist as a propitiatory sacrifice. Moreover, once this change was made, Cranmer never looked back. Any further changes tightened the reformed nature of the liturgy, ensuring it against Gardiner's conservative interpretation and incorporating some of Bucer's suggestions.[135] 'Cranmer was obsessed by the need to emphasize the truth that the Eucharist is not a vicarious sacrifice.'[136]

What drove Cranmer to deny the propitiatory sacrifice of the mass? A number of factors contributed. He wanted to exalt the priesthood and sacrifice of Christ, protecting them from human incursions. His understanding of justification by faith pivoted on his understanding that the benefits of the unique sacrifice of Christ could be appropriated only by the divine gift of personal faith. Yet, Cranmer also had a high view of the Fathers, and their eucharistic language embraced sacrifice. How could he reconcile his new views with the Fathers? The solution to his dilemma lay in spiritual sacrifices.

Before delving into Cranmer's understanding of universal priesthood and spiritual sacrifices, a review of the historical context would be helpful. The medieval church placed the eucharist at the center of lay piety. The consecrated host was transubstantiated into the body of Christ by the words of the priest. With the presence of Christ, divine power was available for application to both spiritual and corporal needs.[137] The priest was believed, in a sense, to

---

[134] Witness his invitations to Lutherans and Swiss alike to resolve the issue in a synod.

[135] Buchanan, *What Did Cranmer Think?*, 18; Brooks, *Cranmer's Doctrine of the Eucharist*, 73; Dugmore, *Mass and Reformers*, 133, 159-60; Dix, *Shape of the Liturgy*, 646; Brightman, *English Rite*, I, cvi; Procter and Frere, *New History*, 459. The most detailed comparison between *Sarum* and 1549 is found in Clark, *Eucharistic Sacrifice*, 184-7. For Bucer's comments, see *Bucer and the Book of Common Prayer*.

[136] F.C. Long, 'Transubstantiation and Sacrifice', *CQR*, 155 (1954), 234. Trevor Jalland's attempt to read 'propitiatory Atonement' into the 1549 rite should be totally discredited. Jalland, *This Our Sacrifice* (London: Mowbray, 1933), 129-30.

[137] Thomas, *Religion and the Decline of Magic*, 36-40.

become Christ the priest.[138] The sacrifice that the priest offered to the Father was an iteration or perpetuation of the sacrifice of Christ, though an unbloody one.[139] Thus, it was a propitiatory sacrifice, and could be applied by the priest to both living and dead.[140] The Council of Trent reaffirmed these doctrines, though removing some popular superstitions.[141] According to English conservatives, as Christ's priesthood is continued in the clerical priesthood, so Christ's propitiatory sacrifice is continued in the propitiatory sacrifice of the mass. Spiritual sacrifices are in the mass, but do not abrogate mass sacrifice. As Edmund Bonner responded to Cranmer in 1547,

> Q.   What is the oblation and sacrifice of Christ in the Mass?
>
> R.   I think it is the presentation of the very body and blood of Christ being really present in the Sacrament; which presentation the priest maketh at the Mass, in the name of the Church, unto God the Father in memory of Christ's passion and death upon the cross; with thanksgiving therefore and devout prayer that all Christian people, and name they which spiritually join with the priest in the said oblation, and of whom he maketh special remembrance, may attain the benefit of the said passion.[142]

Cranmer disagreed. Christ's sacrifice can in no way be identified with the mass. His sacrifice is unique, unrepeatable, and without participation. 'Christ's sacrifice once offered was sufficient for evermore.' Only Christ may offer himself, and any attempt to add to his sacrifice denigrates it. 'Whosoever shall seek any other sacrifice propitiatory for sin, maketh the sacrifice of Christ of no validity, force, or efficacy.' A person may accept either Christ's sacrifice or the sacrifice of the mass, but not both. By trying to hold both, 'divide we our salvation between Christ and the priest'. Thus, the sacrifice of the mass is 'most contumelious against our only Lord and Saviour Christ Jesus, and a violating of his precious blood, which upon the altar of the cross is the only sacrifice and oblation for the sins of all mankind'.[143] He gave the antithesis between mass and cross legal force in the thirtieth of *Forty-Two Articles*.

---

[138] Gardiner, in Cox, I, 83, 363; Jeanes, *Signs of God's Promise*, 33.

[139] B.J. Kidd, *The Later Mediaeval Doctrine of the Eucharistic Sacrifice* (London: SPCK, 1898), 51, 98; Gardiner, in Cox, I, 364.

[140] Clark, *Eucharistic Sacrifice*, 93–5. Both MacCulloch and Jeanes argue the sacrifice of the mass is not affirmed in the *Rationale*. Cranmer, 276; Jeanes, *Signs of God's Promise*, 50. However, the sacrifice of the mass is later described, without condemnation, as are transubstantiation and application to the dead. *The Rationale of Ceremonial*, 24–6. On the other hand, the evangelical doctrinal emphases on Christ's 'sufficient' sacrifice and faith as its appropriation were earlier affirmed. *The Rationale of Ceremonial*, 18–19. A temporary compromise between conservatives and evangelicals seems to have been reached with the agreement that the priest's role is to 'represent' the mass sacrifice. *The Rationale of Ceremonial*, 24.

[141] David N. Power, *The Sacrifice We Offer: The Tridentine Dogma and its Reinterpretation* (Edinburgh: T&T Clark, 1987), 58–64, 189–97.

[142] Clark conveniently gathers the opinions of Fisher, Tunstall, Gardiner, and Bonner. Clark, *Eucharistic Sacrifice*, 528–9, 536–7, 540–2.

[143] *Defence*, 234; Cox, I, 346, 354, 364, 395, 399.

Cranmer's antithesis alters the traditional doctrine of priesthood. Since Christ's priesthood is continual, it cannot be transferred. 'Christ liveth ever, and hath an everlasting priesthood, that passeth not from him to any man else.' In this priesthood, 'he admitteth neither partner nor successor'. Again, those who try to extend his priesthood denigrate it. 'But all such priests as pretend to be Christ's successors in making a sacrifice of him, they be his most heinous and horrible adversaries.'[144] How, then, does Cranmer reconcile this stark opposition with scriptural and historical precedents? Behind his antithesis lay a distinction between two types of sacrifices. The propitiatory sacrifice brings reconciliation, while the spiritual sacrifice is a response to the offer of reconciliation but itself cannot effect reconciliation. Only Christ is capable of reconciling and only he may offer propitiatory sacrifice.

> One kind of sacrifice there is, which is called a propitiatory or merciful sacrifice, that is to say, such a sacrifice as pacifieth God's wrath and indignation, and obtaineth mercy and forgiveness for all our sins, and is the ransom for our redemption from everlasting damnation.... Another kind of sacrifice there is which doth not reconcile us to God, but is made of them that be reconciled by Christ, to testify our duties unto God and to shew ourselves thankful unto him.[145]

Christ offers the propitiatory sacrifice to God on our behalf. The benefits of that sacrifice are applied through faith. We offer spiritual sacrifices to God, but only through the mediation of Christ, whose priesthood is continual and whose sacrifice makes our sacrifices acceptable.

How then is the eucharist related to sacrifice? The eucharist is a sacrament, or sign, which God gives to the church. Sacrament is distinguished from sacrifice. The church receives the sacrament, and is, when remembering Christ's sacrifice, prompted to respond with spiritual sacrifices. There is a movement toward humanity in the sacrament, described as 'seals of God's promises and gifts', and a responsive Godward movement in spiritual sacrifices.[146] And yet, the offering of spiritual sacrifices is most definitely not confined to eucharistic worship. Neither do the people need the mediation of a priest in their offering of spiritual sacrifices. These sacrifices are offered through Christ, not through the priest and not through the eucharist, although the presence of priest and eucharist are a fit context for their offering.

For Cranmer, priest and people offer spiritual sacrifices together. Cranmer redefines the relationship of priest and laity. The old distinctions disappear. 'Therefore Christ made no such difference between the priest and the layman, that the priest should make oblation and sacrifice of Christ for the layman, and eat the Lord's supper from him all alone, and distribute and apply it as him

---

[144] *Defence*, 233, 235, 240; Cox, I, 345–6, 348.
[145] *Defence*, 235; Cox, I, 346.
[146] *Defence*, 246; Cox, I, 350, 366, 397.

liketh.' But new distinctions arise. 'Christ made no such difference, but the difference that is between the priest and the layman in this matter is only in the ministration.' The priest is now a *publicus ecclesiae administer*, a common minister of the church.[147] This new definition does not diminish 'the estimation and dignity' of the ministers, 'but advanceth and highly commendeth their ministration'. The clerical priesthood has thus made the transition from the role of mediatorial priest by virtue of a sacrificial offering to a mediatorial priest by virtue of Word and sacrament. 'Wherefore the ministers of Christ's church be not now appointed priests to make a new sacrifice for sin, as though Christ had not done that at once sufficiently for ever, but to preach abroad Christ's sacrifice, and to be ministers of his word and sacraments.'[148]

These spiritual oblations, offered by priests and people, are described in both negative and positive terms. Negatively, they include the death of various 'unreasonable lusts and desires of the flesh'; the crucifixion of our own wills, 'in life and inward affection'; and repentance.[149] Positively, they are described as laud, praise, and prophesying, which includes activity by the people;[150] lauds and thanksgiving, harking back to the New Testament εὐχαριστήσας and ὑμνήσαντες;[151] any work, office, or duty done for the glory of God;[152] alms given to the church, or bread and wine offered for use in worship;[153] justice;[154] obedience to all higher human authorities; faith in God, which is described as 'the highest and chiefest sacrifice wherewith God is pleased and worshipped';[155] and 'generally our whole obedience to God, in keeping his laws and commandments', especially in having a contrite heart.[156] In his second Oxford explication, Cranmer indifferently lists them as 'sacrifices of thanksgiving, of praise, of confessing his name, of true amendment, of repentance, of mercifulness towards our neighbours, and of all other good works of charity!'[157] Entirely absent in the mature Cranmer is any reference to bread and cup as a sacrifice, a detail that prompts angst among modern liturgical revisionists.[158]

---

[147] *Defence*, 246; Cox, I, 350; Cox, I, appendix, 94.   [148] Cox, I, 363.
[149] *Defence*, 243; Cox, I, 349.   [150] *Defence*, 248; Cox, I, 351, 369.
[151] Cox, I, 359, 361.   [152] Cox, I, 88, 366; *Homilies*, 19.
[153] Cox, I, 79; *Liturgies*, 83–4; 269–71. Interestingly, it was only after Bucer defined almsgiving as a spiritual sacrifice that Cranmer expanded the 1552 communion service to offer vocally the alms to God. His fear of an incorrect sacrificial interpretation may have prompted him to drop the reference in 1549. *Bucer and Book of Common Prayer*, 36–9; *Liturgies*, 271.
[154] Cox, I, 361.
[155] *Catechism*, 54, 103–4.
[156] *Defence*, 236; Cox, I, 346.
[157] Cox, I, 399.
[158] A.H. Couratin, 'The Tradition Received', *Theology*, 69 (1966), 437–42; R.T. Beckwith and C.O. Buchanan, '"This Bread and This Cup": An Evangelical Rejoinder', *Theology*, 70 (1967), 265–71.

Cranmer also equates spiritual sacrifice with *anamnesis* and *repraesentatio*. His *Commonplace Books* quote Chrysostom to that effect, which quotation eventually found its way into *Defence*.[159] His third answer to some 1548 questions concerning abuses reads:

Q.   What is the oblation and sacrifice of Christ in the mass?

R.   The oblation and sacrifice of Christ in the mass is not so called, because Christ is there offered and sacrificed by the priest and the people, (for that was done but once by himself upon the cross;) but it is so called, because it is a memory and representation of that very true sacrifice and immolation which before was made upon the cross.[160]

In arguing with Gardiner about Peter Lombard's definition of the mass, Cranmer concludes the memorial of Christ's sacrifice is radically distinct from Christ's sacrifice. The cross is propitiatory; the mass is not. Against Cranmer, Gardiner argued the mass was both a memorial and a propitiatory sacrifice.[161] Whenever Cranmer is confronted with a patristic text that correlates sacrifice and eucharist, he falls back on the hermeneutic of purely memorial sacrifice. 'Therefore when the old fathers called the mass or supper of the Lord a sacrifice, they meant that it was a sacrifice of lauds and thanksgiving, (and so as well the people as the priest do sacrifice,) or else that it was a remembrance of the very true sacrifice propitiatory of Christ.'[162]

This understanding is incorporated directly into the 1549 and 1552 communion rites. In 1549, before the reception, and bracketing the petition of consecration, is an affirmation of Christ's unique sacrifice and an elaboration of responsive sacrifice. First, the priest offers a prayer of humble access on behalf of the whole church. God is thanked for the 'full, perfect, and sufficient sacrifice' of Christ's passion. Next, the petition and institution narrative are recited. Then, 'without any elevation, or shewing the Sacrament to the people', the spiritual sacrifices of priest and people are offered. There are three oblations. First, 'our Sacrifice of praise and thanksgiving'. Second, 'ourself, our souls, and bodies, to be a reasonable, holy, and lively sacrifice unto thee'. Third, 'our bounden duty and service, and ... our prayers and supplications'.[163] The 1552 rite strengthens the distinction between Christ's propitiatory sacrifice and our spiritual sacrifices. The prayer of humble access and the affirmation of Christ's sacrifice remain, but the petition excludes consecration and the prayer of threefold oblation comes after reception. Moreover, the prayer of oblation becomes an alternative rather than necessary part of the rite. These changes serve to emphasize Christ's unique priesthood and sacrifice.[164]

---

[159] BL Royal MS 7B, XI, fol. 52ᵛ; *Defence*, 250–1; Cox, I, 351–2.
[160] Cox, II, 150.   [161] Cox, I, 357–9.   [162] Cox, I, 353, 356, 359.
[163] *Liturgies*, 87–9.   [164] *Liturgies*, 278–80, 89.

Although we have enumerated the variety of these sacrifices, what was their nature? During worship, they are offered by priest together with people, as opposed to the Gardiner/Smith understanding that they are offered by priest on behalf of people.[165] Offering is not confined to eucharistic worship, for people should offer 'in what place so ever they be', 'whether it be in the Lord's supper, in their private prayers, or in any work they do at any time or place to the glory of God'.[166] The variety of sacrifices is explained in three ways. They can be identified with one another under the category of 'laud and praise'.[167] They can function as the responsive part of an *ordo salutis*: the sacrament spurs memory, which inspires faith, which brings comfort, which results in thanksgiving and the wholesale offering of one's life.[168] Or they can be indifferently listed, as above. What Cranmer is adamant about is their complete separation from Christ's sacrifice and non-propitiatory nature.[169] We offer spiritual oblations in response to Christ's sacrifice. 'For by such sacrifices we shall declare ourselves neither ungrateful to God, nor altogether unworthy of this holy sacrifice of Christ.'[170] Finally, they can only be offered to God through Christ. They are 'accepted of God through the sacrifice of Christ, by whose blood all their filth and unpureness is clean sponged away'.[171]

Sources for Cranmer's Doctrine of Spiritual Sacrifices

Where did Cranmer learn to relate royal priesthood primarily with spiritual sacrifices? Most obviously, from his reading of Scripture. His *Commonplace Books* cite I Peter 2.5, the foundational text connecting royal priesthood with spiritual sacrifices, in a list of other texts from the Old and New Testaments under the heading, *De Sacrificiis Christianorum*, concerning the sacrifices of Christians.[172] In addition to Chrysostom, his citations of Bede refer to baptism as a mystical chrism conferring priesthood upon all Christians, who offer spiritual sacrifices.[173] He also owned a copy of Wyclif's *Trialogus*, who was a concern in his Cambridge days, whom he highly praised, and whose book deals with the subject.[174] He knew of Luther's 1520 *Babylonian Captivity*,

---

[165] Cox, I, 359, 362, 369. *Pace* John Cosin's later division of priestly sacrifice from people's sacrifice. Geoffrey Cuming, 'The English Rite', *Theology*, 69 (1966), 449.

[166] *Defence*, 248; Cox, I, 351, 366.

[167] *Defence*, 251–2; Cox, I, 352.

[168] *Defence*, 251; Cox, I, 352.

[169] Cox, I, 359, 361.

[170] Cox, I, 399.

[171] Cox, I, 362, 366.

[172] BL Royal MS 7B, XI, fol. 50.

[173] BL Royal MS 7B, XI, fol. 189.

[174] Selwyn, 'Cranmer's Library', in *C&S*, 40, 53, 55n, 63. 'And as for John Wickliff, he was a singular instrument of God in his time to set forth the truth of Christ's gospel.' Cox, I, 14.

having read Henry's and Fisher's criticisms. He also annotated his own copy of *Babylonian Captivity*, wherein Luther criticized the mass, distinguished sacrament from sacrifice, allowed for only non-propitiatory spiritual sacrifices, specifically prayers and alms, and equated priests with laity.[175]

Cranmer knew Melanchthon's *Apology* and owned a copy of his 1535 *Loci Communes*, both of which extensively treat spiritual sacrifice as an alternative to the sacrifice of the mass. Like Cranmer, Melanchthon allows orders to be called a sacrament but replaces priestly application with self-application.[176] He, too, differentiates manward sacrament from Godward sacrifice and propitiatory sacrifice from spiritual sacrifice.[177] Melanchthon's undifferentiated list is strikingly similar to Cranmer's exclamation in his second Oxford explication.[178] In his *Apology*, Melanchthon treats several controversial passages, giving the spiritual sacrifice interpretation to each, making much of memorial sacrifice.[179] He also offers the thanksgiving interpretation of the Fathers.[180] Jeanes says Cranmer appropriated a passage on spiritual sacrifices from Melanchthon's *Loci Communes* in both his *Commonplace Books* and *'De Sacramentis'*.[181]

However, although Cranmer knew Melanchthon's theology and mirrored much of it, his was a sporadic development that cannot be strictly attributed to Luther's disciple. In *'De Sacramentis'*, although he rejects the popular view of a propitiatory mass, rejects priestly application, and exalts Christ's sacrifice, he retains the traditional views that it is a sacrifice for living and dead and an unbloody offering.[182] In a paper from the 1538 conference, *'De Missa Privata'*, all of the points on which Melanchthon and the later Cranmer agree are spelled out; however, Cranmer only made marginal notes.[183] After the Germans sent a similar refutation of the sacrifice of the mass to Henry, Tunstall's official response rebutted the agreement and the Henrician experiment with Lutheranism came to an abrupt halt.[184] Cranmer may have continued to contemplate Lutheran views but he could only with private circumspection promote them until Edward's reign.

---

[175] *Cranmer*, 26–9; Selwyn, 'Cranmer's Library', 70. *LW*, XXXVI, 50–6.
[176] *Corpus Reformatorum*, XXI, 470, 485.
[177] *Fayth of the Germaynes*, sig. Svii.
[178] *Fayth of the Germaynes*, sig. Sviii^v.
[179] *Fayth of the Germaynes*, sigs Ti–Tv, Uii.
[180] *Corpus Reformatorum*, XXI, 484; *Fayth of the Germaynes*, sig. Ui^r.
[181] Jeanes, 'Reformation Treatise', 160, 176–7n.
[182] 'Concord', in 'Reformation Treatise', 176, 188.
[183] Cox, II, 480–2; translation in Bray, *Documents*, 208–13. *'De Privata Missa'* cites Augustine in support of spiritual sacrifices. Cox, II, 482. Cf. Dugmore, *Mass and Reformers*, 17.
[184] Portion of German letter devoted to private mass in Burnet, I, ii, 335–41. Portion of Henry's response devoted to private mass in Burnet, I, ii, 352–5; partial translation in Clark, *Eucharistic Sacrifice*, 536–7.

If, as Hope suspects and MacCulloch maintains, Richard Bonner is a pseudonym for Cranmer,[185] then Bucer reinforced Cranmer's spiritual sacrifice theology. The pseudonymous 1548 treatise incorporates much of Bucer's *Constans Defensio*. If 'Bonner' had continued translating, he would have next come to Bucer's delineation of four oblations in the mass.[186] 1548 is also the year in which the famous Lords' Debate occurred. On the second day of that December debate, Thirlby began by objecting that, in their 'book of agreements', there was 'Oblation, which is left out now'.[187] This was extremely problematic to the conservative bishops. D.G. Selwyn has identified the two books in question. The second book parallels the first, except that the final third of the first book, which includes a conservative definition of the sacrifice of the mass, is omitted.[188]

Although Peter Martyr Vermigli also replaced the sacrifice of the mass with spiritual sacrifices in the May 1549 debate at Oxford, it is doubtful Cranmer was greatly indebted to him. Vermigli held many of the same positions that Bucer and Melanchthon held. He taught spiritual sacrifice in his inaugural Corinthian lectures as Regius Professor of Divinity at Oxford, where he displaced Richard Smith, and in his treatise on sacrifice. Cranmer's doctrine of spiritual sacrifice correlates closely with Vermigli's.[189] Cranmer and Vermigli remained close, the latter contributing a prayer to the 1552 communion rite[190] and resorting to Cranmer in the early part of Mary's reign.[191] They likely reinforced each other's conclusions.

It should be evident by this chronological approach that Cranmer was first indebted to Luther and Melanchthon and later to those Reformed theologians who stood on the border between the competing eucharistic theologies of Luther and Zwingli. Calvin also stood on that border. His *Institutes*, first composed during his sojourn with Bucer in Strasbourg, brushed on the idea of spiritual sacrifices, and this was duly quoted in Cranmer's *Commonplace Books*. Brian Gerrish's excellent study of Calvin's eucharistic theology makes much of Calvin's twofold view of eucharistic sacrifice. Communion offers both a gift to believers and serves as a means for believers to return thanksgiving.[192]

---

[185] Hope, 'An English Version', 99; *Cranmer*, 399–403.

[186] Hope, 'An English Version', 109n.

[187] Gasquet and Bishop, *Edward and the Book of Common Prayer*, 404–5.

[188] Selwyn, 'The "Book of Doctrine", The Lords' Debate and the First Prayer Book of Edward VI', *JTS*, 40 (1989), 462–80; Selwyn, 'A New Version of a Mid-Sixteenth-Century Vernacular Tract on the Eucharist', *JEH*, 39 (1988), 228–9.

[189] Joseph C. McLelland, *The Visible Words of God* (London: Oliver and Boyd, 1957), 251–4.

[190] Alan Beesley, 'An Unpublished Source of the Book of Common Prayer: Peter Martyr Vermigli's *Adhortatio ad Coenam Domini Mysticam*', *JEH*, 19 (1968), 83–8.

[191] On Cranmer's relations with Vermigli, see Cox, I, 373–4, 391, 429; McLelland, *Visible Words*, 16–44, 268–71.

[192] Gerrish, *Grace and Gratitude* (Edinburgh: T&T Clark, 1993), 134–56.

However, those Reformed churches closest to the English generally excluded any reference to spiritual sacrifices in their eucharistic liturgy.[193]

Cranmer owed little to Zwingli for his view of spiritual sacrifices. For one, Zurich's more thorough rejection of corporal presence, in comparison with the Lutherans and the moderating views of Bucer and Vermigli, effectively dispelled any idea of eucharistic sacrifice. Spiritual sacrifices served primarily to differentiate Lutheran from traditional understandings of presence. With only a spiritual presence, nobody could accuse Zwingli of retaining the sacrifice of the mass, though Zwingli could accuse Luther of such.[194] Zwingli affirmed universal priesthood as the offering up of oneself, but, other than a summary reference, there is no clear exposition of spiritual sacrifices in his works.[195] We may conclude, therefore, that if not in presence, then in sacrifice, Cranmer was closer to Wittenberg than Zurich.[196] Liturgically, however, Cranmer was dependent on neither the Lutherans nor the Swiss. His exquisite prayer of oblation is entirely his composition.[197]

Common Intercession[198]

Cranmer's views on intercession by ordinary Christians can be seen in simply reading through his book of *common* prayers. During the Reformation, Cardinal Francesco de Quinones revised the Breviary, the singing of the daily offices, to reinvigorate prayers by the clergy. Cranmer borrowed heavily from Quinones' breviary, and turned the clergy's Latin breviary into a vernacular book of prayers for priests and people together.[199] According to Cranmer, the clergy were especially stirred to prayer only so they could teach the people. His ultimate goal was to help the people 'understand and

[193] Dugmore found no mention of spiritual sacrifices in the liturgies of London's Stranger Churches during Edward's reign. *Mass and Reformers*, 163–71. John à Lasco's rite, *Forma ac Ratio*, said communion should replace the idolatrous sacrifice. There is some vague talk about spiritual sacrifices as 'mortifying our olde man' and 'renewing of our mynds', but this was to be accomplished 'before the communion daye'. English translation of *Forma ac Ratio* in Bodleian Barlow MS 19, fols 100ᵛ–105ʳ.

[194] *LW*, XXXVIII, 51.

[195] Yarnell, 'Reformation Development', 50; Clark, *Eucharistic Sacrifice*, 171. Zwingli considers the mass a 'memorial' of Christ's sacrifice, which is 'not a sacrifice'. W.P. Stephens, *The Theology of Huldrych Zwingli* (OUP, 1986), 219. Cf. Richardson, *Zwingli and Cranmer*, 8–36.

[196] Bullinger included spiritual sacrifices in his discussion of royal priesthood, but he also moved towards Calvin's views about this time. Heinrich Bullinger, *The Decades*, ed. by Thomas Harding, 4 vols (PS, 1849–1851), IV, 288–91.

[197] Basil Hall, 'Cranmer, the Eucharist and the Foreign Divines in the Reign of Edward VI', in *C&S*, 240–1.

[198] *LW*, XL, 29.

[199] David Cutts and Harold Miller, *Whose Office? Daily Prayer for the People of God* (Bramcote: Grove Books, 1982), 17–18.

have profit in prayer'.[200] As he explained in 'An exhortation unto prayer' attached to his 1544 *Litany*, he wanted 'neighbour and neighbour' to gather for 'comon prayer'. The vernacular is necessary because prayer is not to be perfunctory but 'mind–heart prayer'.[201]

Common Judgment[202]

As for judgment of doctrine, Cranmer never appreciated Luther's early definition. Although the people must be encouraged to read Scripture,[203] they must simply submit to public authority in the matter of doctrine. Under 'judgment', Luther included the election and discipline of ministers. The extent of Cranmer's move in a 'democratic' direction was to allow the people to object to an ordinand if they knew of an 'impediment, or notable crime'. If objections arose, the ceremony was to cease until the accusation was cleared.[204] Normally, patrons offered a candidate, the clergy examined, and bishops ordained.[205] Although Cranmer promoted teaching as the premier ministerial task, the people had little say over that teaching. Complaints could be, and were, made to the ecclesiastical courts about errant teaching, but the final decision was up to the court.

However, religious policy was increasingly opened to lay participation. As the standard study on the church courts during the Reformation states, 'Successive governments entrusted lay agents with much of the burden of enforcing the religious policies of the crown, either by including them in mixed commissions for the exercise of its ecclesiastical jurisdiction or by creating concurrent lay jurisdiction over offences hitherto under ecclesiastical cognisance.'[206] Cranmer may have been behind the 1545 parliamentary act allowing laymen to exercise ecclesiastical jurisdiction. He promoted William Cooke, a married layman, into high positions in his diocesan administration soon after.[207] But his was not an exercise in egalitarianism. During Cranmer's Reformation, lay participation may have increased but lay initiative, other

---

[200] *Liturgies*, 17–19, 193–6.

[201] *Cranmer's First Litany, 1544*, ed. by Eric Hunt (London: SPCK, 1939), 68, 78–82.

[202] *LW*, XL, 31.

[203] Cox, II, 155.

[204] *Liturgies*, 162, 174, 332, 344.

[205] None of the major writers on clerical life in this period considers election. Appointment seems to have been entirely by presentation. Cf. Cooper, *Last Generation*, 13–18. The *Sarum* rite allows for objections to be raised against a candidate, but this was in Latin. *Monumenta Ritualia Ecclesiae Anglicanae*, III, 161. Bradshaw says the early church's concern to base the ministry in a local community was almost entirely lost in the Middle Ages, where the concern was the transferral of power. 'Medieval Ordinations', 377.

[206] Houlbrooke, *Church Courts and People*, 221.

[207] Ayris, 'God's Vicegerent and Christ's Vicar', in *C&S*, 138–9.

than at the highest levels, declined. Much of this can be pinned on the dissolution of mass institutions (monasteries, chantries, and guilds), which had allowed lay initiative in foundation and discipline, and on governmental enforcement of religion.[208] Religious uniformity as a guarantor of social unity was the order of the day.[209]

And yet, Cranmer insinuated primitive church government allowed greater participation in discipline at the local level. The thirty-first question during the private examination of a priest in Bucer's *De Ordinatione Legitima* interpreted royal priesthood according to Matthew 18 and I Corinthians 14. Although the people were admonished to honor their ministers and work within the parochial system, they should also 'mutually teach and admonish each other'.[210] In 'A Commination against Sinners', Cranmer recognized 'there was a Godly discipline' in the early church. However, this discipline has yet to 'be restored again (which thing is much to be wished)'.[211] In his 1548 Articles of Visitation, he employed the people in the enforcement of marital laws.[212] John à Lasco, Cranmer's superintendent for the Strangers Churches of London, was highly interested in discipline. His *Forma ac Ratio* laboriously details the disciplinary liturgy of the Stranger Churches.[213] The desire for a godly discipline would be furthered by some Elizabethan Protestants, specifically on the basis of Matthew 18 in discipline, and I Corinthians 14 in prophecies.

SUMMARY

Thomas Cranmer embraced the doctrine of royal priesthood and it permeated his theology, politics, and worship. Yet that doctrine cannot be glibly classified as egalitarian or anticlerical, nor can it be relegated to some minor arena. Cranmer's version of universal priesthood envisioned the harmonious cooperation of king, clergy, and people in fulfilling their divine vocations. He gave kings wide latitude in areas previously restricted to bishops and priests, except when it came to formulating doctrine. He successfully defended the position of the clergy, yet he radically redefined their role in terms of vocation to a ministry of Word and sacrament. He granted the people personal access to

---

[208] Gervase Rosser, 'Parochial Conformity and "Voluntary" Religion in Late Medieval England', *TRHS*, 6th series, 1 (1991), 188–9; Scarisbrick, *Reformation and People*, 165; Haigh, 'Anticlericalism and Reformation', 406–7.

[209] Conrad Russell, 'Arguments for Religious Unity in England, 1530–1650', *JEH*, 18 (1967), 201–6.

[210] *Scripta Anglicana*, 252. Wright's translation is inadequate. *Common Places of Bucer*, 267.

[211] *Liturgies*, 150, 323.

[212] Cox, II, 157.

[213] Bodleian Barlow MS 19, fols 187ᵛ–263ᵛ; Rodgers, *John à Lasco in England*, 74–6.

God while reinforcing human community in Christ. The laity should have their vernacular Bibles but they must use them appropriately. By allowing people to offer spiritual sacrifices, he successfully excised traditional views of priesthood and sacrifice, and encouraged the integration of the spiritual into daily life. Yes, Cranmer embraced the doctrine of royal priesthood, but we must be extremely careful with what we mean by such an assertion [see Plate 6].

8

The Reformation of the Queens

We have reviewed various presentations of the biblical doctrine of royal priesthood held during the English Reformation, beginning with John Wyclif and the late medieval period, progressing through the debates between traditionalists and evangelicals, and dwelling upon the innovative ideas utilized by Henry VIII, Thomas Cromwell, and especially Thomas Cranmer. But the struggle for reformation continued. Anne Hudson's 'Premature Reformation' in the fourteenth century[1] provided the *terminus a quo* for our study of the English Reformation in order to establish the background for the transformations of the early sixteenth century. As for an appropriate *terminus ad quem*, Nicholas Tyacke advocates a 'Long Reformation' ending with the eighteenth century.[2] But Dickens favored designating the important religious developments of the seventeenth century a 'second English Reformation' and those of the eighteenth 'a third'.[3] Most contemporary scholars present the English Reformation's finale with the reign of Elizabeth I.[4] Concurring with this consensus we conclude with a study of how the royal priesthood was conceived in the final Tudor decades.

In the beginning of this book, we noted that Reformation historiography often presents the doctrine of royal priesthood as a function of anticlericalism that fostered the growth of Protestant individualism. We also recognized the dominant historiography's disconnect from the sacred role of the monarchy. In a challenge to the dominant paradigm, we found that even when elements of anticlericalism and individualism appeared, the biblical doctrine of royal priesthood was typically construed with more subtlety. We also discovered that contemporaries were compelled to address the claims of priestly monarchs. In this final chapter, we will consider whether the various presentations of the subject doctrine in the later Reformation continue to reinforce these

[1] Hudson, *Premature Reformation*.
[2] 'Re-thinking the "English Reformation"', in *England's Long Reformation: 1500–1800*, ed. by Hudson (London: UCL Press, 1998), 1–32.
[3] Dickens, *The English Reformation*, 391–2.
[4] Diarmaid MacCulloch, *The Later Reformation in England, 1547–1603*, 2d edn (London: Macmillan, 2001), 5–6; Haigh, *English Reformations*; Heal, *Reformation in Britain and Ireland*.

earlier discoveries: the priesthood of the monarchy must receive an accounting, universal priesthood was not necessarily the key to anticlericalism, and individualism did not necessarily arise with the evangelical presentation of this doctrine. The doctrine of royal priesthood in its varied and often conflicting and conflicted applications to and by the monarchy, the clergy, and the people of the later Reformation is our final concern.

THE ROYAL PRIESTHOOD OF THE TUDOR QUEENS

When the doctrine that all Christians are priests and kings appeared in the mouths of contemporaries, it was typically qualified by appeals to vocation in order to dampen its egalitarian potential. But the doctrine still functioned within the ideologies of claimants arguing over the proper grant and exercise of authority. Dogmaticians within each tradition, whether they favored Roman primacy, English conformity, or further reformation, were compelled to address the nature and function of the monarchy. The 'place of theology amid the language of politics' has not always sat well with historians,[5] but theology, especially the doctrine of royal priesthood, was used to buttress political claims. As we have seen, developing a proper theology of the relative authorities of priests and kings presented difficulties to Christian theologians during the early English Reformation. As we shall see, developing a proper theology of royal priesthood presented even greater challenges to Christian theologians during the later English Reformation, for the kings were now queens. Although preparatory in the case of Katherine Parr, paradoxical in the case of Mary I, and equivocal in the case of Elizabeth I, the various formulations of a queen's royal priesthood merited attention.[6] We begin with England's first queen regnant.

Mary I

After Edward's death and Jane Grey's short reign, Cranmer's theological revolution stalled with Mary's accession. Mary wanted royal supremacy rejected and papal supremacy restored quickly but Parliament stood in her way. Even the Catholic laity balked at restoring papal supremacy without

---

[5] Charles W.A. Prior, 'Ecclesiology and Political Thought in England, 1580–*c*.1630', *HJ*, 48 (2005), 856.

[6] Although arguments for women's priesthood have been derived from Tudor history, the theological claims of the last Tudor queens themselves have not been adequately examined. John W. Houghton, 'No Bishop, No Queen: Queens Regnant and the Ordination of Women', *Anglican and Episcopal History*, 67 (1998), 2–25.

assurance that lay appropriators of ecclesiastical wealth might keep their spoils. In the end, eighteen months passed before the papal legate, Reginald Pole, was properly received and the nation's excommunication removed. The clergy finally agreed to forgo the return of ecclesiastical wealth for a restoration of orthodox doctrine, especially the restoration of priestly jurisdiction and the daily sacrifice of the mass. The Roman Catholic clergy considered the priesthood's *potestates iurisdictionis et ordinis* inseparable and would not accept the restoration of one without the other.[7]

Mary's groundbreaking role in the progress of female monarchy has only recently been appreciated,[8] but less has been made of the fact that, during her reign, a monarchical priesthood involving both sacerdotal powers— jurisdiction and order—continued in some sense. First, with regard to jurisdiction, Parliament was early on compelled to define Mary's rule as equivalent to that of England's previous male monarchs. This outlook was widely, though not universally, received, such that at Mary's death the officiating bishop dubbed her 'a queen and by the same title a king also', just as Elizabeth was 'now both king and queen'.[9] As one Catholic apologist later declared, the nation's jurisdictions reside 'as absolutelie in the Prince female, as in the male', bringing Constance Jordan to conclude, 'Politically, she is male.'[10] In a novel incongruity, the political nation was careful to symbolize Mary's queenship as regnant and Charles' kingship as that of a prince consort. In a further incongruity, in spite of her disdain for England's royal supremacy, Mary used her full regal authority to advance her conception of the church. She deprived seven bishops and provided eleven new ones in the interim on her own authority before Pole's legation.[11] While she deferred to Parliament to repeal egregious laws for the restoration of papal supremacy, she precipitously ignored laws that offended her conscience, encouraging her subjects to emulate her actions.[12] One of her first instructions, after the restoration, was that every bishop should deprive those clergy who had married. Ironically, she also enjoined the bishops

---

[7] Judith M. Richards, *Mary Tudor* (London: Routledge, 2008), 169–73; *Documents Illustrative of English Church History*, 396, 412.

[8] Richards, 'Mary as "Sole Quene"? Gendering Tudor Monarchy', *HJ*, 40 (1997), 895–924.

[9] Richards, *Mary Tudor*, 122, 156–7.

[10] John Leslie, *A Defence of the Honour of Marie Quene of Scotland* (London, 1569), sig. R7; Jordan, 'Woman's Rule in Sixteenth-Century British Political Thought', *RQ*, 40 (1987), 428, 443.

[11] David Loades argues, 'In fact Mary had not repudiated the supremacy, except in her own conscience.' Loades, *The Oxford Martyrs* (Bangor: Headstart History, 1992), 116–17, 124. However, Mary did communicate privately with Pole about these episcopal appointments. Loades, 'The Marian Episcopate', in *The Church of Mary Tudor*, ed. by Eamon Duffy and David Loades (Aldershot: Ashgate, 2006), 36. William Wizeman argues that early in her reign, Mary showed 'overt involvement in the religious affairs of her kingdom', but later her influence 'became more discreet or was largely exercised through personal patronage and example.' Wizeman, 'The Religious Policy of Mary I', in *Mary Tudor: Old and New Perspectives*, ed. by Susan Doran and Thomas S. Freeman (Basingstoke: Palgrave Macmillan, 2011), 153–4.

[12] Loades, 'The Personal Religion of Mary I', in *The Church of Mary Tudor*, 19.

to cease using the Henrician legal phrase, *Regia auctoritate fulcitus*, supported by royal authority, in their ecclesiastical documents.[13] In early 1554, she personally ordered obedience to Cardinal Pole.[14] Later, when Pole was recalled by the papacy to answer charges of heresy,[15] she refused the papal nuncio's letters of revocation, retorting she would refer the charges to her own ecclesiastical courts 'in observance of the laws and privileges of her realm'.[16]

Second, with regard to the power of orders, Mary's priests never directly accorded her sacramental authority, but they elevated her religiously through comparisons with the Virgin. Robert Wingfield referred to Mary as *diva*, sacred, who obviously deserved semi-divine adoration.[17] Wingfield praised her 'pure and fertile womb'; Richard Smith believed she would conceive through divine intervention; and Doctor Chedzey placed the announcement of her pregnancy in the context of the Annunciation.[18] Wizeman concluded, 'one Mary possessed an essential role in salvation, so the other possessed an essential role in England's participation in salvation. Both Marys were intercessors, acting on behalf of others' redemption.'[19] The second Mary, during the interim, took it upon herself to declare those priests ordained under Cranmer's *Ordinal* 'were not ordered in very deed', commanding the bishops to 'supply that thing which wanted in them before' in reference to the episcopal conferral of sacrificial power. Edmund Bonner followed this declaration in his subsequent injunctions for the diocese of London, and Pole did likewise in his legatine constitutions. Mary's bishops thus paradoxically affirmed her doctrinal conclusion that 'the power of offering sacrifice' must be restored to ordinands.[20] Finally, it must be noted that Mary's use of the healing touch evoked a 'quasi-priestly' apologetic first put forward by the French [see Plate 7A].[21] In these ways, in spite of her own claims, Mary could and did function as a royal priest, touching upon both *iurisdictionis* and *ordinis*.

---

[13] *VAI*, II, xlvii, 2 and 7.   [14] *TRP*, no. 417.

[15] Richards, *Mary Tudor*, 216–18; Dermot Fenlon, *Heresy and Obedience in Tridentine Italy* (CUP, 1972).

[16] Loades, 'Relations between the Anglican and Roman Catholic Churches in the 16th and 17th Centuries', in *Rome and the Anglicans*, ed. by Wolfgang Haase (Berlin: Walter de Gruyter, 1982), 20.

[17] 'The *Vita Mariae Angliae Reginae* of Robert Wingfield of Brantham', transl. by MacCulloch, in *Camden Miscellany*, 4th series, 29 (London: Royal Historical Society, 1984), 196, 213, 216.

[18] *Camden Miscellany*, 293; King, *Tudor Royal Iconography*, 216–18.

[19] William Wizeman, *The Theology and Spirituality of Mary Tudor's Church* (Aldershot: Ashgate, 2006), 232.

[20] *VAI*, II, xlvii, 12; II, xlviii, 29; *The Anglican Canons, 1529–1947*, ed. by Gerald Bray (Woodbridge: Boydell, 1998), 88–91, 112–15, 150–3.

[21] 'When the French justified their Salic law, they had argued that monarchy was a quasi-priestly function, as demonstrated by the power to cure certain conditions. Being therefore a quasi-priestly office, they concluded, it was obviously one that no woman could occupy. Mary, however, exercised that healing power throughout her reign'. Richards, *Mary Tudor*, 138 and plate 10.

Mary and her clergy thus equivocated in the retention of some aspects of the royal priestly powers claimed for and by her predecessors. But Mary's rule was novel in an important way: she was the first queen regnant recognized as such in England. Although women previously sought to exercise authority in medieval England, their efforts were handicapped by the universal belief that divine sanction forbade such.[22] The turmoil of the Wars of the Roses was furthered by arguments about the propriety of the throne being transmitted through a woman, although Henry VII's own claim was derived through his mother, Margaret Beaufort.[23] The latter part of her grandson's reign was defined by the effort to assure a male heir, providing a major impetus for the break with Rome. Yet the search for dynastic stability was undermined by the Tudor inability to conceive enough males. England was forced (see 'Lawyers', pp. 50–4) to consider other options. Even then, 'queenly reigns' were still considered 'extended moments of suspension in the normal working of political, social, cultural, and gender history.'[24] It was simply inconceivable that a woman could really be a king, much less a priest.

However, a number of social factors came together to induce a slow change in gender expectations, such that women's roles began to encroach subtly upon the traditional preserves of the intercessory offices of both kings and priests. These encroachments were propelled by a growth in literacy and legal rights among early modern women as well as the shock of adjusting to the novelty of queens regnant. Literacy among women was rare, yet advancing, during the early modern period.[25] But early in the sixteenth century, both Margaret Beaufort and Catherine of Aragon modeled a passion for learning. Beaufort was a patron of education and printed books, and is credited with translating two devotional works into English.[26] Catherine, who was praised by Erasmus as 'astonishingly well read, far beyond what would be surprising in a woman',[27] ensured Mary's education in the humanities. She sponsored Luis Vives, who 'broke molds by urging that girls be educated in more than just

---

[22] Helen Castor, *She-Wolves: The Women Who Ruled England Before Elizabeth* (New York: HarperCollins, 2011), 25–33.

[23] Pearl Hogrefe, *Women of Action in Tudor England: Nine Biographical Sketches* (Ames, IA: Iowa State University Press, 1977), 136–54.

[24] Robert Bucholz and Carole Levin, 'It's Good to Be Queen', in *Queens & Power in Medieval and Early Modern England*, ed. by Robert Bucholz and Carole Levin (London: University of Nebraska Press, 2009), xiv.

[25] Only five per cent of women (slightly more in London) were able to sign their own names on ecclesiastical documents. David Cressy, 'Literacy in Pre-industrial England', *Societas*, 4 (1974), 229–40. However, the ability to read was more widespread than the ability to write. Women, moreover, were often taught to read but not write. Margaret Spufford, *Small Books and Pleasant Histories: Popular Fiction and its Readership in Seventeenth-Century England* (CUP, 1981), 32–5.

[26] Hogrefe, *Women of Action*, 145–9; Elizabeth Norton, *Margaret Beaufort: Mother of the Tudor Dynasty* (Stroud: Amberly, 2011), 184–205.

[27] Erasmus to Paolo Bombace, 26 July 1518; James P. Carley, *The Books of King Henry VIII and his Wives* (London: British Library, 2004), 111.

domestic skills and dancing.'[28] In a dedicatory letter to Vives' book, Richard Hyrde queried, 'what is more frutefull than the good education and ordre of women, the one halfe of all mankind'?[29] One may assume women composed more than half the laity.

Yet Vives carefully limited what women could do with their education and exalted the feminine virtue of quiescence. 'I gyve no license to a woman to be a teacher nor to have authoritie of the man but to be in silence.' Women could use their learning only to teach young children and other women.[30] Evangelicals agreed completely. Hugh Latimer preached to his 'sisters': 'Thou shalt be subject. Women are subjects; ye be subjects to your husbands.' At first women were equal with men, but after the fall, 'it is a part of your penance to be subjects unto your husbands: ye are underlings, underlings, and must be obedient.' Women should wear a sign of the power over their heads, 'for she is not immediately under God, but mediately.'[31] Across the religious spectrum, feminine subservience ostensibly disqualified women from serving as mediators, with either royal or spiritual authority.

Katherine Parr

Despite this profound handicap, women were nonetheless thrust into the role of mediation through both literacy and office. As Margaret Hannay reports, 'Paradoxically, women were permitted to break the rule of silence only to demonstrate their religious devotion by using their wealth to encourage religious education and publication by men, by translating the religious works of other (usually male) writers, and, more rarely, by writing their own devotional meditations.'[32] Upper class women, both traditionalists and evangelicals, were the first to gain literacy and break the mediatoral ceiling. After Margaret Beaufort, female translators became more frequent, for example, with More's daughter, Margaret Roper.[33] In the private 'Protestant salon' of Katherine Parr, Henry's last queen, exercises in translation were common as both young men and women of nobility (including the future Edward VI, Mary I, and Elizabeth I) received instruction from some of the leading

[28] Giles Tremlett, *Catherine of Aragon: The Spanish Queen of Henry VIII* (New York: Walker, 2010), 210. However, such humanist proclamations could 'easily become yet another means of restricting [women's] behavior and intellectual growth.' Valerie Wayne, 'Some Sad Sentence: Vives' *Instruction of a Christian Woman*', in *Silent But for the Word*, 19.

[29] Vives, *The Instruction of a Christian Woman* (London, 1529), sig. A2ᵛ, cited in *Silent But for the Word*, 17.

[30] *The Instruction of a Christian Woman*, sig. E2ᵛ.

[31] Latimer, *Sermons*, 252–3.

[32] Margaret P. Hannay, 'Introduction', in *Silent But for the Word*, 4.

[33] Rita M. Verbrugge, 'Margaret More Roper's Personal Expression in the *Devout Treatise Upon the Pater Noster*', in *Silent But for the Word*, 30–42.

humanist tutors of the sixteenth century, many of whom were evangelical.[34] Parr sponsored the English translation of Erasmus' *Paraphrases*, a commentary on the New Testament that included a contribution by Mary on the Gospel of John.[35] Parr also engaged in the mediation of prayer, at first by composing a public prayer for Cranmer's use during the king's final hostilities against the French,[36] and later by publishing two devotional books.

Parr's first publication was her 1544 translation of John Fisher's *Psalmi Seu Precationes*.[37] In her 1545 *Prayers or Meditacions*, the first book of prayers authored by an English woman, she verified her Christian humanism while ignoring the traditional priesthood. At the time, she instituted daily sermons as queen, including the unique use of vernacular worship. But this confident feminine voice courted disaster after Gardiner confronted Henry with evidence of her forward religious attitude. Parr quickly and successfully submitted herself to her husband's headship, embarrassing court conservatives and cementing the evangelical hold over the education of Edward and Elizabeth.[38] After Henry's death, in her 1547 *The Lamentacion of a Sinner*, Parr displayed her evangelical convictions publicly, affirming that personal access to God in Christ is only through the Word and the Spirit as one is justified by faith alone.[39] Nicholas Udall praised Parr for her efforts in helping 'to sowe abrode the woord of God',[40] and in his preface to her *Lamentacion*, William Cecil lauded her as 'a guyde' to the reader to repent, thereby conceding her mediatoral role.[41] As Susan James notes, 'The evangelical need to bear witness forced the private conscience to assume a public voice. It also gave women something to say.'[42]

Elizabeth Tudor, deprived of her birth mother's presence, consistently referred to herself as Parr's 'daughter' during the latter's lifetime.[43] In a letter to her father, prefacing her translation of Parr's *Prayers or Meditacions* into three languages, Elizabeth simultaneously exalted Henry's divine kingship and lauded

---

[34] John N. King, 'Patronage and Piety: The Influence of Catherine Parr', in *Silent But for the Word*, 47. Cf. McConica, *English Humanists and Reformation Politics*, ch. 7.

[35] This book has been labelled 'the most influential single contribution of Renaissance Christianity to the English reformation.' William P. Haugaard, 'Katherine Parr: The Religious Convictions of a Renaissance Queen', *RQ*, 22 (1969), 349. On Mary's translation, see Aysha Pollnitz, 'Religion and Translation at the Court of Henry VIII: Princess Mary, Katherine Parr and the *Paraphrases* of Erasmus', in *Mary Tudor: Old and New Perspectives*, 123–37.

[36] Brandon G. Withrow, *Katherine Parr* (Phillipsburg, NJ: P&R Publishing, 2009), 35–7.

[37] Susan James, *Catherine Parr: Henry VIII's Last Love* (Stroud: Tempus, 2008), 167–8.

[38] Haugaard, 'Katherine Parr', 352–3. Even Latimer lauded Parr for her leadership in family worship, ordaining that which her last husband overlooked. Latimer, *Sermons*, 228.

[39] Parr, *The Lamentacion of a Sinner* (London, 1547), sig. B2^r–B4.

[40] Udall, Preface to Acts, in Erasmus, *The First Tome or Volume of the Paraphrase of Erasmus* (London: Fletestreet, 1548).

[41] But he restricted the assumed readership to 'ladies of estate'. Cecil, 'The Preface', in Parr, *Lamentacion*.

[42] James, *Catherine Parr*, 191.   [43] *ECW*, Letters 1, 2, 4, 8, 10.

Parr's spiritual mediation, affirming personal deification through the queen's words: *Nam nihil acceptius esse debet regi, quem philosophi deum in terris esse sentiunt, quaum illud opus animi, quod nos in coelum tollit, et in terra coelestes, atque in caren diuinos facit.*[44] She likewise avowed Parr's evangelical under-standing of the mediative work of the Word: *Ainsy que nous voyons que dieu par sa parolle, et éscriture peut estre veu, ouy, et congneu quel il est ... lequel autrement ne peut estre congneu, ny veu.*[45] These early lessons helped Elizabeth develop her evangelical religious self-understanding as a godly monarch.

Elizabeth I

Elizabeth's self-understanding dwells upon her placement between God and the people. Early on, she expounded her intimate relation with God in an unusual manner: 'Thou dost handle my soul (if so I durst say) as a mother, daughter, sister, and wife.'[46] Her intimacy with God was, however, not con-fined to the domestic sphere, as multifaceted as it obviously was for her, because in becoming a monarch she became a public mediator leading a defined hierarchy. She prayed for herself as the divinely constituted 'head and governess' of England.[47] She instructed Parliament never to confuse who occupied 'first', 'second', and 'third', and warned, in a poignant rebuttal of previous arguments, 'it is monstrous that the feet should direct the head.'[48] The 'prince' is 'head of all the body' and 'may command the feet' even as she preserved the 'lawful liberties' of her subjects.[49] Like her father and brother, she drew upon biblical allusions to justify her place, often emphasizing female mediators: 'I, like another Deborah, like another Judith, like another Esther'.[50] Her bishops mimicked such claims in their sermons.[51] Her portraits also stress her locus between heaven and earth, most spectacularly in the dramatic

---

[44] *ECAF*, Letter 3. 'For nothing ought to be more acceptable to a king, whom philosophers regard as a god on earth, than this labor of the soul, which raises us up to heaven and on earth makes us heavenly and divine in the flesh'. *ECW*, Letter 3.

[45] *ECAF*, Letter 4. 'Thus also we see that God by His Word and Scripture can be seen, heard, and known for who He is ... who otherwise cannot be known or seen.' *ECW*, Letter 4. Intended to accompany her translation of the first part of Calvin's *Institutes*.

[46] Marc Shell, *Elizabeth's Glass* (London: University of Nebraska Press, 1993), 117. Cf. *ECW*, Letter 2; *ECAF*, Letter 2.

[47] *ECW*, Prayer 21.

[48] *ECW*, Speech 9, Version 2.

[49] *ECW*, Speech 10, Version 1.

[50] *ECW*, Prayer 22.

[51] Edward O. Smith, Jr., 'The Elizabethan Doctrine of the Prince Reflected in the Sermons of the Episcopacy, 1559–1603', *Huntington Library Quarterly*, 28 (1964), 1–17; Dale Hoak, 'A Tudor Deborah? The Coronation of Elizabeth I, Parliament, and the Problem of Female Rule', in *John Foxe and His World*, ed. by Christopher Highley and John N. King (Aldershot: Ashgate, 2002), 73–88.

Ditchley Portrait, where her dress spans the nation and, like a 'prince of light' and 'sonne' of God, she is the instrument of either sunny grace or thunderous judgment [see Plate 7B].[52] The Rainbow Portrait similarly paints Elizabeth as personally related to the ruling Christ, who brings peace to England through her pious embrace of his divine covenant.[53]

To broadcast her mediation, Elizabeth continued Parr's practice of publishing popular works. Her personal intercessions and poetry, alongside translations of classical philosophers and theologians,[54] became part of this 'learned' queen's strategy 'to do what was almost unthinkable in this period: present an unmarried woman as a capable leader, not only of a strong nation but also of global Protestantism.'[55] Elizabeth's speeches in response to Parliament, national crises, and special occasions also functioned as a public means for Elizabeth to lead the people to embrace God's will for them, a will manifested through her religio-political leadership. She argued before the nation's other leaders that her political qualifications were rooted in her religious training: 'It is said I am no divine. Indeed, I studied nothing else but divinity till I came to the crown, and then I gave myself to the study of that which was meet for government.'[56] In other words, Elizabeth's authorization for rule was explicitly and consciously theological in foundation.

Elizabeth's theological system requires further elaboration, but for our purposes it is noticeable that she utilized ministerial notions to bolster her monarchy. In a speech to an early Parliament, recognizing her gender might weaken her ability to govern, she found strength in the fact that God 'constituted' her to this 'princely seat and kingly throne'. Alluding to the eschatological royal priesthood of Revelation 20, she anticipated the day when her difficult earthly reign would be exchanged for a 'better' heavenly reign.[57] In a prayer of communal Trinitarian participation, she painted a verbal picture of her royal supremacy akin to that etched in the Great Bible of her father. She asked for the Holy Spirit to grant her both 'faithful councillors' (lay magistrates) and 'good shepherds' (bishops and priests) to help her govern and the people obey: 'That I myself may rule over each one of them by Thy Word in

---

[52] Portrait by Marcus Gheeraerts the Younger, National Portrait Gallery, London. Kevin Sharpe, *Selling the Tudor Monarchy: Authority and Image in Sixteenth-Century England* (YUP, 2009), 382–4.

[53] Portrait by Marcus Gheeraerts the Younger, Hatfield House, Hertfordshire. René Graziani, 'The "Rainbow Portrait" of Queen Elizabeth I and Its Religious Symbolism', *Journal of the Warburg and Courtauld Institutes*, 35 (1972), 247–59.

[54] *Queen Elizabeth's Englishings*, ed. by Caroline Pemberton, EETS 113 (London: Paul, Trench, Trübner, 1899); *Elizabeth I: Translations, 1544–1589*, ed. by Janel Mueller and Joshua Scodel (London: University of Chicago Press, 2009); *Elizabeth I: Translations, 1592–1598*, ed. by Janel Mueller and Joshua Scodel (London: University of Chicago Press, 2009).

[55] Linda Shenk, *Learned Queen: The Image of Elizabeth I in Politics and Poetry* (New York: Palgrave Macmillan, 2010), 4.

[56] *ECW*, Speech 9, Version 2.   [57] *ECW*, Speech 5.

care and diligence, infuse the Spirit of Thy love, by which both they to me may be joined together very straightly, and among themselves also, as members of one body.'[58] Elizabeth's reference to God's Word is intentional.

In a second Trinitarian prayer, she identifies the Word of God as the means for ruling the commonwealth. His Word moves inwardly to transform the soul for proper action.[59] She classified herself with the evangelical pastors who preach the Word. Although a mere 'handmaid', England was nevertheless 'my flock',[60] and she was 'mother and nurse' to God's 'children'.[61] Her 'ministry' was to restore Christ's rule over 'this flock of ours'.[62] She prayed that God would help her present to Him 'a perfect reformed Church',[63] a church that came into existence as she, His sacred 'instrument', 'set forth the glorious Gospell of thy deare Sonne Christ Ihesus.'[64] She reminded the University of Oxford that her care for the kingdom is comprised not only of a *curam corporum* but also a *curam animarum*.[65] While Elizabeth rejected the sacrifice of the mass,[66] she could also present herself poetically as 'Amongst Thy priests, offering to Thee, Zeal for incense, reaching the skies; Myself and scepter, sacrifice.'[67] Elizabeth conceived of herself as a priest according to a broadly evangelical definition, a publicly authoritative preaching minister, who disdained 'private men's expositions' of the Word of God and was more than willing to reprimand and even pull the licenses of unruly priests.[68]

Elizabeth's self-conception as an evangelical royal priest did not go unchallenged. While Elizabeth's exact preference for the 1559 settlement of religion has been subject to debate, laypeople were doubtless the driving force behind it.[69] (Once enacted, she remained unfailingly committed to the settlement, making

---

[58] *ECW* and *ECAF*, Prayer 6.   [59] *ECW* and *ECAF*, Prayer 33.
[60] *ECW* and *ECAF*, Prayer 19.   [61] *ECW* and *ECAF*, Prayer 31.
[62] *ECW* and *ECAF*, Prayer 24.   [63] *ECW*, Prayer 29.
[64] *ECAF*, Prayer 30.   [65] *ECW* and *ECAF*, Speech 20.
[66] *ECW* and *ECAF*, Prayer 24.

[67] *ECW*, Poem 14. John Jewel similarly painted Elizabeth in sacerdotal colors, granting her more of a priestly ministry than that of the Roman clergy. 'They talk much of an unbloody sacrifice. It is not theirs to offer it. Queen Elizabeth shall offer it upon unto God; even her unbloody hands, an unbloody sword, an unbloody people, and an unbloody government. This is an unbloody sacrifice. This sacrifice is acceptable to God.' Jewel, *Seditious Bull*, in *The Works of John Jewel*, ed. by John Ayre, 4 vols (PS, 1845–1850), IV, 1155; Gary W. Jenkins, *John Jewel and the English National Church: The Dilemmas of an Erastian Reformer* (Aldershot: Ashgate, 2006), 107.

[68] *ECW*, Speech 16. Margaret Christian, 'Elizabeth's Preachers and the Government of Women: Defining and Correcting a Queen', *SCJ*, 24 (1993), 562–5.

[69] J.E. Neale believed Elizabeth preferred the more traditional 1549 prayer book, but was forced into a more Protestant settlement by radicals in the House of Commons. *Elizabeth I and Her Parliaments 1559–1581* (London: Cape, 1953), 33–84. Norman Jones has shown that Elizabeth probably preferred the more Protestant 1552 prayer book but was forced into a more traditional settlement by conservatives in the House of Lords. *Faith by Statute* (London: Royal Historical Society, 1982). Both agree the settlement was formulated by three laypersons— Elizabeth, William Cecil, and Nicholas Bacon—and enacted by a lay-dominated Parliament.

it her own and the nation's standard.[70]) During these early parliamentary struggles over the acts of supremacy and uniformity, the conservative clergy in Convocation and the bishops in the House of Lords strongly objected to the proposed settlement, specifically because it gave divine authority to a woman. Cuthbert Scot, Bishop of Chester, believed a disastrous chain of events was being set loose: the laity were defining away the sacrifice of the mass; and without the mass's continual external sacrifice, there is no priesthood; and without a priesthood, there is no New Testament religion; and, 'if we have no religion, then be we *Sine Deo in hoc mundo*'.[71] Nicholas Heath, Archbishop of York and Lord Chancellor, argued against a female supremacy for four principal reasons: a woman cannot wield the keys of binding and loosing; she cannot feed the flock with the Word; she cannot preach or administer the sacraments; and she 'is not called to be an Apostle, nor Evangelist, nor to be a Pastor (as much as to say, a Shepherd), nor a Doctor, or a Preacher; therefore she canot be Supream Head of Christ's Militant Church; nor yet of any Part thereof'.[72] John Feckenham, Abbot of Westminster, appealed to a variation of universal priesthood, the consensus and unity of the Christian people. As far as he was concerned, the consensus of the faithful throughout history allowed neither the heretical liturgy nor any royal supremacy.[73] The bishops subsequently resigned *en masse* in protest.

Particularly galling to Catholics was the oath required by the 1559 Act of Supremacy. It granted Elizabeth ultimate jurisdiction in both spiritual and ecclesiastical causes, although it transformed her title to 'Supreme Governor' from 'Supreme Head'.[74] William Allen believed the oath made a monarch into a priest: 'This can have no excuse, neither true or likely sense in the world, making indeed a king and priest all one: no difference betwixt the state of the church and a temporal commonwealth.' Allen said Catholics were right to reject this oath, for the idea of a woman heading the church and defining doctrine is 'monstrous'.[75] Similarly, Edward Rishton, writing on behalf of Nicolas Sander, assumed the oath granted the queen 'priestly power, even that of administering sacraments'.[76]

From the other extreme, advanced Protestants also raised the issue of female priesthood in their arguments with the Elizabethan bishops. After correlating the surplice with the priesthood of Antichrist, a Mr Axton told

[70] MacCulloch, *Later Reformation in England*, 28–9, 44.

[71] That is, without God in this world. 'Speech of Bishop Scot', in Henry Gee, *The Elizabethan Prayer-Book & Ornaments* (London: Macmillan, 1902), 236–52.

[72] 'A Speech made in the Upper House of Parliament', in *Third Collection of Scarce and Valuable Tracts*, 10–16.

[73] '*Populi Christiani consensus et unitas*'. 'Speech of Abbot Feckenham', in Gee, *Elizabethan Prayer-Book*, 235.

[74] *Documents*, 323.

[75] *A True, Sincere and Modest Defence of English Catholics*, 6–10, in Claire Cross, *The Royal Supremacy in the Elizabethan Church* (London: Allen & Unwin, 1969), doc. 17.

[76] Rishton completed Sander's history. Nicolas Sander, *The Rise and Growth of the Anglican Schism*, transl. by David Lewis (Rockford, Illinois: Tan Books, 1988), 237–40, 244–6.

Thomas Bentham, Bishop of Lichfield and Coventry, that each congregation should have the right to elect its pastor. Quoting Scripture and the fathers, Axton also questioned the queen's position in the church, specifically her ability to preach and administer sacraments. Bentham excoriated Axton for his 'arrogant spirit'.[77] When Edmund Grindal, then Bishop of London, debated members of an illegal conventicle in 1567, the issue was raised as to whether the monarch may teach the Word of God. Grindal snapped at the questioner, wanting to know if he really believed kings should teach. He then severely limited the king's involvement with the Word to obedience. The 'king'—contemporaries continued to employ the masculine in abstract discussions of female monarchy—may only legislate concerning 'things indifferent'.[78] It was over this same issue, the monarch's involvement with the Word, specifically whether Elizabeth could restrict the preaching of the Word in those disputed exercises called 'prophesyings', that Grindal learned a queen could and would suspend even an archbishop of Canterbury. Contrary to his expectations, Grindal proved a lesser force than Ambrose, and Elizabeth, a royal priest, proved a worthier opponent than Theodosius.[79]

THE RIVAL PRIESTHOODS OF THE CLERGY

'Anticlericalism', as we have seen, is more complex than the term, at least as it is traditionally understood, suggests, and the situation intensifies with the late Tudors. Among the clergy, clericalism and anticlericalism—one is ever the function of the other—manifested themselves in intense rivalry between opposing parties [see Plate 8]. Conformists in the Elizabethan Church of England faced opposition from Rome and from more advanced Protestants. Roman Catholics challenged the validity of ordinations performed with Cranmer's *Ordinal*, but also pushed against each other: Jesuits versus secular priests.[80] Catholics denied any ordination not performed by orthodox bishops and for the purpose of sacrificing the mass. Elizabethan conformists tended to allow non-episcopal ordinations by continental Protestants,[81] but objected when puritans deliberately went to the continent to avoid episcopal consecration, as in the case

---

[77] Axton was likely arguing that Elizabeth's right to appoint clergy gave her power over Word and sacraments, as he earlier objected to nobles filling offices. *Seconde Parte of a Register*, 68–74.

[78] *The Remains of Edmund Grindal*, ed. by William Nicholson (PS, 1843), 206–7.

[79] Patrick Collinson, *Archbishop Grindal 1519–1583* (London: Cape, 1979), 233–52; *Remains of Grindal*, 376–90.

[80] MacCulloch, *Later Reformation in England*, 121–2; Haigh, 'Revisionism, the Reformation and the History of English Catholicism', *JEH*, 36 (1985), 398–405.

[81] Sykes, *Old Priest and New Presbyter*, 87–100.

of Walter Travers.[82] The hottest Protestants challenged the conformists for being too close to popery. Thomas Cartwright demanded ordination by presbyters alone following election by the congregation.[83] Sadly, the monarchs' efforts to establish their own diverging religions seem only to have reinforced this clerical rivalry. Mary saw to it that unrepentant evangelical bishops, like Cranmer, were defrocked and burnt, as she willingly submitted her nation to Cardinal Pole, who contended obedience to the pope was her only hope.[84] Elizabeth could likewise be accused of clericalism, by advanced Protestants and recusant Catholics, who disliked her bishops, and of anticlericalism, by the very fact she kept those same bishops poor.[85] Ironically, the use of the state to enforce conformity often seems merely to have hardened the views of the survivors.[86]

At stake in the midst of these controversies was not the existence of a distinction between clergy and laity but the nature and form of the clergy. Peter Lake describes the debates between puritan Cartwright and leading conformist John Whitgift as the manifestation of a wider competition between 'two rival clerical interest groups', 'Anglicans and Puritans'.[87] Elizabethan Anglicans generally wanted to retain episcopal jurisdiction and royal supremacy, with the monarch deciding ceremonial matters of an 'indifferent' nature. Many puritans wanted to localize power in the parish, characterized by an alliance between upper laity and priest, and believed godly consciences should decide 'indifferent' matters. Both puritans and conformists agreed the ministry should be redefined in the direction of preaching the Word and away from sacrificing the mass. However, Catholics also believed in preaching as long as it followed the restoration of the mass and papal discipline. We here summarize the teachings about the clergy within these three rival groups: Counter-Reformation 'Catholics',[88] Elizabethan 'Conformists',[89] and Elizabethan 'Puritans'.[90]

---

[82] Dawley, *Whitgift*, 176–9.

[83] A.F. Scott Pearson, *Thomas Cartwright and Elizabethan Puritanism 1535–1603* (CUP, 1925), 28–9.

[84] Thomas F. Mayer, *Reginald Pole: Prince & Prophet* (CUP, 2000), 211.

[85] Andrew Foster, 'The Clerical Estate Revitalized', in *The Early Stuart Church, 1603–1642*, ed. by Kenneth Fincham (London: Macmillan, 1993), 139–60.

[86] Harrison Crumrine, 'The Oxford Martyrs and the English Protestant Movement, 1553–58', *Historian*, 70 (2008), 75–90.

[87] *Anglicans and Puritans?* (London: Unwin Hyman, 1988), 26.

[88] Many conformist and puritan theologians also wanted 'Catholic' unity, but without submission to Rome. Franklin Le Van Baumer, 'The Church of England and the Common Corps of Christendom', *Journal of Modern History*, 16 (1944), 21.

[89] 'Conformist' indicates those in the early modern period willing to comply with the established church and liturgy. Maltby, *Prayer Book and People in Elizabethan and Early Stuart England* (CUP, 1998), 5–19.

[90] Concerning the use of 'Anglican' and 'Puritan' and the need to distinguish these terms from later associations, see Patrick Collinson, *The Elizabethan Puritan Movement* (OUP, 1967), 13.

Counter-Reformation Catholicism

Duffy and Wizeman argue that Marian Catholics invented the Counter-Reformation outlook that characterizes late Tudor Catholicism.[91] The leading figure in England's Catholic 'reformation'[92] was Reginald Cardinal Pole. Pole's doctrine of royal priesthood was first outlined in his *Defense of the Unity of the Church*, written after the executions of More and Fisher as a definitive call for Henry to repent. Pole explains the different origins, natures, and roles of kingship and priesthood in order to undermine the royal supremacy and recover papal primacy. Pole's understanding of the scope of the church is key to subsequent discussions. The church is not to be confused with any kingdom; rather, the universal church is the 'body', England is one 'member', and the pope is the 'head'.[93] He believes God created human beings for community and the best means of governing such a community is monarchy tempered with aristocracy. Henry has broken the unity of the church by subverting its divine structure.

Pole's primary question is, 'Is the church governed by kings or priests?'[94] To begin, he warns Henry that his theologians' arguments raise the specter of an egalitarian royal priesthood. The same Peter who commanded, 'Honor the king', also commanded, 'Honor all men' (I Peter 2.17): 'we can conclude from your argument that all men are Vicars of Christ, that all men hold the office of supreme head of the Church.'[95] Against such hideous chaos, Pole makes an aesthetic case for papal primacy: the church's 'most beautiful order' is hierarchical, where 'all things lead up to the government and control of one man . . . who acts in the place of Christ'. This one man is Peter, the rock upon which the church is built (Matthew 16), and although all Christians are also rocks (I Peter 2.5), 'all do not hold equal positions of excellence in this edifice'. Later, he again warns Henry's theologians that neither all Christians nor the king but the pope alone possesses a cure of souls, which he shares only with the priesthood.[96]

Pole argued that priesthood and kingship are separated and ranked due to Scripture, reason, and tradition. Christ 'appointed priests over all the rulers of this world' and rulers like Constantine 'recognized that bishops held a supreme position in the Church'. First, kings originated in the choice of the people, who granted the king power to judge and wage war. Man is communal by nature and communities disintegrate without one leader, so the king 'exists on behalf of the people, not the people on behalf of the king.' He should take

---

[91] For the historiography of late Tudor Catholicism, see Duffy, *Fires of Faith: Catholic England under Mary Tudor* (YUP, 2009), 188–90. Wizeman, 'Religious Policy', 153–70.

[92] *VAI*, II, xlvii, preface.

[93] *Unity*, 208; Mayer, *Reginald Pole*, 223.

[94] *Unity*, 14, 29.   [95] *Unity*, 33. Cf. 235.   [96] *Unity*, 92–3, 98–118, 141–2.

counsel with priests in order to avoid becoming a tyrant, because kings rely upon fallible human prudence and civil laws in order to rule, while priests rely on divine wisdom and laws. Second, priests originated with the mysterious Melchisedek, or God, and are sent to lead in divine worship. The priest holds such an exalted place that Pole vacillates between calling them 'ambassadors of the people to God, ambassadors of God to the people, or even gods.' 'In every way he is greater than the king': the priest anoints the king; he is a father to the king; he represents the Supreme King of all; he prescribes the king's duties; and the king never instructs him. In summary, 'the function of the emperor is to be a servant to the priestly function'.[97] Pole then describes the punishment that came on biblical kings who would be priests. The priest's power of jurisdiction may not be transferred. The holy fathers would never grant 'the King to be head of the Church', for that would entail granting him the power of 'binding and loosing the sins of men' and 'administering the sacraments'. They could not imagine something so 'abhorrent to the divine will.' Pole appeals at length for Henry to repent or face judgment. In the end, if Henry will emulate Joshua, who put priests foremost, God will exalt him.[98]

While promoting papal primacy, Pole was not a 'high papalist', limiting it in two ways. First, the pope's office must be carried out in the midst of the bishops, for all bishops share equally in the succession, as papal inerrancy 'inhered in the college of cardinals, not the pope.'[99] The church's nobility of cardinals and bishops reforms the papacy as needed, just as England's nobility curbs royal power. The nobility are thus essential for the reformation of church and realm.[100] Second, Pole's papal primacy, as Benedict XVI commented, is manifested in the imitation of Christ. *Sedes crucem*: the 'chair' of the vicar of Christ is the 'cross' of Christ.[101] This communal–mystical view of the papacy, however, failed the cardinal more than once. Pole informed the Tridentine fathers that conscience must be followed until a conciliar majority rules and the pope confirms; afterwards, obedience is the only option. But after Trent's withering decree on justification was promulgated, Pole's conscience was greatly distressed.[102] Likewise, Pole's unsuccessful appeal for Paul IV to cancel his inquisitorial recall demonstrated the limit of the church's nobility to restrain an abusive pontiff.[103]

Although not a high papalist, Pole was definitely a high clericalist. Pole's elitism did not blind him to the problems of the priesthood; it compelled him to reform the clergy. During the second session at Trent, he blasted shepherds

---

[97] *Unity*, 49–63.   [98] *Unity*, 91, 209, 335–6.
[99] Mayer, *Reginald Pole*, 16, 145, 179, 319.   [100] *Reginald Pole*, 45, 98, 221.
[101] Joseph Ratzinger, *Church, Ecumenism, and Politics: New Endeavours in Ecclesiology*, transl. by Michael J. Miller et al (San Francisco: Ignatius, 1987), 36–50.
[102] Mayer, *Reginald Pole*, 150–3.   [103] Fenlon, *Heresy and Obedience*, 276–8.

'who differ from lay-folk only in dress', clothing themselves with sin.[104] At the London Synod of 1556, Pole argued the *reformatio* of the church must begin with the deformities of the clergy. The bishops should rectify their non-residency and preach the gospel to the flocks they should love.[105] The synod's first decree ordained sermons every St Andrew's day to celebrate the return of the mass with the restoration of papal primacy. The second decree reinstituted canon law and the seven sacraments while banning heretical books. The 'person of the minister' is one of three essentials in the sacraments; there can be no sacrament without a priest. In the all-important sacrament of the mass, the priest occupies the central place, 'For it is the priest, speaking in the person of Christ, who solemnizes this rite' to bring about the Christian's union with Christ through the sacrifice. The decree elaborates that the *animarum cura* is committed to clergy alone. The fourth decree requires preaching for all those with cure of souls and forbids common proclamation. Official homilies and catechisms 'composed by pious and learned men under the direction of the synod' are also promised. The fifth decree requires vestments as a means of distinguishing clergy from laity. The eleventh decree establishes and provides the outline for the structure of cathedral seminaries, a Counter-Reformation innovation for which Pole deserves credit.[106] At the close of the synod, Pole reminded the clergy they were his 'undershepherds' whom he would hold accountable. Priests must teach the people, but their discipline of the laity is prerequisite to such.[107]

The sermons of Thomas Watson, Bishop of Winchester, reinforce Pole's high clericalism. Christ becomes present through the priests, who are ordained to be ministers of the Word. When the Word is proclaimed by true priests, 'the priest in the person of Christe doth open the eares.'[108] While Marian Catholicism affirmed what might sound like Lutheran *fides ex auditu*, Scripture depends upon the ordained priesthood to make Christ present. Similarly, Watson proclaimed that while preaching, the sacraments, and discipline (three Reformation marks of the church) are necessary, it is the priest who edifies the church through them. Wizeman agrees with Duffy that the Marian church exhibits an 'enormously high doctrine of priesthood'.[109] This high view

---

[104] Michael Hutchings, *Reginald Cardinal Pole, 1500–1558: The Last Archbishop of Canterbury* (Midhurst: Saint Joan, 2008), 42.

[105] Mayer, *Reginald Pole*, 238–9.

[106] *Anglican Canons*, 68–161. After restoring the papacy in England, he required any clergy ordained under Cranmer's *Ordinal* to be examined and re-ordained. Mayer, *Reginald Pole*, 238–9.

[107] *Reginald Pole*, 243.

[108] William Wizeman, 'The Theology and Spirituality of a Marian Bishop: The Pastoral and Polemical Sermons of Thomas Watson', in *The Church of Mary Tudor*, 273.

[109] *The Church of Mary Tudor*, 274.

was also evident in Bonner's decision to reverse yet again the order of obedience in official catechesis on the fifth commandment.[110] The Marian bishops were influenced by humanism and some Reformation emphases, but they were intent on restoring the traditional priesthood's honor, an honor that evinced itself in the central Marian sacrament of the mass, where Christ was believed to abide eternally and order society temporally.[111]

Conformity

In response to accusations of female priesthood, the apologists of the Elizabethan regime resurrected the *potestates* distinctions buried by Henry. John Aylmer asserted a distinction between two offices, the greater ecclesiastical and the lesser civil. Civil rulers should not meddle with 'any such thing as belonged to the priesthood', and yet, they have the responsibility of redressing priestly faults. Although women cannot be priests, they can be magistrates. Elizabeth may oversee the church, but she may not function as a priest: 'she hath thauthority and ouersight but not the function and practise'.[112] John Jewel, Bishop of Salisbury, said Elizabeth was given no new power that her predecessor, Constantine, did not have. The magistrate is 'the nurse of God's religion' and may make ecclesiastical laws, and even 'hear and take up cases and questions of the faith', commit jurisdiction over such cases to the learned, and commit bishops and priests to their duties, or remove them.[113] In other words, the clergy retained *potestas ordinis*, while the monarch wielded *potestas iurisdictionis*.[114] Awkwardly, the Elizabethan apologists vacillated over whether defining the faith came under *ordo* or *iurisdictio*.

This equivocation made the *potestates* distinctions fluid. In 1569, Pope Pius V supported the northern rebellion with a bull excommunicating Elizabeth for suppressing the faith and abolishing the sacraments. The need to pacify traditionalist laity thus obliged the Elizabethan apologists to reconfigure the distinctions. In 1568, Jewel assigned the determination of faith to Elizabeth,

---

[110] *Bishops' Book* placed spiritual fathers before magistrates; *King's Book* noticeably reversed the order; Bonner restored the priority of the clergy 'as fyrst they which haue cure, and charge of our soules, who by theyr offyce, doo begette us to the faythe of Chryst'. *Doctryne*, sigs Ooiii–Ppiii. Elizabeth later reversed the order once again, in bidding the prayers. *VAI*, III, iii, 'Form of bidding'.

[111] Wizeman, 'Theology and Spirituality', 265; Loades, 'The Personal Religion of Mary I', 20–1; Lucy Wooding, 'The Marian Restoration and the Mass', in *The Church of Mary Tudor*, 227–57.

[112] *An Harbarowe for Faithfull and Trewe Subiectes* (Strassburg, 1559), sig. I4.

[113] *A Defence of the Apology* (Louvain, 1568), in *Works of John Jewel*, III, 167.

[114] Cf. Walter Haddon, *An Answer Apologetical, Against Jerome Osorius, Bishop of Silvan, in Portugal*, transl. by James Bell (Latin 1565; English 1581), in *The Fathers of the English Church*, vol. 8 (London: Hatchard, 1812), 278, 300–1, 305, 311–12.

but immediately after the bull, Jewel denies it to her, saying she necessarily leaves such matters to 'learned divines'. 'She preacheth not, she ministereth not the sacraments, she doth neither excommunicate nor absolve from excommunication, she sitteth not to give sentence in spiritual causes, she challengeth not the dispensation of the keys of the kingdom of heaven.'[115] Elizabeth herself earlier helped oversee the addition of a denial of proclamatory and sacramental power to the magistrate in the 1563 reconfiguration of Cranmer's *Forty-Two Articles*.[116] After the northern rebellion, she reinforced this point by denying herself any authority 'to define or determine any article or point of the Christian faith and religion', alter ceremonies, or use the priestly functions of preaching and administering sacraments.[117] To mollify her political subjects, Elizabeth might rhetorically restrict her *potestas ordinis*, but she continued inter alia her intercessory role in public prayer and exercised her authority over the definition of doctrine.

In 1574, John Whitgift, Elizabeth's third Archbishop of Canterbury (1583–1604), denied the queen a right to *potestas ordinis*.[118] But in 1595, her 'little black husband' was forced to modify his opinion. Whitgift tried to settle a dispute at Cambridge over Calvinistic predestinarianism by composing nine articles at Lambeth Palace. Elizabeth learned of his effort to define doctrine and required him to suppress his own articles.[119] Likewise, when advanced Protestants thought they could compel doctrinal changes, she reminded them she was anointed their queen and no changes could be forced upon her.[120] In the end, those who relied on the *potestates* distinctions were finally unable to decide whether the definitive teaching of doctrine fell under the category of *ordo* or *iurisdictio*. The Elizabethan settlement never settled this question and the queen's royal priesthood remained indefinite yet potent. Elizabeth, like all the Tudors, felt free to control preaching through licensing[121] and the dissemination of propaganda.[122] She also felt free to 'supply' anything lacking in Matthew Parker's consecration as Archbishop of Canterbury, just in case Catholics objected to the unusual provenance of his *ordine*.[123]

---

[115] *A View of a Seditious Bull* (1570), in *Works of Jewel*, IV, 1145.
[116] *Thirty-Nine Articles*, art. 37; *Documents*, 308. Christopher Haigh, *Elizabeth I*, 2d edn (London: Longman, 1998), 37.
[117] William Edward Collins, *Queen Elizabeth's Defence of Her Proceedings in Church and State* (London: Church Historical Society, 1899), 45–7.
[118] *The Works of John Whitgift*, ed. by John Ayre, 3 vols (PS, 1851–1853), I, 22.
[119] Powell Mills Dawley, *John Whitgift and the English Reformation* (New York: Scribner, 1954), 208–15; V.J.K. Brook, *Whitgift and the English Church* (London: English Universities Press, 1957), 164–5.
[120] Neale, *Elizabeth I and Her Parliaments 1559–1581*, 149.
[121] *TRP*, nos 122, 186, 303, 390, 451.
[122] *TRP*, nos 158, 287, 398, 601.
[123] Norman Sykes, *Old Priest and New Presbyter* (CUP, 1956), 112–13.

The Elizabethan episcopate may be characterized as composed of two tendencies: progressive and monarchical.[124] At the beginning of her reign, Elizabeth needed to replace the episcopal bench, and William Cecil, her Secretary, helped her acquire a slate of evangelicals, many of whom had become enamored with the continental Reformed churches during their Marian exile. Cecil's influence was instrumental on their behalf until the rise of a more monarchical group led by John Whitgift under the court influence of Christopher Hatton in the 1570s.[125] The 'progressive bishops' engaged with the queen during the 1560s over the eradication of images, concerning clerical marriage, and regarding vestments. Although desiring further reformation, they were slowly but surely transformed through her indomitable will into an instrument of her fixed settlement. Elizabeth might keep her preference for the crucifix private and acquiesce to clerical marriage, but she was adamant that the clergy retain their distinction from the laity through the wearing of vestments, and she refused to see her dominance of the church through episcopal governance undermined by the novel system of presbyterianism.[126] The bishops were intended to enforce the religious settlement as agreed by the queen in Parliament. After Grindal's suspension from office and Whitgift's effective elevation to church leadership, the monarchical bishops came into the lead and the enforcement of religious uniformity became the leading characteristic of the Elizabethan episcopate.

Jewel, 'both a Puritan and a Prelate',[127] wrote what became a definitive work for conformists, *An Apology of the Church of England*. He divided the church's ministry into 'divers degrees' along the lines of Cranmer's *Ordinal*: 'some be deacons, some priests, some bishops'. By 'priests', however, he did not intend those who sacrifice the mass. Rather, the clergy are 'committed the office to instruct the people and the whole charge and setting forth of religion.' The clergy are not mediators—'Christ is ever present to assist his church and needeth not any man to supply his room'—but preachers of his Word. Preachers are appointed 'orderly and comely' and the church does not 'allow every man to be a priest, to be a teacher, and to be an interpreter of the Scriptures.' The 'minister' is granted the 'power to bind, to loose, to open, to shut'. These keys are exercised through the preaching of the Word, for 'the keys' are 'the word of God'. When the minister preaches the Word, it works

---

[124] Elizabethan governance has been characterized as falling into two periods, an early emphasis on mixed polity and a later imperial monarchy. Stephen Alford, *The Early Elizabethan Polity: William Cecil and the British Succession Crisis, 1558–1569* (CUP, 1998), 1–8.

[125] Brett Usher, *William Cecil and Episcopacy, 1559–1577* (Aldershot: Ashgate, 2003).

[126] Scott A. Wenig, *Straightening the Altars: The Ecclesiastical Vision and Pastoral Achievements of the Progressive Bishops under Elizabeth I, 1559–1579* (Oxford: Peter Lang, 2000), 99–136.

[127] Jenkins, *John Jewel*, 246.

upon men's consciences either to open or shut them.[128] The English ministry also dispenses the two sacraments but rejects 'shows' and 'vain and superfluous ceremonies', 'because we know that men's consciences were encumbered about them'. The church's prayers are offered in the people's language so that they may 'take common commodity by common prayer'.[129] While the Catholics 'have innumerable sorts of mediators', the only mediator in the Church of England is Jesus Christ, who grants access to God through his 'one only sacrifice which he once offered upon the cross'. Jewel's understanding of mediation lacks subtlety, but his purpose is clear. Jewel is interested in inculcating truly personal faith among the people when their consciences respond to the Word of God proclaimed by the minister.[130]

The progressive Elizabethan bishops saw their primary responsibility as reforming the ministry so that the land would be filled with preachers.[131] In order to have an effective preaching ministry, ministers should be highly educated in biblical knowledge and rhetorical eloquence. There was a twofold strategy for the development of such preachers. First, a 'graduate ministry' was fashioned through the two universities, enhanced with the queen's endowment of lectureships and the bishops' endowment of new colleges as seminaries.[132] Second, 'prophesyings' or 'exercises' affiliated with a 'classis' were established locally or allowed by the bishops as a sort of 'in-service training' for those clergy already in the parishes. While Elizabeth suppressed the prophesyings due to their chaotic effect on the people and their emboldening of radical clergy, the royal and episcopal effort through the universities eventually created a transformed ministry by the seventeenth century. No longer a priesthood offering sacrifices, the clergy became a graduate ministry preaching sermons. Because vernacular Scripture was now widely available, as part of what Andrew Pettegree deems that 'most explicitly anticlerical theological concept, the priesthood of all believers', the laity had access directly to the means of grace. Pettegree believes the ministry needed to find a way of maintaining its distinctiveness. Thus, evangelical clergy were transformed into a 'graduate ministry' that was elite and professional. Through education in preaching, ministers became 'an occupational group with special expertise who could assist and guide lay people in their fumbling quest to divine the

---

[128] *An Apology of the Church of England*, ed. by John Booty (Ithaca, NY: Cornell University Press, 1963), 24–8.

[129] *An Apology of the Church of England*, 31–7.

[130] *An Apology of the Church of England*, 38–9.

[131] Wenig, *Straightening the Altars*, 147–53, 159–61, 222–3, 228.

[132] Rosemary O'Day, 'The Reformation of the Ministry, 1558–1642', in *Continuity and Change: Personanel and Administration of the Church in England 1500–1642*, ed. by O'Day and Felicity Heal (Leicester: Leicester University Press, 1976), 62–3.

mysteries of God and the afterlife.'[133] Collinson corroborates the conclusions of Pettegree and O'Day in perceiving the rise of a 'neo-clericalism' alongside 'lay emancipation' in the later Reformation.[134] However, with the influx of such confident priests expectations arose for yet further reformation.

Puritanism

The appearance of two major affinities within Elizabeth's church began during the 'Vestiarian Controversy', but the impetus for puritanism's independent attitude in governance has its origin in the reign of Mary.[135] Living outside the government's will due to their religious convictions, many English evangelicals contemplated new ideas about authority, whether they escaped into exile on the continent or remained in England. In England, John Hooper, evangelical Bishop of Gloucester, considered a new ecclesiology without a basis in royal supremacy. J.W. Martin identifies Hooper as the episcopal father of English nonconformity because of Hooper's call for the formation of illegal congregations.[136] Dickens detects a number of illegal, self-governing conventicles, led not only by Protestant clerks but also lay preachers.[137] George Withers, during Elizabeth's reign, believed that in these self-governing conventicles, 'the church of God was again restored entire, and, in a word, complete in all its parts'.[138] Brett Usher shows how one London congregation ordained its own ministers without episcopal involvement. Grindal validated several of these ministers' ordinations as the new Elizabethan bishop of London.[139]

Among the exiles, self-government became a way of life. While debating proper liturgical forms, some future conformists even practiced congregational self-government. For instance, the future Archbishop of York, Edwin Sandys, specifically approved congregational election and discipline of ministers.[140] A few exiles also began experimenting with theological arguments in

---

[133] Andrew Pettegree, 'The Clergy and the Reformation: From "Devilish Priesthood" to New Professional Elite', in *The Reformation of the Parishes: The Ministry and the Reformation in Town and Country*, ed. by Pettegree (Manchester: Manchester University Press, 1993), 5, 11–13, 16.

[134] *Religion of Protestants*, 96.

[135] Ronald J. Vander Molen, 'Anglican against Puritan: Ideological Origins during the Marian Exile', *CH*, 42 (1973), 45–57.

[136] *Religious Radicals in Tudor England* (London: Hambledon Press, 1989), 25, 126.

[137] *English Reformation*, 301–7.

[138] *[E]cclesia Dei denuo renovatur omnibus suis numeris (ut uno verbo dicam) absoluta et perfectissima.* Withers to Frederick III, mid-1567; *The Zurich Letters*, 2d series, ed. by Hastings Robinson (PS, 1845), 156–64; *Epistolae Tigurinae*, 95.

[139] '"In a Time of Persecution": New Light on the Secret Protestant Congregation in Marian London', in *John Foxe and the English Reformation*, ed. by Loades (Hampshire: Scolar Press, 1997), 233–51.

[140] William Whittingham, *A Brief Discourse of the Troubles at Frankfort* (London, 1908), 186, 202, 207–8.

support of civil rebellion. John Ponet, a bishop under Henry and Edward, retained the concept of the communication of divine power as the basis for legitimate government, but in a novel way. He rechanneled its distribution through the people. 'Common wealthes and realmes may liue, whan the head is cut of, and may put on a newe head, that is, make them a newe gouernour, whan they see their olde head seke to much his will and not the wealthe of the hole body, for which he was only ordained.'[141] Ponet follows what Skinner identifies as the private law argument of active resistance, which generally allowed private individuals to remove tyrants. Constitutional forms of active resistance, preferred by continental Calvinists, allowed only the lesser magistrates to intervene, and that by virtue of their office.[142] English Calvinists, such as Ponet[143] and Christopher Goodman, tended towards the more revolutionary private law argument. According to Goodman, only prophets, priests, and kings may be anointed. Since Mary is a woman, she obviously cannot be anointed; therefore, a new monarch must be elected.[144] John Knox, a Scotsman expecting advancement under a future Protestant monarch in England, wrote against the governments of Mary Tudor and Mary of Guise since, 'Hereof it is plain that the administration of the grace of God is denied to all women'. This includes the administration of the church's sacraments and the state's justice.[145] Knox's timing could not have been worse, for his work appeared when Mary died and Elizabeth was coming to the throne. Elizabeth took the matter personally and long held a grudge against Knox and John Calvin, the latter for allowing the publication of Knox's treatise in Geneva, and against Calvin's successor in Geneva, Theodore Beza.[146]

Although the most radical views of the exiles were not repeated in Elizabeth's reign,[147] the people were increasingly granted more consideration in discussions of governance. In his response to Knox, Aylmer argued that England's government was not 'a mere monarchie', but 'a rule mixte of all these': 'Democraties', 'Aristories', and 'monarchies'.[148] Sir Thomas Smith, privy councillor to

---

[141] *A Shorte Treatise of Politike Power* (1556), in Winthrop S. Hudson, *John Ponet (1516?-1556)* (Chicago: University of Chicago Press, 1942), II, 61.

[142] *Foundations of Modern Political Thought*, II, 210–11.

[143] *Shorte Treatise*, 47, 111–18.

[144] *How Svperior Powers Oght to be Obeyd of their subiects* (Geneva, 1558), 51–6.

[145] *The First Blast of the Trumpet against the Monstrous Regiment of Women* (Geneva, 1558), in *On Rebellion*, ed. by Roger A. Mason (CUP, 1994), 19.

[146] Calvin to William Cecil, 29 January 1559; Beza to Bullinger, 3 September 1566. *Zurich Letters*, 2d series, 34–6, 127–36; *Epistolae Tigurinae*, 20–1, 75–80.

[147] On the three late Tudor Protestant theories of rebellion—passive resistance, revolt by lesser magistrates, and tyrranicide by the people—see Richard L. Greaves, 'Concepts of Political Obedience in Late Tudor England: Conflicting Perspectives', *JBS*, 22 (1982), 23–34. Knox's views are particularly difficult to nail down. John R. Gray said Knox had 'clearly no coherent and consistent theory', because his primary concern was religious reformation. 'The Political Theory of John Knox', *CH*, 8 (1939), 132–47.

[148] *An Harborowe for Faithfull and Trewe Subiectes*, sigs G2ʳ, H2ᵛ–H3ʳ.

both Edward and Elizabeth, began his treatise on England's 'maner of gouerne-ment' with the same axiom, and he went on to argue that England was 'united by common accord and covenauntes of themselves'.[149] The arguments between Elizabeth and her council and Parliament over the succession and the potential for Mary Stuart to lead a Catholic insurgency brought Cecil to lead in the adoption of the Bond of Association. This bond created a society on a 'quasi-republican' basis to defend Elizabeth, which led Collinson to describe Elizabeth as the head of a 'monarchical republic'. Elizabeth recognized that her people 'showed great conscience' with the bond but would not let it go further.[150] While Elizabeth affirmed her sacred monarchy and her bishops ruled the church, the realm was often convulsed with efforts from below to exercise influence. The records of her parliaments indicate a relentless yet relentlessly stymied effort to institute further reform.[151]

Although Archbishop Parker's requirement of his clergy to wear vestments has been described as a 'calling into question the Protestant notion of the priesthood of all believers',[152] those who objected to vestments usually ex-pressed revulsion toward the idolatry of the papal priesthood rather than a desire for common priesthood. In a section of the *Admonition* entitled 'A View of Popishe Abuses', the puritan authors argued that vestments 'serve not to edification' but 'kepe the memorie' of the abominable popish priesthood before the weak people.[153] When discussing the priesthood, they advocated neither a universal priesthood nor a particular priesthood, but the nonexistence of any Christian priesthood, 'seeing the offyce of Priesthode is ended, Christe being the last priest that ever was.'[154] The critical issue for the earliest puritans was not defending the priesthood of all believers but sup-pressing the rags of popery in order not to offend the tender consciences of 'simple Christians' nor encourage 'obstinate papists'.

But it was in the arena of formal polity that the division between conform-ists and puritans became evident. From vestments in the 1560s, attention shifted to church government in the 1570s. The bishops responded that vestments were really *adiaphora*, indifferent things, and, therefore, subject to magisterial definition. The bishops believed allowing puritans to decide what is offensive and what is not would only give 'to every man in his parish an absolute authority'. Cartwright led the effort at Cambridge to teach a new type

---

[149] *De Republica Anglorum* (London, 1583), 1, 57.

[150] 'The Monarchical Republic of Queen Elizabeth I', *Bulletin of the John Rylands Library*, 49 (1987), 394–424; *ECW*, Speech 17, Version 1.

[151] Neale, *Elizabeth I and Her Parliaments, 1559–1581* and *Elizabeth I and Her Parliaments, 1584–1601* (New York: Norton, 1958).

[152] Eppley, *Defending Royal Supremacy*, 147.

[153] *Puritan Manifestoes: A Study of the Origin of the Puritan Revolt*, ed. by W.H. Frere and C.E. Douglas (London: SPCK, 1954), 35.

[154] *Puritan Manifestoes*, 25.

of polity, appealing to the upper laity to join with the priest as lay elders in bringing godliness to the church at the parish level. Even after early losses to Whitgift at Cambridge, Cartwright wielded his pen to support the authors of *Admonition*. The ensuing debate between Cartwright and Whitgift ran into thousands of pages, allowing them to debate such things as the usefulness of the word 'priest' as well as matters of polity and hermeneutics.[155] In calling for 'an equality of ministers' and for the *classis* to oversee not just the education but the governance of the parishes, the puritans shifted from meddling in the realm of conscience to meddling with the queen's realm. Elizabeth took note and empowered, first, Parker, then the monarchical bishops under John Whitgift to discover and suppress the presbyterian movement.[156]

While Cartwright might appeal for lay participation, he ultimately opted for a clerical elitism that limited lay participation to consent to the decisions of the elders.[157] The authors of the first and second *Admonitions* to Parliament might argue for common 'consentes' in the election of clergy on the basis of the laity's participation in the covenant, but they were clear that the initiative in election and the discipline of clergy was something handled 'in that con-sistorie or in some one of the councils'. In 1591, Cartwright admitted that the presbyterians made the laity's participation in government passive.[158] However, more radical puritans were willing to experiment with governance through an active laity.

It was in the realm of covenantal ecclesiology that Robert Browne, the theological father of separatism,[159] made his unique contribution. Browne

---

[155] Cartwright disliked the term 'priest' as a description of the ministry, arguing that the only priest Christians have is Christ. Whitgift argued that the term should be retained but its definition changed: 'As heretofore use hath made it to be taken for a sacrificer, so will use now alter that signification, and make it to be taken for a minister of the gospel.' *The Works of John Whitgift*, ed. by John Ayre, 3 vols (PS, 1851–1853), II, 310–11, 350–2. Richard Hooker agreed with Cartwright that the name priest does have an odious reference, 'a clergyman which offereth sacrifice to God', to some people. He personally prefers 'presbyter', which signifies 'fatherly guides', but the answer is not simple. Language in itself is difficult to delimit because meanings are multiple and transitional. Paul used the term 'flesh' in different senses and the fathers displayed a 'like security of speech' in referring to ministry as priesthood. 'Wherefore to pass by the name, let them use what dialect they will, whether we call it a Priesthood, a Presbytership, or a Ministry, it skilleth not.' *Of the Laws of Ecclesiastical Polity*, V, lxxviii, 2–3, in *The Works of Richard Hooker*, ed. W. Speed Hill, 5 vols (London: Harvard University Press, 1977–1990), II, 437–40; Nigel Atkinson, *Richard Hooker and the Authority of Scripture, Tradition and Reason: Reformed Theologian of the Church of England?* (Carlisle: Paternoster, 1997), 72–5.
[156] V.J.K. Brook, *A Life of Archbishop Parker* (OUP, 1962), 196–8; Collinson, *Elizabethan Puritan Movement*, 92–108.
[157] Peter Iver Kaufman, *Thinking of the Laity in Late Tudor England* (Notre Dame, IN: University of Notre Dame, 2004), 107–9.
[158] *Puritan Manifestoes*, 118–20; Kaufman, *Thinking of the Laity*, 114–18.
[159] There were Elizabethan semi-separatist and separatist congregations before Browne, but he was the first to formulate their theological principles. H. Gareth Owen, 'A Nursery of Elizabethan Nonconformity, 1567–72', *JEH*, 17 (1966), 65–76. On the relationship of Richard Fitz's separatist congregation (c. 1571) with Browne's theological development, first made

first published his views in the famous *A Treatise of reformation without tarying for anie* (1582).[160] Mimicking Gelasian dualism, Browne removed the monarch from her pivotal position in the church, though he retained her civil supremacy, and made her one of the congregation, subjecting the monarch to ministerial oversight and congregational discipline. Browne constructed his theology through a Ramist division of Elizabethan Calvinism. The church and the kingdom of Christ are coterminous; therefore, King Jesus is the only monarch in the church. Christ exercises his threefold office of kingship, priesthood, and prophecy—*triplex munus Christi*—within the congregation. On the basis of the gathering passages of Matthew 18, Browne believed Christ was present in a local remnant, the covenanted congregation. Where Christ is present, his power is exercised; therefore, local congregations are empowered to handle their own discipline, worship, and preaching. He argued that 'here by is the foundacion [of the church] laied, when we make & hould the couenant with the Lord to be vnder his gouernment, when we haue the power of the Lord . . . amongst vs, & the septer of Christ Iesus amongst vs'.[161] As in heavenly Jerusalem, so in the disciplined congregation, '*The Lord is there*', and he rules from his congregational throne.[162] Browne led what Richard Bancroft wryly described as 'theire new Kindome of Christe' into exile in the Low Countries. But the congregation soon employed Browne's doctrine of congregational kingship to dismiss him.[163] The disappointed ideologue of covenantal congregationalism subsequently reconciled with Archbishop Whitgift through the mediation of his relative, Lord Burghley.[164]

Separatists after Browne continued to affirm the self-contained kingship of covenanted congregations. In *A Brief Discoverie of the False Church*, his last writing before being executed for treason in 1593, Henry Barrow defended covenantal ecclesiology from the perspective of the enlightened conscience. Covenantal congregationalism is preferable to conformity for four reasons: the elect are few and must covenant to worship God according to his Word alone; the conformist priesthood represents a return to Rome while congregational election and ordination are necessary for a preaching ministry; due to their external ritualism the Church of England suppresses personal faith, but because the elect have their consciences awakened through preaching, they

apparent in 1582, see B.R. White, *The English Separatist Tradition* (OUP, 1971), 27–32. Treatments of Browne's life and thought are available in Frederick J. Powicke, *Robert Browne* (London: Congregational Union, 1910); Dwight C. Smith, 'Robert Browne, Independent', *CH*, 6 (1937), 289–349; H. Foreman, 'Robert Browne and Education', *Baptist Quarterly*, 30 (1983), 4–14; Diane Parkin-Speer, 'Robert Browne: Rhetorical Iconoclast', *SCJ*, 18 (1987), 519–29.

[160] *RH&RB*, 150–70.
[161] *A Trve and Short Declaration* (1583?), in *RH&RB*, 421.
[162] *An Answere to Master Cartwright* (1585?), in *RH&RB*, 459.
[163] Stuart Barton Babbage, *Puritanism and Richard Bancroft* (London: SPCK, 1962), 24.
[164] Submission and Commentary, 7 October 1585, in *RH&RB*, 507–8.

alone truly worship God; and ministerial functions are 'committed to the whole church and euerie member thereof', whereas the Church of England exercises a 'spiritual dictatorship'.[165] In spite of such revolutionary claims, Elizabethan congregational kingship was always strictly limited to the ecclesiastical arena.[166]

THE PLACE OF THE PEOPLE

In the latter part of the English Reformation, the monarchy maintained a claim to a sacred priesthood, though Mary sought to exalt Rome and Elizabeth was willing to temporize for political expediency. The clergy, on the other hand, fractured into rival parties that fortified existing clericalisms, as in Counter-Reformation Catholicism, or developed new clericalisms, as among Reformed puritans. These new clericalisms revealed bitter divisions between the squabbling gaggles of clergy: Catholics, conformists, and puritans anathematized one another and seemed all too ready to appeal to state powers to enforce their claims to authority. Rival clericalisms reinforced old types of anticlericalism and gave voice to new ones. Now, we must ask, whither the people? Was the laity ready to utilize the Reformation doctrine of royal priesthood as a tool to garner authority? Did this doctrine, with its roots in Scripture and its temporary radicalization under Luther, foster individualism among the people? Having considered sacred monarchy and anticlericalism in our discussions of the monarchy and the clergies, we will seek to answer this third major question through surveying theological claims regarding the people.

Haigh and Duffy rightly called for renewed interest in the popular aspects of Mary's reign, including the Marian theologians' use of the vernacular to restore true religion.[167] Part of their task of restoration included a renewed understanding of the orthodox doctrine of universal priesthood. The Council of Trent condemned any who believed all Christians are priests 'without distinction' or have 'equal spiritual power', went on to reassert orders as a sacrament that imprints an indelible character through the hierarchy, and denied the need for ministers to preach or receive the 'consent or call of the

---

[165] David W. Atkinson, 'A Briefe Discoverie of the False Church: Henry Barrow's Last Spiritual Statement', *Historical Magazine of the Protestant Episcopal Church*, 48 (1979), 265–78.

[166] It was only in the turbulent 1640s that there was a concerted attempt to introduce universal kingship into the civil arena when the Fifth Monarchy Men sought to make Jesus the King of England. Murray Tolmie, *The Triumph of the Saints* (CUP, 1977); B.S. Capp, *The Fifth Monarchy Men* (London: Faber and Faber, 1972); Louise Fargo Brown, *The Political Activities of the Baptists and the Fifth Monarchy Men* (OUP, 1912).

[167] Haigh, *English Reformations*, 203–34; Duffy, *Stripping*, 524–64.

people or of the secular power'.[168] In England, Bonner issued an official collection of homilies modeled on the *King's Book*. In his sermon on orders, he admitted, 'in some respecte all chrysten men and women are called priestes', but this primarily concerned 'spirituall sacrifices of fayth, prayer, and other godly vertues'. Besides that 'generall preisthode', there is 'a certayne speciall and singuler vocation or function of preisthode and ministeration' that requires the episcopal imposition of hands.[169]

Thomas Watson said, 'Wherefore as the sacraments be necessary to man's salvation, so it is necessary for certain men to be ordained and authorised of God to minister the same.'[170] Bonner agreed, for the priest is 'a mediatour unto God', who 'in the stede of God' is 'arbiter or judge', especially at the altar. Lay prayers become more effective, *ex opere operato*, if presented by the priest during the mass.[171] Watson went further, saying God receives the people's spiritual sacrifices only when they are perfected by the priest's sacrifice. Watson believed social existence was dependent on the priest sacrificing the mass. Without his sacrifice, heaven and earth remain unreconciled and the earth becomes a dangerous place to live.[172] While defending clerical celibacy, Thomas Martin lamented the Protestant doctrine of universal priesthood, which made 'This difference betwixt a clerke, and a laie man, to be but a mere ordeinaunce, or tradition of man, & therfore not necessarie to be kept, or beleued'. Martin denied all Christians receive priestly power at baptism.[173] Gardiner agreed with his fellow prelates, but went further by arguing that vernacular Scripture, vernacular preaching, and personal mental appropriation were dispensable.[174]

Cardinal Pole, eulogized at his death as 'the second apostle of the English',[175] does not seem to have addressed the lay priesthood beyond warning Henry of its egalitarian potential. His clerical elitism could be dismissive of a laity he wanted passive. In a vernacular sermon to London's leaders, he pitted the 'imbecyllyte and wekeness' of the laity against the wisdom and meekness of Christ and his church. They must now honor the priesthood they once dishonored. Those who oppose the priests are heretics and must be disciplined: 'to him that dothe not obeye the pryste, the lawe appoyntethe no lesse payne

---

[168] *Canons and Decrees of the Council of Trent*, Session 23, ch. 4 and Canons 1–8. The later Tridentine Catechism allowed only an internal universal priesthood. *The Catechism of the Council of Trent*, transl. by J. Donovan (Dublin, 1829), 316–17.

[169] *A profitable and necessarye doctryne, with certayne homelies adioyned* (London, 1555), sig. Aaii^v.

[170] *Sermons on the Sacraments*, ed. by T.E. Bridgett (London: Burns & Oates, 1876), 285–7.

[171] *Doctryne*, sigs Pi, Riii, Sii, Zi–Aiii (variable pagination).

[172] *Sermons*, 124–36; A&M, VIII, 284; *Twoo notable sermons* (London, 1554), sig. Rvii.

[173] *A Traictise declaryng and plainly prouyng* (London, 1554), sig. Aiii^r. Thanks to John Jackson for providing this reference.

[174] Muller, *Letters of Gardiner*, 307, 355.

[175] Mayer, *Reginald Pole*, 347.

than deathe' according to 'the wrathe of God'. He defended the burning of heretics in London, because they are 'undermynynge the chefe foundacyon of all commonwelthe, whiche ys religion'. National order and unity depend upon religion, which is bound with the sacraments, which depend upon the priesthood, which cannot exist without the papacy. The priesthood's ceremonies are more important than Scripture, for they give more light than Scripture and it may not be understood properly until the people obediently adhere to the sacraments.[176] Yet Pole was also concerned with the people personally, for individual belief is necessary for justification.[177] Individual souls, not the church, are 'brides of Christ'. Since faith must not be divorced from good works, the people must obey their superiors.[178] The second apostle to the English wanted the people to hear preaching and receive vernacular Scripture, but only within strict limits and after the laity obediently received the sacraments from the reformed clergy.

During Elizabeth's reign, the prosecution and execution of Catholic priests was defended at the highest levels as a matter of state policy.[179] In many cases, Catholic laypeople, discouraged from resorting to the sacraments of the parish churches, were left without access to sacramental means of grace. The new order of the Society of Jesus with seminaries on the continent trained the shock troops for a Catholic resurgence in England. When he established the Jesuits, Ignatius Loyola made his *Spiritual Exercises* foundational. These exercises, in continuity with the late medieval mystical tradition, focus on 'personal spiritual renewal' through intense examination of the conscience. During the period when the Inquisition investigated suspicions about this 'uneducated layman', Loyola added his 'Rules for Thinking with the Church' as an appendix to animate obedience to the hierarchy.[180] Two of the most popular books in Elizabethan England were the Jesuit Robert Parsons' intensely personal *Christian Exercise* and *Christian Directorie*. They were so successful in converting people to Catholicism that Edmund Bunny published Calvinized editions of Parsons' devotionals.[181] Ironically, English Catholicism

---

[176] Strype, III, ii, 482–510. On priestly elitism and the passiveness of the laity as well as the priority of liturgy and discipline over preaching in Pole's theology, cf. Rex H. Pogson, 'Reginald Pole and the Priorities of Government in Mary Tudor's Church', *HJ*, 18 (1975), 3–20; Eamon Duffy, 'Cardinal Pole Preaching: St Andrew's Day 1557', in *The Church of Mary Tudor*, 176–200; Hutchings, *Reginald Cardinal Pole*, 60–4.

[177] Fenlon, *Heresy and Obedience*, 114, 122, 143, 169.

[178] Mayer, *Reginald Pole*, 121, 138, 184, 217.

[179] William Cecil, *The Execution of Iustice in England* (London, 1583).

[180] Loyola, *The Spiritual Exercises*, 4th edn (Westminster, MD: Newman, 1943), 121–5; Robert E. McNally, 'The Council of Trent, the Spiritual Exercises and the Catholic Reform', *CH*, 34 (1965), 36–49.

[181] McNulty, 'The Protestant Version of Robert Parsons' *The First Booke of the Christian Exercise*', *Huntington Library Quarterly*, 22 (1959), 271–300; John P. Driscoll, 'The Second Parte: Another Protestant Version of Robert Persons' *Christian Directorie*', *Huntington Library Quarterly*, 25 (1962), 139–46.

became individualistic through their dependence upon such inward devotional books, for the texts turned interpretation over to the lay reader. These books became known as 'domme preachers', substitutes for priests and sacraments. Due to these historical factors, English Catholics turned inward even as they maintained fidelity to the papacy as the guarantor of universal orthodoxy.[182] On the other hand, it is commonplace that there was a definite inward turn among puritans concerned with proving their eternal election during Elizabeth's reign, as evidenced in the highly popular works of William Perkins.[183]

Within the English church, disagreements between conformists and puritans rarely extended to their views of the people's priesthood. For instance, drawing upon humanist teachings from the early Reformation, both parties approved of householders teaching their dependents. The family was pictured as 'a little church', and the father was 'priest-like' and, for William Perkins, akin to a bishop.[184] Although episcopal authorities were leery about illegitimate priests functioning in the households or neighbors participating,[185] both conformists and puritans encouraged household religious instruction well into the early Stuart period. While men who were householders were elevated through such sacerdotal comparisons, women also found themselves subtly raised. As a religion of the book, Protestantism encouraged literacy among both men and women, and women were expected to catechize their children. The Geneva Bible commented on Deuteronomy 21.18, 'it is the mothers dutie also to instruct her children'.[186]

While the expectations for women to embrace silence as a virtue remained, there were profound exceptions to the rule. Thomas Freeman, carefully comparing the eyewitness accounts of Marian Protestants with the reports of John Foxe and Henry Bull, discovered that the martyrologists concealed the active pastoral role that evangelical women gave to male martyrs. Women lectured, advised, and argued theology with men. Such activity, alongside verbal prayers and material support, led one evangelical martyr to exclaim, 'God... doth supply my spiritual lack by the good ministry of godly and virtuous women'.[187] Under Elizabeth, evangelicals were more reserved in

---

[182] Alexandra Walsham, '"Domme Preachers"? Post-Reformation English Catholicism and the Culture of Print', *P&P*, 168 (2000), 72–123.

[183] 'Weak Christians, Backsliders, and Carnal Gospelers: Assurance of Salvation and the Pastoral Origins of Puritan Practical Divinity in the 1580s', *CH*, 70 (2001), 462–81.

[184] Citing Henry Niclaes and the Family of Love, Christopher Hill concluded, 'This elevation of the father thus prepared the way for Independency and separatism.' *Society and Puritanism in Pre-Revolutionary England* (London: Secker & Warburg, 1964), 454–66.

[185] Cardwell, *Documentary Annals*, II, 7; *Anglican Canons*, 200–1.

[186] *Geneva Bible* (London, 1594). 'Books written for women at the time and earlier agreed that this was the most essential part of the woman's role.' Alison Sim, *The Tudor Housewife* (Stroud: Sutton, 1996), 108.

[187] Freeman, '"The Good Ministrye of Godlye and Vertuous Women": The Elizabethan Martyrologists and the Female Supporters of the Marian Martyrs', *JBS*, 39 (2000), 8–33. Foxe

their empowerment of women. Richard Greaves noted the increasing number of women, including those in the lower classes, who served as translators, authors, and printers, as well as supporters of nonconformity.[188] Bernard Capp argues that women exercised more authority than is commonly recognized. Women led some twenty per cent of households and could ingenuously resort to 'quasi-judicial' or informal forms of church discipline, in spite of early modern role assumptions.[189] Margo Todd believes that the humanist attitude toward the woman's conscience could be seen as 'the beginnings of the modern notion of sexual equality'.[190]

There are relatively few recorded instances of appeals being made to the royal priesthood in order to justify common preaching or teaching. Foxe reports that Edmund Allin, a miller, was accused of leading his own religious services. His parish priest inquired, 'Why didst thou teach the people, being no priest'? Allin responded, 'Because ... we are all kings to rule our affections, priests to preach the virtues and word of God, as Peter writeth, and lively stones to give light to others. ... Shall every artificer be suffered, yea commanded, to practise his faculty and science, and a Christian forbidden to exercise his?'[191] Under Elizabeth, the rector of Congerston claimed that he could preach without a preaching license, because 'it is lawfull for every Christien man having habilitie by learning to preache the Worde as he is commanded'. However, this cleric did not refer to the royal priesthood directly and appealed to this argument when caught in a lie about a previous preaching license.[192] Due to the lack of available clergy, Elizabeth's first Archbishop of Canterbury experimented with lay readers in 1561, but outlawed the practice in 1571.[193] Some prophesyings apparently allowed lay participation. Grindal said gifted laymen may preach, but they are no longer considered 'mere Plebeian or Laymen' at that point anyway. Women most definitely should not preach.[194] Whitgift argued that women could preach but only where there was no other means for the gospel to reach infidels.[195]

---

did not suppress all pastoral activities in which women engaged. Edith Wilks Dolnikowski, 'Feminine Exemplars for Reform: Women's Voices in John Foxe's Acts and Monuments', in *Women Preachers and Prophets through Two Millennia of Christianity*, ed. by Beverly Mayne Kienzle and Pamela J. Walker (London: University of California Press, 1998), 199–211.

[188] Greaves, 'The Role of Women in Early English Nonconformity', *CH*, 52 (1983), 299–311.

[189] Capp, 'Separate Domains? Women and Authority in Early Modern England', in *The Experience of Authority in Early Modern England*, ed. by Paul Griffiths et al (London: Palgrave, 1996), 117–45.

[190] Todd, 'Humanists, Puritans and the Spiritualized Household', *CH*, 49 (1980), 18–34.

[191] *A&M*, VIII, 321–2; Kaufman, *Thinking of the Laity*, 56.

[192] *Lincoln Episcopal Records, in the Time of Thomas Cooper*, ed. by C.W. Foster (London: Canterbury and York Society, 1913), 135–6.

[193] Brook, *A Life of Archbishop Parker*, 90–1, 101–3; *Anglican Canons*, 174–7.

[194] Strype, *The History of ... Edmund Grindal* (London, 1710), II, doc. 12; Collinson, *Grindal*, 239, 247.

[195] Greaves, 'The Role of Women', 307.

As for the sacraments, some puritans objected to the practice of lay baptism, both because of its private nature and because it was not performed by presbyters but by deacons, laymen, and women.[196] In 1576, convocation tried to end the practice but dropped the issue when Elizabeth personally objected.[197] Whitgift defended baptism by women against Cartwright, though he was clearly uncomfortable doing so. After Elizabeth's death, Whitgift concurred with the abolition of the practice by the Hampton Conference.[198] Neither group allowed lay presidency, but Cartwright objected to the prayer book's private communion for the sick, as it was not public. Whitgift retorted that where two or three are gathered, Christ is present and communion may be administered.[199] Both groups promoted spiritual sacrifices as indicative of universal priesthood and both limited any further lay initiative through the Protestant concept of vocation.[200]

As for church governance, the presbyterians wanted to establish a local disciplinary structure through lay eldership, a limited office intended only for the godly, but they were hindered by the episcopate. Except in rare cases, they ceased pressing their plans for the laity after the 1580s.[201] In some cases, radical Protestantism expressed itself, neither in presbyterianism nor in separatism, but in local oversight of parish clergy through donative curacies and lecturers through town corporations. In the case of Ipswich, local laity continued their late medieval tradition of lay oversight of clergy and expressed little enthusiasm for the 'new clericalism' of the presbyterian classis.[202] The bishops primarily encouraged local lay involvement in discipline through the churchwardens. The 1559 injunctions required churchwardens to present absentee parishioners. The 1571 canons called for the election of two churchwardens in each parish by the consent of both minister and parishioners. Responsible to the episcopal courts for disciplinary referrals, they could also present their priests. In 1604, churchwardens were even protected from lawsuits for presentation. Their use of their powers seems to have been muted by the need to live with their fellow parishioners. A number of lesser offices were open to lay occupation and election, too.[203]

---

[196] *Puritan Manifestoes*, 11, 13–15, 26.

[197] *Anglican Canons*, 214. Cf. Doyle, 'Lay Administration', 328.

[198] *Works of Whitgift*, II, 494–9, 519–40, 540n; Nicholas Tyacke, *Anti-Calvinists* (OUP, 1987), 15–25.

[199] *Works of Whitgift*, II, 508–18, 547–9.

[200] *The Sermons of Edwin Sandys*, ed. by John Ayre (PS, 1842), 403–17; *Geneva Bible*, Beza's marginal notes on Romans 12.1, transl. by L. Tomson.

[201] Kaufman, *Thinking of the Laity*, 150–7.

[202] Diarmaid MacCulloch and John Bletchly, 'Pastoral Provision in the Parishes of Tudor Ipswich', *SCJ*, 22 (1991), 457–74.

[203] *Anglican Canons*, 190–7, 384–5, 414–15; Christopher Marsh, *Popular Religion in Sixteenth-Century England* (London: Macmillan, 1998), 69–79; Eric Carlson, 'The Origins, Function, and Status, of Churchwardens', in *The World of Rural Dissenters 1520–1725*, ed. by Margaret Spufford (CUP, 1995), 164–207.

In all these cases, whether it was with regard to preaching or the sacraments or parish discipline, the laity received limited avenues of exercise for their royal priesthood, but references to the relevant scriptural passages were rarely used to justify such lay initiative. Except in the case of a few separatists and in the limited space of the spiritualized household, laypeople simply were not granted much of a role as a royal priesthood beyond that which was established earlier in the English Reformation. On the basis of research into the English Reformation, it could be argued that the doctrine of royal priesthood had little effect on the attitudes of contemporaries toward the community and the individual's role therein. Much less was the royal priesthood of the people an agent in the rise of religious or political individualism. If one wanted to identify theological conceptions that shaped people's attitudes about the relation of community and individual persons during the Reformation, then 'covenant' and 'conscience' or 'public' and 'private' are more likely candidates than the doctrine of royal priesthood. But that is the subject of a different study.

From the premature reformation of John Wyclif and the Lollards through the later reformations of Mary and Elizabeth, the biblical teaching about a royal priesthood was a concern for people across the religious spectrum. In spite of the claims of recent historians and theologians that the doctrine fostered individualism and anticlericalism, theorists and practitioners in Reformation England rarely allowed the doctrine to drift in those directions. Indeed, early modern individualism in its theological forms is more likely related to the devotional practices and appeals to conscience found among both traditionalists and evangelicals. As for anticlericalism, that phenomenon was more a function of its counterposition, clericalism, than of royal priesthood. Rather than propagating anticlericalism and individualism, our subject doctrine of royal priesthood appears to have found its most concrete expression in the roles of those leading laity, the sacred monarchs, male and female.

Bibliography

Manuscripts

Bodleian Library, Oxford
Barlow MS 19: Anonymous English translation of John à Lasco's *Forma ac Ratio*
  (Frankfurt, 1555)
Quarto Rawlinson 245: Henry VIII, Annotations on *The Institution of a Christian Man*
  (London, 1537)

British Library, London
Cotton MS Cleopatra E, V: Ecclesiastical documents from the reign of Henry VIII
Cotton MS Cleopatra E, VI: Ecclesiastical documents from the reign of Henry VIII
Cotton MS Cleopatra F, II: Ecclesiastical documents from the reigns of Henry VIII and
  Elizabeth I
Harley MS 31: Ecclesiastical documents from late medieval England
Harley MS 6079: Heraldic and genealogical tracts
Royal MS 6E, VI: *Omne Bonum*
Royal MS 7B, XI: Thomas Cranmer, *Commonplace Books*, volume I
Royal MS 7B, XII: Thomas Cranmer, *Commonplace Books*, volume II
Royal MS 7C, XI: Ecclesiastical documents from the reign of Henry VIII
Royal MS 18E, I: Jean Froissart, *Chroniques de France et d'Angleterre*, Book II
Stowe MS 141: Documents from the reign of Henry VIII

Public Records Office, London
SP 1/101: State Papers, Domestic Series
SP 1/105: State Papers, Domestic Series
SP 6/1: State Papers, Domestic Series
SP 6/2: State Papers, Domestic Series, including Robert Trueman and Thomas Derby,
  'The thre maners of preisthod'
SP 6/4: State Papers, Domestic Series
SP 6/7: State Papers, Domestic Series
SP 6/8: State Papers, Domestic Series

Westminster Cathedral, London
Treasury MS 7: Queen Mary's Manual

Unpublished Theses
Catto, Jeremy I., 'William Woodford, O.F.M. (c.1330–c.1397)' (University of Oxford
  D.Phil., 1969)
H.H.W. Kramm, 'Church Order and Ministry under Luther, and in the Early Lutheran
  Church, Considered in the Light of Non-Roman Christianity in Germany, Scandi-
  navia and the British Isles Today' (University of Oxford D.Phil., 1941)

McCristal, John F., 'A Study of John Wyclif's Treatise *De Mandatis Divinis*' (University of Oxford B.Litt., 1958)

Yarnell, Malcolm B., 'The Reformation Development of the Priesthood of All Believers' (Duke University Th.M., 1996)

Primary Sources and Translations

Acts of the Privy Council of England, new series, vol. 2, ed. by John Roche Dasent (London: Her Majesty's Stationery Office, 1890)

Advocates of Reform: From Wyclif to Erasmus, ed. by Matthew Spinka, *LCC*, XIV (London: SCM Press, 1953)

Alane [Alesius], Alexander, *Of the auctorite of the word of god agaynst the bisshop of London* ([n.p.], [n.d.])

The Anglican Canons 1529–1947, ed. by Gerald Bray (Woodbridge, Suffolk: Boydell Press, 1998)

Anglican Orders: The Documents in the Debate, ed. by Christopher Hill and Edward Yarnold (Norwich: Canterbury Press, 1997)

An Apology for Lollard Doctrines, ed. by James Henthorn Todd (London: Camden Society, 1842)

Aquinas, Thomas, *The Summa Theologica of St Thomas Aquinas*, transl. by the Fathers of the English Dominican Province, 20 vols (London: Washbourne, 1912–1922)

——, *The Summa Contra Gentiles of St Thomas Aquinas*, transl. by the English Dominican Fathers, 4 vols in 5 books (London: Burns, Oates & Washbourne, 1924–1929)

——, *Summa Theologica*, 5 vols (Madrid: Biblioteca de Autores Cristianos, 1951)

Der Authentische Text der Leipziger Disputation, ed. by Reinhold Otto Seitz (Berlin: Schwetschke und Sohn, 1903)

Augustine of Hippo, *Writings in Connection with the Donatist Controversy*, ed. by Marcus Dods (Edinburgh: T&T Clark, 1872)

——, *On Christian Teaching*, transl. by R.P.H. Green (OUP, 1997)

——, *The City of God against the Pagans*, transl. by R.W. Dyson (CUP, 1998)

——, *The Trinity*, transl. by Edmund Hill (Brooklyn, New York: New City Press, 1991)

Barnes, Robert, *A supplicacion unto the most gracious prince King Henry VIII* (London: John Byddell, 1534)

——, *A Supplicatyon made by Robert Barnes doctoure in diunite vnto the most excellent and redoubted prince Kinge Henry VIII* (Antwerp: S. Cock, 1534)

Bateman, Stephen, *A Christall glasse of christian reformation* (London: John Day, 1569)

Bede, St, [Commentaries on I Peter and Revelation], in *Patrologia Latina*, ed. by J.P. Migne (Paris: [n.pub.], 1844–1855), XCIII.

Bible, *[Geneva Bible] The Bible, Translate according to the Ebrew and Greeke, and conferred with the best translations in diuers Languages. With most profitable Annotations vpon all the hard places, and other things of great importance, as may appeare in the Epistle to the Reader* (London: Christopher Barker, 1594)

Bonner, Edmund, *A profitable and necessarye doctryne, with certayne homelies adioyned* (London: John Cawood, 1555)

Bonner, Richard, [Thomas Cranmer?], *A treatyse of the ryght honourynge and wourshyppyng of our saviour Jesus Christe in the sacrament of breade and wyne* (London: Gawlter Lynne, 1548)

Browne, Robert, *The Writings of Robert Harrison and Robert Browne*, ed. by Albert Peel and Leland H. Carlson (London: Allen & Unwin, 1953)

Bucer, Martin, *Scripta Anglican Fere Omnia* (Basil: Petri Pernae Officina, 1577)

——, *Common Places of Martin Bucer*, ed. by David F. Wright (Abingdon: Sutton Courtenay Press, 1972)

——, *Martin Bucer and the Book of Common Prayer*, ed. by E.C. Whitaker (Chester: Alcuin Club, 1974)

Bullinger, Heinrich, *The Decades of Henry Bullinger, Minister of the Church of Zurich. Translated by H.I.*, ed. by Thomas Harding, 4 vols (Cambridge: PS, 1849–1851)

Calendar of State Papers, Spanish, ed. by G.A. Bergenroth et al., 15 vols (1862–1964)

Calvin, John, *Institutes of the Christian Religion*, ed. by John T. McNeill and transl. by Ford Lewis Battles, 2 vols (London: SCM Press, 1960)

Catholic Church, *The Catechism of the Council of Trent*, transl. by J. Donovan (Dublin, 1829)

——, *The Sarum Missal in English*, transl. by Frederick E. Warren (London: Alexander Moring, 1911)

Certain Sermons or Homilies (1547) and A Homily against Disobedience and Wilful Rebellion (1570): A Critical Edition, ed. by Ronald B. Bond (London: University of Toronto Press, 1987)

Chronicles of the Revolution 1397–1400: The Reign of Richard II, ed. by Chris Given-Wilson (Manchester: Manchester University Press, 1993)

Church of England, *The Byble in Englyshe, that is to saye the content of all the holy scrypture, both of ye olde and newe testament, truly translated after the veryte of the Hebrue and Greke textes* (London: Rychard Grafton and Edward Whitchurch, 1539)

——, *The Reformation of the Ecclesiastical Laws of England, 1552*, transl. by James C. Spalding (Kirksville, Missouri: Sixteenth Century Journal Publishers, 1992)

——, *The Ordination of Women to the Priesthood: A Report by the House of Bishops*, General Synod, 764 (London: Church House, 1987)

The Cloud of Unknowing and Other Works, ed. by Clifton Wolters (London: Penguin, 1961)

Colet, John, *A Treatise on the Sacraments of the Church*, ed. by J.H. Lupton (London: Bell and Daldy, 1867)

——, *Enarratio in Epistlam S. Pauli ad Romanos*, ed. by J.H. Lupton (London: Bell and Daldy, 1873)

——, *Opuscula Quaedam Theologica*, ed. by J.H. Lupton (London: George Bell, 1876)

Commentarivs in Apocalypsin. Ante Centum Annos Editus, ed. by Martin Luther (Wittenberg: [n.pub.], 1528)

Concilia Magnae Britanniae et Hiberniae, ed. by David Wilkins, 4 vols (London: R. Gosling et al, 1737)

The Coronation Order of King James I, ed. by J. Wickham Legg (London: F.E. Robinson, 1902)

Cranmer, Thomas, *Writings and Disputations of Thomas Cranmer, Archbishop of Canterbury, Martyr, 1556, Relative to the Sacrament of the Lord's Supper*, ed. by John Edmund Cox (Cambridge: PS, 1844)

Cranmer, Thomas, *Miscellaneous Writings and Letters of Thomas Cranmer, Archbishop of Canterbury, Martyr, 1556*, ed. by John Edmund Cox (Cambridge: PS, 1846)

——, *Archbishop Cranmer on the True and Catholic Doctrine and Use of the Sacrament of the Lord's Supper* [1550], ed. by Henry Wace (London: Thynne, 1907)

——, *Cranmer's First Litany, 1544 and Merbecke's Book of Common Prayer Noted, 1550*, ed. by Eric Hunt (London: SPCK, 1939)

——, *The Work of Thomas Cranmer*, ed. by G.E. Duffield (Abingdon: Sutton Courtenay Press, 1964)

The Divorce Tracts of Henry VIII, ed. by Edward Surtz and Virginia Murphy (Angers: Moreana, 1988)

Documentary Annals of the Reformed Church of England, ed. by Edward Carnell, 2 vols (OUP, 1844)

Documents Illustrative of English Church History Compiled from Original Sources, ed. by Henry Gee and William John Hardy (London: Macmillan, 1896)

Documents of the English Reformation, ed. by Gerald Bray (Cambridge: James Clarke, 1994)

The Documents of Vatican II: All Sixteen Official Texts Promulgated by the Ecumenical Council 1963–1965, ed. by Walter M. Abbot and transl. by Joseph Gallagher (New York: Guild Press, 1966)

Documents Relating to the Revels at the Court in the Time of King Edward VI and Queen Mary, ed. by Albert W. Feuillerat (Louvain: A. Uystpruyst, 1914)

Dymmok, Roger, *Liber Contra XII Errores et Hereses Lollardorum*, ed. by H.S. Cronin (London: WLW, 1922)

Edgeworth, Roger, *Sermons very fruitfull, godly and learned by Roger Edgeworth: Preaching in the Reformation, c.1535–c.1553*, ed. by Janet Wilson (Woodbridge, Suffolk: Brewer, 1993)

Edward VI, *Literary Remains of King Edward the Sixth*, ed. by John Gough Nichols, 2 vols (London: Roxburghe Club, 1857)

——, *The Chronicle and Political Papers of King Edward VI*, ed. by W.K. Jordan (London: Allen & Unwin, 1966)

England, Parliament, *Journals of the House of Lords*, 10 vols (London: [n.pub.], 1771)

An English Chronicle of the Reigns of Richard II., Henry IV., Henry V., and Henry VI., Written before the Year 1471, ed. by John Silvester Davies (London: Camden Society, 1856; reprint, London: AMS Press, 1968)

English Coronation Records, ed. by Leopold G. Wickham Legg (Westminster: A. Constable, 1901)

The English Levellers, ed. by Andrew Sharp (CUP, 1998)

The English Works of Wyclif Hitherto Unprinted, ed. by F.D. Matthew, EETS 74 (London: Trübner, 1880)

Erasmus of Rotterdam, *Opus Epistolarum Des. Erasmi Roterodami*, ed. by P.S. Allen et al., 12 vols (OUP, 1906–1958)

——, *Praise of Folly*, transl. by Betty Radice (London: Penguin, 1971)

——, *The Collected Works of Erasmus*, ed. by Richard J. Schoeck and Beatrice Corrigan (Toronto: University of Toronto Press, 1974–)

——, *Christian Humanism and the Reformation: Selected Writings of Erasmus*, 3d edn, ed. by John C. Olin (New York: Fordham University Press, 1987)

——, *The Education of a Christian Prince*, ed. by Lisa Jardine and transl. by Neil M. Cheshire and Michael J. Heath (CUP, 1997)

Fasciculi Zizaniorum Magistri Johannis Wyclif Cum Tritico, ed. by Walter Waddington Shirley (London: Rolls Series, 1858)

Fasciculus Rerum Expetendarum & Fugiendarum, ed. by Edward Brown, 2 vols (London: Richard Chiswell, 1690)

Fish, Simon, *The Summe of the holye Scripture . . . with an informacyon howe all estates shulde lyve accordynge to the Gospell* (London: [n.pub.], 1529: reprint, London: Scolar Press, 1973)

——, *A Supplicacyon for the Beggars*, ed. by J.M. Cowper, EETS extra series, 13 (London: Trübner, 1871)

Fisher, John, *Assertionis Lutheranae Confutatio* (Antwerp: Michael Hillen, 1523)

——, *A sermon had at Paulis by the commandment of the most reuernd father in god my lorde legate* (London: Thomas Berthelet, 1528)

——, *The English Works of John Fisher: Bishop of Rochester*, ed. by John E.B. Mayor, EETS extra series, 27 (London: Trübner, 1876)

——, *The Life of Fisher Transcribed from MS Harleian 6382*, ed. by Ronald Bayne, EETS extra series, 117 (OUP, 1921)

——, *Sacri Sacerdotii Defensio Contra Lutherum* (1525), in *Corpus Catholicorum: Werke Katholischer Schriftseller in Zeitalter der Glaubensspaltung*, vol. 9 (Münster: Aschendorff, 1925)

——, *The Defence of the Priesthood*, transl. by P.E. Hallett (London: Burns, Oates & Washbourne, 1935)

——, *Exposition of the Seven Penitential Psalms in Modern English*, ed. by Anne Barbeau Gardiner (San Francisco: Ignatius Press, 1998)

Fitz-James, Richard, *Sermo Die Lune in Ebdomada Pasche* (Westminster: Wynkyn de Worde, 1495; reprint, CUP, 1907)

Formularies of the Faith put forth by Authority during the Reign of Henry VIII, ed. by Charles Lloyd (OUP, 1856)

Fortescue, John, *The Works of Sir John Fortescue, Knight, Chief Justice of England and Lord Chancellor to Henry the Sixth*, ed. by Thomas Fortescue, Lord Clermont, 2 vols (London: Private, 1869)

——, *The Governance of England: Otherwise Called the Difference between an Absolute and a Limited Monarchy*, ed. by Charles Plummer (OUP, 1885)

——, *De Laudibus Legum Anglie*, ed. by S.B. Chrimes (CUP, 1942)

——, *On the Laws and Governance of England*, ed. by Shelley Lockwood (CUP, 1997)

Foxe, Edward, *Opus Eximium, De Vera Differentia Regiae Potestatis et Ecclesiasticae, Et Quae Sit Ipsa Veritas ac Virtus Utriusque* (London: Thomas Berthelet, 1534)

——, *The true dyfferes betwen the regall power and the Ecclesiastical power*, transl. by Henry Lord Stafforde (London: William Copland, 1548)

Foxe, John, *The Ecclesiastical history contayning the Actes and Monumentes* (London: John Day, 1563)

——, *The Ecclesiastical history contayning the Actes and Monumentes* (London: John Day, 1570)

——, *The Ecclesiastical history, contayning the Actes and Monumentes* (London: John Day, 1576)

Foxe, John, *The Ecclesiastical history contayning the Actes and Monumentes* (London: John Day, 1580)

——, *The Acts and Monuments*, 4th edn, ed. by Josiah Pratt, 8 vols (London: Religious Tract Society, 1877)

Frith, John, *The Work of John Frith*, ed. by N.T. Wright (Oxford: Sutton Courtenay Press, 1978)

From Irenaeus to Grotius: A Sourcebook in Christian Political Thought, ed. by Oliver O'Donovan and Joan Lockwood O'Donovan (Cambridge: Eerdmans, 1999)

Gardiner, Stephen, *Obedience in Church and State: Three Political Tracts*, ed. by Pierre Janelle (CUP, 1930)

——, *The Letters of Stephen Gardiner*, ed. by James Arthur Muller (CUP, 1933)

St German, Christopher, *Here after foloweth a lytell treatise called the newe addicions* (London: Berthelet, 1531)

——, *A Treatise concernynge generall councilles, the Byshoppes of Rome, and the Clergy* (London: Berthelet, 1538)

——, *Doctor and Student*, ed. by T.F.T. Plucknett and J.L. Barton (London: Selden Society, 1974)

——, *On Chancery and Statute*, ed. by J.A. Guy (London: Selden Society, 1985)

The German Peasants' War: A History in Documents, ed. by Tom Scott and Robert Scribner (Atlantic Highlands, New Jersey: Humanities Press International, 1991)

Gest, Edmund, *A Treatise againste the preuee Masse in the behalfe and furtheraunce of the mooste hylye communyon* (London: Thomas Raynald, 1548)

Goodman, Christopher, *How Svperior Powers Oght To Be Obeyd Of Their Subiects: and Wherin they may lawfully by Gods Worde be disobeyed and resisted* (Geneva: Jean Crispin, 1558)

Grindal, Edmund, *The Remains of Edmund Grindal, D.D., Successively Bishop of London, and Archbishop of York and Canterbury*, ed. by William Nicholson (Cambrdige: PS, 1843)

Hall, Edward, *Hall's Chronicle* (London: J. Johnson, 1809)

——, *Henry VIII*, ed. by Charles Whibley, 2 vols (London: T.C. & E.C. Jack, 1904)

Helwys, Thomas, *A Short Declaration of the Mystery of Iniquity*, ed. by Richard Groves (Macon, Georgia: Mercer University Press, 1998)

Henry VIII, *Assertio Septem Sacramentorum adversus Martinum Lutherum* (London: Richard Pynson, 1521; reprint, Ridgewood, New Jersey: Gregg Press, 1966)

——, *Answere Unto A Certaine Letter of Martyn Lther* (London: Richard Pynson, 1527; reprint, New York: De Capo Press, 1971)

——, *Miscellaneous Writings of Henry the Eighth, King of England, France & Ireland*, ed. by Francis Macnamara (Berkshire: Golden Cockerel Press, 1924)

——, *State Papers Published under the Authority of His Majesty's Commission, King Henry VIII*, 11 vols (London: John Murray, 1830–1852)

Heresy Trials in the Diocese of Norwich, 1428–31, ed. by Norman P. Tanner (London: Royal Historical Society, 1977)

Hilton, Walter, *The Ladder of Perfection*, transl. by Leo Sherley-Price (London: Penguin, 1957)

A History of Conferences and Other Proceedings Connected with the Book of Common Prayer, From the Year 1558 to the Year 1690, 3d edn, ed. by Edward Cardwell (OUP, 1849)

Hooper, John, *Early Writings of John Hooper, D.D., Lord Bishop of Gloucester and Worcester, Martyr, 1555*, ed. by Samuel Carr (Cambridge: PS, 1843)

Hus, John, *Documenta Mag. Joannis Hus: Vitam, Doctrinam, Causam in Constantiensi Concilio Actam et Controversias de Religione in Bohemia 1403–1418*, ed. by Franciscus Palacky (Prague: Tempsky, 1869)

——, *The Church*, transl. by David S. Schaff (London: Allen & Unwin, 1915)

——, *Tractatus de Ecclesia*, ed. by S. Harrison Thomson (Cambridge: Heffer, 1956)

James of Viterbo, *On Christian Government: De Regimine Christiano*, ed. by R.W. Dyson (Woodbridge, Suffolk: Boydell Press, 1995)

Jewel, John, *The Works of John Jewel, Bishop of Salisbury*, ed. by John Ayre, 4 vols (Cambridge: PS, 1848–1850)

John of Paris, *On Royal and Papal Power*, transl. by John A. Watt (Toronto: Pontifical Institute of Mediaeval Studies, 1971)

Jonas, Justus, *A Short Instruction into Christian Religion Being a Catechism Set Forth by Archbishop Cranmer in MDXLVIII: Together with the Same in Latin* (OUP, 1829)

Kempe, Margery, *The Book of Margery Kempe*, transl. by B.A. Windeatt (London: Penguin, 1985)

A Kempis, Thomas, *The Imitation of Christ*, ed. by Leo Sherley-Price (London: Penguin, 1952)

Kent Heresy Proceedings 1511–12, ed. by Norman Tanner (Maidstone: Kent Archaeological Society, 1997)

Knighton's Chronicle 1337–1396, ed. by G.H. Martin (OUP, 1995)

Knox, John, *On Rebellion*, ed. by Roger A. Mason (CUP, 1994)

Langland, William, *Piers Plowman: A New Translation of the B-Text*, transl. by A.V.C. Schmidt (OUP, 1992)

The Lanterne of Ligt, ed. by L.M. Swinburn, EETS 151 (OUP, 1917)

Latimer, Hugh, *Sermons by Hugh Latimer*, ed. by George Elwes Corrie (Cambridge: PS, 1844)

The Lay Folks Mass Book, ed. by Thomas Frederick Simmons, EETS 71 (London: Trübner, 1879)

Letters and Papers, Foreign and Domestic, of the Reign of Henry VIII, ed. by J.S. Brewer et al. (London: Longman, Green, 1862–1932)

Liber Regie Capelle: A Manuscript in the Biblioteca Publica, Evora, ed. by Walter Ullmann (London: Henry Bradshaw Society, 1961)

Luther, Martin, *Luther's Reply to King Henry VIII, Now First Englished after the Lapse of Four Centuries*, transl. by E.S. Buchanan (New York: [n. pub.], 1928)

——, *D. Martin Luthers Werke. Kritische Gesamtausgabe: Briefwechsel* (Weimar: H. Böhlau, 1930–)

——, *Luther's Works*, ed. by Jaroslav Pelikan and Helmut T. Lehmann, 55 vols (Philadelphia: Fortress Press; St Louis: Concordia, 1955–1986)

——, *Three Treatises: To the Christian Nobility of the German Nation, The Babylonian Captivity of the Church, and The Freedom of A Christian*, transl. by Charles M. Jacobs, A.T.W. Steinhäuser and W.A. Lambert (Philadelphia: Fortress Press, 1989)

Lyndwood, William, *Provinciale* (Oxford: Richard Davis, 1679)

Lyndwood, William, *Lyndwood's Provinciale: The Text of the Canons Therein Contained, Reprinted from the Translation Made in 1534*, ed. by J.V. Bullard and H. Chalmer Bell (London: Faith Press, 1929)

Martin, Thomas, *A Traictise declaryng and plainly prouyng, that the pretensed marriage of Priestes, and professed persones, is no mariage, but altogether unlawful, and in all ages, and al countreies of Christendome, bothe forbidden, and also punyshed* (London: R. Caly, 1554)

Melanchthon and Bucer, ed. by Wilhelm Pauck, *LCC*, XIX (London: SCM Press, 1969)

Melanchthon, Philip, *Widder die Artikel der Bawrschaft* ([n.p.], 1525)

——, *The confessyon of the fayth of the Germaynes exhibited to the most victorious Emperour Charles the V. in the Councell or assemble holden at Augusta the yere of our lorde 1530. To which is added the Apologie of Melanchthon*, transl. by Rycharde Taverner (London: Robert Redman, 1536; reprint, Amsterdam: Walter J. Johnson, 1976)

——, 'Epistola Nuncupatoria Mel. ad Henricum VIII. Angliae Regem', in *Corpus Reformatorum*, ed. by Henry Ernest Bindseil et al., 101 vols (1834–), XXI, 333–9

——, *Loci Communes* (1535), in *Corpus Reformatorum*, ed. by Henry Ernest Bindseil et al, 101 vols (1834–), XXI, 341–560

——, *Melanchthon on Christian Doctrine: Loci Communes 1555*, ed. by Clyde L. Manschreck (OUP, 1965)

The Middle English Translation of the Rosarium Theologie, ed. by Christina von Nolcken (Heidelberg: Carl Winter, 1979)

Monumenta Ritualia Ecclesiae Anglicanae or Occasional Offices of the Church of England according to the Ancient Use of Salisbury, the Prymer in English and Other Prayers and Forms with Dissertations and Notes, ed. by William Maskell, 3 vols (London: Pickering, 1846–1847)

More, Thomas, *The Correspondence of Sir Thomas More*, ed. by E.F. Rogers (PUP, 1947)

——, *The Complete Works of St Thomas More* (YUP, 1963–)

——, *Utopia*, transl. by Paul Turner (London: Penguin, 1965)

Morice, Ralph, 'Anecdotes and Character of Archbishop Cranmer', in *Narratives of the Reformation*, ed. by John Gough Nichols (London: Camden Society, 1859)

Narratives of the Reformation, ed. by John Gough Nichols (London: Camden Society, 1859)

Netter, Thomas, *Doctrinale Fidei Catholicae*, 3 vols (Venice: [n.pub.], 1757; reprint, Farnborough: Gregg Press, 1967)

Original Letters Relative to the English Reformation, Written during the Reigns of King Henry VIII., King Edward VI., and Queen Mary: Chiefly from the Archives of Zurich, ed. by Hastings Robinson, 2 vols (Cambridge: PS, 1846–1847)

The Pageant of Medieval England: Historical and Literary Sources to 1485, ed. by Francis Godwin James (Gretna, LA: Pelican Publishing, 1975)

A parte of a register, contayninge sundrie memorable matters, written by diuers godly and learned in our time (Middelburg: Richard Schilders, 1593?)

Pecock, Reginald, *The Reule of Crysten Religion*, EETS 171 (OUP, 1927)

Ponet, John, *A Short Treatise of Politike Power* (1556), facsimile in Hudson, Winthrop S., *John Ponet (1516?–1556): Advocate of Limited Monarchy* (Chicago: University of Chicago Press, 1942)

Powell, Edward, *Propugnaculum Summi Sacerdotii evangelici, ac septenarii sacramentorum* (London: Richard Pynson, 1523)

Ptolemy of Lucca and Thomas Aquinas, *On the Government of Rulers, De Regimine Principum*, transl. by James M. Blythe (Philadelphia: University of Pennsylvania Press, 1997)

Puritan Manifestoes: A Study of the Origin of the Puritan Revolt with a Reprint of the Admonition to the Parliament and Kindred Documents, 1572, ed. by W.H. Frere and C.E. Douglas (London: SPCK, 1954)

The Rationale of Ceremonial, 1540–1543: With Notes and Appendices and an Essay on the Regulation of Ceremonial during the Reign of King Henry VIII, ed. by Cyril S. Cobb, Alcuin Club Collections 18 (London: Longmans, Green and Co, 1910)

The Records of the Northern Convocation, ed. by Dean Kitchin, Surtees Society 113 (Durham: Andrews, 1907)

Records of the Reformation: The Divorce 1527–1533, ed. by Nicholas Pocock, 2 vols (OUP, 1870)

The Reformation of the Ecclesiastical Laws as Attempted in the Reigns of King Henry VIII, King Edward VI, and Queen Elizabeth, ed. by Edward Cardwell (OUP, 1850)

The Register of John Stafford, Bishop of Bath and Wells, 1425–1443, 2 vols, ed. by Thomas Scott Holmes (London: Somerset Record Society, 1915–1916)

The Registers of Cuthbert Tunstall, Bishop of Durham 1530–59, and James Pilkington, Bishop of Durham, 1561–76, ed. by Gladys Hinde, Surtees Society 161 (London: Andrews, 1952)

Registrum Johannis Trefnant, Episcopi Herefordensis, ed. by William W. Capes (London: Canterbury and York Society, 1916)

Ricart, Robert, *The Maire of Bristowe is Kalendar*, ed. by Luch Toulmin Smith (Westminster: Camden Society, 1872)

Ridley, Nicholas, *The Works of Nicholas Ridley, D.D., Sometime Lord Bishop of London, Martyr, 1555*, ed. by Henry Christmas (Cambridge: PS, 1851)

Rolle, Richard, *The Fire of Love*, transl. by Clifton Wolters (London: Penguin, 1972)

Roper, William, *A Man of Singular Virtue Being a Life of Sir Thomas More by His Son-in-Law William Roper and a Selection of More's Letters*, ed. by A.L. Rowse (London: Folio Society, 1980)

St German, Christopher, *Here after foloweth a lytell treatise called the newe addicions* (London: Berthelet, 1531)

——, *A Treatise concernynge generall councilles, the Byshoppes of Rome, and the Clergy* (London: Berthelet, 1538)

Sanders, Nicholas, and Edward Rishton, *The Rise and Growth of the Anglican Schism*, transl. by David Lewis (Rockford, Illinois: Tan Books, 1988)

Sandys, Edwin, *The Sermons of Edwin Sandys, D.D., Successively Bishop of Worcester and London, and Archbishop of York; To Which Are Added Some Miscellaneous Pieces, By the Same Author*, ed. by John Ayre (Cambridge: PS, 1842)

The Seconde Parte of a Register, Being a Calendar of Manuscripts under That Title Intended for Publication by the Puritans about 1593, ed. by Albert Peel, 2 vols (CUP, 1915)

Select English Works of John Wyclif, ed. by Thomas Arnold, 3 vols (OUP, 1869–1871)

Selections from English Wycliffite Writings, ed. by Anne Hudson (CUP, 1978)

Smith, Richard, *The Assertion and Defence of the Sacramente of the aulter* (London: John Herforde, 1546)

——, *A Defence of the Sacrifice of the masse* (London: John Herforde, 1547)

——, *A Confutation of a certen Booke, Called a defence of the true, and Catholike doctrine of the sacrament, &c. sette fourth of late in the name of Thomas Archebysshoppe of Canterburye* ([n.p.], 1550)

Starkey, Thomas, *An Exhortation to the people, instructynge theym to Unitie and Obedience* (London: Thomas Berthelet, 1536)

——, *A Dialogue between Pole and Lupset*, ed. by T.F. Mayer, Camden Society, 4th series, 37 (London: Royal Historical Society, 1989)

Statutes of the Realm, ed. by Alexander Luders et al., 11 vols (London: George Eyre and Andrew Strahan, 1810–1828)

A Third Collection of Scarce and Valuable Tracts, on the Most Interesting and Entertaining Subjects, ed. by Lord Somers (London: F. Cogan, 1751)

Three Coronation Orders, ed. by J. Wickham Legg (London: Henry Bradshaw Society, 1900)

Trevisa, John, *Trevisa's Dialogus inter Militem et Clericum*, ed. by Aaron Jenkins Perry, EETS 167 (OUP, 1925)

Troubles Connected with the Prayer Book of 1549, ed. by Nicholas Pocock (London: Camden Society, 1884)

Tudor Royal Proclamations, ed. by Paul L. Hughes and James F. Larkin, 2 vols (YUP, 1964, 1969)

The Two Liturgies, A.D. 1546, and A.D. 1552: With Other Documents Set Forth by Authority in the Reign of King Edward VI, ed. by Joseph Ketley (Cambridge: PS, 1844)

Two Wycliffite Texts, ed. by Anne Hudson, EETS 301 (OUP, 1993)

Tyndale, William, *A compendious introduccion vnto the pistle to the Romayns* ([n.p.], 1526)

——, *Doctrinal Treatises and Introductions to Different Portions of the Holy Scriptures by William Tyndale, Martyr, 1536*, ed. by Henry Walter (Cambridge: PS, 1848)

——, *Expositions and Notes on Sundry Portions of the Holy Scriptures Together With the Practice of Prelates by William Tyndale, Martyr, 1536*, ed. by Henry Walter (Cambridge: PS, 1849)

——, *An Answer to Sir Thomas More's Dialogue, the Supper of the Lord After the True Meaning of John VI. and I Cor. XI. and Wm. Tracy's Testament Expounded by William Tyndale, Martyr, 1536*, ed. by Henry Walter (Cambridge: PS, 1850)

Vermigli, Peter Martyr, *A discourse or traictise of Petur Martyr Uermilla Florentine, the publyque reader of diuinitee in the Uniuersitee of Oxford wherin he openly declared his whole and determiniate iudgemente concernynge the Sacrament of the Lordes supper in the sayde Uniuersitee*, transl. by Nicholas Udall (London: Robert Stoughton, 1550)

—— *The Common Places of the most famous and renowned Diuine Doctor Peter Martyr*, transl. by Anthony Marten ([n.p.], 1574)

Visitation Articles and Injunctions of the Period of the Reformation, ed. by Walter Howard Frere and William McClure Kennedy, 3 vols (London: Longmans, Green and Company, 1910)

Watson, Thomas, *Twoo notable sermons, made the thirde and fyfte Fridayes in Lent last past, before the quenes highnes* (London: J. Cawood, 1554)

——, *Sermons on the Sacraments*, ed. by T.E. Bridgett (London: Burns & Oates, 1876)

Whitgift, John, *The Works of John Whitgift, D.D., Master of Trinity College, Dean of Lincoln, &c. Afterwards Successvely Bishop of Worcester and Archbishop of Canterbury*, ed. by John Ayre, 3 vols (Cambridge: PS, 1851–1853)

Whittingham, William, *A Brief Discourse of the Troubles at Frankfort, 1554–1558*, ed. by E. Arbor (London: Elliot Stock, 1908)

Wingfield, Robert, 'The *Vita Mariae Angliae Reginae* of Robert Wingfield of Brantham', ed. by Diarmaid MacCulloch, in *Camden Miscellany*, 4th series, 29 (London: Royal Historical Society, 1984), 181–301

Wriothesley, Charles, *A Chronicle of England During the Reigns of the Tudors*, ed. by William Douglas Hamilton, 2 vols (London: Camden Society, 1875–1877)

Wyclif, John, *Tracts and Treatises of John de Wycliffe, D.D.*, transl. by Robert Vaughan (London: Wycliffe Society, 1845)

——, *De Officio Pastoralis*, ed. by Gotthard Victor Lechler (Leipzig: [n.pub.], 1863)

——, *Trialogus Cum Supplemento Trialogi*, ed. by Gotthard Lechler (OUP, 1869)

——, *Polemical Works*, ed. by Rudolf Buddenseig, 2 vols (London: WLW, 1883)

——, *Sermones*, ed. by Johann Loserth, 4 vols (London: WLW, 1887–1890)

——, *De Officio Regis*, ed. by Alfred W. Pollard and Charles Sayle (London: WLW, 1887)

——, *De Apostasia*, ed. by Michael Henry Dziewicki (London: WLW, 1889)

——, *De Eucharistia*, ed. by Johann Loserth (London: WLW, 1892)

——, *De Simonia*, ed. by Michael Henry Dziewicki and Dr Herzberg-Frankel (London: WLW, 1899)

——, *De Civili Dominio*, ed. by Reginald L. Poole and Johann Loserth, 3 vols (London: WLW, 1900)

——, *De Veritate Sacrae Scripturae*, ed. by Rudolf Buddenseig, 3 vols (London: WLW, 1906)

——, *Opera Minora*, ed. by Johann Loserth (London: WLW, 1913)

——, *On Universals (Tractatus de Universalibus)*, transl. by Anthony Kenny (OUP, 1985)

——, *On Simony*, transl. by Terrence A. McVeigh (New York: Fordham University Press, 1992)

York Mystery Plays: A Selection in Modern Spelling, ed. by Richard Beadle and Pamela M. King (OUP, 1984)

The Zurich Letters, Comprising the Correspondence of Several English Bishops and Others, with some of the Helvetian Reformers, During the Early Part of the Reign of Queen Elizabeth, [with *Epistolae Tigurinae* in an appendix] ed. by Hastings Robinson (Cambridge: PS, 1842)

The Zurich Letters (Second Series) Comprising the Correspondence of Several English Bishops and Others, with some of the Helvetian Reformers, During the Reign of Queen Elizabeth, [with *Epistolae Tigurinae* in an appendix] ed. by Hastings Robinson (Cambridge: PS, 1845)

Zwingli, Huldrych, *Writings*, ed. by E.J. Furcha (Allison Park, Pennsylvania: Pickwick, 1984)

Secondary Sources

Ackroyd, Peter, *The Life of Thomas More* (London: Chatto & Windus, 1998)

Adams, Robert, 'Langland's Theology', in *A Companion to Piers Plowman*, ed. by John A. Alford (London: University of California Press, 1988), 87–114

Aers, David, *Community, Gender, and Individual Identity: English Writing 1360–1430* (London: Routledge, 1988)

——, 'Walter Brut's Theology of the Sacrament of the Altar', in *Lollards and Their Influence in Late Medieval England*, ed. by Fiona Somerset, Jill C. Havens, and Derrick G. Pitard (Woodbridge: Boydell & Brewer, 2003), 115–26

Althaus, Paul, *The Theology of Martin Luther*, transl. by Robert C. Schultz (Minneapolis: Fortress Press, 1966)

——, *The Ethics of Martin Luther*, transl. by Robert C. Schultz (Philadelphia: Fortress Press, 1972)

Anglo, Sydney, *Spectacle, Pageantry and Early Tudor Policy*, 2d edn (OUP, 1997)

Archer, Rowena E., and Simon Walker, eds., *Rulers and Ruled in Late Medieval England: Essays Presented to Gerald Harriss* (London: Hambledon Press, 1995)

Aston, Margaret, *Thomas Arundel: A Study of Church Life in the Reign of Richard II* (OUP, 1967)

——, *Lollards and Reformers: Images and Literacy in Late Medieval Religion* (London: Hambledon Press, 1984)

——, 'Wyclif and the Vernacular', *SCH*, Subsidia 5 (1987), 281–330

——, '*Corpus Christi* and *Corpus Regni*: Heresy and the Peasants' Revolt', *P&P*, 143 (1994), 3–47

Aston, Margaret, and Colin Richmond, eds., *Lollardy and the Gentry in the Later Middle Ages* (Stroud: Sutton Publishing, 1997)

Avis, Paul D.L., *The Church in the Theology of the Reformers* (London: Marshall, Morgan & Scott, 1981)

Ayris, Paul, 'God's Vicegerent and Christ's Vicar: The Relationship between the Crown and the Archbishopric of Canterbury, 1533–53', in *Thomas Cranmer: Churchman and Scholar*, ed. by Paul Ayris and David Selwyn (Woodbridge, Suffolk: Boydell Press, 1993), 115–36

Ayris, Paul, and David Selwyn, eds., *Thomas Cranmer: Churchman and Scholar* (Woodbridge, Suffolk: Boydell Press, 1993)

Babbage, Stuart Barton, *Puritanism and Richard Bancroft* (London: SPCK, 1962)

Babbit, Susan M., '*Praeter Politicos Principatus Ponendum*: Priests as Magistrates and Citizens in Medieval Texts Using Aristotle's *Politics*', in *Popes, Teachers, and Canon Law in the Middle Ages*, ed. by James Ross Sweeney and Stanley Chodorow (London: Cornell University Press, 1989), 145–59

Bagchi, David V.N., '*Eyn Mercklich Underscheyd*: Catholic Reactions to Luther's Doctrine of the Priesthood of All Believers, 1520–25', *SCH*, 26 (1989), 155–65

——, *Luther's Earliest Opponents: Catholic Controversialists 1518–1525* (Minneapolis: Fortress Press, 1991)

Bagge, Sverre, 'The Individual in Medieval Historiography', in *The Individual in Political Theory and Practice*, ed. by Janet Coleman (OUP, 1996)

Baker, J.H., *The Order of Serjeants at Law: A Chronicle of Creations with Related Texts and a Historical Introduction* (London: Selden Society, 1984)

Ban, Joseph D., 'English Reformation: Product of King or Minister?' *CH*, 41 (1972), 186–97

Barbee, C. Frederick, and Paul F.M. Zahl, *The Collects of Thomas Cranmer* (Cambridge: Eerdmans, 1999)

Barth, Karl, *Church Dogmatics*, transl. by G.W. Bromiley, T.F. Torrance et al., 4 parts in 14 vols (Edinburgh: T&T Clark, 1958–1977)

Le Van Baumer, Franklin, *The Early Tudor Theory of Kingship* (YUP, 1940)

Beattie, J.H.M., 'On Understanding Sacrifice', in *Sacrifice*, ed. by M.F.C. Bourdillon and Meyer Fortes (London: Academic Press, 1980)

Beckingsale, B.W., *Thomas Cromwell: Tudor Minister* (London: Macmillan, 1978)

Beckwith, R.T., *Priesthood and Sacraments: A Study in the Anglican–Methodist Report* (Abingdon: Marcham Manor Press, 1964)

——, 'Thomas Cranmer and the Prayer Book', in *The Study of Liturgy*, revised edn, ed. by Cheslyn Jones et al. (OUP, 1992), 101–6

Beckwith, R.T., and C.O. Buchanan, '"This Bread and This Cup": An Evangelical Rejoinder', *Theology*, 79 (1967), 265–71

Beckwith, Sarah, 'A Very Material Mysticism: The Medieval Mysticism of Margery Kempe', in *Medieval Literature: Criticism, Ideology and History*, ed. by David Aers (Brighton: Harvester Press, 1986), 34–57

——, *Christ's Body: Identity, Culture and Society in Late Medieval Writings* (London: Routledge, 1993)

Beesley, Alan, 'An Unpublished Source of the Book of Common Prayer: Peter Martyr Vermigli's *Adhortatio ad Coenam Domini Mysticam*', *JEH*, 19 (1968), 83–8

Bellah, Robert, *Habits of the Heart: Individualism and Commitment in American Life* (London: University of California Press, 1987)

Bernard, G.W., 'The Pardon of the Clergy Reconsidered', *JEH*, 37 (1986), 258–87

——, 'The Making of Religious Policy, 1533–1546: Henry VIII and the Search for the Middle Way', *HJ*, 41 (1998), 321–49

——, *The King's Reformation: Henry VIII and the Remaking of the English Church* (YUP, 2005)

Biller, Peter, 'Confession in the Middle Ages: Introduction', in *Handling Sin: Confession in the Middle Ages*, ed. by Peter Biller and A.J. Minnis (York: York Medieval Press, 1998)

Birnbaum, Pierre, and Jean Leca, eds., *Individualism: Theories and Methods*, transl. by John Gaffrey (OUP, 1990)

Black, Antony, 'The Individual and Society', in *The Cambridge History of Medieval Political Thought c.350–c.1450*, ed. by J.H. Burns (CUP, 1988)

Blench, J.W., *Preaching in England in the Late Fifteenth and Sixteenth Centuries: A Study of English Sermons 1450–c.1600* (Oxford: Blackwell, 1964)

Blickle, Peter, *The Revolution of 1525: The German Peasants' War from a New Perspective*, transl. by Thomas A. Brady, Jr. and H.C. Erik Midelfort (London: Johns Hopkins University Press, 1981)

——, *Communal Reformation: The Quest for Salvation in Sixteenth-Century Germany*, transl. by Thomas Dunlap (London: Humanities Press, 1992)

——, 'Reformation and Communal Spirit: The Reply of the Theologians to Constitutional Change in the Late Middle Ages', in *The German Reformation: The Essential Readings*, ed. by C. Scott Dixon (Oxford: Blackwell, 1999), 133–68

Blickle, Steven Ellis and Eva Österberg, 'The Commons and the State: Representation, Influence and the Legislative Process', in *Resistance, Representation and Community*, ed. by Peter Blickle (OUP, 1997)

Bloch, Marc, *The Royal Touch: Sacred Monarchy and Scrofula in England and France*, transl. by J.E. Anderson (London: Routledge, 1973)

Block, Edward A., *John Wyclif: Radical Dissenter* (San Diego, California: San Diego State College Press, 1962)

Block, Joseph S., *Factional Politics and the English Reformation 1520–1540* (Woodbridge, Suffolk: Boydell Press, 1993)

Boehrer, Bruce, 'Tyndale's *The Practyse of Prelates*: Reformation Doctrine and the Royal Supremacy', *Renaissance and Reformation* 3 (1986), 257–76

Bose, Mishtooni, 'Reginald Pecock's Vernacular Voice', in *Lollards and Their Influence in Late Medieval England*, ed. by Fiona Somerset, Jill C. Havens, and Derrick G. Pitard (Woodbridge: Boydell & Brewer, 2003), 217–36

Bostick, Curtis V., *The Antichrist and the Lollards: Apocalypticism in Late Medieval and Reformation England* (Leiden: E.J. Brill, 1998)

Bossy, John, 'The Mass as a Social Institution 1200–1700', *P&P*, 100 (1983), 29–61

——, *Christianity in the West 1400–1700* (OUP, 1985)

——, 'Prayers', *TRHS*, 6th series, 1 (1991), 137–50

Bourne, E.C.E., 'Cranmer and the Liturgy of 1552', *CQR*, 155 (1954), 382–90

Bowker, Margaret, *The Secular Clergy in the Diocese of Lincoln 1495–1520* (CUP, 1968)

——, 'The Supremacy and the Episcopate: The Struggle for Control, 1534–1540', *HJ*, 18 (1975), 227–43

——, 'The Henrician Reformation and the Parish Clergy', *BIHR*, 50 (1977), 30–47

——, *The Henrician Reformation: The Diocese of Lincoln under John Longland 1521–1547* (CUP, 1981)

Brachlow, Stephen, *The Communion of Saints: Radical Puritan and Separatist Ecclesiology 1570–1625* (OUP, 1988)

Bradshaw, Christopher, 'David or Josiah? Old Testament Kings as Exemplars in Edwardian Religious Polemic', in *Protestant History and Identity in Sixteenth-Century Europe*, ed. by Bruce Gordon, 2 vols (Hants: Scolar Press, 1996), II, 77–90

Bradshaw, Paul F., *The Anglican Ordinal: Its History and Development from the Reformation to the Present Day* (London: SPCK, 1971)

——, 'Medieval Ordinations', in *The Study of Liturgy*, revised edn, ed. by Cheslyn Jones et al. (OUP, 1992), 369–79

——, 'Ordination as God's Action through the Church', in *Anglican Orders and Ordinations: Essays and Reports from the Interim Conference at Jarvenpää, of the International Anglican Liturgical Consultation, 4–9 August 1997*, ed. by David R. Holeton, Joint Liturgical Studies 39 (Cambridge: Grove Books, 1997), 8–15

Brigden, Susan, 'Popular Disturbance and the Fall of Thomas Cromwell and the Reformers, 1539–1540', *HJ*, 24 (1981), 257–78

——, 'Tithe Controversy in Reformation London', *JEH*, 32 (1981), 285–301

——, 'Thomas Cromwell and the "Brethren"', in *Law and Government Under the Tudors*, ed. by Claire Cross, David Loades and J.J. Scarisbrick (CUP, 1988), 31–49

——, 'Youth and the English Reformation', in *The Impact of the English Reformation 1500–1640*, ed. by Peter Marshall (London: Arnold, 1997), 55–84

Brightman, F. E., *The English Rite: Being a Synopsis of the Sources and Revisions of the Book of Common Prayer with an Introduction and an Appendix*, 2 vols (London: Rivingtons, 1921)

Brilioth, Yngve, *Eucharistic Faith and Practice: Evangelical and Catholic*, transl. by A.G. Hebert (London: SPCK, 1961)

Brockwell, Jr., Charles W., *Bishop Reginald Pecock and the Lancastrian Church: Securing the Foundations of Cultural Authority* (Lewiston, New York: Edwin Mellen Press, 1985)

Bromiley, G.W., *Thomas Cranmer Theologian* (London: Lutterworth Press, 1956)

Brook, V.J.K., *Whitgift and the English Church* (London: English Universities Press, 1957)

——, *A Life of Archbishop Parker* (OUP, 1962)

Brooks, Peter Newman, *Thomas Cranmer's Doctrine of the Eucharist: An Essay in Historical Development*, 2d edn (London: Macmillan, 1992)

——, 'Saint Martin and Saint Thomas: A Comparison', *Faith and Worship*, 47 (1999), 3–8

Brown, Louise Fargo, *The Political Activities of the Baptists and Fifth Monarchy Men in England During the Interregnum* (OUP, 1912)

Brundage, James A., *Medieval Canon Law* (London: Longman, 1995)

Buchanan, Colin, *What Did Cranmer Think He Was Doing?*, Grove Liturgical Study 7 (Bramcote, Nottinghamshire: Grove Books, 1976)

——, 'Anglican Orders and Unity', in *Anglican Orders and Ordinations: Essays and Reports from the Interim Conference at Jarvenpää, of the International Anglican Liturgical Consultation, 4–9 August 1997*, ed. by David R. Holeton, Joint Liturgical Studies 39 (Cambridge: Grove Books, 1997), 16–28

——, 'Anglican Ordination Rites: A Review', in *Visible Unity and the Ministry of Oversight: The Second Theological Conference between the Church of England and the Evangelical Church in Germany* (London: Church House Publishing, 1997), 120–9

——, 'Editorial: Lay Presidency in Sydney', *News of Liturgy*, 299 (1999), 1–2, 11–12

Buck, Stephanie, *Hans Holbein 1497/98–1543* (Cologne: Könemann, 1999)

Buddenseig, Rudolf, *John Wiclif, Patriot and Reformer* (London: Allen & Unwin, 1884)

Burckhardt, Jacob, *The Civilization of the Renaissance*, transl. by S.G.C. Middlemore (London: Allen & Unwin, 1944)

Burkhard, John J., '*Sensus Fidei*: Theological Reflection since Vatican II', *Heythrop Journal*, 34 (1993), 41–59, 123–36

Burnet, Gilbert, *The History of the Reformation of the Church of England*, 3 vols (London: Richard Chiswell and John Churchill, 1681, 1715)

Burnett, Amy Nelson, 'Confirmation and Christian Fellowship: Martin Bucer on Commitment to the Church', *CH*, 64 (1995), 202–17

——, 'The Social History of Communion and the Reformation of the Eucharist', *P&P*, 211 (2011), 77–119

Burns, J.H., 'Fortescue and the Political Theory of *Dominium*', *HJ*, 28 (1985), 777–97

——, ed., *The Cambridge History of Medieval Political Thought c.350–c.1450* (CUP, 1988)

Butterworth, Charles C., and Allan G. Chester, *George Joye, 1495?–1553: A Chapter in the History of the English Bible and the English Reformation* (Norwich: Fletcher, 1962)

Calhoun, C.J., 'Community: Toward a Variable Conceptualization for Comparative Research', *Social History*, 5 (1980), 105–29

Canning, Joseph, *A History of Medieval Political Thought 300–1450* (London: Routledge, 1996)

Capp, B.S., *The Fifth Monarchy Men: A Study in the Seventeenth-Century English Millenarianism* (London: Faber and Faber, 1972)

Carlson, Eric, 'The Origins, Function, and Status, of Churchwardens, With Particular Reference to the Diocese of Ely', in *The World of Rural Dissenters 1520–1725*, ed. by Margaret Spufford (CUP, 1995), 164–207

Carre, Meyrick H., *Realists and Nominalists* (OUP, 1946)

Castor, Helen, *She-Wolves: The Women Who Ruled England Before Elizabeth* (New York: HarperCollins, 2011)

Cate, Fred H., 'Thomas Cranmer's Eucharistic Doctrine and the Prayer Books of Edward VI', *Historical Magazine of the Protestant Episcopal Church*, 55 (1986), 95–111

Catto, Jeremy I., 'John Wyclif and the Cult of the Eucharist', *SCH*, Subsidia 4 (1985), 269–86

——, 'Religious Change under Henry V', in *Henry V: The Practice of Kingship*, ed. by G.L. Harriss (OUP, 1985)

——, 'Wyclif and Wycliffism at Oxford 1356–1430', in *The History of the University of Oxford*, vol. 2, *Late Medieval Oxford*, ed. by idem and Ralph Evans (OUP, 1992)

——, 'The King's Government and the Fall of Pecock, 1457–58', in *Rulers and Ruled in Late Medieval England: Essays Presented to Gerald Harriss*, ed. by Rowena E. Archer and Simon Walker (London: Hambledon Press, 1995), 201–22

Champion, J.A.I., *The Pillars of Priestcraft Shaken: The Church of England and Its Enemies 1660–1730* (CUP, 1992)

Chaney, William A., *The Cult of Kingship in Anglo-Saxon England: The Transition from Paganism to Christianity* (Manchester: Manchester University Press, 1970)

Chodorow, Stanley, *Christian Political Theory and Church Politics in the Mid-Twelfth Century: The Ecclesiology of Gratian's Decretum* (London: University of California Press, 1972)

Chrimes, S.B., *English Constitutional Ideas in the Fifteenth Century* (CUP, 1936)

Christian, Margaret, '"I knowe not howe to preache": The Role of the Preacher in Taverner's Postils', *SCJ*, 24 (1998), 377–97

Clark, Francis, *Eucharistic Sacrifice and the Reformation* (London: Darton, Longman & Todd, 1960)

Clark, J.P.H., 'Late Fourteenth-Century Cambridge Theology and the English Contemplative Tradition', in *The Medieval Mystical Tradition in England, Exeter Symposium V*, ed. by Marion Glasscoe (London: Brewer, 1993), 1–16

Clebsch, William A., *England's Earliest Protestants 1520–1535* (YUP, 1964)

Coleman, Janet, ed., *The Individual in Political Theory and Practice* (OUP, 1996)

Collier, Jeremy, *An Ecclesiastical History of Great Britain, Chiefly of England, From the First Planting of Christianity, To the End of the Reign of King Charles the Second; With a Brief Account of the Affairs of Religion in Ireland*, new edn, ed. by Francis Barham, 9 vols (London: Straker, 1840–1841)

Collins, William Edward, *Queen Elizabeth's Defence of Her Proceedings in Church and State with an Introductory Essay on the Northern Ireland Rebellion* (London: Church Historical Society, 1899)

Collinson, Patrick, *The Elizabethan Puritan Movement* (London: Jonathan Cape, 1967)

——, *Archbishop Grindal 1519-1583: The Struggle for a Reformed Church* (London: Jonathan Cape, 1979)

——, *The Religion of Protestants: The Church in English Society 1559-1625* (OUP, 1982)

——, *Godly People: Essays on English Protestantism and Puritanism* (London: Hambledon Press, 1983)

Cooper, J.R., 'The Supplication against the Ordinaries Reconsidered', *EHR*, 72 (1957), 616-41

Cooper, Tim, *The Last Generation of English Catholic Clergy: Parish Priests in the Diocese of Coventry and Lichfield in the Early Sixteenth Century* (Woodbridge, Suffolk: Boydell Press, 1999)

Cook, William R., 'John Wyclif and Hussite Theology', *CH*, 42 (1973), 335-49

Cosgrove, Richard A., 'English Anticlericalism: A Programmatic Assessment', in *Anticlericalism in Late Medieval and Early Modern Europe*, ed. by Peter A. Dykema and Heiko A. Oberman (Leiden: E.J. Brill, 1993)

Costigiane, Helen, 'A History of the Western Idea of Conscience', in *Conscience in World Religions*, ed. by Jayne Hoose (Herefordshire: Gracewing, 1999)

Coulton, G.G., *Ten Medieval Studies, with Four Appendices* (CUP, 1906)

Couratin, A.H., 'The Tradition Received: "We Offer this Bread and Cup": 2', *Theology*, 69 (1966), 437-42

Courtenay, William J., 'Cranmer as a Nominalist *Sed Contra*', *HTR*, 57 (1964), 367-80

Craig, John, and Caroline Litzenberger, 'Wills as Religious Propaganda: The Testament of William Tracy', *JEH*, 44 (1993), 415-31

Cressy, David, 'Literacy in Pre-industrial England', *Societas*, 4 (1974), 229-40.

——, *Literacy and the Social Order: Reading and Writing in Tudor and Stuart England* (CUP, 1980)

Crompton, James, 'Fasciculi Zizaniorum I', *JEH*, 12 (1961), 34-45

——, 'Fasciculi Zizaniorum II', *JEH*, 12 (1961), 155-66

Cross, Claire, *The Royal Supremacy in the Elizabethan Church* (London: Allen & Unwin, 1969)

——, '"Great Reasoners in Scripture": The Activities of Women Lollards 1380-1530', *SCH*, Subsidia 1 (1978), 359-80

——, 'Priests into Ministers: The Establishment of Protestant Practice in the City of York, 1530-1630', in *Reformation Principle and Practice: Essays in Honour of Arthur Geoffrey Dickens*, ed. by Peter Newman Brooks (London: Scolar Press, 1980), 203-25

——, David Loades and J.J. Scarisbrick, eds., *Law and Government Under the Tudors* (CUP, 1988)

——, *Church and People: England 1450-1660*, 2d edn (Oxford: Blackwell, 1999)

Cuming, G.J., 'The English Rite: "We Offer this Bread and Cup": 4', *Theology*, 69 (1966), 447-52

Cross, Claire, *A History of Anglican Liturgy* (London: Macmillan, 1969)

Cunningham, David S., *Faithful Persuasion: In Aid of a Rhetoric of Christian Theology* (Notre Dame, Indiana: University of Notre Dame Press, 1991)

——, *These Three Are One: The Practice of Trinitarian Theology* (Oxford: Blackwell, 1998)

Cutts, David, and Harold Miller, *Whose Office? Daily Prayer for the People of God*, Grove Liturgical Study 32 (Bramcote, Nottinghamshire: Grove Books, 1982)

D'Alton, Craig W., 'The Suppression of Lutheran Heretics in England, 1526–1529,' *JEH*, 54 (2003), 228–53

Dabin, Paul, *Le Sacerdoce Royal des Fidèles dans la Tradition Ancienne et Moderne* (Paris: Desclèe de Brouwer, 1950)

Dahmus, Joseph H., *The Prosecution of John Wyclif* (YUP, 1952)

Daly, L.J., *The Political Theory of John Wyclif* (Chicago: Loyola University Press, 1962)

Daniell, David, *William Tyndale: A Biography* (YUP, 1994)

Davies, E.T., *Episcopacy and the Royal Supremacy in the Church of England in the XVI Century* (Oxford: Blackwell, 1950)

Davies, Richard G., 'Richard II and the Church', in *Richard II: The Art of Kingship*, ed. by Anthony Goodman and James Gillespie (OUP, 1999)

Davis, John F., 'The Trials of Thomas Bylney and the English Reformation', *HJ*, 24 (1981), 775–90

——, 'Joan of Kent, Lollardy and the English Reformation', *JEH*, 33 (1982), 225–33

——, 'Lollardy and the Reformation in England', in *The Impact of the English Reformation 1500–1640*, ed. by Peter Marshall (London: Arnold, 1997), 37–44

Dawley, Powell Mills, *John Whitgift and the English Reformation* (New York: Charles Scribner, 1954)

Deanesly, Margaret, *The Lollard Bible and Other Medieval Biblical Versions* (CUP, 1920)

Dickens, A.G., *Lollards and Protestants in the Diocese of York 1509–1558* (OUP, 1959)

——, *Thomas Cromwell and the English Reformation* (London: Hodder and Stoughton, 1959)

——, 'The Early Expansion of Protestantism in England 1520–1558', *ARG*, 78 (1987), 187–221

——, 'The Shape of Anti-clericalism and the English Reformation', in *Politics and Society in Reformation Europe: Essays for Geoffrey Elton on his Sixty-fifth Birthday*, ed. by E.I. Kouri and Tom Scott (London: Macmillan, 1987), 379–410

——, *The English Reformation*, 2d edn (University Park, Pennsylvania: Pennsylvania State University Press, 1989)

Dix, Gregory, *The Shape of the Liturgy* (Westminster: Dacre Press, 1945)

Dobbins, Sharon K., 'Equity: The Court of Conscience or the King's Command, the Dialogues of St German and Hobbes Compared', *Journal of Law & Religion*, 9 (1991), 113–49.

Dobson, R. Barrie, *The Peasants' Revolt of 1381*, 2d edn (London: Macmillan, 1983)

——, ed., *The Church, Politics and Patronage in the Fifteenth Century*, ed. by R. Barrie Dobson (Gloucester: Alan Sutton, 1984)

Doe, Norman, *Fundamental Authority in Late Medieval English Law* (CUP, 1990)

Doernberg, Erwin, *Henry VIII and Luther: An Account of Their Personal Relations* (London: Barrie and Rockliff, 1961)

Dolnikowski, Edith Wilks, 'FitzRalph and Wyclif on the Mendicants', *Michigan Academician*, 19 (1987), 87–100

Dowling, Maria, *Humanism in the Age of Henry VIII* (London: Croom Helm, 1986)

——, 'Cranmer as Humanist Reformer', in *Thomas Cranmer: Churchman and Scholar*, ed. by Paul Ayris and David Selwyn (Woodbridge, Suffolk: Boydell Press, 1993), 89–114

Doyle, Eric, 'William Woodford on Scripture and Tradition', in *Studia Historico-Ecclesiastica, Festgabe fur Prof. Luchesius G. Spatling*, ed. by Isaac Vazquez (Rome: Pontificum Athenaeum Antonianum, 1977), 481–504

Doyle, Robert C., '"Lay Administration" and the Sixteenth Century', *Churchman*, 113 (1999), 319–30

Drury, John, *Painting the Word: Christian Pictures and Their Meanings* (YUP, 1999)

Duckett, Eleanor Shipley, *Saint Dunstan of Canterbury: A Study of Monastic Reform in the Tenth Century* (London: Collins, 1955)

Duffy, Eamon, *The Stripping of the Altars: Traditional Religion in England 1400–1580* (YUP, 1992)

——, 'Cranmer and Popular Religion', in *Thomas Cranmer: Churchman and Scholar*, ed. by Paul Ayris and David Selwyn (Woodbridge, Suffolk: Boydell Press, 1993), 199–216

——, *Saints & Sinners: A History of the Popes* (YUP, 1997)

——, *Marking the Hours: English People & Their Prayers 1240–1570* (YUP, 2006)

Duffy, Eamon, and David Loades, eds., *The Church of Mary Tudor* (Aldershot: Ashgate, 2006)

Dugmore, C.W., *The Mass and the English Reformers* (London: Macmillan, 1958)

Dunnill, John, *Covenant and Sacrifice in the Letter to the Hebrews* (CUP, 1992)

Dykema, Peter A., and Heiko A. Oberman, eds., *Anticlericalism in Late Medieval and Early Modern Europe* (Leiden: E.J. Brill, 1993)

Eastwood, Cyril, *The Priesthood of All Believers: An Examination of the Doctrine from the Reformation to the Present Day* (London: Epworth Press, 1960)

——, *The Royal Priesthood of the Faithful: An Investigation of the Doctrine from Biblical Times to the Reformation* (London: Epworth Press, 1963)

Echlin, Edward P., *The Story of Anglican Ministry* (Slough: St Paul Publications, 1974)

Elliott, John Hall, *The Elect and the Holy: An Exegetical Examination of I Peter 2:4–10 and the Phrase βασίλειον ἱεράτευμα* (Leiden: E.J. Brill, 1966)

——, *A Home for the Homeless: A Sociological Exegesis of I Peter, Its Situation and Strategy* (London: SCM Press, 1982)

Elton, Geoffrey R., 'The Commons' Supplication of 1532: Parliamentary Manoeuvres in the Reign of Henry VIII', *EHR*, 66 (1951), 507–34

——, *The Tudor Constitution: Documents and Commentary* (CUP, 1965)

——, *Policy and Police: The Enforcement of the Reformation in the Age of Thomas Cromwell* (CUP, 1972)

——, *Reform and Renewal: Thomas Cromwell and the Common Weal* (CUP, 1973)

——, *Star Chamber Stories*, 2d edn (London: Methuen, 1974)

——, *Studies in Tudor and Stuart Politics and Government*, 4 vols (CUP, 1974–1992)

Elton, Geoffrey R., *Reform and Reformation: England 1509–1558* (London: Edward Arnold, 1977)

Emmison, F.G., *Tudor Secretary: Sir William Petre at Court and Home* (London: Phillimore, 1961)

Eppley, Daniel, *Defending Royal Supremacy and Discerning God's Will in Tudor England* (Aldershot: Ashgate, 2007)

Evans, G.R., 'Wyclif on Literal and Metaphorical', *SCH*, Subsidia 5 (1987), 259–66

——, *Problems of Authority in the Reformation Debates* (CUP, 1992)

——, *Philosophy and Theology in the Middle Ages* (London: Routledge, 1993)

——, *John Wyclif: Myth and Reality* (Oxford: Lion Hudson, 2005)

Farnsley, A.E., *Southern Baptist Politics: Authority and Power in the Restructuring of an American Denomination* (University Park, Pennsylvania: Pennsylvania State University Press, 1994)

Farr, William, *John Wyclif as Legal Reformer* (Leiden: E.J. Brill, 1974)

Fenlon, Dermot, *Heresy and Obedience in Tridentine Italy: Cardinal Pole and the Counter Reformation* (CUP, 1972)

——, 'Thomas More and Tyranny', *JEH*, 32 (1981), 453–76

Fife, Robert Herndon, *The Revolt of Martin Luther* (New York: Columbia University Press, 1957)

Figgis, John N., *The Divine Right of Kings*, 2d edn (1914; reprint, Bristol: Thoemmes Press, 1994)

Fines, J., 'Heresy Trials in the Diocese of Coventry and Lichfield, 1511–12', *JEH*, 13 (1962), 160–74

——, *A Biographical Register of Early English Protestants and Others Opposed to the Roman Catholic Church 1525–1558 A–C* (Abingdon: Sutton Courtenay Press, 1981)

——, 'Bishop Reginald Pecock and the Lollards', in *Studies in Sussex Church History*, ed. by M.J. Kitch (Sussex: Leopard's Head Press, 1981)

Fisher, R.M., 'Reform, Repression and Unrest at the Inns of Court, 1518–1558', *HJ*, 20(1977), 783–801

Fitzpatrick, P.J., 'On Eucharistic Sacrifice in the Middle Ages', in *Sacrifice and Redemption: Durham Essays in Theology*, ed. by S.W. Sykes (CUP, 1991), 129–56

Fletcher, Anthony, and Diarmaid MacCulloch, *Tudor Rebellions*, 4th edn (London: Longman, 1997)

Fletcher, Richard, *The Conversion of Europe from Paganism to Christianity 371–1386AD* (London: HarperCollins, 1997)

Ford, Simon N., 'Social Outlook and Preaching in a Wycliffite *Sermones Dominicales* Collection', in *Church and Chronicle in the Middle Ages: Essays Presented to John Taylor*, ed. by Ian Wood and G.A. Loud (London: Hambledon Press, 1991), 179–91

Foster, Andrew, 'The Clerical Estate Revitalized', in *The Early Stuart Church, 1603–1642*, ed. by Kenneth Fincham (London: Macmillan, 1993)

Fox, Alistair, *The English Renaissance: Identity and Representation in Elizabethan England* (Oxford: Blackwell, 1997)

Franklin, R. William, ed., *Anglican Orders: Essays on the Centenary of Apostolicae Curae, 1896–1996* (London: Mowbray, 1996)

Freeman, Thomas S., 'The Importance of Dying Earnestly: The Metamorphosis of the Account of James Bainham in "Foxe's Book of Martyrs"', *SCH*, 33 (1997), 267–88

——,'Texts, Lies, and Microfilm: Reading and Misreading Foxe's "Book of Martyrs"', *SCJ*, 30 (1999), 23–46

Fritze, Ronald H., 'Root or Link? Luther's Position in the Historical Debate over the Legitimacy of the Church of England, 1558–1625', *JEH*, 37 (1986), 288–302

Fryde, E.B., ed., *Handbook of British Chronology*, 3rd edn (CUP, 1986)

Garrett, Jr., James Leo, 'The Biblical Doctrine of the Priesthood of the People of God', in *New Testament Studies: Essays in Honor of Ray Summers in his Sixty-fifth Year*, ed. by Huber L. Drumwright and Curtis Vaughan (Waco, Texas: Baylor University Press, 1975)

——, 'The Pre-Cyprianic Doctrine of the Priesthood of All Christians', in *Continuity and Discontinuity in Church History: Essays Presented to George Huntston Williams*, ed. by F.F. Church and Timothy George (Leiden: E.J. Brill, 1979)

——, 'The Priesthood of All Christians: From Cyprian to John Chrysostom', *Southwestern Journal of Theology*, 30 (1988), 22–33

Gasquet, Francis Aidan, and Edmund Bishop, *Edward VI and the Book of Common Prayer: An Examination into Its Origin and Early History with an Appendix of Unpublished Documents* (London: John Hodges, 1890)

Gee, Henry, *The Elizabethan Prayer-Book & Ornaments with an Appendix of Documents* (London: Macmillan, 1902)

Genet, Jean-Philippe, 'Ecclesiastics and Political Theory in Late Medieval England: The End of a Monopoly', in *The Church, Politics and Patronage in the Fifteenth Century*, ed. by R. Barrie Dobson (Gloucester: Alan Sutton, 1984), 23–43

Gerrish, Brian A., 'Priesthood and Ministry in the Theology of Martin Luther', *CH*, 34 (1965), 404–22

——, *Grace and Gratitude: The Eucharistic Theology of John Calvin* (Edinburgh: T&T Clark, 1982)

Gill, Paul E., 'Politics and Propaganda in Fifteenth-Century England: The Polemical Writings of Sir John Fortescue', *Speculum*, 46 (1971), 333–47

Glasscoe, Marion, *English Medieval Mystics: Games of Faith* (London: Longman, 1993)

Gleason, John B., *John Colet* (London: University of California Press, 1989)

Goertz, Harald, *Allgemeines Priestertum und Ordiniertes Amt bei Luther* (Marburg: Elwart Verlag, 1997)

Gogan, Brian, *The Common Corps of Christendom: Ecclesiological Themes in the Writings of Sir Thomas More* (Leiden: E.J. Brill, 1982)

Gossip, Giles, *Coronation Anecdotes* (London: Robert Jennings, 1823)

Gribbin, Joseph A., 'Lay Participation in the Eucharistic Liturgy of the Later Middle Ages', in *Ministerial and Common Priesthood in the Eucharistic Celebration: The Proceedings of the Fourth International Colloquium of Historical, Canonical and Theological Studies on the Roman Catholic Liturgy* (London: Saint Austin Press, 1999), 51–70

Gross, Anthony, *The Dissolution of the Lancastrian Kingship: Sir John Fortescue and the Crisis of Monarchy in Fifteenth-Century England* (Stamford, Lincolnshire: Paul Watkins, 1996)

Guggisberg, Hans R., 'The Secular State of the Reformation Period and the Beginnings of the Debate on Religious Toleration', in *The Individual in Political Theory and Practice*, ed. by Janet Coleman (OUP, 1996), 79–98

Gunther, Karl, and Ethan H. Shagan, 'Protestant Radicalism and Political Thought in the Reign of Henry VIII', *P&P*, 194 (2007), 35–74

Gurevich, Aaron, *The Origins of European Individualism*, transl. by Katharine Judelson (Oxford: Blackwell, 1995)

Guy, John, 'Scripture as Authority: Problems of Interpretation in the 1530s', in *Reassessing the Henrician Age: Humanism, Politics and Reform 1500–1550*, ed. by Alistair Fox and John Guy (Oxford: Blackwell, 1986), 203–20

——, 'Thomas Cromwell and the Intellectual Origins of the Henrician Revolution', in *The Tudor Monarchy*, ed. by John Guy (London: Arnold, 1997), 213–33

——, ed., *The Tudor Monarchy* (London: Arnold, 1997)

——, 'Tudor Monarchy and Its Critiques', in *The Tudor Monarchy*, ed. by John Guy (London: Arnold, 1997), 78–109

Gwynn, Aubrey, *The English Austin Friars in the Time of Wyclif* (OUP, 1940)

Haas, S.W., 'Simon Fish, William Tyndale, and Sir Thomas More's "Lutheran Conspiracy"', *JEH*, 23 (1972), 125–36

——, 'The *Disputatio Inter Clericum et Militem*: Was Berthelet's 1531 Edition the First Henrician Polemic of Thomas Cromwell?', *Moreana*, 14 (1977), 65–72

——, 'Henry VIII's *Glasse of Truthe*', *History*, 64 (1979), 353–62

——, 'Martin Luther's "Divine Right" Kingship and the Royal Supremacy: Two Tracts from the 1531 Parliament and Convocation of Clergy', *JEH*, 31 (1980), 317–25

Haendler, Gert, *Luther on Ministerial Office and Congregational Function*, transl. by Ruth C. Gritsch and ed. by Eric W. Gritsch (Philadelphia: Fortress Press, 1981)

Hague, Dyson, *The Life and Work of John Wycliffe*, 2d edn (London: Church Book Room, 1935)

Haigh, Christopher, 'The Recent Historiography of the English Reformation', *HJ*, 25 (1982), 995–1007

——, 'Anticlericalism and the English Reformation', *History*, 68 (1983), 391–407

——, 'Revisionism, the Reformation and the History of English Catholicism', *JEH*, 36 (1985), 394–405

——, *English Reformations: Religion, Politics and Society under the Tudors* (OUP, 1993)

——, *Elizabeth I*, 2d edn (London: Longman, 1998)

Haines, Roy M., '"Wilde Wittes and Wilfulnes": John Swetstock's Attack on those "Poyswunmongeres", the Lollards', *SCH*, 8 (1972), 143–53

Viscount Halifax, *Leo XIII and Anglican Orders* (London: Longmans Green, 1912)

Hall, Basil, *Humanists and Protestants 1500–1900* (Edinburgh: T&T Clark, 1990)

——, 'Cranmer's Relations with Erasmianism and Lutheranism', in *Thomas Cranmer: Churchman and Scholar*, ed. by Paul Ayris and David Selwyn (Woodbridge, Suffolk: Boydell Press, 1993), 3–38

——, 'Cranmer, the Eucharist and the Foreign Divines in the Reign of Edward VI', in *Thomas Cranmer: Churchman and Scholar*, ed. by Paul Ayris and David Selwyn (Woodbridge, Suffolk: Boydell Press, 1993), 217–58

Hannay, Margaret Patterson, ed., *Silent But for the Word: Tudor Women as Patrons, Translators and Writers of Religious Works* (Kent, Ohio: Kent State University Press, 1985)

Hanson, R.P.C., *Eucharistic Offering in the Early Church*, Grove Liturgical Study 19 (Bramcote, Nottinghamshire: Grove Books, 1979)

Harnack, Adolf, *History of Dogma*, transl. by Neil Buchanan et al., 7 vols (London: Williams & Norgate, 1894–1899)

Harper-Bill, Christopher, 'Dean Colet's Convocation Sermon and the Pre-Reformation Church in England', in *The Impact of the English Reformation 1500–1640*, ed. by Peter Marshall (London: Arnold, 1997), 17–36

Hatch, Nathan O., *The Democratization of American Christianity* (YUP, 1989)

Heal, Felicity, *Of Prelates and Princes: A Study of the Economic and Social Position of the Tudor Episcopate* (CUP, 1980)

——, *Reformation in Britain and Ireland* (OUP, 2003)

Heath, Peter, *The English Parish Clergy on the Eve of the Reformation* (London: Routledge, 1969)

Hendrix, Scott H., '"We are All Hussites"? Hus and Luther Revisited', *ARG*, 65 (1974), 134–61

——, *Luther and the Papacy: Stages in a Reformation Conflict* (Philadelphia: Fortress Press, 1981)

Hill, Christopher, *The World Turned Upside Down: Radical Ideas during the English Revolution* (London: Maurice Temple Smith, 1972)

Hinton, R.W.K., 'English Constitutional Doctrines from the Fifteenth Century to the Seventeenth: I. English Constitutional Theories from Sir John Fortescue to Sir John Eliot', *EHR*, 75 (1960), 410–25

Hoak, Dale, 'A Tudor Deborah? The Coronation of Elizabeth I, Parliament, and the Problem of Female Rule', in *John Foxe and His World*, ed. by Christopher Highley and John N. King (Aldershot: Ashgate, 2002), 73–88

Holeton, David R., ed., *Anglican Orders and Ordinations: Essays and Reports from the Interim Conference at Jarvenpää, of the International Anglican Liturgical Consultation, 4–9 August 1997*, Joint Liturgical Studies 39 (Cambridge: Grove Books, 1997)

Holmes, P., 'The Last Great Tudor Councils', *HJ*, 33 (1990), 1–22

Hope [Hopf], C., 'An English Version of Parts of Bucer's Reply to the Cologne *Antididagma* of 1544', *JTS*, 11 (1960), 94–110

Hopf [Hope], Constantine, *Martin Bucer and the English Reformation* (Oxford: Blackwell, 1946)

Hornbeck II, J. Patrick, *What is a Lollard? Dissent and Belief in Late Medieval England* (OUP, 2010)

Horne, Brian, 'The Republic, the Hierarchy, and the Trinity', in *Order and Ministry*, ed. by Christine Hall and Robert Hannaford (Leominster, Herefordshire: Gracewing, 1996)

Houlbrooke, Ralph A., *Church Courts and the People during the English Reformation 1520–1570* (OUP, 1979)

Hoyer, Siegfried, 'Lay Preaching and Radicalism in the Early Reformation', in *Radical Tendencies in the Reformation: Divergent Perspectives*, ed. by Hans J. Hillerbrand (Kirksville, Missouri: Sixteenth Century Journal Publishers, 1986), 84–97

Hudson, Anne, *Lollards and Their Books* (London: Hambledon Press, 1985)

——, 'Wyclif and the English Language', in *Wyclif in His Times*, ed. by Anthony Kenny (OUP, 1986)

——, *The Premature Reformation: Wycliffite Texts and Lollard History* (OUP, 1988)

——, '"Laicus Litteratus": The Paradox of Lollardy', in *Heresy and Literacy 1000–1530*, ed. by Peter Biller and Anne Hudson (CUP, 1994), 222–36

Hudson, Winthrop S., *John Ponet (1516?–1556): Advocate of Limited Monarchy* (Chicago: University of Chicago Press, 1942)

Hughes, Jonathan, *Pastors and Visionaries: Religion and Secular Life in Late Medieval Yorkshire* (Woodbridge, Suffolk: Boydell & Brewer, 1988)

Hughes, Philip Edgcumbe, *Theology of the English Reformers*, new edn (Grand Rapids: Baker, 1980)

Huizinga, Johan, *Erasmus and the Age of Reformation with a Selection from the Letters of Erasmus* (PUP, 1984)

Hurley, Michael, '*Scriptura Sola*: Wyclif and His Critics', *Traditio*, 16 (1960), 275–352

Ives, E.W., *Anne Boleyn* (Oxford: Blackwell, 1986)

——, 'The Common Lawyers in Pre-Reformation England', *TRHS*, 5th series, 18 (1968), 145–73

——, *The Common Lawyers of Pre-Reformation England: Thomas Kebell: A Case Study* (CUP, 1983)

Jacob, E.F., *Archbishop Henry Chichele* (London: Thomas Nelson, 1967)

Jalland, Trevor, *This Our Sacrifice: A Brief Theological and Historical Study of the Eucharistic Oblation* (London: A.R. Mowbray, 1933)

Jayne, Sears, *John Colet and Marsilio Ficino* (OUP, 1963)

Jeanes, Gordon, 'A Reformation Treatise on the Sacraments', *JTS*, 46 (1995), 149–90

——, *Signs of God's Promise: Thomas Cranmer's Sacramental Theology and the Book of Common Prayer* (London: T&T Clark, 2008)

Cheslyn Jones et al., eds., *The Study of Liturgy* (OUP, 1992)

Joyce, Jerry, *The Laity: Help or Hindrance?* (Dublin: Mercier Press, 1994)

Jurkowski, Maureen, 'New Light on John Purvey', *EHR*, 110 (1995), 1180–90

——, 'Lawyers and Lollardy in the Early Fifteenth Century', in *Lollardy and the Gentry in the Later Middle Ages*, ed. by Margaret Aston and Colin Richmond (Stroud: Sutton Publishing, 1997), 155–82

Justice, Steven, *Writing and Rebellion: England in 1381* (London: University of California Press, 1994)

Kaminsky, Howard, 'Wyclifism as Ideology of Revolution', *CH*, 32 (1963), 57–74

Kantorowicz, Ernst H., *The King's Two Bodies: A Study in Medieval Political Theology* (PUP, 1957)

Kaufman, Peter Iver, 'John Colet's *Opus de Sacramentis* and Clerical Anticlericalism', *JBS*, 22 (1983), 1–22

——, *The 'Polytyque Churche': Religion and Early Tudor Political Culture, 1485–1516* (Macon, Georgia: Mercer University Press, 1986)

Keating, Daniel A., *Deification and Grace* (Naples, FL: Sapientia Press, 2007)

Keble, Edward, *St Mary's Church*, 3d edn (Shropshire: R.J.L. Smith, 1997)

Keen, Maurice, 'Wyclif, the Bible, and Transubstantiation', in *Wyclif in His Times*, ed. by Anthony Kenny (OUP, 1986), 1–16

——, *English Society in the Later Middle Ages 1348–1500* (London: Penguin, 1990)

Kelly, M.J., 'The Submission of the Clergy', *TRHS*, 5th series, 15 (1965), 97–119

Kempf, Friedrich, 'Innocent III's Claim to Power', in *Innocent III: Vicar of Christ or Lord of the World?*, 2d edn, ed. by James M. Powell (Washington, DC: Catholic University of America Press, 1994), 173–77

Kenny, Anthony, *Wyclif* (OUP, 1985)

——, 'The Realism of *De Universalibus*', in *Wyclif in His Times*, ed. by Anthony Kenny (OUP, 1986), 17–29

——, ed., *Wyclif in His Times* (OUP, 1986)

——, 'Realism and Determinism in the Early Wyclif', *SCH*, Subsidia 5 (1987), 165–77

——, *A Brief History of Western Philosophy* (Oxford: Blackwell, 1998)

Khomiakoff, A.-S., *L'Église Latine et le Protestantisme au Point de Vue de l'Église d'Orient* (Lausanne: B. Benda, 1872; reprint, Farnborough: Gregg Press, 1969)

Kidd, B.J., *The Later Mediaeval Doctrine of the Eucharistic Sacrifice* (London: SPCK, 1898)

Kienzle, Beverly Mayne, and Pamela J. Walker, eds., *Women Preachers and Prophets through Two Millennia of Christianity* (London: University of California Press, 1998)

King, John N., *Tudor Royal Iconography: Literature and Art in an Age of Religious Crisis* (PUP, 1989)

Kitching, C.J., 'The Probate Jurisdiction of Thomas Cromwell as Vicegerent', *BIHR*, 46 (1973), 102–6

Kittelson, James, 'Martin Bucer and the Ministry of the Church', in *Martin Bucer: Reforming Church and Community*, ed. by D.F. Wright (CUP, 1994), 83–94

Knowles, David, *The English Mystical Tradition* (London: Burns & Oates, 1961)

Kreider, Alan, *English Chantries: The Road to Dissolution* (London: Harvard University Press, 1979)

Küng, Hans, *The Church*, transl. by Ray and Rosaleen Ockenden (London: Burns & Oates, 1968)

Lahey, Stephen E., *Philosophy and Politics in the Thought of John Wyclif* (CUP, 2003)

——, *John Wyclif* (OUP, 2009)

Lake, Peter, *Anglicans and Puritans? Presbyterianism and English Conformist Thought from Whitgift to Hooker* (London: Unwin Hyman, 1988)

Lambert, Malcolm, *Medieval Heresy: Popular Movements from the Gregorian Reform to the Reformation*, 2d edn (Oxford: Blackwell, 1992)

Land, Stephen K., *Kett's Rebellion: The Norfolk Rising of 1549* (Woodbridge, Suffolk: Boydell Press, 1977)

Lander, J.R., *The Limitations of English Monarchy in the Later Middle Ages* (London: University of Toronto Press, 1989)

Lechler, Gotthard, *John Wiclif and His English Precursors*, transl. by Peter Lorimer, 2 vols (London: Kegan Paul, 1878)

Leff, Gordon, 'Wyclif and Hus: A Doctrinal Comparison', in *Wyclif in His Times*, ed. by Anthony Kenny (OUP, 1986), 105–26

——, 'The Place of Metaphysics in Wyclif's Theology', *SCH*, Subsidia 5 (1987), 217–32

——, 'John Wyclif: The Path to Dissent', *Proceedings of the British Academy*, 52 (1966), 143–80

——, *Heresy in the Later Middle Ages: The Relation of Heterodoxy to Dissent, c.1250–c.1450* (Manchester: Manchester University Press, 1967)

Le Goff, Jacques, ed., *Medieval Callings*, transl. by Lydia G. Cochrane (London: University of Chicago Press, 1990)

Lehmberg, Stanford E., *The Reformation Parliament 1529–1536* (CUP, 1970)

Lehmberg, Stanford E., *The Later Parliaments of Henry VIII 1536–1547* (CUP, 1977)

——, 'The Religious Beliefs of Thomas Cromwell', in *Leaders of the Reformation*, ed. by Richard L. DeMolen (London: Associated University Presses, 1984), 134–52

Lewis, Ewart, *Medieval Political Ideas*, 2 vols (New York: Cooper Square, 1974)

Lightfoot, J.B., 'The Christian Ministry', in *St Paul's Epistle to the Philippians* (London: Macmillan, 1891), 181–269

Lindsay, Thomas M., *The Church and Ministry in the Early Centuries*, 2d edn (London: Hodder and Stoughton, 1903)

——, *A History of the Reformation* (Edinburgh: T&T Clark, 1906)

Litzenberger, Caroline, *The English Reformation and the Laity: Gloucestershire, 1540–1580* (CUP, 1997)

Lloyd, Trevor, ed., *Lay Presidency at the Eucharist?* Grove Liturgical Study 9 (Bramcote, Nottinghamshire: Grove Books, 1977)

Loades, David M., 'Relations between the Anglican and Roman Catholic Churches in the 16th and 17th Centuries', in *Rome and the Anglicans: Historical and Doctrinal Aspects of Anglican–Roman Catholic Relations*, ed. by Wolfgang Haase (Berlin: Walter de Gruyter, 1982), 1–53.

——, *The Oxford Martyrs*, 2d edn (Bangor: Headstart History, 1992)

Logan, F. Donald, 'Thomas Cromwell and the Vicegerency in Spirituals: A Revisitation', *EHR*, 103 (1988), 658–67

Lohse, Bernard, *Martin Luther's Theology: Its Historical and Systematic Development*, transl. by Roy A. Harrisville (Minneapolis: Fortress Press, 1999)

Long, F.C., 'Transubstantiation and Sacrifice', *CQR*, 155 (1954), 229–34

Lovatt, Roger, '*The Imitation of Christ* in Late Medieval England', *TRHS*, 5th series, 18 (1968), 97–121

Lupton, J.H., *A Life of John Colet, D.D., Dean of St Paul's, and Founder of St Paul's School, with an Appendix of Some of His English Writings* (London: George Bell, 1887)

Luscombe, David, 'Wyclif and Hierarchy', *SCH*, Subsidia 5 (1987), 233–44

Lutton, Robert, *Lollardy and Orthodox Religion in Pre-Reformation England: Reconstructing Piety* (Woodbridge: Boydell & Brewer, 2006)

Lytle, Guy Fitch, 'John Wyclif, Martin Luther and Edward Powell: Heresy and the Oxford Theology Faculty at the Beginning of the Reformation', *SCH*, Subsidia 5 (1986), 465–80

MacCulloch, Diarmaid, *The Later Reformation in England 1547–1603* (London: Macmillan, 1990)

——, 'Review', *JEH*, 44 (1993), 308–10

——, 'Two Dons in Politics: Thomas Cranmer and Stephen Gardiner, 1503–1533', *HJ*, 37 (1994), 1–22

——, 'Henry VIII and the Reform of the Church', in *The Reign of Henry VIII: Politics, Policy and Piety*, ed. by Diarmaid MacCulloch (London: Macmillan, 1995), 159–80

——, 'Archbishop Cranmer: Concord and Tolerance in a Changing Church', in *Tolerance and Intolerance in the European Reformation*, ed. by Ole Peter Grell and Robert Scribner (CUP, 1996), 199–215

——, *Thomas Cranmer: A Life* (YUP, 1996)

——, *Tudor Church Militant: Edward VI and the Protestant Reformation* (London: Penguin, 1999)

MacIntyre, Alasdair, *After Virtue: A Study in Moral Theory*, 2d edn (London: Duckworth, 1985)

Maccarrone, Michele, 'Innocent III Did Not Claim Temporal Power', in *Innocent III: Vicar of Christ or Lord of the World?*, 2d edn, ed. by James M. Powell (Washington, DC: Catholic University of America Press, 1994), 73–8

Macek, Ellen A., 'Richard Smith: Tudor Cleric in Defense of Traditional Belief and Practice', *Catholic Historical Review*, 72 (1986), 383–402

Macfarlane, Alan, *The Origins of English Individualism: The Family, Property and Social Transition* (Oxford: Blackwell, 1978)

Macy, Gary, 'The Dogma of Transubstantiation', *JEH*, 45 (1994), 11–22

Maltby, Judith, *Prayer Book and People in Elizabethan and Early Stuart England* (CUP, 1998)

Marc'hadour, Germain, 'Erasmus as Priest: Holy Orders in His Vision and Practice', in *Erasmus' Vision of the Church*, ed. by Hilmar M. Pabel (Kirksville, Missouri: Sixteenth Century Journal Publishers, 1995), 115–50

Maring, Norman H., and Winthrop S. Hudson, *A Baptist Manual of Polity and Practice*, revised edn (Valley Forge, Pennsylvania: Judson Press, 1991)

Marius, Richard, *Thomas More: A Biography* (London: Collins, 1986)

Marsh, Christopher, *Popular Religion in Sixteenth-Century England: Holding Their Peace* (London: Macmillan, 1998)

Marshall, Peter, *The Catholic Priesthood and the English Reformation* (OUP, 1994)

——, ed., *The Impact of the English Reformation 1500–1640* (London: Arnold, 1997)

Martin, J.W., *Religious Radicals in Tudor England* (London: Hambledon Press, 1989)

Mayer, Thomas F., 'Starkey and Melanchthon on Adiaphora: A Critique of W. Gordon Zeeveld', *SCJ* 11 (1980), 39–50

——, 'Thomas Starkey, an Unknown Conciliarist at the Court of Henry VIII', *JHI* 49 (1988), 207–27

——, *Thomas Starkey and the Commonweal: Humanist Politics and Religion in the Reign of Henry VIII* (CUP, 1989)

McConica, James Kelsey, *English Humanists and Reformation Politics under Henry VIII and Edward VI* (OUP, 1965)

——, *Erasmus* (OUP, 1991)

McEntegart, Rory, *Henry VIII, The League of Schmalkalden and the English Reformation* (Woodbridge: Boydell Press, 2002)

McFarlane, K.B., *John Wycliffe and the Beginnings of English Nonconformity* (London: English Universities Press, 1952)

——, *Lancastrian Kings and Lollard Knights* (OUP, 1972)

McGee, Eugene K., 'Cranmer and Nominalism', *HTR*, 57 (1964), 189–216

——, 'Cranmer's Nominalism Reaffirmed', *HTR*, 59 (1966), 192–6

McGrath, Alister E., *Luther's Theology of the Cross: Martin Luther's Theological Breakthrough* (Oxford: Blackwell, 1985)

——, *The Intellectual Origins of the European Reformation* (Oxford: Blackwell, 1987)

——, *Iustitia Dei: A History of the Christian Doctrine of Justification*, 2d edn (CUP, 1998)

McHugh, J.F., 'The Sacrifice of the Mass at the Council of Trent', in *Sacrifice and Redemption: Durham Essays in Theology*, ed. by S.W. Sykes (CUP, 1991), 157–81

McLelland, Joseph C., *The Visible Words of God: An Exposition of the Sacramental Theology of Peter Martyr A.D.1500–1562* (London: Oliver and Boyd, 1957)

McSheffrey, Shannon, *Gender & Heresy: Women and Men in Lollard Communities, 1420–1530* (Philadelphia: University of Pennsylvania Press, 1995)

Merriman, Roger Bigelow, *The Life and Letters of Thomas Cromwell*, 2 vols (OUP, 1902)

Mertes, R.G.K.A., 'The Household as a Religious Community', in *People, Politics and Community in the Later Middle Ages*, ed. by Joel Rosenthal and Colin Richmond (Gloucester: Alan Sutton, 1987), 123–39

Messenger, Ernest C., *The Lutheran Origin of the Anglican Ordinal* (London: Burns, Oates & Washbourne, 1934)

——, *The Reformation, the Mass and the Priesthood: A Documented History with Special Reference to the Question of Anglican Orders*, 2 vols (London: Longmans, 1936–1937)

Meyer, Carl S., 'Henry VIII Burns Luther's Books, 12 May 1521', *JEH*, 9 (1958), 173–87

Miles, Leland, *John Colet and the Platonic Tradition* (London: Allen & Unwin, 1962)

Milton, Anthony, *Catholic and Reformed: The Roman and Protestant Churches in English Protestant Thought, 1600–1640* (CUP, 1995)

Mitchell, Leonel L., *Baptismal Anointing* (London: SPCK, 1966)

Moberly, R.C., *Ministerial Priesthood: Chapters (Preliminary to a Study of the Ordinal) on the Rationale of Ministry and the Meaning of Christian Priesthood, with an Appendix upon Roman Criticism of Anglican Orders* (London: John Murray, 1897)

Moltmann, Jürgen, *The Trinity and the Kingdom of God: The Doctrine of God*, transl. by Margaret Kohl (London: SCM Press, 1981)

Moorman, John R.H., 'The Medieval Parsonage and its Occupants', *Bulletin of the John Rylands Library*, 28 (1944), 3–19

Moran, J.A.H., *The Growth of English Schooling 1340–1548* (PUP, 1985)

Morris, Colin, *The Discovery of the Individual 1050–1200* (London: SPCK, 1972)

Muessig, Carolyn, 'Prophecy and Song: Teaching and Preaching by Medieval Women', in *Women Preachers and Prophets through Two Millennia of Christianity*, ed. by Beverly Mayne Kienzle and Pamela J. Walker (London: University of California Press, 1998), 146–58

Muller, James Arthur, *Stephen Gardiner and the Tudor Reaction* (London: Macmillan, 1926)

Mullins, E.Y., *The Axioms of Religion: A New Interpretation of the Baptist Faith* (Philadelphia: Judson Press, 1908; reprint, Nashville: Broadman & Holman, 1997)

Murray, Alexander, *Reason and Society in the Middle Ages* (OUP, 1978)

Neale, J.E., *Elizabeth I and Her Parliaments 1559–1581* (London: Jonathan Cape, 1953)

Newman, John Henry, *On Consulting the Faithful in the Matters of Doctrine*, ed. by John Coulson (London: Collins, 1961)

Nicholson, Graham, 'The Act of Appeals and the English Reformation', in *Law and Government under the Tudors*, ed. by Claire Cross, David Loades and J.J. Scarisbrick (CUP, 1988)

Norton, Elizabeth, *Margaret Beaufort: Mother of the Tudor Dynasty* (Stroud: Amberly, 2011)

Null, Ashley, *Thomas Cranmer's Doctrine of Repentance: Renewing the Power to Love* (OUP, 2000)

Oakley, Francis, 'Conciliarism in England: St German, Starkey and the Marsiglian Myth', in *Reform and Renewal in the Middle Ages and the Renaissance*, ed. by Thomas M. Izbicki and Christopher Bellitto (Leiden: E.J. Brill, 2000)

Oberman, Heiko A., *Luther: Man between God and the Devil* (London: Doubleday, 1992)

——, 'Anticlericalism as an Agent of Change', in *Anticlericalism in Late Medieval and Early Modern Europe*, ed. by Peter A. Dykema and Heiko A. Oberman (Leiden: E.J. Brill, 1993)

O'Day, Rosemary, *The English Clergy: The Emergence and Consolidation of a Profession 1558–1642* (Leicester: Leicester University Press, 1979)

O'Donovan, Oliver, *On the Thirty-Nine Articles: A Conversation with Tudor Christianity* (Exeter: Paternoster Press, 1986)

——, *The Desire of the Nations: Rediscovering the Roots of Political Theory* (CUP, 1996)

Orme, Nicholas, *Education and Society in Medieval and Renaissance England* (London: Hambledon Press, 1989)

Owen, Dorothy M., *The Medieval Canon Law: Teaching, Literature and Transmission* (CUP, 1990)

Owst, Gerald R., *Preaching in Medieval England: An Introduction to Sermon Manuscripts of the Period, c.1350–1450* (CUP, 1926)

——, *Literature and Pulpit in Medieval England: A Neglected Chapter in the History of English Letters and of the English People*, revised edn (Oxford: Blackwell, 1961)

Ozment, Steven, *Protestants: The Birth of a Revolution* (London: Doubleday, 1993)

Pabel, Hilmar M., ed., *Erasmus' Vision of the Church* (Kirksville, Missouri: Sixteenth Century Journal Publishers, 1995)

——, 'The Peaceful People of Christ: The Irenic Ecclesiology of Erasmus of Rotterdam', in *Erasmus' Vision of the Church*, ed. by Hilmar M. Pabel (Kirksville, Missouri: Sixteenth Century Journal Publishers, 1995), 57–94

Pantin, W.A., *The English Church in the Fourteenth Century* (CUP, 1955)

Payne, John B., *Erasmus: His Theology of the Sacraments* (Richmond, Virginia: John Knox Press, 1970)

Pearson, A.F. Scott, *Thomas Cartwright and Elizabethan Puritanism 1535–1603* (CUP, 1925)

Peters, Christine, *Patterns of Piety: Women, Gender and Religion in Late Medieval and Reformation England* (CUP, 2003)

Phillips, Heather, 'John Wyclif and the Optics of the Eucharist', *SCH*, Subsidia 5 (1987), 45–58

Pickthorn, Kenneth, *Early Tudor Government: Henry VII* (CUP, 1949)

Pollard, A.F., *Wolsey* (London: Longmans, Green, 1953)

Poole, Reginald, *Illustrations of the History of Medieval Thought and Learning* (London: SPCK, 1920)

Powell, James M., ed., *Innocent III: Vicar of Christ or Lord of the World?*, 2d edn (Washington, DC: Catholic University of America Press, 1994)

Power, David N., *The Sacrifice We Offer: The Tridentine Dogma and its Reinterpretation* (Edinburgh: T&T Clark, 1987)

Powicke, Frederick J., *Robert Browne: Pioneer of Modern Congregationalism* (London: Congregational Union, 1910)

Powicke, Maurice, *The Reformation in England* (OUP, 1941)

Pragman, James H., 'The Augsburg Confession in the English Reformation: Richard Taverner's Contribution', *SCJ*, 11 (1980), 75–85

Procter, Francis, and Walter Howard Frere, *A New History of the Book of Common Prayer with a Rationale of Its Offices* (London: Macmillan, 1941)

Pronger, Winifred A., 'Thomas Gascoigne: I', *EHR*, 53 (1938), 606–26

——, 'Thomas Gascoigne: II', *EHR*, 54 (1939), 20–37

Raffield, Paul, 'A Discredited Priesthood: The Failings of Common Lawyers and Their Representation in Seventeenth Century Satirical Drama', *Law & Literature* 17 (2005), 365–95

Rapp, Claudia, 'Imperial Ideology in the Making: Eusebius of Caesarea on Constantine as "Bishop"', *JTS*, 49 (1998), 685–95

Ratcliff, E.C., 'The English Usage of Eucharistic Consecration 1548–1662', *Theology*, 60 (1957), 229–36, 273–80

Rea, James Edward, *The Common Priesthood of the Members of the Mystical Body: An Historical Survey of the Heretical Concepts of the Doctrine as Compared with the True Catholic Concept* (Westminster, Maryland: Newman, 1947)

Reardon, Bernard M.G., *Religious Thought in the Reformation*, 2d edn (London: Longman, 1995)

Redworth, Glyn, 'A Study in the Formulation of Policy: The Genesis and Evolution of the Act of Six Articles', *JEH*, 37 (1986), 42–67

——, *In Defence of the Church Catholic: The Life of Stephen Gardiner* (Oxford: Blackwell, 1990)

Rex, Richard, 'The English Campaign against Luther in the 1520s', *TRHS*, 5th series, 39 (1989), 85–106

——, *The Theology of John Fisher* (CUP, 1991)

——, *Henry VIII and the English Reformation* (London: Macmillan, 1993)

——, 'The New Learning', *JEH*, 44 (1993), 26–44

——, 'The Crisis of Obedience: God's Word and Henry's Reformation', *HJ*, 39 (1996), 863–94

——, 'Jasper Fyloll and the Enormities of the Clergy: Two Tracts Written during the Reformation Parliament', *SCJ*, 31 (2000), 1043–62

——, *The Lollards* (Basingstoke: Palgrave, 2002)

Richards, Judith, *Mary Tudor* (London: Routledge, 2009)

Richardson, Cyril C., *Zwingli and Cranmer on the Eucharist: Cranmer Dixit et Contradixit* (Evanston, Illinois: Seabury-Western Theological Seminary, 1949)

Richmond, Colin, 'Religion and the Fifteenth-Century English Gentleman', in *The Church, Politics and Patronage in the Fifteenth Century*, ed. by R. Barrie Dobson (Gloucester: Alan Sutton, 1984), 193–208

Ridley, Jasper, *Thomas Cranmer* (OUP, 1962)

Roberts, Dunstan C.D., 'An Annotated and Revised Copy of *The Institution of a Christen Man* (1537)', *BIHR*, 84 (2011), 28–52

Robson, J.A., *Wyclif and the Oxford Schools: The Relation of the 'Summa de Ente' to Scholastic Debates at Oxford in the Later Fourteenth Century* (CUP, 1961)

Rodgers, Dirk W., *John à Lasco in England* (New York: Peter Lang, 1994)

Rogers, Charles, *Life of George Wishart, the Scottish Martyr, with his Translation of the Helvetian Confession* (Edinburgh: Paterson, 1876)

Rollison, David, *A Commonwealth of the People: Popular Politics and England's Long Social Revolution, 1066–1649* (CUP, 2010)

Rosser, Gervase, 'Parochial Conformity and "Voluntary" Religion in Late-Medieval England', *TRHS*, 6th series, 1 (1991), 173–89

Rubin, Miri, *Corpus Christi: The Eucharist in Late Medieval Culture* (CUP, 1991)

——, 'Small Groups: Identity and Solidarity in the Late Middle Ages', in *Enterprise and Individuals in Fifteenth-Century England*, ed. by Jennifer Kermode (Gloucester: Alan Sutton, 1991), 132–50

——, 'The Eucharist and the Construction of Medieval Identities', in *Culture and History 1350–1600: Essays on English Communities, Identities and Writing*, ed. by David Aers (London: Harvester, 1992), 43–63

Rupp, E.G., *Studies in the Making of the English Protestant Tradition (Mainly in the Reign of Henry VIII)* (CUP, 1947)

Russell, Conrad, 'Arguments for Relgious Unity in England, 1530–1650', *JEH*, 18 (1967), 201–26

Russell, G.H., 'Vernacular Instruction of the Laity in the Later Middle Ages in England: Some Texts and Notes', *Journal of Religious History*, 2 (1962), 98–119

Saul, Nigel, 'Richard II and the Vocabulary of Kingship', *EHR*, 110 (1995), 854–77

——, 'The Kingship of Richard II', in *Richard II: The Art of Kingship*, ed. by Anthony Goodman and James Gillespie (OUP, 1999), 37–57

Sawada, P.A., 'Two Anonymous Tudor Treatises on the General Council', *JEH*, 12 (1961), 197–214

Sayers, Jane, *Innocent III: Leader of Europe 1998–1216* (London: Longman, 1994)

Scarisbrick, J.J., 'The Pardon of the Clergy, 1531', *HJ*, 12 (1956), 22–39

——, *The Reformation and the English People* (Oxford: Blackwell, 1984)

——, *Henry VIII* (University of California Press, 1968; new edn, YUP, 1997)

Scase, Wendy, *Piers Plowman and the New Anticlericalism* (CUP, 1989)

——, 'Reginald Pecock', in *English Writers of the Late Middle Ages*, ed. by M.C. Seymour (Aldershot, Hants: Variorum, 1996), 69–146

Schaff, Philip, *Modern Christianity: The German Reformation, A.D. 1517–1530*, 2 vols (Edinburgh: T&T Clark, 1888)

Schoeck, R.J., 'The Use of St John Chrysostom in Sixteenth-Century Controversy: Christopher St German and Sir Thomas More in 1533', *HTR*, 54 (1961), 21–7

Schramm, Percy Ernst, *A History of the English Coronation*, transl. by Leopold G. Wickham Legg (OUP, 1937)

Schwarz, Marc L., 'Some Thoughts on the Development of a Lay Religious Consciousness in Pre-Civil-War England', *SCH*, 8 (1972), 171–78

Sedlak, Jan, *M. Jan Hus*, 2 parts (Prague: Tiskem B. Stybla, 1915)

Selwyn, D.G., 'A Neglected Edition of Cranmer's Catechism', *JTS*, 15 (1964), 76–91

——, 'A New Version of a Mid-Sixteenth-Century Vernacular Tract on the Eucharist: A Document of the Early Edwardian Reformation?', *JEH*, 39 (1988), 217–39

——, 'The "Book of Doctrine", the Lords' Debate and the First Prayer Book of Edward VI: An Abortive Attempt at Doctrinal Consensus?', *JTS*, 40 (1989), 446–80

——, 'Cranmer's Library: Its Potential for Reformation Studies', in *Thomas Cranmer: Churchman and Scholar*, ed. by Paul Ayris and David Selwyn (Woodbridge, Suffolk: Boydell Press, 1993), 39–72

Shagan, Ethan H., 'Clement Armstrong and the Godly Commonwealth: Radical Religion in Early Tudor England', in *The Beginnings of English Protestantism*, ed. by Peter Marshall and Alec Ryrie (CUP, 2002), 60–83

Sharpe, Kevin, *Selling the Tudor Monarchy: Authority and Image in Sixteenth-Century England* (YUP, 2009)

Shurden, Walter B., *The Baptist Identity: Four Fragile Freedoms* (Macon, Georgia: Smyth & Helwys, 1993)

Skeeters, Martha, *Community and Clergy: Bristol and the Reformation c.1530–c.1570* (OUP, 1993)

Skinner, Quentin, *The Foundations of Modern Political Thought*, 2 vols (CUP, 1978)

Smalley, Beryl, 'The Biblical Scholar', in *Robert Grosseteste, Scholar and Bishop: Essays in Commemoration of the Seventh Centenary of his Death*, ed. by D.A. Callus (OUP, 1955), 70–97

——, 'The Bible and Eternity: John Wyclif's Dilemma', *Journal of the Warburg and Courtauld Institutes*, 27 (1964), 73–89

Smith, Dwight C., 'Robert Browne, Independent', *CH*, 6 (1937), 289–349

Somerset, Fiona, 'Answering the *Twelve Conclusions*: Dymmok's Halfhearted Gestures towards Publication', in *Lollardy and the Gentry in the Later Middle Ages*, ed. by Margaret Aston and Colin Richmond (Stroud: Sutton Publishing, 1997), 52–76

Southern, Richard W., *Western Society and the Church in the Middle Ages* (London: Penguin, 1980)

——, *Robert Grosseteste: The Growth of an English Mind in Medieval Europe*, 2d edn (OUP, 1992)

Sowerby, Tracey A., *Renaissance and Reform in Tudor England: The Careers of Sir Richard Morison c.1513–1556* (OUP, 2010)

Spaemann, Robert, *Persons: The Difference between Someone and Something*, transl. by Oliver O'Donovan (OUP, 2006)

Spinka, Matthew, *John Hus: A Biography* (PUP, 1968)

Spufford, Margaret, *Small Books and Pleasant Histories: Popular Fiction and its Readership in Seventeenth-Century England* (CUP, 1981)

Starkey, David, 'Representation through Intimacy: A Study in the Symbolism of Monarchy and Court Office in Early Modern England', in *The Tudor Monarchy*, ed. by John Guy (London: Arnold, 1997), 42–78

Steiner, Emily, 'Lollardy and the Legal Document', in *Lollards and Their Influence in Late Medieval England*, ed. by Fiona Somerset, Jill C. Havens, and Derrick G. Pitard (Woodbridge: Boydell & Brewer, 2003), 155–74

Stephens, W.P., *The Theology of Huldrych Zwingli* (OUP, 1986)

——, *Zwingli: An Introduction to His Thought* (OUP, 1992)

Strong, Roy, *Coronation: A History of Kingship and the British Monarchy* (London: HarperCollins, 2005)

Strype, John, *Ecclesiastical Memorials; Relating Chiefly to Religion and its Reformation, Under the Reigns of King Henry VIII, King Edward VI, and Queen Mary the First*, 7 vols (OUP, 1816)

——, *The History of the Life and Acts of the Most Reverend Father in God, Edmund Grindal, The First Bishop of London, and the Second Archbishop of York and*

Canterbury successively, in the Reign of Q. Elizabeth (London: John Watt and John Hartley, 1710)

Surtz, Edward, *The Works and Days of John Fisher: An Introduction to the Position of St John Fisher (1469–1535), Bishop of Rochester, in the English Renaissance and Reformation* (Cambridge, Massachusetts: Harvard University Press, 1967)

Swanson, R.N., *Church & Society in Late Medieval England* (Oxford: Blackwell, 1989)

——, 'Problems of the Priesthood in Pre-Reformation England', *EHR*, 417 (1990), 845–69

——, *Religion and Devotion in Europe, c.1215–c.1515* (CUP, 1995)

Sykes, Norman, *Old Priest and New Presbyter: The Anglican Attitude to Episcopacy, Presbyterianism and Papacy Since the Reformation* (CUP, 1956)

Sykes, Stephen, ed., *Sacrifice and Redemption: Durham Essays in Theology* (CUP, 1991)

——, '"To the Intent that these Orders May Be Continued": An Anglican Theology of Orders', in *Anglican Orders: Essays on the Centenary of Apostolicae Curae, 1896–1996*, ed. by R. William Franklin (London: Mowbray, 1996), 48–63

Szittya, Penn, *The Antifraternal Tradition in Medieval Literature* (PUP, 1986)

Tawney, R.H., *Religion and the Rise of Capitalism: A Historical Study* (London: Penguin, 1922)

Taylor, Charles, *Sources of the Self: The Making of the Modern Identity* (CUP, 1989)

——, *A Secular Age* (HUP, 2007)

Tentler, Thomas N., 'The *Summa* for Confessors as an Instrument of Social Control', in *The Pursuit of Holiness in Late Medieval and Renaissance Religion: Papers from the University of Michigan Conference*, ed. by Charles Trinkaus and Heiko A. Oberman (Leiden: E.J. Brill, 1974)

——, *Sin and Confession on the Eve of the Reformation* (PUP, 1977)

Teetaert, Amédée, *La Confession aux Laïques dans L'Eglise Latine depuis le VIIIe jusq'au XIVe Siècle* (Paris: Gabalda, 1926)

Thomas, Keith, *Religion and the Decline of Magic: Studies in Popular Beliefs in Sixteenth- and Seventeenth-Century England* (London: Penguin, 1973)

Thompson, A. Hamilton, *The English Clergy and their Organization in the Later Middle Ages* (OUP, 1947)

Thomson, John A.F., *The Later Lollards 1414–1520* (OUP, 1965)

——, *The Transformation of Medieval England 1370–1529* (London: Longman, 1983)

Thomson, S., 'The Philosophical Basis of Wyclif's Theology,' *Journal of Religion*, 11 (1931), 86–116

—— Harrison, 'Luther and Bohemia', *ARG*, 44 (1953), 160–81

Thomson, Williell R., *The Latin Writings of John Wyclyf: An Annotated Catalog* (Toronto: Pontifical Institute of Mediaeval Studies, 1983)

Tierney, Brian, *Church Law and Constitutional Thought in the Middle Ages* (London: Variorum, 1979)

Tjernagel, Neelak Serawlook, *Henry VIII and the Lutherans: A Study in Anglo-Lutheran Relations from 1521 to 1547* (Saint Louis: Concordia Publishing House, 1965)

Todd, Margo, *Christian Humanism and the Puritan Social Order* (CUP, 1987)

Tolmie, Murray, *The Triumph of the Saints: The Separate Churches of London 1616–1649* (CUP, 1977)

Tönnies, Ferdinand, *Community and Society (Gemeinschaft und Gesellschaft)*, transl. by Charles P. Loomis (East Lansing, Michigan: Michigan State University Press, 1957)

Torrance, Alan J., *Persons in Communion: An Essay in Trinitarian Description and Human Participation with Special Reference to Volume One of Karl Barth's Church Dogmatics* (Edinburgh: T&T Clark, 1996)

Torrance, Thomas F., *Kingdom and Church: A Study in the Theology of the Reformation* (Edinburgh: Oliver and Boyd, 1956)

——, *Royal Priesthood: A Theology of Ordained Ministry*, 2d edn (Edinburgh: T&T Clark, 1993)

Troeltsch, Ernst, *The Social Teaching of the Christian Churches*, transl. by Olive Wyon, 2 vols (London: Allen & Unwin, 1931)

Trueman, Carl R., *Luther's Legacy: Salvation and English Reformers 1525–1556* (OUP, 1994)

Tyacke, Nicholas, *Anti-Calvinists: The Rise of English Arminianism c.1590–1640* (OUP, 1987)

——, 'Introduction: Re-thinking the "English Reformation"', in *England's Long Reformation: 1500–1800*, ed. by Nicholas Tyacke (London: UCL Press, 1998), 1–32

Ullmann, Walter, *Principles of Government and Politics in the Middle Ages* (London: Methuen, 1961)

——, *The Individual and Society in the Middle Ages* (London: Methuen, 1967)

——, 'This Realm of England is an Empire', *JEH*, 30 (1979), 175–203

Underwood, William, 'Thomas Cromwell and William Marshall's Protestant Books', *HJ*, 47 (2004), 517–39

Usher, Brett, '"In a Time of Persecution": New Light on the Secret Protestant Congregation in Marian London', in *John Foxe and the English Reformation*, ed. by David Loades (Hants: Scolar Press, 1997), 233–51

Volf, Miroslav, *After Our Likeness: The Church as the Image* (Cambridge: Eerdmans, 1998)

De Vooght, Paul, *Les Sources de la Doctrine Chrétienne d'après les Théologiens du XIV Siècle et du Début du XVe* (Paris: Desclèe de Brouwer, 1954)

——, 'Wyclif et la *Scriptura Sola*', *Ephemerides Theologicae Lovanienses*, 39 (1963), 50–86

Wabuda, Susan, 'Equivocation and Recantation During the English Reformation: The "Subtle Shadows" of Dr Edward Crome', *JEH*, 44 (1993), 224–42

——, 'Setting Forth the Word of God: Archbishop Cranmer's Early Patronage of Preachers', in *Thomas Cranmer: Churchman and Scholar*, ed. by Paul Ayris and David Selwyn (Woodbridge, Suffolk: Boydell Press, 1993), 75–88

Walker, Greg, *Persuasive Fictions: Faction, Faith and Political Culture in the Reign of Henry VIII* (London: Scolar Press, 1996)

Walker, Simon, 'Richard II's Views on Kingship', in *Rulers and Ruled in Late Medieval England: Essays Presented to Gerald Harriss*, ed. by Rowena E. Archer and Simon Walker (London: Hambledon Press, 1995), 49–63

Watkins, Oscar D., *A History of Penance: Being a Study of the Authorities: (A) For the Whole Church to A.D. 450 (B) For the Western Church from A.D. 450 to A.D. 1215*, 2 vols (London: Longmans Green, 1920)

Watt, Diane, *Secretaries of God: Women Prophets in Late Medieval and Early Modern England* (Cambridge: Brewer, 1997)

Watt, John A., *The Theory of Papal Monarchy in the Thirteenth Century: The Contribution of the Canonists* (New York: Fordham University Press, 1965)

——, 'Spiritual and Temporal Powers', in *The Cambridge History of Medieval Political Thought c.350–c.1450*, ed. by J.H. Burns (CUP, 1988), 367–423

Waugh, W.T., 'Sir John Oldcastle', *EHR*, 20 (1905), 434–56, 637–58

Weber, Max, *The Protestant Ethic and the Spirit of Captialism*, (London: Allen & Unwin, 1930) transl. by Talcott Parsons

——, 'The Sociology of Charismatic Authority', in *From Max Weber: Essays in Sociology*, transl. by H.H. Gerth and C. Wright Mills (London: Routledge & Kegan Paul, 1948), 245–52

Werrell, Ralph S., *The Theology of William Tyndale* (Cambridge: James Clarke, 2006)

White, B.R., *The English Separatist Tradition: From the Marian Martyrs to the Pilgrim Fathers* (OUP, 1971)

Wilkinson, Bertie, 'The Deposition of Richard II and the Accession of Henry IV', *EHR*, 54 (1939), 215–39

——, *Constitutional History of England in the Fifteenth Century 1399–1485, with Illustrative Documents* (London: Longmans, 1964)

Wilks, Michael, 'Predestination, Property, and Power: Wyclif's Theory of Dominion and Grace', *SCH*, 2 (1965), 220–36

——, 'Royal Priesthood: The Origins of Lollardy', in *The Church in a Changing Society: Conflict—Reconciliation or Adjustment? CIHEC Conference in Uppsala 1977* (Uppsala, Sweden: Swedish Society of Church History, 1978), 63–70

——, 'Royal Patronage and Anti-Papalism from Ockham to Wyclif', *SCH*, Subsidia 5 (1987), 135–63

——, 'Wyclif and the Great Persecution', *SCH*, Subsidia 10 (1994), 39–63

Williams, Neville, *The Cardinal and the Secretary* (London: Weidenfeld and Nicolson, 1975)

Williams, Rowan, *The Wound of Knowledge: Christian Spirituality from the New Testament to St John of the Cross* (London: Darton, Longman & Todd, 1979)

——, *Eucharistic Sacrifice: The Roots of a Metaphor*, Grove Liturgical Study 31 (Bramcote, Nottinghamshire: Grove Books, 1982)

——, *Arius: Heresy and Tradition* (London: Darton, Longman & Todd, 1987)

——, 'Religious Experience in the Era of Reform', in *Companion Encyclopedia of Theology*, ed. by Peter Byrne and Leslie Houlden (London: Routledge, 1995), 576–93

——, *On Christian Theology* (Oxford: Blackwell, 2000)

Wingren, Gustav, *The Christian's Calling: Luther on Vocation*, transl. by Carl C. Rasmussen (London: Oliver and Boyd, 1957)

Wizeman, William, *The Theology and Spirituality of Mary Tudor's Church* (Aldershot: Ashgate, 2006)

Woodhouse, H.F., *The Doctrine of the Church in Anglican Theology 1547–1603* (London: SPCK, 1954)

Wood-Legh, K.L., *Perpetual Chantries in Britain* (CUP, 1965)

Woodward, G.W.O., *The Dissolution of the Monasteries* (Andover, Hampshire: Pitkin, 1975)

Workman, Herbert, *John Wyclif: A Study of the English Medieval Church*, 2 vols (OUP, 1926)

Yarnell, Malcolm B., III, 'The First Evangelical Sinner's Prayer Published in English', *Southwestern Journal of Theology*, 47 (2004), 27–43

Zeeveld, W. Gordon, *Foundations of Tudor Policy* (London: Methuen, 1969)

Zell, Michael L., 'The Personnel of the Clergy in Kent, in the Reformation Period', *EHR*, 89 (1974), 513–33

Zizioulas, John D., *Being as Communion: Studies in Personhood and the Church* (Crestwood, New York: St Vladimir's Seminary Press, 1985)

——, 'The Doctrine of God the Trinity Today', in *The Forgotten Trinity: 3. A Selection of Papers Presented to the BCC Study Commission on Trinitarian Doctrine Today* (London: Inter-Church House, 1991), 33–46

Index